T0138308

The Changing Hospital Industry

**A National Bureau
of Economic Research
Conference Report**

Contents

Acknowledgments

The research papers collected in this volume were presented at a National Bureau of Economic Research conference held in Palm Beach, Florida, in November 1997. I am grateful to Jason Barro and Mark Duggan for serving as rapporteurs and to Kirsten Foss Davis for planning and organizing the meeting.

The Changing Hospital Industry

Comparing Not-for-Profit and For-Profit Institutions

Edited by **David M. Cutler**

The University of Chicago Press

Chicago and London

DAVID M. CUTLER is professor of economics at Harvard University
and a research associate of the National Bureau of Economic
Research.

The University of Chicago Press, Chicago 60637
The University of Chicago Press, Ltd., London
© 2000 by the National Bureau of Economic Research
All rights reserved. Published 2000
Printed in the United States of America
09 08 07 06 05 04 03 02 01 00   1 2 3 4 5
ISBN: 0-226-13219-6 (cloth)

Library of Congress Cataloging-in-Publication Data

The changing hospital industry : comparing not-for-profit and for-
    profit institutions / edited by David M. Cutler.
        p.   cm.—(A National Bureau of Economic Research
    conference report)
    Includes bibliographical references and index.
    ISBN 0-226-13219-6 (alk. paper)
    1. Hospitals—Economic aspects—United States. I. Cutler,
David M.   II. Series: Conference report (National Bureau of
Economic Research)
RA971.3.C48   2000
338.4′736211′0973—DC21   99-27207
                                                              CIP

Introduction

David M. Cutler

Most industries in the United States comprise either for-profit firms, not-for-profit firms, or government enterprises. For-profits predominate in manufacturing, for example, while higher education is almost entirely not-for-profit (at least for four-year colleges) and elementary education is almost exclusively public. The hospital industry, however, includes a mix of the three modes of production. In 1995, 65 percent of acute care hospital beds were in private not-for-profit institutions, 24 percent were in public institutions, and 11 percent were in for-profit institutions. Indeed, not-for-profit, for-profit, and government hospitals provide similar services and compete in the same markets. Not-for-profit and for-profit hospitals, for example, engage in joint ventures, and firms of one organization form have subsidiaries of another form.

In recent years, the hospital market has been in a state of flux. Technological innovation and the spread of managed care have led to striking reductions in inpatient demand. Between 1980 and 1995, hospital days in the United States fell by 35 percent, when the population was both growing and growing older. In response to such large demand reductions, the number of independent, acute care hospitals fell from 6,102 in 1980 to 5,258 in 1995, a decline of 14 percent. Further, many remaining hospitals merged with other hospitals, cut their inpatient capacity, or converted status (primarily to for-profit form). Between 1980 and 1995, 263 not-for-profit hospitals (5 percent of the 1980 number) converted to for-profit form.

David M. Cutler is professor of economics at Harvard University and a research associate of the National Bureau of Economic Research.

These changes raise two fundamental questions: (1) What determines a hospital's choice of for-profit or not-for-profit organizational form? and (2) How does that form affect patients and society?

The Choice of Organizational Form

What determines a hospital's organizational form—for-profit, private not-for-profit, or government? The answer is in some part historical. Many not-for-profit hospitals, for example, were founded by religious orders and have remained not-for-profit because of religious affiliation. There is more to the story, however, than just history. Hospitals do not always retain their historical form; they sometimes convert from one organizational form to another (including hospitals founded by religious institutions).

Several nonhistorical factors may explain the choice of organizational form. One factor is profits. Public and private not-for-profit hospitals can, of course, earn a profit. These institutions may not, however, pay out their profits to a residual claimant. When fund balances are high, hospitals may decide to convert to for-profit form so that future profits can be paid out. Increased profits may also convince hospitals to remain in not-for-profit status, however, because not-for-profit hospitals frequently use profits to finance activities that managers or boards of directors consider important—uncompensated care, teaching, and medical research.

Organizational form also determines access to financing. For-profit firms have access to different financial instruments than not-for-profit firms, since they can use equity financing. Equity capital is most readily available to hospitals affiliated with large for-profit corporations. Not-for-profit hospitals may decide to convert to for-profit form if they have exhausted their ability to issue tax-exempt debt and other available instruments and still need working capital.

A final theory of organizational form is information signaling. Medical care is rife with information imperfections. It is difficult for patients to identify valuable procedures before they become sick, and patients often have little time to do so after they become sick. Thus, information imperfections often force patients to trust that providers will provide high quality medical care. But what ensures that providers will not skimp on care? For-profit firms might skimp more than not-for-profit firms, if skimping raises profits without harming business. Not-for-profit hospitals, in contrast, may have less incentive to skimp on care since they do not have shareholders who demand the highest possible returns. Thus, organizational form may provide a way to signal quality to imperfectly informed consumers.

The Implications of Organizational Choice

These explanations for the choice between for-profit and not-for-profit form have different implications for the appropriateness of and society's views about not-for-profit and for-profit institutions.

Organizational choice affects public sector budgets. The effect is easily recognized in the case of public hospitals, which are part of government budgets. Private not-for-profit organizations also affect public revenues, since they are exempt from federal and state corporate income taxes and local property taxes. This lost revenue has not gone unnoticed. Proposals have periodically been made to eliminate the favorable tax treatment of private not-for-profit institutions, particularly when they are not seen as providing substantial public goods.

Further, hospitals have substantial indirect effects on government budgets. Hospitals provide a number of public goods that are generally associated with governments, including caring for the uninsured, training medical residents, and facilitating medical research. Traditionally, hospitals have financed these activities by charging more than marginal cost to people with insurance. The "tax" on those with insurance offsets the cost of the "public goods." By financing these activities privately, the costs of these public goods are kept off of the public budget.

Not-for-profit and for-profit hospitals may differ in their willingness to provide public goods. Government hospitals are frequently hospitals of last resort for the very poor. Public goods provision may also be a specific objective of private not-for-profit hospitals; not-for-profit hospitals have mission statements and charters commonly enumerating the public goods as goals. For-profit hospitals are unlikely to value public goods directly, however, or at best, the relationship would be indirect—provide public goods if needed, but minimize the amount of provision if possible. Thus, as hospitals move from one organizational form to another, the amount of privately provided public goods may change, and that change has implications for patient health and public budgets.

In addition, the choice of organizational form may affect the quality of medical care for insured people. As noted above, for-profit hospitals have greater incentives to skimp on patient care than do not-for-profit hospitals, if skimping on care is hard to detect and thus does not result in the hospital receiving an adverse reputation or being sued. On the other hand, greater pay may lead to better managerial ability in for-profit than in not-for-profit hospitals, potentially leading to better outcomes. Medical care is a complex activity, requiring precise coordination of physicians, nurses, and hospital facilities. A well-run organization is likely to have much better outcomes than does a poorly run organization, and high pay might motivate organizations to be more efficient.

Concerns about quality and the potential loss of public goods have weighed heavily in the public sector. In response, some states have made it difficult for for-profit hospitals to enter. And not-for-profit hospital managers frequently feed this perception, arguing that quality will suffer if for-profit hospitals become dominant.

Given the dramatic recent changes in the hospital industry and these substantial policy questions, it is important to consider the role of not-for-profit hospitals in the medical care system. The papers in this volume present such an examination, focusing on the two issues discussed above: the choice between for-profit and not-for-profit organizational form and the implications of this choice for patients and society.

Hospital Conversions to For-Profit Form

The first set of papers examines the reasons for hospital conversions from not-for-profit to for-profit status and the purchase prices paid for converting hospitals. In a case study of 10 hospital conversions that occurred in North Carolina and South Carolina since 1981, Frank A. Sloan, Donald H. Taylor, and Christopher Conover investigate whether communities receive a fair price when selling a hospital. For their analysis, the authors obtained detailed information about hospital purchase prices, the use of the funds received, and the commitments made by the buyers to the local communities. They calculate appropriate prices under different assumptions about future cash flows and take into account any community benefits that are not reflected in the transaction price. To estimate these benefits, they use parameter estimates from regression analyses of Tennessee hospital conversions.

They conclude that for-profit hospital corporations paid a price substantially above the fair price to acquire not-for-profit hospitals. Interestingly, the authors find the reverse when communities transact with not-for-profit or government organizations. Finally, they find that hospitals that convert to for-profit status do not reduce their provision of community benefits. Because the authors examine a limited time horizon, they acknowledge that these for-profit facilities may behave quite differently in the years ahead. The authors also suggest that further research needs to be done on the social benefits associated with the foundations formed as a result of hospital conversions.

In the second chapter, David M. Cutler and Jill R. Horwitz also use a case-study approach to explain why two not-for-profit hospitals converted to for-profit status and identify the effects of the conversions. They study two large hospitals that both converted more than a decade ago, allowing the authors to examine both the short- and long-term consequences of these conversions. For their analysis, Cutler and Horwitz use several sources of information, including interviews with hospital personnel, newspaper articles, Medicare cost reports, and legal documents.

Their results suggest two primary motivations for conversions to for-profit status. The first is a financial one—not-for-profit hospitals with substantial amounts of debt may convert to gain access to cheaper sources of capital. Second, the culture of a not-for-profit hospital can have an important effect on the decision to convert, as hospitals run by businessmen may be much more likely than religiously affiliated or physician-run hospitals to convert. Their findings also show that the conversions have improved the financial performance of these hospitals by cutting hospital costs and by increasing public sector reimbursement. The authors suggest that this second factor is due to skillful exploitation of Medicare loopholes by for-profit hospitals. Finally, they find that nearby not-for-profit hospitals also begin to game the Medicare program after entry by a for-profit hospital. The authors suggest that future research in this area should examine the effect of not-for-profit hospital conversions on medical care quality.

Medical Care Quality in For-Profit and Not-for-Profit Organizations

The second group of papers examines quality differences between for-profit and not-for-profit hospitals. Medical care quality has historically been difficult to measure. There are several reasons for this. First, it is difficult to identify the relevant measures of quality. A complete measure would include patient health, satisfaction, and process of care, among other factors. Second, until quite recently there were no reliable data sets that gave detailed information about long-term health outcomes for a substantial share of the population. Third, because of inadequate information about the mix of patients at different hospitals, it was difficult to know if differences across facilities in health outcomes were due to hospital quality or differences in patient mix. Finally, measures of health outcomes, particularly when comparing individual facilities within a market, are quite noisy.

As a result, the papers in this section of the volume take a number of approaches to measuring hospital quality. Improving significantly upon previous work in this area, Mark McClellan and Douglas Staiger use a generalized method-of-moments (GMM) framework to compare quality at for-profit and not-for-profit hospitals. The authors use a data set that contains all elderly Medicare beneficiaries who were (1) hospitalized from 1984 through 1994 following their first heart attack (acute myocardial infarction, or AMI) or (2) hospitalized with ischemic heart disease (IHD) from 1984 through 1991. The authors use 90-day mortality as their outcome measure, and emphasize that the severity of AMI and IHD limits the scope for selection across hospitals and thus enables them to more precisely estimate differences in hospital quality. Moreover, because the outcome measures are noisy estimates of hospital quality, the authors use data from many years to construct filtered risk-adjusted mortality rates (RAMRs) for each hospital.

Their results suggest that (1) there is a strong negative relationship between hospital volume and mortality rates, (2) not-for-profit hospitals have lower mortality than both for-profit and government hospitals, and (3) differences in mortality rates between not-for-profit and for-profit hospitals increased between 1985 and 1994. The authors conclude with case studies of three counties and find evidence that, within a market, for-profit hospitals actually have higher quality than do not-for-profit hospitals. The small average difference in mortality rates between not-for-profit and for-profit hospitals that the authors uncover, coupled with the large variation within each hospital type, suggests that there may be other factors that affect hospital quality and are significantly more important than ownership type.

After suffering from an acute, emergency condition, many individuals' first contact with the health care system is not the hospital but the emergency 911 system that helps to get them to the facility. Because previous research has shown that the time between the onset of an emergency condition and the initiation of appropriate medical procedures can have an important effect on mortality for certain conditions, it may be the case that changes in funding for 911 systems lead to substantial changes in average health outcomes. Moreover, the quality of the response system may have an important effect on the appropriate choice of medical care inputs for nearby hospitals.

Susan Athey and Scott Stern explore the causes and effects of differences across communities in prehospital and in-hospital emergency services. Initially, the authors use a data set with every ambulance ride in Pennsylvania during 1995 to explore the direct productivity benefits that arise when a community adopts a basic or advanced 911 system. Focusing on cases of cardiac incident, they find that both the time to reach an emergency site and the time that elapses from the site to the hospital is decreasing in the adoption of advanced 911 services. However, there is little evidence to suggest that mortality rates from cardiac incidents are related to the adoption of 911 services.

Next, the authors investigate the effect of 911 systems on both the allocation of patients across hospitals and the adoption of cardiac technologies by hospitals. They find that a hospital's level of cardiac technology has an important effect on its share of cardiac patients within a market, but little evidence that the 911 system influences hospitals' technology investments. Finally, using a national-level data set on the adoption of 911 technologies across communities, the authors analyze the determinants of 911 adoption by communities. They find that places with a more conservative political orientation are less likely to adopt advanced 911 systems and that state legislation governing the adoption of 911 has an important effect on communities' adoption decisions.

Previous authors have shown that health care practice patterns vary significantly across geographic areas within the United States. Jonathan Skinner and John E. Wennberg use this variation to investigate the productive and allocative efficiency of end-of-life medical care. The authors compare Medicare expenditures and physician visits in the last six months of life across communities in the United States. Initially, the authors focus on Miami and Minneapolis and find that average Medicare costs are substantially higher (by approximately a two-to-one margin) in Miami. Finding that the variation is even larger for intensive medical care, they ascribe much of the variation in expenditures to differences in the treatment of the chronically ill in the two areas.

Next, the authors conduct a cross-sectional analysis of the 306 hospital referral regions in the United States, and they find that the variation in end-of-life medical spending does not appear to be driven by differences in underlying health status across areas. The authors then explore whether the additional spending in certain areas leads to improved health outcomes, as measured by mortality rates. They find no evidence that the areas with relatively high expenditures have better health outcomes than do those areas with significantly lower spending. Finally, the authors argue that patients frequently prefer less intensive treatment than physicians advocate, identifying another potential source of inefficiency in the provision of medical care.

Previous research suggests that recent changes in the health care marketplace have forced not-for-profit hospitals to behave quite similarly to their for-profit counterparts. As inpatient demand has fallen, not-for-profit hospitals have diversified into other activities and entered into joint ventures with for-profit firms. Richard G. Frank and David S. Salkever explore the causes and effects of this recent diversification of activities, and its implications for charitable giving and care to the poor. The authors report on the results of three focus group discussions with executives from 14 (mainly not-for-profit) hospitals in Boston and Chicago, and they use these results in constructing a model of not-for-profit hospital diversification and charitable giving.

They find that nonteaching not-for-profit hospitals diversify their activities and enter into joint ventures not only to offset reductions in inpatient revenues but also to gain market share, strengthen ties with physicians, and reduce the uncertainty in demand for care. Their focus group discussions revealed that philanthropy constitutes a very small share (approximately 1 percent) of a typical not-for-profit hospital's budget, and suggest that these private donations fall when a hospital's financial performance improves. Frank and Salkever find no evidence that diversification or a decline in private donations has reduced the supply of public goods (i.e., charity care) by not-for-profit hospitals. This may be due to not-for-profits' success in keeping their profits relatively high, allowing them to continue to cross-subsidize care for unprofitable patients.

Managed Care and Hospital Quality

The third part of the book focuses directly on the relationship between managed care and hospital quality. As noted above, managed care has fundamentally changed the medical care landscape. Thus, determining its effect on hospital operations is a central problem in health economics research.

Using a unique approach and a rich data set, Sarah Feldman and David Scharfstein compare the quality of care received by cancer patients insured by fee-for-service and managed care insurers. They use provider volume as a proxy for quality, taking the result from many previous studies that the patients of high-volume physicians and hospitals have better clinical outcomes than do other patients. They use a data set containing all Massachusetts hospital discharges in 1995 (including physician identifiers for each discharge) to compare the providers of fee-for-service and managed care patients with breast cancer, colorectal cancer, and gynecologic cancer. The authors choose these three types of cancer because they are typically treated surgically, and thus there are unlikely to be significant differences in the type of treatments received by fee-for-service and managed care patients.

The authors find that managed care patients tend to be treated by physicians who perform relatively fewer surgeries, and that these patients receive their treatment in lower-volume hospitals. The differences across the seven managed care plans are substantial, with one of the plans actually sending their patients to higher volume providers than the fee-for-service providers. Furthermore, their results suggest that there is substantial variation in quality within a typical managed care plan, as some plans appear to offer higher quality care for one type of cancer than for another. The authors conclude that, if provider volume is an accurate measure of quality, then managed care plans may indeed offer lower quality health care than fee-for-service plans.

The second paper in this section aims to explain how insurance status affects the type of care that an individual receives *within a particular institution*. David Meltzer, Frederick L. Hiltz, and David Bates use a case-study approach to analyze the effect of a managed care institution on the type of care provided in a large academic medical center. They use data on all admissions to the teaching hospital's internal medicine service over a one-and-a-half-year period to investigate the effect of the attending physician's financial incentives on the costs of care. Within the hospital, some attendings are employed by the managed care organization (MCO) while all others are employed by the hospital. The MCO attendings, whose patients are almost all MCO patients, have much stronger financial incentives to reduce costs than do the physicians employed by the hospital.

The authors find that the patients of MCO-employed attendings have significantly lower costs than do similar patients of hospital-employed physicians. The majority of this cost saving is accomplished through shorter lengths-of-stay. The authors also find that physician workload has a significant effect on patient discharge probabilities, and they suggest that hospitals may increase their attending physicians' incentives to discharge patients quickly by reducing their house staff rather than through actual financial incentives. Both of these papers build substantially on previous research concerning the effects of managed care on health care quality.

Taxation and Information

The final section of the volume examines the tax implications of the difference between not-for-profit and for-profit ownership and the signaling value of different forms of ownership. As noted above, the differential tax treatment received by not-for-profit hospitals has attracted considerable recent attention, as many health care analysts claim that these facilities are behaving no differently from their for-profit counterparts. Using a detailed data set on the financial status of not-for-profit hospitals, William M. Gentry and John R. Penrod estimate the magnitude of these tax benefits. Not-for-profit hospitals are exempt from corporate income taxes (federal and state) and property taxes (state and local), have access to tax-exempt bond financing, and can receive charitable donations that are tax deductible for the donor.

Using data from the Health Care Financing Administration's 1995 public use file of Medicare cost reports, the authors estimate that the income tax exemption is worth $4.6 billion to not-for-profit hospitals while the value of their property tax exemption is $1.6 billion. Additionally, the authors' results suggest that the net benefit of access to tax-exempt bonds is quite small and does not significantly reduce the cost of borrowing for not-for-profit hospitals. The authors note, however, that if not-for-profit hospitals engage in tax arbitrage by borrowing at tax-exempt interest rates and investing in financial assets with greater returns, the magnitude of this benefit could be substantial. Data limitations prevent the authors from carefully estimating the value of the tax deduction for charitable gifts. However, their preliminary analysis of cost report data reveals that these contributions are substantial only for a small number of hospitals, with 44 percent of all not-for-profit hospitals having zero charitable contributions in 1995.

Finally, Tomas Philipson examines whether consumers are willing to pay significantly higher prices for not-for-profit nursing home care than for similar care in for-profit facilities. If not-for-profit nursing homes solve the asymmetric information problem between consumers and producers better than their for-profit counterparts, these two types of institutions are not perfect substitutes. More specifically, not-for-profit nursing homes should sell at a premium because consumers would value the not-for-profit status more highly.

Using data from the U.S. National Nursing Home Surveys in 1985 and 1995, Philipson finds no support for the presence of a not-for-profit premium. Instead, he finds a 5 percent for-profit premium in 1985 and no significant difference in price in 1995. These results suggest that there is perfect substitution on the demand side between not-for-profit and for-profit production, and that asymmetric information is relatively less important in health care markets than many economists have previously suggested. Finally, Philipson points out that future theoretical work on the effect of organizational form within the health care market should aim to explain why the hospital market is served mainly by not-for-profit firms while the nursing home market is dominated by for-profit facilities.

A Concluding Thought

The economics of the hospital industry are changing rapidly and dramatically. Reduced demand, lower profit margins, and more intense competition make the hospital industry of today very different from the hospital industry of the past.

Already, the changes in the industry have reached the public sector. Antitrust policy has been forced to evaluate the costs and benefits of hospital mergers. Tax policy has to consider the revenue consequences of different organizational forms. And perceptions that care for the uninsured will suffer as the industry changes will place pressure on public hospitals and public insurance programs.

The demands for economic analysis are great. The papers in this volume, and the subsequent research they are certain to stimulate, will have enormous implications for public policy toward this vital industry.

I

Hospital Conversions to For-Profit Form

1

Hospital Conversions
Is the Purchase Price Too Low?

Frank A. Sloan, Donald H. Taylor, Jr.,
and Christopher J. Conover

1.1 Introduction

Conceptually, the appropriate decision as to assignment of ownership rights is that arrangement that minimizes transactions costs between the firm and its various contractors. For various reasons, including asymmetric information between buyers (patients) and sellers (hospitals and others), the dominance of third-party payment, and consumption externalities, it is widely believed among experts in the health field and many in the public that the for-profit organizational form does not minimize transactions cost in the hospital sector (e.g., Relman 1980; Gray 1991).

The for-profit (FP) hospital is in the minority numerically in all industrialized countries. In the United States presently, only 10 percent of hospital beds are in FP hospitals, with 70 percent being in private not-for-profit (NFP) and 20 percent in public institutions (Claxton et al. 1997). For-profit hospitals fall into two groups—small, independent, privately held hospitals, often physician owned, and hospitals that are part of publicly

Frank A. Sloan is the J. Alexander McMahon Professor of Health Policy and Management and professor of economics at Duke University and a research associate of the National Bureau of Economic Research. He is also the director of the Center for Health Policy, Law, and Management at Duke. Donald H. Taylor, Jr., is assistant research professor of public policy studies, Terry Sanford Institute of Public Policy, in the Center for Health Policy, Law, and Management, Duke University. Christopher J. Conover is assistant research professor of public policy studies, Terry Sanford Institute of Public Policy, and Senior Fellow, Center for Health Policy, Law, and Management at Duke University. He also serves as director of the Duke Health Policy Certificate Program.

This research was supported in part by grants from the Duke Endowment, the Fullerton Foundation, the Self Foundation, and the Robert Wood Johnson Foundation. The authors thank Lan Liang, Peter Rankin, and Yaoping Wang for research assistance, and conference participants.

owned corporations. Although the for-profit share has been quite stable historically, for-profit chain hospitals have grown both numerically and in influence in many communities since they first appeared in the late 1960s. The growth of these hospital companies has not been steady, but rather has been characterized by cycles of growth (Gray and Schlesinger 1997). Most of the 1990s have been a growth period for the hospital companies, with many NFP and government hospitals being acquired by these firms (Kuttner 1996a, 1996b; Needleman, Chollet, and Lamphere 1997). The remaining for-profit hospitals that are independent free-standing organizations command much less interest because they are small in terms of bed capacity and are a vanishing breed.

The growth of for-profit chains in particular has elicited substantial concern, especially among some health care leaders. They have argued that consolidation of hospitals under the aegis of publicly owned corporations will mean higher priced and lower quality care, lower rates of production of outputs that—although unprofitable to hospitals—have high marginal social benefit, and less accessible care to those with low ability to pay (see, e.g., Relman 1980). As Gray and Schlesinger explained, the reasons for eschewing the for-profit ownership form for hospitals comes down to two issues: trust and community benefits. Others see much potential for market-driven health care to deliver personal health care services efficiently (Herzlinger 1997).

Conversions from public to NFP hospital status are also manifestations of a trend of assigning the responsibility of public goals to private organizations. A similar trend is occurring in primary and secondary education and to a lesser extent in corrections and in certain municipal services (Kuttner 1997, 356–61).

A related development is the increased commercialization of some large public hospital systems, perhaps reflecting reduced public subsidies. As large public hospital systems seek to improve their competitiveness through acquisition of smaller public, quasi-public, or even NFP facilities, local communities are faced with reduced control and potential loss of a public asset and/or the benefit flows from this asset (Bell et al. 1997; Gray 1997).

Buying and selling of hospitals is receiving a considerable amount of public interest and scrutiny, both in the media and by public regulatory agencies (Horwitz 1998). Aside from antitrust scrutiny to gauge the effect on competition, the vast majority of mergers and acquisitions are not subject to public scrutiny because both buyer and seller are believed to be reasonably empowered to conduct the transaction in their own self-interests.

In this context, however, sellers—the communities in the case of public and NFP hospitals—may not be sufficiently empowered or knowledgeable to act in their own self-interests. One reason is that the sellers may not have the requisite expertise. Such transactions occur very infrequently. The process of determining fair value is made difficult because of the multidimensional attributes of the transactions and the heterogeneous preferences of various stakeholders in the communities. Various rules of thumb exist for establishing a "fair" price for hospitals, such as a multiple of earnings before interest, taxes, depreciation, and amortization (EBITDA); but these rules must in fact be quite imprecise. Also, various stakeholders at the hospital being sold may have self-interests—such as job preservation and/or acquiring an equity interest in the enterprise—that may not coincide with the broader public interest.

Differential bargaining power is commonplace and does not necessarily provide a rationale for public oversight or even intervention since such intervention also inevitably has unintended adverse side effects. But the merit want nature of hospital care strengthens the argument for some type of public scrutiny. Some states require assessment of such transactions by the state attorney general or another regulatory body, and the proportion of states imposing such scrutiny is rapidly increasing, as is the activity of attorneys general in this field (Matzke 1997; Shactman and Fishman 1996; Horwitz 1998).

Hospital ownership conversions take several forms. In this study, we consider a "conversion" to be any change in ownership type, either FP, NFP, or government.

In the most straightforward case, one hospital or parent company purchases a NFP or public community hospital outright. In some, a hospital's assets and liabilities are transferred to another organization at a zero purchase price. Alternatively, a facility may be leased by another organization, through which control of the hospital assets is ceded to the lessor for long time periods—often for several decades. Sometimes, ownership conversion is coincident with a horizontal merger. Such mergers represent full integration of two or more hospital entities. Joint ventures involve less complete integration than full mergers. Joint ventures may be broad or limited in scope, such as for the provision of a single service.

The objective of this article is to investigate whether communities have received a fair price for the hospitals they have sold or leased. To answer this question, we analyzed 10 recent transactions involving hospitals in North Carolina and South Carolina in depth. The case studies provided critical information that cannot be obtained from secondary sources. Most important were the financial and nonfinancial terms of the transactions. Among the financial terms were (1) purchase and lease prices, (2) recipient organizations of funds, which may be foundations, (3) various commitments made about provision of services, and (4) the time path of outlays and commitments. Among the nonfinancial terms were organizational changes, such as in board membership and composition. Statements by various community members about reasons for the conversion and community benefits involved have helped to guide and provide a cross-check on our own empirical analysis.

To gauge whether the transactions prices were fair, we computed private rates of return under alternative assumptions about future cash flows that reflect both revenue accruing to the facility post transaction and possible efficiency gains. Normally, the price is fair if the cash flows yield a rate of return equal to the cost of capital. Since the net value to the community includes a range of social benefits, some of which are intangible, comparisons of private rates of return with cost of capital provide an inadequate indication of value of the transaction to the seller. Therefore, we have also assessed community benefits that may not be reflected in the transaction price.

Rate of return analyses were conducted by some, or perhaps all, of the parties prior to the transactions, but undoubtedly not using a consistent methodology. Also, assumptions may have been made to support a particular view about the attractiveness of the transactions. However, the parties' calculations may have been more accurate than ours because of insider knowledge or more access to detailed information about local market conditions. In any event, these calculations have not been made available to us or, more generally, to the public at large.

There is very little empirical evidence on changes that occur in hospital behavior postconversion or on the process of selection into a hospital conversion. Relevant behavioral responses include changes in pricing practices; efficiency gains, which in turn affect hospital profitability; and the provision of uncompensated care and services judged essential or highly beneficial to the communities. Thus, as part of this study, we provide new empirical evidence on how ownership conversion affects these behaviors.

In section 1.2, we describe our methodology. Section 1.3 presents evidence from the 10 case studies. In section 1.4, we present empirical evidence on the effects of conversions on profitability, and on provision of uncompensated care and particular hospital services. Data on uncompensated care were not collected for North Carolina. For this reason, and because a larger number of conversions occurred in Tennessee than in the Carolinas, our empirical analysis of conversions based on secondary data includes Tennessee as well as North Carolina and South Carolina. Some parts of the analysis were limited to Tennessee due in part to data availability. Section 1.5 presents our analysis of rates of return on the investments that the buyers made as well as of the cost of capital prevailing at the time of the transactions in the 10 case-study hospitals; this discussion is followed by a more general assessment of benefit in section 1.6. Finally, section 1.7 discusses conclusions and implications.

1.2 Methods

1.2.1 Case Study Sample and Site Visits: North Carolina and South Carolina

We identified all ownership changes that occurred in North Carolina and South Carolina between 1985 and 1996 using public use tapes from the American Hospital Association's *Annual Survey of Hospitals,* information supplied by the two state hospital associations, and, finally, telephone calls to hospitals when we found inconsistencies between the first two sources. This process yielded 29 changes.

We prepared a table that compared past with present ownership status. This table was presented to our study's board of advisors. The board was highly knowledgeable about the hospital industry in the two states and was representative of the various community interests there.

In consultation with the board, we selected 10 cases for in-depth study (table 1.1). Selection was guided by these criteria: inclusion of all major types of ownership conversions that occurred; representation of hospitals in both states; year of conversion (pre- versus post-1990), and type of transaction (acquisition, lease, joint venture). Many conversions occurred after 1994, limiting the amount of information we were able to obtain on these hospitals postconversion. Conversions taking place during the earlier period ("older conversions") afforded more time to measure cash flows postconversion and other impacts on the community that the conversion may have had. More recent conversions made it more likely that we could clearly capture the details of each conversion. Among the details were motives for converting, the process itself, and terms of charitable foundations related to hospital conversions. Foundations were only created as part of the recent conversions.

These 10 hospitals ranged in size from 64 acute care beds (Hilton Head Hospital) to 725 beds (Wake Medical Center), with half having fewer than

Table 1.1   **Ten Hospitals Studied in North and South Carolina**

	Final Status		
Original Status	Private Not-for-Profit	Government	For-Profit
Private not-for-profit		Cleveland Regional Medical Center 1994 Roanoke/Chowan 1997	Hilton Head 1995 Byerly 1995 Providence 1995 Cape Fear 1996 Mary Black 1996
Government	Wake County 1997		Piedmont 1981 Upstate 1984

150 beds and four having between 200 and 300 beds. Four facilities are located in metropolitan statistical areas (MSAs) with more than 500,000 population, one is in an MSA with roughly 250,000, and the remainder are located outside of MSAs entirely. Although some facilities have teaching residents, none is considered a major teaching hospital. For each of the 10 hospitals selected, we conducted a two-day site visit. During the site visit we spoke with various stakeholders representing the hospital, the broader medical community, public health/social services officials, employers, churches, and community advocates.

1.2.2   Analysis of Secondary Data

Overview

To supplement the case-study data, we used information for North Carolina, South Carolina, and Tennessee from the American Hospital Association's (AHA's) Annual Hospital Survey (1987–1995), Medicare Cost Reports (1983–1995), and Tennessee Joint Annual Reports of Hospitals (1990–96). The AHA surveys provided information on hospital outputs, concentration of output at the market level, and provision of particular services by the nonfederal short-term general hospitals in the three states. From the Medicare cost reports, we obtained prices, cost, cash flows, and balance-sheet information. The Tennessee joint annual reports (JARs) provided more detailed financial data than was available from either of the two other sources, including information on provision of uncompensated care and on taxes paid by the for-profits. We also attempted to collect financial statements from the 10 case-study hospitals. Only two facilities, however, were willing to release such information. Fortunately, most pertinent information from income statements and balance sheets was available from the Medicare cost reports.

Analysis Based on Joint Annual Report Data: Tennessee

We analyzed pricing, changes in average cost, profitability, and provision of uncompensated care pre- and postownership change in Tennessee using data from Tennessee JARs. Dependent variables were net patient revenue and total expense per adjusted patient day; profit as a fraction of total hospital revenue, including and, alternatively, excluding interest, depreciation, and taxes; and uncompensated care charges as a fraction of total charges and, alternatively, of net patient revenue. In the analysis of pricing and cost, the dependent variables were expressed in natural logarithm form.

The key explanatory variables were binary variables for ownership in the base year (1990); for government and NFP ownership, with for-profit the omitted reference group; and for specific types of ownership conversions (government or NFP to FP and FP to NFP or government); and for other conversions. We had to combine the other types of conversions (e.g., government to NFP) into a single variable because the number of observations was insufficient to permit a more detailed specification. To measure the effects of conversions, we specified separate variables for the pre- and postconversion years. The effect of conversion was measured as the difference between two coefficients, postconversion minus preconversion. This differencing eliminated time-invariant, otherwise unspecified hospital effects of the hospitals that converted. To determine whether or not there was a trend in profitability postconversion, we substituted trend variables as an alternative to the binary variables for postconversion in the analysis of profitability.

In addition, we included explanatory variables for hospital output concentration, a Herfindahl-Hirschman Index (HHI) for adjusted patient days in the hospital's market area, real per capita income, the fraction of the population over age 65, the fraction of the population enrolled in health maintenance organizations, the fraction of hospital admissions in the market covered by Medicaid, the unemployment rate, population density, and a time trend. In the uncompensated care analysis, if the observation was for an NFP or FP facility, we included a binary variable to indicate whether or not there was a government hospital in the county. To account for implementation of Medicaid managed care in Tennessee—TennCare—in 1994, we included a second Medicaid variable to indicate the Medicaid share during the years TennCare was in effect (1994 onward); otherwise, this variable was set equal to zero. We split the time trend into two variables—one for 1990–93 and the other for 1994–96. For hospitals located in metropolitan areas, we considered the Standard Metropolitan Statistical Area (SMSA) to be the market area. For other hospitals, we specified the county as the market area. All monetarily expressed variables were converted to 1995 dollars using the Consumer Price Index for all items.

Analysis Based on American Hospital Association Surveys:
Tennessee, North Carolina, and South Carolina

With AHA data, we assessed the impacts of conversions on emergency room visits, on births, and on the availability of selected services. We classified services into three categories: (1) "unprofitable, essential" community services: HIV/AIDS treatment, community health and education, emergency room, and labor/delivery; (2) elderly oriented services that may be adopted in response to Medicare Prospective Payment System: home health, rehabilitation, and skilled nursing facility; and (3) services likely to be profitable: sports medicine, magnetic resonance imaging (MRI), and open heart surgery (Waters 1992). The dependent variables in the analysis of emergency room and labor/delivery output were the log of emergency room visits and births. We used logit to estimate the service availability equations. Finally, we estimated equations for the share of admissions covered by (1) Medicaid and (2) Medicare to further assess impacts of ownership conversions on case mix.

1.2.3   Analysis of Rates of Return

Measurement of Investment

From the interviews, we obtained information on purchase prices and lease payments, terminal values when specified (one case), and commitments to invest in the community or hospital facility (e.g., taking over indigent care obligations or debt payments previously financed by the county). These were specified as negative cash flows in the year such expenditures occurred or were expected to occur, expressed in 1995 dollars.

Time Horizon

For leases, we took the time horizon to be the term of the lease. Otherwise, we based the rates of return on, alternatively, a 20- and a 30-year period, with the terminal value being 25 percent of the 1995 value of the facility as reported in the Medicare cost reports. Alternative calculations assumed different terminal values.

Measurement of Returns

For two hospitals, we could measure returns for some years postconversion. For the eight others, we observed no postconversion years. However, in all cases, we had to project returns for at least some years. For our projections, we used the parameter estimates from the regression for total margin based on Tennessee data to project future cash flows. To link the projection with historical cash flows, we formed an index with the projected 1995 margin as the base value. We multiplied this index by the mean cash flow for the hospital for years 1993–95. We used a three-year average because of the volatility of cash flows and because the 1995 year was the year immediately preconversion for several hospitals. Alternative calculations used two- and five-year averages.

For future values of HHI and unemployment, we took values for 1995 and assumed a constant value throughout. We projected population, population over age 65, HMO and Medicaid patient shares, and real per capita income in the hospital's market area based on annual growth rates actually observed between 1987 and 1995. We capped the area HMO share at 75 percent and limited the Medicaid share to be within ±25 percent of the 1995 value. When the HMO share was zero in 1995 (which occurred in four cases), we assumed a 1 percent per year growth in share starting in 1996, with a maximum set at a 25 percent share. For the time trend, we took the midpoint of the two coefficients for the 1990–93 and 1994–96 periods, respectively. In the base case, we used the trend coefficient after 15 years postconversion. Thereafter the trend was assumed to stop. Alternative calculations capped the trend at 10 years and 20 years. We used the coefficients from the relevant pre- and postconversion binary variables when the conversion occurred after 1995. For example, if a conversion occurred on July 1, 1996, we used the preconversion value for a half a year and the postconversion value for the other half.

For depreciation, we computed a rate of depreciation based on the hospital's fixed assets for 1995. We used straight-line depreciation until the terminal value was reached. For interest, we computed an interest rate for 1995 by dividing each hospital's interest payments by its long-term debt obligations. That interest rate was assumed to be constant in the future. Liabilities were decreased over time as the loan was paid back. For taxes paid by for-profit hospitals, we applied the federal and state statutory rates for corporate income taxes to annual net earnings (after interest and depreciation). We obtained property tax rates from the county in which the for-profit hospital was located for 1996 tax year and used these rates for all years to estimate property taxes based on the value of total assets. The rate for all other taxes (2.4 percent) was calculated from Tennessee JARs data and was applied to annual net earnings.

Cost of Capital to Hospitals

Estimates of the weighted cost of capital were computed using a method reported in Sloan et al. (1988). For for-profit organizations, we used an estimate of beta from the capital asset pricing model of 1.41. To estimate the real cost of equity capital, we added the risk premium to the nominal risk-free interest rate for the year in which the transaction occurred (from Sloan et al. 1988). The sum was the nominal cost of equity capital, which we converted to real terms using the inflation rate for all items. The nominal interest rate was taken to be the rate on 30-year U.S. Treasury bonds, again expressed in real terms using the inflation rate. The weighted cost of capital estimate used the hospital's debt-to-assets ratio in the year before the conversion occurred as weights. In Sloan et al. (1988), the estimated cost of capital for the hospital sector was slightly higher when an estimate based on arbitrage pricing theory was used.

For the nonprofit sector, the first task was to adjust the beta used for for-profit hospitals. This beta took account of the leverage in the NFP versus the FP hospital companies. The adjusted beta was 1.46. With this beta and the same risk-free interest rate information used above, we estimated the real cost of equity capital. We used a 30-year municipal bond for the cost of debt. Again, we used information on the debt-to-assets ratio to obtain a weighted real cost of capital. The NFP cost of capital was also used for government facilities. Another benchmark used for comparison was the ratio of the purchase price to average earnings before interest, taxes, depreciation, and amortization (EBITDA) in the three years prior to conversion.

Sensitivity Analysis

In addition to testing alternative values to use for the terminal value of the facility, when to make the trend factor constant, and which base years to use in projecting earnings, we examined the impact on rate of returns of assuming that hospitals were able to achieve an additional 5 or 20 percent reduction in hospital expenses. That is, because our model was designed to project the average increase in earnings resulting from a particular type of conversion, it is conceivable that for any given facility, this projection failed to fully account for either cost-cutting opportunities or revenue-enhancing possibilities that would provide better earnings. The prospect of increasing earnings plausibly would come from cost reductions beyond that reflected in the historical data postconversion. Previous cost analysis based on data from a much earlier period indicated that FP companies achieve cost reductions several years after the conversion occurs (Becker and Sloan 1985). Studies of hospital efficiency have found substantial slack (e.g., 15 percent in Zuckerman et al. 1994). Several nonacademic accounts have maintained that FP companies achieve sizable margins (Japsen 1996; Moore 1997). In our calculations, we assumed the cost reductions began in the third post-conversion year and were fully realized by the end of the seventh year.

1.2.4   Assessing Community Benefit

In addition to the empirical analysis described above, we obtained perceived benefits from various stakeholders in the communities. We assessed these benefits in qualitative terms.

1.3   Evidence from Case Studies of Converting Hospitals

The case studies from the 10 North Carolina and South Carolina hospitals that converted provided information not available from various secondary sources, including the rationale for converting; details about the terms of the conversions; disposition of proceeds from the sale or lease of the facility; changes in the hospital, such as renovation and expansion or deletion of services; plans for provision of uncompensated care; and views about the advantages and disadvantages of the conversion. This section summarizes this descriptive material.

1.3.1   Reasons for the Conversion

In every case, the stated rationale for the conversion was to preserve the financial viability of the hospital for the benefit of the health care of local citizens and to preserve local jobs. Both benefits were viewed as particularly important for hospitals in rural areas. The alternative to the conversion was seen as either increased public subsidy, mainly in the form of investment in plant or equipment, or closure of the facility.

One mechanism stated for improving financial viability was to increase bargaining power with managed care organizations by affiliating with a network of facilities. The desire to build hospital networks and referrals to existing hospitals also applied to the acquiring organizations. Another motive was to improve hospital efficiency, either by assigning property rights to profits to investors or, in the case of public to private, not-for-profit conversions, to give hospitals additional flexibility in input use than is possible in a government-run organization.

The motive of forestalling investment in hospitals by converting is more complex. Conceptually, hospital and community leaders might be stating that the cost of capital funds to the communities exceeded that of others—either hospital companies or hospitals in other locations. It is not clear, however, that the communities viewed the issue in such terms. Rather, some seem to have thought of capital supplied by these external sources as essentially "free" instead of being included in the price of hospital care paid by the local citizenry. In the case of government facilities, some public officials viewed running a hospital and/or the cost of raising funds through bond referenda or in some other way as a political liability, one that conversion would alleviate.

1.3.2   Terms of Conversions

We studied two conversions of government (county) to FP facilities; one from government to NFP; five from NFP to FP status, with for-profit companies the acquiring organization; and two acquisitions of NFP hospitals by larger public hospitals/systems, one a hospital authority in the largest city in the Carolinas (Charlotte), and the other a teaching hospital serving a rural population in eastern North Carolina (table 1.2). For the last two transactions, the major negative consideration to the community was loss of community control. For the others, potential efficiency gains in marketing and in operations and the benefit of not having to infuse capital funds into the facility were balanced against concern about loss of community control, as well as a possible change in mission. In two of the NFP to FP conversions, survey respondents said the community did not accept the most favorable financial offer, opting instead to sell to organizations providing greater long-term stability. We did not obtain specific information on the multiple offers or on the efforts communities made to secure and scrutinize multiple offers.

The earliest conversion we studied first occurred in 1981, with a resale occurring in 1988. In our rate-of-return analysis, we considered the transaction year to be 1981 and then did backward extrapolation of relevant

Table 1.2 Description of Conversion Arrangements

Hospital and Terms of Conversion	Year	Financial Terms	Investment/ Expansion Plans	Other Terms
Government to For-Profit				
Purchase of Piedmont Memorial Hospital by Tenet	Jan. 1981	$10 million	Built new $32.2 million hospital in 1983; $20 million expansion from 1995–98	County had buyback options in 1988 and 1995; now 50-year-term, at which time the contract must be renegotiated
Purchase of Cherokee Memorial Hospital (Upstate Carolina Medical Center) by National Medical Enterprises	Feb. 1984	$1.2 million + $5 million in lease payments over 3 years	Built a new hospital for $18 million	Must maintain hospital emergency room, ambulance service, and indigent care
Not-for-Profit to For-Profit				
Purchase of Byerly Hospital by Health Management Associates	Aug. 1995	$31 million	Currently building new hospital for $45 million	
50/50 joint venture between Sisters of Charity of St. Augustine (Providence Hospital) and Columbia/HCA	Nov. 1995	$80 million	$7.9 million investment	Must maintain hospital and religious mission

Purchase of Hilton Head Hospital by Tenet (then AMI)	May 1995	$26 million	Current $7 million expansions in services	Foundation
Purchase of Cape Fear Memorial Hospital by Columbia/HCA	May 1996	$55 million	$4.8 million expansion	Foundation
Purchase of Mary Black Hospital by Quorum	July 1996	$58.5 million	$7.6 million expansion in 1996–97	Foundation
Governmental to Private Not-for-Profit				
Transfer of assets from Wake County to Wake County Hospital System, Inc.	April 1997	Assumption of $100 to $118 million debt		County appoints majority of board
Private Not-for-Profit to Government				
Lease of Cleveland Regional Medical Center by Charlotte/Mecklenburg Health Authority	July 1994	Lease of $1.7 million per year; term is 11 years		Affiliation with and contract management by lessor in July 1994; lease began Oct. 1997; $1.4 million of lease proceeds into county general fund
Lease of Roanoke/Chowan Hospital by Pitt County Memorial Hospital	Feb. 1997	$1 million + assumption of long-term debt; term is 23 years	$1 million per year in unspecified capital foundations	Foundation; Pitt can buy outright for $100,000 in 2021

variables to recover the stream of cash flows prior to 1987. The most recent conversion occurred in 1997.

The only leases were for the two NFP hospitals that were acquired by public hospital systems. The term of one lease was 23 years; the other was 11 years. In one case, the buyer committed to an annual lease payment plus assumption of the hospital's long-term debt. In the other, the acquiring organization just paid a fixed lease payment. The ownership conversions involved some form of purchase; in one case, this was organized as a joint venture to preserve the hospital's religious mission. In one of the NFP to FP conversions, the foundation that was created as a result of the transactions acquired a 20 percent equity position in the hospital. This gave the community some continued input into hospital decision making. Subsequently, the foundation sold its equity to the hospital company that had purchased the hospital. Foundation directors said that they felt comfortable with the progress the new owners had made and believed that the foundation could earn a higher return on its equity if its funds were invested elsewhere. In one of the public-to-FP conversions, the terms of the contract must be renegotiated in 50 years.

Eight of the 10 transactions included an explicit commitment to invest in the hospital. In some, the buyer committed to build a new facility. In others, commitments were made to expand specific services, such as rehabilitation and obstetrics. In fact, with the exception of one hospital, every facility had either undertaken investment or had explicit plans to do so at the time the interviews were conducted. Two new hospitals, both resulting from public to for-profit conversions, had been built, and at one of the other hospitals recently converted to for-profit status, plans had been developed for constructing a new hospital and medical office complex. Other facilities had expanded existing services or had entered into new services.

A key issue in most of the conversions was some form of guarantee of continued provision of uncompensated care. Nine agreements specified a minimum dollar amount or a catchment area for which the hospital was to accept patients irrespective of ability to pay. In the tenth case (Cape Fear), the agreement specified that uncompensated care was to be provided at the level of comparable hospitals.

1.3.3   Disposition of Proceeds from Sale or Lease

Six foundations, organized to allocate the proceeds, were created from these 10 transactions. These included all of the NFP to FP cases and one of the two leases. The majority of these foundations stipulated that the funds be used not only for health-related initiatives but also for community-oriented activities. However, several charters limited the types of community-oriented activities the foundation could support. An exception to this broader community focus was the one with the lowest level of funding (Roanoke/Chowan), which stipulated that all monies generated from lease payments be allocated to capital improvements in the hospital, hospital-owned physician practices, or other hospital-based programs, such as hospice care. Funds were not to be used to fund uncompensated care. A second foundation containing cash reserves of the old NFP hospital ($14 million) may be created in the future, but its focus in terms of giving is undetermined.

One of the foundations conducted a needs assessment and strategic planning jointly with the city in which it was located to determine education and economic development issues that were the highest priority to the community as a whole.

1.3.4   Satisfaction after the Sale or Lease

We did not interview individuals in the parent organization that purchased or leased the facilities (although some of the hospital CEOs or others were employed by these companies). However, for those conversions for which we could compare pre- versus postconversion profitability, profits rose in each case. The vast majority of persons we interviewed in the communities affected by the conversions were generally satisfied with the transaction. Hospital viability had been maintained, and purchasers had invested in local facilities. However, a persistent concern was loss of local control to an organization controlled by outsiders.

1.4   Empirical Evidence on Effects of Conversions

1.4.1   Profitability and Uncompensated Care: Tennessee Hospitals

We analyzed profitability without and with interest and depreciation using JAR data on Tennessee hospitals (table 1.3). The first regression was used in our analysis of the rates of return to the 10 case-study conversions that occurred in North Carolina and South Carolina. Both regressions revealed essentially the same result. Our discussion focuses on the second regression.

On average, NFP and government hospitals in Tennessee were less profitable than those under for-profit ownership. Margins of NFP and government hospitals were, respectively, 3.0 percent and 5.9 percent below those of for-profit hospitals. Those NFP hospitals that converted were less profitable on average than their counterparts that did not convert (8.7 percent less). Those NFP facilities that converted to for-profit experienced an increase in their profit rate (5.6 percent). Those hospitals that converted from for-profit to either NFP or government status also experienced an increase in profitability (4.6 percent). For all other conversions, there was a small pre- versus postconversion difference (0.6 percent decrease)

Table 1.3 **Effects of Conversion on Profit and Uncompensated Care: Tennessee Hospitals, 1990–1996**

Explanatory Variables	Profit Rate Excluding Interest and Depreciation	Profit Rate with Interest and Depreciation	Uncompensated Care
Intercept	0.182	0.158	0.124
	(0.047)	(0.051)	(0.031)
Private, not-for-profit	−0.036	−0.026	0.030
	(0.007)	(0.008)	(0.005)
Government	−0.071	−0.053	0.041
	(0.008)	(0.009)	(0.006)
Other government	—	—	−0.018
hospitals in county	—	—	(0.005)
NFP to FP (pre)	−0.042	−0.078	−0.019
	(0.015)	(0.016)	(0.010)
NFP to FP (post)	−0.019	−0.024	−0.008
	(0.019)	(0.021)	(0.0013)
NFP to FP, diff	**0.023**	**0.054**	**0.011**
F-value (Prob $> F$)	**0.877 (0.349)**	**4.054 (0.044)**	**0.521 (0.471)**
FP to NFP or G (pre)	−0.036	−0.028	0.030
	(0.020)	(0.022)	(0.013)
FP to NFP or G (post)	−0.015	−0.018	0.004
	(0.020)	(0.021)	(0.013)
FP to NFP or G, diff	**0.021**	**0.010**	**−0.026**
F-value (Prob $> F$)	**0.569 (0.451)**	**0.108 (0.743)**	**2.025 (0.155)**
Other conversion (pre)	−0.003	0.018	−0.040
	(0.022)	(0.024)	(0.015)
Other conversion (post)	0.010	0.024	−0.002
	(0.032)	(0.035)	(0.021)
Other conversion, diff	**0.013**	**0.006**	**0.038**
F-value (Prob $> F$)	**0.116 (0.734)**	**0.021 (0.885)**	**2.219 (0.137)**
HMO share	−0.066	−0.090	−0.021
	(0.039)	(0.043)	(0.025)
HHI	−0.027	−0.025	0.020
	(0.009)	(0.010)	(0.006)
Medicaid share	0.051	−0.006	−0.115
	(0.111)	(0.122)	(0.073)
Medicaid share 1994–96 (TN)	0.112	0.165	0.101
	(0.153)	(0.167)	(0.100)
Per capita income ('0000)	0.096	0.079	0.007
	(0.024)	(0.026)	(0.016)
Unemployment rate	0.008	0.008	0.002
	(0.002)	(0.002)	(0.001)
Population over 65 (%)	0.691	0.386	−0.513
	(0.184)	(0.201)	(0.120)
Population density ('000)	0.087	0.099	0.015
	(0.041)	(0.045)	(0.027)
Time	−0.007	0.001	−0.002
	(0.004)	(0.005)	(0.003)
Time * 94–96 (TN)	−0.001	0.004	−0.005
	(0.005)	(0.005)	(0.003)
	$R^2 = 0.25$	$R^2 = 0.23$	$R^2 = 0.14$
	$\overline{R}^2 = 0.23$	$\overline{R}^2 = 0.22$	$\overline{R}^2 = 0.12$
	$F(18, 796) = 14.49$	$F(18,796) = 13.45$	$F(19, 795) = 6.69$

Source: Tennessee Joint Annual Report of Hospitals, 1990–1996.

in margins. In only two instances (NFP to FP hospitals, col. 2, table 1.3; and FP to NFP, col. 1, table 1.3) were the pre- versus postconversion changes in margins statistically significant at conventional levels (F-test).

We tested for trends in profitability after conversion, and we could not detect any. However, the length of postconversion period in the Tennessee hospital sample was often quite short (one to three years). The coefficient on the time-trend variable indicates that provision of uncompensated care increased over time (significant at the 10 percent level).

Several other factors contributed to profitability. In particular, increased HMO share decreased profitability. Higher real per capita income increased margins, as did population density. Surprisingly, judging from the HHI parameter estimate, profits were lower in markets with less output concentration. Comparing net patient revenue with the cost results (not shown), the lower margin appears to be attributable to lower per hospital demand.

Both NFP and government hospitals in Tennessee provided more uncompensated care than did for-profit hospitals. Uncompensated care as a percentage of net patient revenue (the variant of the uncompensated care equation presented in table 1.3) was 3.1 percent higher for FP and 3.9 percent higher for government facilities. NFP or FP hospitals located in Tennessee counties with a government hospital provided less uncompensated care on average. Hospitals that converted from NFP to FP status increased uncompensated care by 0.9 percent. By contrast, hospitals converting from FP to either NFP or government facilities decreased their provision of uncompensated care, and the marginal effect was over twice as large (2.2 percent versus 0.9 percent) as that for conversions in the other direction. There was also an increase in uncompensated care among the other hospitals that changed ownership status (1.8 percent). None of these changes, however, were statistically significant. Most noteworthy, conversions to for-profit status did not result in reduced uncompensated care; in fact, in such situations, provision of such care may have increased, albeit slightly.

1.4.2 Effects of Conversions on Availability of Services: Hospitals in North Carolina, South Carolina, and Tennessee

Both NFP and government hospitals in the three states were more likely to provide AIDS, community health, and patient education services, ceteris paribus (table 1.4). (To conserve space, only the results for the ownership and the conversion variables are shown.) Conversion from NFP to FP status decreased the probability of having an AIDS program by 0.10 and community health by 0.04, but it did not change the probability of having a patient education program. However, none of these changes were statistically significant at conventional levels (chi-square test). Interestingly, those hospitals that converted from FP to NFP or government status

Table 1.4   Logit Analysis of Effects of Conversion on Availability of Services: North Carolina, South Carolina, and Tennessee Hospitals 1987–1995

Explanatory Variables	AIDS	Community Health	Patient Education	Home Health	Rehabilitation	Skilled Nurse Facility	Sports Medicine	Open Heart Surgery	MRI
Private, not-for-profit	0.65 (0.12) [0.16]	0.40 (0.12) [0.08]	0.76 (0.13) [0.11]	1.53 (0.15) [0.30]	0.50 (0.12) [0.12]	0.56 (0.16) [0.08]	0.16 (0.16) [0.02]	-0.66 (0.29) [-0.02]	-0.59 (0.17) [0.09]
Government	0.48 (0.14) [0.11]	0.16 (0.14) [0.03]	0.74 (0.15) [0.11]	1.27 (0.16) [0.25]	0.30 (0.14) [0.07]	0.25 (0.18) [0.04]	-0.22 (0.20) [-0.03]	-0.13 (0.37) [-0.00]	-0.30 (0.20) [0.04]
G or NFP to FP (pre)	0.20 (0.21) [0.05]	0.06 (0.23) [0.01]	0.16 (0.26) [0.02]	0.00 (0.22) [0.00]	0.71 (0.20) [0.18]	0.01 (0.25) [0.00]	-0.25 (0.28) [-0.03]	1.70 (0.44) [0.04]	0.46 (0.30) [0.07]
G or NFP to FP (post)	-0.22 (0.31) [-0.05]	-0.15 (0.31) [-0.03]	0.13 (0.32) [0.02]	0.56 (0.33) [0.11]	0.26 (0.29) [0.06]	-2.42 (0.73) [-0.34]	0.89 (0.31) [0.10]	-0.96 (0.82) [-0.02]	0.63 (0.34) [0.09]
G or NFP to FP, diff	**-0.10**	**-0.04**	**-0.00**	**0.11**	**-0.12**	**-0.34**	**0.13**	**-0.06**	**0.02**
χ²	**1.31**	**0.33**	**0.00**	**2.12**	**1.73**	**9.86**	**7.57**	**8.41**	**0.15**
(P-value)	**(0.25)**	**(0.57)**	**(0.94)**	**(0.15)**	**(0.19)**	**(0.00)**	**(0.01)**	**(0.00)**	**(0.70)**
FP to G or NFP (pre)	0.37 (0.36) [0.09]	-0.09 (0.35) [-0.02]	0.01 (0.34) [0.00]	0.86 (0.39) [0.17]	-1.33 (0.62) [-0.33]	—	—	—	-1.06 (1.04) [-0.15]
FP to G or NFP (post)	-0.64 (0.84) [-0.15]	-0.01 (0.62) [-0.00]	1.04 (0.59) [0.15]	1.59 (0.55) [0.31]	-0.58 (0.59) [-0.14]	—	—	—	-1.80 (1.06) [-0.26]
FP to G or NFP, diff	**-0.24**	**0.02**	**0.15**	**0.14**	**0.19**	—	—	—	**-0.11**
χ²	**1.25**	**0.01**	**2.31**	**1.28**	**0.80**	—	—	—	**0.25 (0.62)**
(P-value)	**(0.26)**	**(0.91)**	**(0.13)**	**(0.26)**	**(0.37)**	—	—	—	

Source: American Hospital Association, Annual Hospital Survey, 1987–1995.

Note: Standard errors are in parentheses unless otherwise indicated. Marginal effects are in brackets. Only ownership and conversion results are shown in table.

also dropped AIDS programs, but they added patient care programs. Again, however, these changes were not statistically significant.

Among services oriented toward the elderly, conversions from NFP or government to FP facilities increased the probability of offering home health by 0.11 but decreased the probability of having rehabilitation by 0.12 and of having a skilled nursing unit by 0.34. The third change was statistically significant at the 1 percent level.

For the conversions to government or NFP from for-profit status, there were increases in the probability of offering home health by 0.14 and of rehabilitation by 0.19. However, neither difference was statistically significant. We could not estimate the effects of this type of ownership conversion on provision of a skilled nursing facility because of an inadequate number of observations.

The final category included services that are likely to be profitable and oriented to a more general population. Among these, for those facilities converting to for-profit status, the probability of offering sports medicine increased by 0.13 and the probability of having MRI increased by 0.02 after the conversion, but the probability of doing open heart surgery decreased by 0.06. The first and third changes in probability were statistically significant at the 1 percent level.

1.4.3 Effects of Conversions on Emergency Room Visits, Deliveries, and Medicare and Medicaid Shares: Hospitals in North Carolina, South Carolina, and Tennessee

Conversion from NFP or government to for-profit status resulted in a 12 percent increase in emergency room visits and a 20 percent increase in the fraction of admissions covered by Medicaid (table 1.5). There were much more substantial decreases in the volume of deliveries (27 percent on average) but a slight decrease in the fraction of patients on Medicare (3 percent). Only the change in the Medicaid share was statistically significant at conventional levels. However, conversions from FP to NFP or government status resulted in larger percentage increases in numbers of visits to emergency rooms. Following such conversions, the volume of deliveries increased. Only in the case of the Medicaid patient share were decreases observed. But none of these changes were statistically significant at conventional levels.

In sum, conversions resulted in a mixed pattern of adoption of services. Judging from the empirical evidence, it would be inappropriate to attribute much of the change in service offerings or volume to a particular type of change in ownership status.

Table 1.5 Effects of Conversion on Emergency Room Visits, Deliveries, and Medicare and Medicaid Shares: North Carolina and South Carolina Hospitals, 1987–1995

Explanatory Variables	$\log_e$ (ER Visits)	$\log_e$ (Deliveries)	$\log_e$ (Medicaid Share)	$\log_e$ (Medicare Share)
Private, not-for-profit	-0.08	-0.30	0.07	0.07
	(0.03)	(0.07)	(0.03)	(0.02)
Government	-0.03	-0.46	0.12	0.06
	(0.04)	(0.08)	(0.04)	(0.02)
G or NFP to FP (pre)	-0.03	-0.33	-0.22	0.06
	(0.05)	(0.12)	(0.05)	(0.02)
G or NFP to FP (post)	0.08	-0.64	-0.04	0.03
	(0.07)	(0.16)	(0.07)	(0.04)
G or NFP to FP, diff	**0.11**	**-0.31**	**0.18**	**-0.03**
F-value	**1.38**	**2.48**	**4.16**	**0.69**
(Prob > F)	**(0.24)**	**(0.12)**	**(0.04)**	**(0.41)**
FP to G or NFP (pre)	-0.36	-0.36	-0.14	0.01
	(0.21)	(0.21)	(0.10)	(0.05)
FP to G or NFP (post)	-0.16	-0.16	-0.19	0.12
	(0.37)	(0.37)	(0.15)	(0.07)
FP to G or NFP, diff	**0.20**	**0.20**	**-0.05**	**0.11**
F-value	**2.97**	**0.24**	**0.07**	**1.53**
(Prob > F)	**(0.09)**	**(0.63)**	**(0.79)**	**(0.22)**
	$R^2 = 0.18$	$R^2 = 0.16$	$R^2 = 0.42$	$R^2 = 0.24$
	$\bar{R}^2 = 0.17$	$\bar{R}^2 = 0.15$	$\bar{R}^2 = 0.41$	$\bar{R}^2 = 0.23$
	$F(21, 2699) = 27.49$	$F(21, 2066) = 18.37$	$F(21, 2728) = 93.16$	$F(21, 2734) = 41.12$

Source: American Hospital Association, Annual Hospital Survey, 1987–1995.

Note: Standard errors are in parentheses unless otherwise noted. Only ownership and conversion results are shown in table.

1.5   Rates of Return and Cost of Capital: 10 Hospital Conversions in North Carolina and South Carolina

1.5.1   Base Case

Real rates of return were computed under alternative assumptions described above (table 1.6). With some notable exceptions, the rates of return, especially those involving a for-profit purchaser, generally were low. Unless otherwise stated, we discuss the base case rate with a 30-year time horizon or the lease, whichever applied. Results were fairly insensitive to variations in key assumptions—term and terminal value.

The two cases with the most postconversion experience were Piedmont (1981) and Upstate (1984). For these, much of the postconversion experience was actually observed. For Piedmont and Upstate, respectively, the rates of return were 9.4 percent and 6.7 percent. This was above the estimated real cost of capital to Piedmont (6.3 percent) at the time these transactions occurred, but it was lower than that to Upstate (7.6 percent). Piedmont was able to earn this return despite a buyback provision that was highly favorable to the seller. We learned from our case studies that such buyback arrangements are now uncommon. Upstate is located in a highly competitive market marked by other recent for-profit acquisitions and merger activities. Moreover, the purchase terms were established through a bidding process involving at least six other firms, including Hospital Corporation of America, which had previously managed the hospital under contract. The original purchaser, National Medical Enterprises (NME), sold the hospital shortly after building a new facility due to a strategic change in company focus. NME either may have been willing to forgo some profitability in order to gain access to a new market or may have miscalculated the difficulty of turning this hospital around (the somewhat low returns are in spite of considerable efficiency improvements, expansion of facilities, and success in attracting new physicians to the community).

Among the NFP to FP conversions, the most favorable rate of return was for Providence Hospital, which was a joint venture between the Sisters of Charity of St. Augustine and Columbia/HCA. In this case, the rate of return of 9.4 percent was above the estimated cost of capital to Columbia/HCA of 7.7 percent. In all other cases in this category, the real rate of return was appreciably below the real cost of capital.

For example, in the Cape Fear case, the hospital was slightly profitable. But prior to conversion, it lost some key managed care contracts to a crosstown rival. Since Columbia/HCA acquired the hospital, the hospital has regained some of the lost business. However, none of these special considerations were considered in our rate-of-return calculations. The area has been growing; we accounted for population growth in our calculations.

Table 1.6   Rates of Return and Cost of Capital (Base Case): 10 North Carolina and South Carolina Transactions

	Conversion Date	Base Case Real Rate of Return (IRR) % Calculated Over			Weighted Real Cost of Capital	Ratio of Purchase Price to Preconversion EBITDA[a]	
		30 Years	20 Years	Lease Period		Cash Price[b]	Full Price[c]
Public to for-profit							
Piedmont	1/1/81	9.41	9.20	—	6.27	—	—
Upstate	2/1/84	6.73	6.15	—	8.18	—	—
Not-for-profit to for-profit							
Byerly	8/1/95	1.83	0.71	—	7.15	4.4	8.9
Cape Fear	5/1/96	0.63	(1.02)	—	5.89	8.6	10.2
Hilton Head	5/1/95	(1.76)	(3.01)	—	6.77	8.4	10.9
Mary Black	7/1/96	(0.53)	(1.85)	—	6.30	8.6	10.0
Providence	8/1/95	9.42	9.20	—	7.65	4.8	5.5
Public to not-for-profit							
Wake County	4/1/97	253.03	253.03	—	4.71	Transfer	2.6
Not-for-profit to quasi-public							
Cleveland	10/1/97	Lease	—	196.03	5.02	Lease	1.3
Roanoke/Chowan	2/1/97	Lease	(4.86)	(4.19)	4.62	Lease	5.6

Note: Base case measures internal rate of return (IRR) of all cash flow, including purchase price, lease payments, and any new obligations taken on by the purchaser (i.e., taking over indigent care payments or debt obligations previously financed by county) in the lease arrangements; rate of return is calculated over lease period only. In base case, trend variable (= 1 in 1990) is assumed to be constant after 15 years (that is, this variable reduces the IRR by the same amount in year 30 as in year 15).

[a] EBITDA = earnings before interest, taxes, depreciation, and amortization. Preconversion EBITDA is the actual average annual amount for the three years prior to the year of conversion (not adjusted for inflation). Note that in the case of Cleveland Hospital, the lease arrangement did not begin until 1997, but the boards merged in 1994. Therefore, the preconversion EBITDA period is 1991–1993.

[b] Cash price equals the total amount paid by purchaser to acquire the hospital, exclusive of other obligations financed over time out of hospital operations.

[c] Total price equals cash price plus all other new obligations financed over time out of hospital operations, including lease payments, service, indigent care, or debt obligations not previously financed by the hospital itself (i.e., formerly subsidized by county).

The lowest rate of return for the NFP to FP conversions was for Hilton Head (−1.8 percent). In this case, the purchaser (Tenet) may have reasoned that it would benefit from construction of a retirement community across the river that eventually would house 40,000 persons, a development not reflected in our calculations.

Much more favorable to the buyer or acquirer were the county government to NFP transaction in Wake County (NC) and the NFP (Cleveland) to the hospital district authority transaction in Charlotte (NC). In Wake, for which the rate of return was 253 percent, compared to a cost of capital of 4.7 percent, the county was highly interested in finding a way to ensure the provision of indigent care without having to use tax funds to pay for those services, but it wanted to avoid selling or leasing to a for-profit organization. Roughly $400 million was transferred to a new NFP organization on apparently highly favorable terms to the new organization. In exchange, this organization guaranteed payment of $159 million in county debt obligations (which it already had been paying off prior to the conversion) and is committed to providing indigent care without the traditional county subsidy (several million annually), but the cost of fulfilling these obligations is considerably below the hospital's net earnings.

In the Cleveland Regional Medical Center situation, a period of leadership instability led to a request for assistance from the Charlotte/Mecklenburg Health Authority; an affiliation agreement and contract management by the Health Authority began in 1994. This interaction led to a leasing arrangement whereby the lessor pays $1.7 million per year for 11 years (starting October 1997) in return for a cash flow that is much larger than this. We estimated a 196 percent rate of return to the lessor on this transaction, compared to a cost of capital of 5.0 percent.

By contrast, in the case of Roanoke/Chowan, for which the rate of return over the lease period was −4.2 percent, the lessor, Pitt County Memorial Hospital—which is the teaching hospital for East Carolina University's medical school—assumed the hospital's debt payments of $25 million over the 23-year life of the lease. In the Cleveland case, the lessor assumed no debt.

Another way to view the purchase price is to compare it to EBITDA— the stream of earnings that the purchaser could be expected to enjoy absent large shifts in the market. If we look only at the cash amount paid (i.e., direct payments paid by the buyer at closing or through lease payments), the ratio to EBITDA was between 4.4 and 8.6. If we use the full price—that is, inclusive of long-term obligations such as covering previously subsidized indigent care—the ratios are much higher. In contrast, the ratios for not-for-profit and quasi-public acquisitions were much lower, and two of these, Wake County at 2.6 and Cleveland at 1.3, were much below the standard EBITDA multiples (typically 4–8) used in hospital acquisitions or those in other private markets.

1.5.2   Sensitivity Analysis

To test the robustness of our findings, we performed several sensitivity analyses. Our findings generally were robust with respect to assumptions about the terminal value of the hospital in the final year of the rate-of-return calculation. In more than half of the cases, rates of return varied by less than one-half of a percentage point. Hilton Head showed a much larger swing in returns, which reflects its relatively low projected stream of net earnings compared to the value of the facility itself. Likewise, it made almost no difference whether the trend factor flattened in year 10 or year 20. Not surprisingly, the base period used to project earnings made more of a difference, reflecting the volatility of hospital earnings in recent years. Nevertheless, changes in this assumption do not alter the overall flavor of our conclusions: For-profits continue to have rates of return at or below their cost of capital, while those for not-for-profit facilities were substantially higher. One final excursion was to see what happened if we assumed that our method somehow had been insufficient to account for the cost savings said to be achieved by for-profit companies. With an assumed cost reduction of 20 percent from the hospital's 1995 base, the Mary Black transactions rate of return equaled the cost of capital (compare the 6.2 percent return in table 1.7 with the 6.3 percent cost of capital in table 1.6). The largest discrepancy was for Hilton Head, with a rate of return of 4.6 percent with a 20 percent expense reduction compared to a cost of capital of 6.8 percent. It may be appropriate to infer equality of returns and costs in this case too because we did not specifically account for relative demand growth in this market.

Overall, with the caveat that we only investigated 10 cases in two states and used parameter estimates from a third, the pattern of the rates of return offers two important implications. First, the communities typically received more than a fair financial return on their assets when they transacted with a for-profit organization (in five out of seven such cases, the for-profit purchaser had returns below their own cost of capital). Despite the limitations of our sample, our findings are consistent with a recent U.S. General Accounting Office analysis of 14 not-for-profit hospital conversions to for-profit status in which it was found that most of the buyers had overpaid for the facilities (Weissenstein 1997). Second, the very high returns occurred when the communities dealt with NFP or quasi-governmental organizations. The lesson is that even private nonprofit and governmental organizations may take advantage of a highly profitable opportunity when they can.

Table 1.7   Rate of Return Sensitivity Analysis: 10 North Carolina and South Carolina Transactions

	If Terminal Value as % of 1995 Value =		If Trend Factor Constant after		If Projected Earnings Based on		If Hospital Expenses Cut an Additional	
	0%	100%	10 Years	20 Years	1994–95	1991–95	5%	20%
Public to for-profit								
Piedmont	9.41	9.42	9.40	9.42	9.52	9.27	NA[a]	NA[a]
Upstate	6.72	6.77	6.69	6.75	6.63	6.58	NA[a]	NA[a]
Not-for-profit to for-profit								
Byerly	1.80	1.96	1.71	1.91	1.28	2.51	3.00	5.15
Cape Fear	0.00	1.69	0.56	0.68	0.64	0.23	2.37	5.40
Hilton Head	(3.72)	(0.22)	(1.79)	(1.74)	(3.25)	(0.23)	0.78	4.56
Mary Black	(1.02)	0.16	(0.61)	(0.46)	(1.13)	0.81	2.18	6.22
Providence	9.41	9.37	9.27	9.47	10.01	8.13	10.56	12.19
Public to not-for-profit								
Wake County	NA[b]		253.03	253.03	227.83	340.54	—[c]	—[c]
Not-for-profit to quasi-public								
Cleveland	NA[d]		196.03	196.03	341.82	244.84	—[c]	—[c]
Roanoke/Chowan	NA[d]		(4.39)	(4.02)	(2.56)	(3.10)	—[c]	—[c]

Note: All rates-of-return calculations based on 30 years, except for lease arrangements, in which case lease period is used. NA = Not applicable.

[a] Efficiency savings not calculated since there is ample actual data on revenues, expenses, and margins in the postconversion period.

[b] Transfer with restrictions on sale. Purchaser presumed not able to sell facility in terminal year.

[c] Efficiency savings only calculated for conversions to for-profit status.

[d] Due to lease arrangement, purchaser not able to sell facility in terminal year.

1.6   Nonfinancial Returns: 10 Hospital Conversions in North Carolina and South Carolina

The above analysis of conversion effects did not reveal that a systematic reduction in services occurs when a government or NFP hospital converts to for-profit status or the converse. Lack of statistical significance may reflect lack of statistical power. However, in many cases, magnitudes of change were not great either.

An alternative approach is to gauge responses of stakeholders in 10 communities (table 1.8). Six of the 10 cases seemed to have been threatened with closure ("had effect" in the table). A paramount issue to community leaders was to keep a hospital in their communities. For both of the government (county) to FP conversions, this was a primary motive for selling the hospitals. In one case, a referendum to allow authorization to issue bonds was rejected by the voters. In the other, county officials were unwilling to raise the capital funds. In the NFP to FP conversion category, three of the five hospitals appeared to have been threatened with closure, the other two having had a fairly strong financial position. Of the remaining three hospitals, one (Roanoke/Chowan) had experienced a declining occupancy rate and had difficulty in recruiting and retaining physicians and desired a link to a larger hospital system.

Foundations were formed in six cases, all recent conversions; five were products of conversions to for-profit facilities. The sixth (Roanoke/Chowan) was limited because of the small size of the lease payments that fund the foundation and the stipulation that this money must be used for unspecified improvements to the hospital or its affiliated enterprises. In this case, another foundation with an unspecified focus may be created in the near future using cash reserves on hand at the time of the lease. Of the six, two charters limited foundation outlays to health (Cape Fear and Mary Black), although even in the case of Mary Black, health is broadly defined and the emphasis will be on health promotion and wellness rather than on traditional medical services. In the remaining agreements, the foundation may fund both health and other activities—mainly education, the arts, and local economic development. Several foundations are among the largest in the state. As another measure of magnitude of giving, one foundation's annual outlays match the level of charitable giving by United Way (Cape Fear), and in two other cases (Mary Black and Providence) outlays will considerably exceed those of United Way.

Hospitals also introduced or expanded cardiac catheterization, rehabilitation, obstetrics/delivery, skilled nursing facility beds, home health services, and/or renovation of emergency room facilities with new 24-hour capabilities. Of course, some of this construction may have occurred absent conversion, but community leaders often attributed this investment to these transactions or, at minimum, believed that conversion resulted

Table 1.8   Nonfinancial Benefits from Key Informant Interviews: 10 North Carolina and South Carolina Transactions

Hospital	Effect on Avoiding Closure	Foundation	Service Expansions	Uncompensated Care
Government to for-profit				
Piedmont	Had effect; county rejected bond referendum in 1979 and new hospital was needed	None	Built new hospital, outpatient facility, neurosurgery, open heart surgery, cardiac catheterization, inpatient psychiatry, and ER	Minimum guarantee for residents of York County (SC) of $475,000/year; hospital pays county Medicaid tax
Upstate	Had effect; county unwilling to invest capital necessary for upkeep and expansion	None	Built new hospital, expanded ER, and guaranteed continuation of ambulance service previously subsidized by county	Guarantee for residents of Cherokee county
Private not-for-profit to government				
Byerly	Had effect; needed capital and improved purchasing power	Foundation created $30 million; funds for health, education, and local economic development	Building a new hospital	Guarantee to continue present indigent level
Providence	No effect; conversion was effort to obtain capital to finance needed expansions	Foundation created $80 million; supports hospital's religious mission, including health	Laser eye surgery, upgraded cardiac catheterization, 18 skilled nurse facility beds, MRI, plans for satellite facility	Guarantee continuation of religious mission, including indigent care, no abortions, etc.
Hilton Head	Had effect; hospital had falling occupancy and defaulted bonds in past that hurt future prospects	Foundation created $21 million in funds for health, education, and the arts	Rehabilitation, cardiac catheterization, 15 skilled nurse facility beds, and obstetrics; future plans to build satellite facility	Guarantee to continue preconversion levels

(continued)

Table 1.8 (continued)

Hospital	Effect on Avoiding Closure	Foundation	Service Expansions	Uncompensated Care
Cape Fear	Had effect; loss of managed care contracts to rival hospital increased need for an outside partner	Foundation created $40 million with focus on health and prevention	Rehabilitation, obstetrics, cardiac catheterization, senior center	No guarantee
Mary Black	No effect; felt that long-term survival enhanced by having better purchasing power	Foundation created $62 million; focuses on wellness and prevention	MRI and cardiac catheterization now fixed, geriatric psych unit, skilled nurse facility, and birthing center	Guarantee at prior levels
Government to private not-for-profit				
Wake County	No effect; primary motivation was to reduce county responsibility and expense of running hospital	None	No guarantee but transfer enables joint ventures outside of county which were previously prohibited	Guarantee at $53 million
Private not-for-profit to government				
Roanoke/Chowan	Had effect; capital needed; falling occupancy and difficulty recruiting physicians; needed partner	Foundation created; $1 million per year in unspecified capital improvements	Total value of lease payment used for unspecified capital improvements each year	Guarantee for residents of 4-county area
Cleveland	No effect; believed, however, that a larger partner with subspecialty services needed for long-term survival	None		$300,000/year from lease to a community indigent care network plus hospital guarantee of historical levels

in such facility improvements occurring more quickly than would have happened otherwise. Further, some services, such as rehabilitation, were likely to be profitable to the facility. In general, the services that were expanded were likely to be profitable.

Provision of uncompensated care is another community benefit. In some contracts, the guarantee was stated as a dollar minimum or as set levels provided prior to the transaction. In others, the buyer guaranteed that residents of specified areas would have access to the facility. One contract specified a guarantee of provision of uncompensated care to a four-county area, the area it served historically, but in general, the areas coincided with the hospital's county. Even in the one case without a guarantee, respondents maintained that uncompensated care had been maintained at prior levels since the conversion. Our findings are consistent with a recent California study showing that of 17 for-profit acquisitions between 1980 and 1991, the conversions did not result in a statistically significant change in the level of uncompensated care or preexisting trends (Young et al. 1997). Likewise, Project HOPE conducted 10 case studies similar to ours, including 8 for-profit acquisitions, and concluded that charity and uncompensated care typically continued at the same or higher levels following conversion (Mark et al. 1997).

Valuing the benefits of foundation activities and expanded hospital services would be difficult at best and was not undertaken here. Such computations would be more important if the financial returns from these transactions had been advantageous to the buyers. Determining the benefits of these foundations is made even more difficult by the large range of projects they could fund.

1.7 Conclusions, Implications, and an Agenda for Future Research

For many conversions, especially those in which a for-profit organization was the purchaser, the purchase price seems to have been right, or perhaps even too high, but not too low. The conversions for which the purchase price was too low involved other types of purchasers. In these cases, the seller desired to sell or lease but did not want to deal with a for-profit organization.

One reason for eschewing a for-profit hospital company might have been a fear that community benefits would be unduly sacrificed. But we did not find that the for-profit hospital companies reduced such benefits after they acquired the facilities. Many of the conversions were recent, and we cannot exclude the possibility of substantial cuts downstream.

One view might be that providing excess returns to a governmental or NFP organization does no harm since the excess return will ultimately be returned to the community, the seller or lessor, in some form. However, such funds need not be allocated in this way, but rather in the form of emoluments to management or to other "insider" stakeholders. Also, when the buyer is an organization in another community, the recipients of any dividend are likely to be citizens of other communities. Finally, acquisition by a not-for-profit purchaser may only be an intermediate step to ultimate conversion to for-profit status.

Our results imply that if there is a case for public scrutiny of these transactions, such scrutiny should not be limited to those cases in which the buyer is a for-profit hospital company. In general, the benefits of such scrutiny should be weighed against the costs. It is not clear that such scrutiny would protect the public any better, and it would probably not protect as well as competitive bidding and/or an open discussion that invites community input into the pros and cons of various alternatives.

Our findings raise at least two important questions. First, do these results generalize? Second, why should publicly held corporations undertake investments for which the rate of return falls far short of the cost of capital?

The results may not generalize. Further research on conversions in other states should be undertaken. It is worth noting, however, that the same companies were involved in conversions in other states during the same time period. Consultants that assisted the parties with these transactions would have been available to similarly situated parties in other states. Tennessee has had among the highest for-profit hospital shares in the United States historically. By contrast, North Carolina and South Carolina have had much lower for-profit shares.

The issue of why some hospital companies may have undertaken unprofitable investments is more difficult to answer. A glib answer would be that we only analyzed a small number of transactions. More likely, the companies may have included returns not included in our calculations, such as network building or establishing new footholds in new markets. But even so, if the communities had been "exploited," one would have expected to observe much higher rates of return. Also, our analysis of changes in profitability of hospitals that converted to for-profit status in Tennessee showed that, on average, the profit rate only increased slightly after the conversions occurred. Perhaps the buyers' intentions were not fully realized. Clearly, observed patterns of returns reflect the relative bargaining strength of the parties. It would be useful to model bargaining explicitly. Of course, to obtain useful quantitative results, it would be necessary to have a much larger sample.

The hospital industry is contracting due to growth of managed care, among other reasons. Running a hospital in a "business as usual" fashion will almost surely be a money-losing proposition, as our regression results indicate.

Finally, both the decision-making process and the decisions of foundations created as a consequence of sale or lease of hospitals have not been documented. Whether or not these foundations truly yield a community benefit is an open question, one worthy of further study.

References

Becker, E., and F. A. Sloan. 1985. Hospital Ownership and Performance. *Economic Inquiry* 23 (1): 21–36.

Bell, J., H. Snyder, C. Tien, and J. Silas. 1997. The Preservation of Charitable Health Care Assets. *Health Affairs* 16 (2): 125–30.

Butler, P. A. 1997. State Policy Issues in Nonprofit Conversions. *Health Affairs* 16 (2): 69–84.

Claxton, G., J. Feder, D. Shactman, and S. Altman. 1997. Public Policy Issues in Nonprofit Conversions: An Overview. *Health Affairs* 16 (2): 9–28.

Gray, B. 1991. *The Profit Motive and Patient Care: The Changing Accountability of Doctors and Hospitals.* Cambridge, Mass.: Harvard University Press.

———. 1997. Conversion of HMOs and Hospitals: What's at Stake? *Health Affairs* 16 (2): 29–47.

Gray, B., and M. Schlesinger. 1997. The Profit Transformation of the Hospital and HMO Fields. Paper presented at a conference on hospital conversions, cosponsored by Healthcare Trustees of New York State and the Milbank Memorial Fund, May.

Hansmann, H. 1996. *The Ownership of Enterprise.* Cambridge, Mass.: Belknap.

Herzlinger, R. 1997. *Market Driven Health Care: Who Wins, Who Loses in the Transformation of America's Largest Service Industry.* Reading, Mass.: Addison-Wesley.

Horwitz, J. 1998. State Oversight of Hospital Conversions: Preserving Trust or Protecting Health? Malcolm Wiener Center for Social Policy Working Paper no. H-98-03. Cambridge, Mass.: Kennedy School of Government, Harvard University.

Japsen, Bruce. 1996. Investor-Owned Chains Seek Rich Rural Harvest. *Modern Healthcare* 26 (27): 32–37.

Kane, N. M. 1997. Managing Charitable Assets from Conversions. *Health Affairs* 16 (2): 229–37.

Kuttner, R. 1996a. Columbia/HCA and the Resurgence of the For-Profit Hospital Business (pt. 1 of 2). *New England Journal of Medicine* 335 (5): 362–67.

———. 1996b. Columbia/HCA and the Resurgence of the For-Profit Hospital Business (pt. 2 of 2). *New England Journal of Medicine* 335 (6): 446–51.

———. 1997. *Everything for Sale.* New York: Knopf.

Mark, T., C. Paramore, E. Rodriguez, C. Good, C. Schur, E. Swalenstocker, P. Neuman, and E. Dorosh. 1997. The Community Impact of For-Profit Hospital Conversions: Results from Ten Case Studies. In *The Community Impact of Hospital Mergers and Conversions.* Bethesda, Md.: Project HOPE.

Matzke, G. E. 1997. A Road Map from Nebraska. *Health Affairs* 16 (2): 89–91.

Miller, L. B. 1997. The Conversion Game: High Stakes, Few Rules. *Health Affairs* 16 (2): 112–17.

Moore, J. Duncan. 1997. Columbia by the Numbers. *Modern Healthcare* 27 (18): 78–96.

Needleman, J., D. J. Chollet, and J. Lamphere. 1997. Hospital Conversion Trends. *Health Affairs* 16 (2): 187–95.

Relman, A. S. 1980. The New Medical-Industrial Complex. *New England Journal of Medicine* 303 (17): 363–69.

Shactman, D., and A. Fishman. 1996. *State Regulations of Health Industry Conversions from Not-For-Profit to For-Profit Status.* Waltham, Mass.: Council on the Economic Impact of Health Care Reform.

Sloan, F., J. Valvona, M. Hassan, and M. A. Morrissey. 1988. Cost of Capital to the Hospital Sector. *Journal of Health Economics* 7 (1): 25–45.

Waters, T. M. 1992. Non-Price and Price Competition in Health Care Markets: Are Consumers Sensitive to Quality and Price Differences? Ph.D. diss. Vanderbilt University, Nashville, Tenn.

Weissenstein, E. 1997. A Favorable Report: GAO Finds Little to Fault in For-Profit Hospital Conversions. *Modern HealthCare* 27 (45): 2, 6.

Young, J. D., K. Desai, and C. Lukas. 1997. Does the Sale of Nonprofit Hospitals Threaten Health Care for the Poor? *Health Affairs* 16 (1): 137–41.

Zuckerman, S., J. Hadley, and L. Iezzoni. 1994. Measuring Hospital Efficiency with Frontier Cost Functions. *Journal of Health Economics* 13 (3): 255–80.

2

Converting Hospitals from Not-for-Profit to For-Profit Status
Why and What Effects?

David M. Cutler and Jill R. Horwitz

The vast majority of American hospitals are organized as charitable, not-for-profit corporations. The public does not own them. Instead, they are private corporations organized to pursue a community health care mission. Their corporate and tax statuses rest on a combination of statutory provisions and revenue service definitions. While many aspects of their organization and regulation distinguish them from for-profit corporations, the fundamental distinction is their purpose to further charitable hospital goals rather than to maximize owners' wealth.

Between 1970 and 1995, 330 (about 7 percent) out of approximately 5,000 not-for-profit hospitals have converted to for-profit corporate form, including a dramatic number in just the past few years. Despite these large changes, there has been almost no empirical research on the reasons for and the effects of conversions.[1] This paper offers a preliminary exploration of the causes and effects of conversions. Throughout the paper, we focus on two case studies: Wesley Medical Center in Wichita, Kansas, and the

David M. Cutler is professor of economics at Harvard University and a research associate of the National Bureau of Economic Research. Jill R. Horwitz is a graduate student in the health policy Ph.D. program at Harvard University.

The authors are grateful to Kathy Kenyon, Edward Parson, Jim Rebitzer, Alan Weil, conference participants, and several anonymous interviewees for helpful discussions. This research was supported by a grant from the National Institute on Aging to the National Bureau of Economic Research. The views in this paper are those of the authors and do not necessarily reflect the views of any interviewees.

1. There has also been little work comparing conversions in the hospital industry to conversions in other medical care industries, such as insurance or physician services, or in other industries outside of the medical sector, such as public utilities. This is a worthy topic for future research.

Columbia/HealthOne system in Denver, Colorado.[2] These two conversions interested us for many reasons. Wesley Medical Center and Columbia/HealthOne are both large, stable hospitals. As of 1995, Wesley, which employed over 3,000 people, was the fifteenth largest for-profit hospital in the United States, and measured by revenues, it was Columbia/HCA's largest hospital. In addition, HealthOne recently entered into a joint venture limited liability company (LLC) with Columbia/HCA, providing a good example of an increasingly popular corporate form. Because both hospitals initially converted over a decade ago, they offered long histories for study. The very factors that attracted us, however, also make the experience of the hospitals somewhat less generalizable. As we discuss below, the typical converting hospital is small and financially weak. Therefore, the motivations for these conversions are more complicated and subtle than those of the ordinary conversion.

The data in this paper are drawn from several sources, including interviews, Medicare cost reports, legal documents, and newspaper articles. In the course of our research we visited both hospitals to interview people familiar with and employed by the sellers, the buyers, the resulting foundations, and the government. Because many details of hospital transactions are confidential, the numbers and deal structures reported below are all derived from public sources. Of course, public sources may not be completely accurate, and several people we interviewed expressed displeasure with public reporting of the transactions involved; still, the public record is often the only one available.

Our case studies suggest two principal factors driving hospital conversions. The first is financial considerations. While profits are certainly important, financial considerations are not limited to concerns about profitability. Having a large debt load and gaining access to cheaper sources of capital are also important in the conversion decision. Second, we find that the culture of the not-for-profit hospital influences the conversion decision. Both of our case study institutions had boards of directors consisting primarily of businessmen, many of whom believed they were ill-trained to run a major hospital. Businessmen may also be more tolerant of the for-profit ownership form than people with a more religious or not-for-profit orientation.

Our evidence on the effects of for-profit and not-for-profit ownership is subtle. Looking at financial measures of hospital performance, we find that for-profit hospitals, particularly those run by Columbia/HCA, were more financially successful than not-for-profit hospitals. In part, this success derives from the for-profits' skill at increasing public sector reim-

2. Columbia-HealthOne operates six general hospitals (Presbyterian/St. Luke's Medical Center, Swedish Medical Center, Aurora Presbyterian Medical Center, Rose Medical Center, Aurora Regional Medical Center, and North Suburban Medical Center). In addition, it operates over 60 medical clinics and employs over 10,000 people.

bursements; in part it is because for-profit hospitals cut costs where not-for-profit hospitals do not. But perhaps most important, not-for-profit hospitals appear to follow for-profit hospitals in the same behavior. A few years after for-profit hospitals exploit Medicare loopholes, not-for-profit hospitals do the same. This pattern has troubling implications as for-profit hospitals become an increasingly large player in the medical care environment.

We are not able to examine the quality of hospital care in any detail. Determining hospital quality requires accurate measures of patient outcomes and adjustments for the health of patients across institutions. Neither of these measures is available to us. Examining the implications of conversions for hospital quality is an important issue for future research.

We begin by defining terms, describing some mechanisms by which hospitals convert, and detailing the transactions of the two case hospitals. In section 2.2, we present trends in the number of conversions over time. In section 2.3, we report and analyze the reasons commonly offered for conversions. In section 2.4, we present two case studies of converted hospitals, examining why they converted and how the conversions affected the hospitals and their markets. Finally, in section 2.5, we offer concluding thoughts.

2.1 The Mechanics of Hospital Conversions

The term "conversion," for the purposes of this paper, is any mechanism by which a hospital changes its essential orientation from not-for-profit to for-profit or vice versa.[3] State law dictates which of many possible mechanisms charitable, not-for-profit hospitals may use to convert to for-profit corporate form. To convert in some states, a not-for-profit hospital may simply file amended articles of incorporation and bylaws with the state secretary or corporations commission. Most conversions, however, involve more than one party. Asset sales, in which the buyer takes all of the seller's assets and only the liabilities specifically contracted for in the sales document, are typical in conversion transactions because buyers are often not permitted to buy some not-for-profit liabilities such as tax-exempt debt. In this type of transaction, a for-profit pays money to a not-for-profit hospital and subsequently owns the hospital and its assets. The not-for-profit hospital generally uses the proceeds from the asset sale to buy back outstanding debt, with remaining amounts directed to other charitable purposes.

Acquisitions, mergers, corporate restructurings that transfer not-for-

---

3. The term "conversion" has also been used to describe privatizations, the process by which a public hospital becomes private or a private hospital becomes public. This paper studies only private hospitals.

profit assets to for-profit subsidiaries, consolidations, lease agreements, and various forms of joint ventures between for-profit and not-for-profit hospitals have all been used to convert hospitals. Some of these transactions, particularly joint ventures, involve ongoing relationships between not-for-profit and for-profit hospitals. A joint venture may involve as little integration as joint marketing of a new service or as much integration as a partnership that looks to the outside world like a single corporation. In some, control is shared between the two entities; in others, one hospital effectively controls the other by dominating the subordinate hospital's board or operating the majority of the subordinate's assets. Joint ventures and asset sales may also differ in their tax implications; for example, passive income to a not-for-profit corporation may be taxed as unrelated income, while for-profit gifts to a not-for-profit are tax deductible.

According to federal tax law, not-for-profit assets may not be used for profit-making purposes. Thus, when not-for-profit hospitals convert to for-profit status, the proceeds must be directed toward another not-for-profit activity; they cannot benefit private individuals or for-profit buyers. If the IRS finds that a transaction involved private inurement, it may force the unwinding of a deal and impose stiff penalties on the participating institutions and individuals. State corporations codes generally dictate the use of charitable assets when a not-for-profit corporation merges, dissolves, or transforms itself in some other way. Statutes typically require that assets be used for purposes similar to those of the selling entity. Foundations established with conversion proceeds must, therefore, pursue community goals similar to those specified by the converting hospital's charter (e.g., community-based health care).

How similar the old and new purposes must be varies according to state corporations and trust laws. Not-for-profit hospitals frequently solicit contributions for particular purposes and receive funds with explicit and implicit restrictions upon their use. When hospitals convert they often are no longer able to comply with these restrictions. Judicial authorization, through a cy pres proceeding, is required for a new foundation to use the restricted funds.[4] A judge must find that the settlor[5] had a broad charitable intent, that the previous use has "become obsolete or impossible or impracticable of execution due to changes in social, economic, political or other conditions,"[6] and that the new use is as near as possible to the intended use. Under some state laws, this test applies not only to formal restricted trusts but also to all charitable donations and, in very restrictive states, even to the charitable corporation itself. In states that have adopted the Uniform Management of Institutional Funds Act, donors may permit

4. Cy pres comes from the French "*cy pres comme possible*," meaning "as near as possible."
5. A person who creates a trust.
6. George T. Bogert, Trusts §147.520 (1987).

a change in the use of institutional funds or the court may order the change under an analysis similar to the cy pres analysis.

State attorneys general are frequently the only government actors who interpret and apply restrictions on conversions and the proceeds they generate; consequently, the rigor with which statutes are applied, or whether they are applied at all, varies dramatically by state (Horwitz 1998). The public has an interest in ensuring adequate oversight of conversions and their proceeds for many reasons. The public allows not-for-profit hospitals to have tax exemptions because it wishes the hospital to perform desirable public services. Thus, the public has an interest in ensuring that the benefits of those exemptions are not appropriated by a for-profit buyer. Conversions may also represent redistributive losses to the extent that for-profits do not provide services that not-for-profits formerly did (such as uncompensated medical care); the public sector may want to minimize the extent of these losses (Horwitz 1998).

To illustrate the nature of hospital conversions, we discuss the details of the conversions for our two case-study institutions.

2.1.1 Wesley Medical Center

The Wesley Medical Center sale was relatively straightforward. (Fig. 2.1 shows the conversion graphically.) In 1985, Wesley's assets were sold to the Hospital Corporation of America (HCA), at the time one of the largest for-profit hospital companies in the United States. Wesley had 786 beds,[7] making it Kansas's second-largest hospital (behind a Veterans Administration hospital) and the largest hospital to have converted from not-for-profit to for-profit corporate status at that time. HCA paid approximately $265 million for the operating assets, including $40 million earmarked to defease outstanding debt. After the debt defeasance, the net proceeds were roughly $225 million. In 1993, HCA merged with Columbia Hospital Corporation, becoming Columbia/HCA, and Wesley changed its name to Columbia Wesley Medical Center. In 1997, as Columbia/HCA faced widespread negative publicity, Wesley dropped "Columbia" from its appellation.

In the Wesley case, the use of the $225 million proceeds from the sale was somewhat complicated. Wesley was founded by and affiliated with the Methodist Church, and there was considerable controversy regarding the role of the church in the sale. Whether the church held formal decision-making authority regarding the sale was never resolved, although the members of the Methodist Kansas West Annual Conference, the governing body for Methodist churches in Kansas, voted to support it. In the final agreement, the church received about 12 percent (approximately $32

---

7. All statistics on number of hospital beds in the paper refer to staffed beds. Hospitals may also have licensed beds that are not staffed.

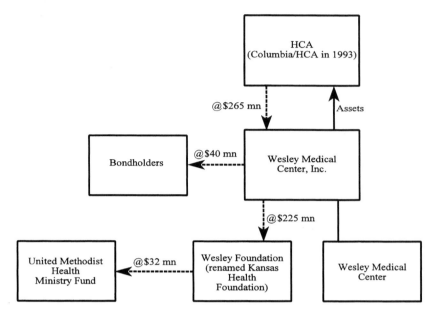

Fig. 2.1   The Wesley Hospital sale

million of the $265 million deal) of the original sale over three years. Thus, two foundations were funded: the Kansas Health Foundation,[8] with the bulk of the money from the Wesley sale (about $200 million); and the United Methodist Health Ministry Fund, with the payments to the Methodist Church. In 1996, the Kansas Health Foundation reported assets of $377 million.

2.1.2   Columbia-HealthOne

Our second case study is the Columbia-HealthOne hospital system in Denver, Colorado. In 1995, the system was Colorado's third-largest private employer (10,000 people) and had estimated annual revenues of $1.2 billion. HealthOne has a much more complicated history of transaction activity. (Figs. 2.2A, 2.2B, and 2.2C detail the ownership activities.) The forerunners to HealthOne were Presbyterian Hospital (sponsored by the Presbytery of Denver) and St. Luke's Hospital (sponsored by the Episcopal Diocese of Colorado), which merged in 1979 to form PSL Healthcare Corporation. In 1985, PSL Healthcare Corporation sold its assets to AMI—a for-profit hospital company—for $173 million. At the time, Pres-

8. The Kansas Health Foundation is the descendant of the foundation previously associated with the medical center, the Wesley Foundation. Restrictions on funds held by that foundation before the conversion were released in state court under the *Kansas Uniform Management of Institutional Funds Act* (K.S.A. @58-3607 (1996)).

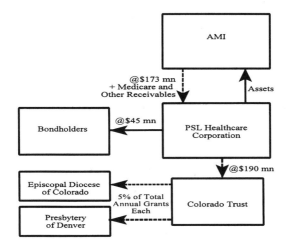

Fig. 2.2A   The HealthOne mergers: AMI

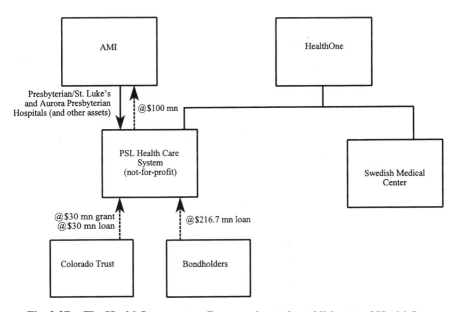

Fig. 2.2B   The HealthOne mergers: Reconversion and establishment of HealthOne

byterian Hospital had 385 beds and St. Luke's Hospital had 284 beds, so that the total institution had 669 beds. After paying off approximately $45 million of outstanding debt and other obligations, PSL Healthcare Corporation was left with roughly $123 million. Subsequent settlements of outstanding Medicare claims and other closing adjustments brought the net proceeds of the sale to nearly $190 million.

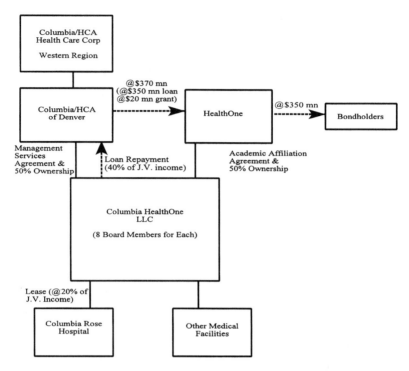

Fig. 2.2C   The HealthOne mergers: The joint venture with Columbia/HCA

This sum was used to establish the Colorado Trust, the state's second-largest private foundation. The Colorado Trust's mission is "to promote the health and well-being of the people in Colorado through programs for affordable and accessible health care and the strengthening of families." The seller imposed two restrictions on the Trust: (1) that it support medical research and education, and (2) that it distribute an amount equal to 10 percent of the preceding year's grants to the Episcopal Diocese of Colorado and the Presbytery of Denver. In addition, the selling board was concerned about health care access for the poor. As a condition to the sale, AMI promised to maintain then-current levels of indigent care.

By 1991, AMI encountered financial trouble because of the high debt it incurred from a leveraged buyout. AMI suspended construction on a partially completed tower at the Presbyterian/St. Luke's hospital complex. Disturbed by the hard luck that befell the hospital, doctors and other community members established a not-for-profit hospital corporation, PSL Healthcare Systems (PSL), to purchase the Colorado assets of AMI.[9]

9. These assets included Presbyterian hospital, St. Luke's Hospital, and Aurora Presbyterian Hospital, among other assets.

Because the new not-for-profit would undertake medical research and education, the Colorado Trust decided that aiding PSL in purchasing AMI's Colorado assets would fulfill its obligation to support medical research and education. Therefore, the Colorado Trust granted $30 million and lent $30 million to PSL for the purchase. With these sources and an additional $216.7 million borrowed from other sources, PSL purchased AMI's Colorado assets and made other investments.[10] The hospital again became a not-for-profit institution. In 1993, PSL merged with Swedish Hospital, another not-for-profit hospital in Denver. Shortly thereafter, the name of the combined institution was changed to HealthOne. The asset value of HealthOne was about $550 million in 1995,[11] although HealthOne had outstanding debt of about $350 million, for a net value of $200 million.

Facing such a large debt burden, HealthOne once again chose corporate organizational change as the answer to its problems. In searching for a merger partner, HealthOne identified Columbia/HCA as the only candidate willing to act quickly. Columbia/HCA already owned two hospitals in the Denver area (North Suburban Hospital and Aurora Regional Hospital), as well as a number of medical clinics, surgery centers, and other medical services. These assets were worth about $180 million. In addition, Columbia was in the process of purchasing a third hospital, Rose Hospital (long affiliated with the Jewish community), which had assets of about $220 million and debt of about $70 million, for a net value of $150 million.

Rather than an outright sale, Columbia and HealthOne formed a joint venture. The joint venture is a for-profit holding company, named Columbia-HealthOne LLC.[12] The assets of the joint venture include Columbia's two existing hospitals and its outpatient facilities, and the hospitals in HealthOne. To equalize the ownership of the joint venture, Columbia/HCA loaned HealthOne approximately $350 million to defease its outstanding debt. The loan was assumed by the LLC, however, so HealthOne's share of the repayment is small. In addition, Columbia/HCA contributed $10–$20 million to the HealthOne Foundation. After the contributions, Columbia/HCA and HealthOne had roughly the same net asset values (about $180 million each), so the two are equal partners in the joint venture. Columbia, through an exclusive management contract with the joint venture, controls the day-to-day operations at the facilities.

10. About $100 million was paid to AMI for the Colorado assets. Most of the remainder was used to complete construction on the patient tower.
11. By this point, HealthOne included the above mentioned hospitals and several outpatient facilities.
12. A limited liability company is a hybrid of a partnership and a business corporation. Like a partnership, profits and losses flow to the members of the company through distributions. Unlike most partnerships, however, members of limited liability companies benefit from some of the protections against personal liability afforded to employees of business corporations. Bankruptcy, death, dissolution, expulsion, resignation, or withdrawal of any member of the LLC usually leads to automatic dissolution of the company.

In addition to its assets, the joint venture leases Columbia Rose Hospital for a 99-year term. Since Columbia owns Rose Hospital, the lease payments of approximately $19 million per year are made to Columbia, but the leasing arrangement preserved the equal ownership of the joint venture ownership.

The claims on the joint venture are therefore at least threefold: (1) some of the money generated goes to Columbia/HCA to repay the loan it extended to HealthOne; (2) some of the money is paid to Columbia/HCA for the Rose lease; and (3) the remaining profits of the joint venture are split equally between Columbia/HCA and HealthOne for the equity role in the joint venture. In 1996, the interest payments to Columbia/HCA were reported to be about $60 million; the lease payments to Columbia/ HCA for Rose Hospital were reported to be $19 million; and profits were reported to be $19 million. HealthOne's 50 percent interest in the LLC includes representation on the board equal to that of Columbia, thus ensuring HealthOne's veto power over Columbia decisions.

HealthOne now concentrates on graduate medical education. It pays the faculty and residents and administers medical education at HealthOne-Columbia facilities.

2.2   The Magnitude of Hospital Conversions

To understand the magnitude of hospital conversions nationwide, we examine the trend of conversions over the past 25 years. We focus on conversions of general medical and surgical institutions. There are a variety of other types of hospitals—rehabilitation, children's, cancer, tuberculosis, and so forth—that may also change organizational form, but our interest is in the nearly 5,000 general hospitals that form the bulk of the U.S. hospital system. We also focus on private, not-for-profit institutions. Federal, and particularly state and local, hospitals may become private and/or for-profit corporations, but their motives to convert to for-profit status may be very different from those of a private hospital.

Figure 2.3 shows the number of private, not-for-profit hospitals converting to for-profit status between 1970 and 1995. Our data are from the American Hospital Association (AHA) annual surveys, compilations of self-reported information by hospitals. We find conversions by matching hospitals in successive years of the survey and determining which hospitals moved from not-for-profit to for-profit control.[13] Between 1970 and 1984 our data are biannual; we assign half of the two-year change to each year.

The number of conversions was low in the 1970s—about 5–10 per year. As table 2.1 shows, the hospitals that converted were relatively small; 52

---

13. This method omits hospitals that changed their AHA identification number at the time of the conversion. We use data provided by the AHA to correct this problem.

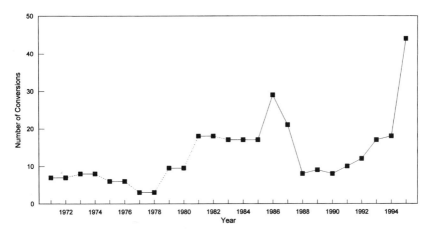

Fig. 2.3   Hospital conversions from not-for-profit to for-profit status, 1970–95
Note: Data prior to 1984 are averages over a two-year period.

Table 2.1   **Not-for-Profit to For-Profit Hospital Conversions by Size**

Number of Beds	Private, Not-for-Profit Hospitals, 1980	Total Conversions by Time Period				
		1970–80	1980–87	1987–91	1991–94	1994–95
All hospitals	4,991	67	137	34	47	44
< 25 beds (%)	4	3	8	0	2	0
25–49 beds (%)	18	21	15	38	15	9
50–99 beds (%)	24	33	29	26	30	9
100–199 beds (%)	22	31	34	18	30	36
200–399 beds (%)	20	10	13	15	19	34
≥ 400 beds (%)	11	1	1	3	4	11

Note: Authors' calculations based on American Hospital Association annual survey.

percent of the hospitals that converted to for-profit status had fewer than 100 beds, compared to 46 percent of hospitals as a whole. Only 1 percent of the largest hospitals converted to for-profit status, well below their 11 percent share of total hospitals.

In the early and, particularly, mid-1980s, conversion activity increased. There were 29 conversions in 1986 alone. Informal conversations we have had with hospital executives suggest that financial concerns drove the merger activity in this period. When the Prospective Payment System (PPS) for Medicare was implemented in fiscal year 1984, for example, hospital executives worried that their revenues would fall. Industry wisdom also predicted that for-profit medical care would gain in importance, and many hospitals were eager to be in the vanguard of this trend.

By 1988, the Prospective Payment System proved to be less damaging to revenues than previously feared. The remaining not-for-profit hospitals were likely more committed to the not-for-profit organizational form. As a result, conversion activity slowed; between 1988 and 1991 there were only 8 or 10 conversions each year.

In the 1990s, and particularly in very recent years, conversions have again increased. There were between 12 and 18 conversions per year up through 1994, and an overwhelming 44 conversions in 1995.

Further, the type of hospital converting from not-for-profit to for-profit status has changed markedly over time. This change is most noticeable in the size of the institution. About one-quarter of the converting hospitals in the 1991–94 period had over 200 beds, as did nearly one-half of the converting hospitals in 1994–95. Hospitals with over 200 beds accounted for only about 15 percent of conversions in the 1970s and early 1980s.

There are also clear regional patterns to hospital conversions, as shown in table 2.2. Conversion activity is most prominent in the Southern Atlantic states (principally Florida) and the West South Central states (principally Texas), both Columbia/HCA strongholds. Despite having only one-quarter of the nation's hospitals in 1980, these two regions account for about one-half of the conversions in each time period. Hospitals in the Pacific region (largely California) are also overrepresented in conversions.

There has been very little conversion activity in the Northeast or Middle Atlantic, however. In our sample, there were only 4 conversions in the entire 25-year period in those states, despite the fact that they accounted for 13 percent of the hospitals in 1980. The relative lack of conversions in the Northeast and Middle Atlantic regions likely reflects several factors: tighter regulation in those states; smaller managed care enrollment; and a sense that the hospital industry is substantially overbuilt in those areas.

Table 2.2   Conversions by Region

Region	Private, Not-for-Profit Hospitals, 1980	Share of Conversions, 1970–95
All	4,991	330
Northeast (%)	5	1
Middle Atlantic (%)	11	0
South Atlantic (%)	13	22
East North Central (%)	18	9
East South Central (%)	8	11
West North Central (%)	15	9
West South Central (%)	13	19
Mountain (%)	7	8
Pacific (%)	11	19

Note: Data on conversions are from the American Hospital Association.

2.3   Why Are Hospitals Converting?

To date there has been no empirical examination regarding why hospitals increasingly prefer the for-profit over the not-for-profit corporate form. One explanation for conversions is generic: Recent years have seen many more hospital mergers in general, and thus we would expect more conversions of hospitals from not-for-profit to for-profit status. Of course, this raises the question of why there have been so many hospital mergers. Rather than citing simply "increased merger activity," we instead consider the changes in the medical care marketplace that might drive such behavior. We focus on six explanations for hospital conversions.

2.3.1   Financial Status

Perhaps the most commonly mentioned factor in hospital conversions is the financial status of the converting hospitals. There are several related financial reasons that motivate not-for-profit hospitals to sell to or partner with for-profit institutions. These include access to capital, current or expected profit reductions, and relief from debt burden.

Access to Capital

The most commonly identified reason for conversions is the need to obtain capital, for operations and capital expenditures such as new equipment and buildings. While there are many permutations of the capital-needs argument, all boil down to an inadequate access to capital for necessary expenditures. First, many not-for-profits face absolute limits on accessing capital. Although not-for-profit corporations have access to forms of capital that are unavailable to for-profits—tax-deductible donations and tax-exempt debt—both sources are limited. Donations are limited by donors' willingness to give, and tax-exempt debt is subject to regulatory restrictions regarding use and amount.[14] Not-for-profit hospitals may find other available financing schemes such as securitization, asset leveraging, and pooling schemes too risky to undertake. Conversions, therefore, may provide needed capital through equity financing and enhanced access to debt.[15] Although not-for-profits may have access to the same sources of taxable debt as do for-profits, many may have unfavorable debt ratings that make the cost of commercial debt prohibitive. Second, equity may also be a cheaper source of capital than those sources easily available to

14. There is a $150 million limitation on nonhospital debt (e.g., related businesses, clinics, buildings for professional services, efforts to integrate). This limit poses a problem for hospitals that operate under a master bond or debenture indenture, a written agreement under which bonds or debentures are issued, setting forth maturity dates, interest rates, and other terms.
15. For-profit hospitals borrow more debt than do not-for-profit hospitals (Frank and Salkever 1994). After accounting for tax deductions, taxable debt can be less expensive for a for-profit than tax-exempt debt is for a not-for-profit.

not-for-profit hospitals. Therefore, even hospitals that have adequate access to debt may prefer equity financing. The market spread between equity and debt, caused in part by bond insurance and state issuing agency fees, may make equity financing more desirable. High debt levels may also lead to agency problems, as managers of highly leveraged institutions engage in excessively risky activities whose costs they can transfer to bondholders (Jensen and Meckling 1976). Third, even if equity is not an inherently more desirable instrument than debt, equity is perceived as an important currency by those involved in conversions and similar transactions. Hospital administrators hoping to become part of a larger system may find that access to equity generates more consolidation options.

Profits

Current and feared revenue declines have also motivated not-for-profit hospitals to convert. Actual and expected declines may be caused by market-specific changes such as overbedding, demographic changes, or increased competition attributable to reorganization by competitors. Conversions may also provide a way for not-for-profit managers to avoid the risks of operating under new regulatory regimes or delivery systems that are expected to cause lower profits or that may increase the riskiness of hospital profits. Conversion activity increased, for example, with the implementation of the Prospective Payment System in 1984, and again in the 1990s, as managed care began to make substantial inroads in health care delivery.

Debt Service

Not-for-profit hospitals generally fund their capital budgets with tax-exempt debt. For various reasons, such as revenue reductions due to market changes, some hospitals find they are not able to service the debt. Selling to a cash-rich, for-profit buyer provides one way of meeting debt obligations.

2.3.2   Increased Efficiency

Patel et al. (1994) suggest that for-profits may achieve greater dynamic efficiency in resource allocation than not-for-profits because they can more quickly enter and exit markets as conditions change. Others maintain that for-profit hospitals are inherently more efficient than their not-for-profit counterparts because of superior management talent. Large for-profit systems also have access to efficiency-producing accounting and data processing systems.

It is important to be clear about the notion of "efficiency." For-profit hospitals are likely to be better at maximizing shareholder value than not-for-profit hospitals are at maximizing operating surpluses. This does not mean that for-profit hospitals are better at promoting *social* interests, or even the interests of the original not-for-profit hospital, than are not-for-profit hospitals (Reinhardt 1996).

Of course, if all that not-for-profit hospitals wanted from conversions was to obtain access to better management, they might just hire management services from a for-profit firm without actually changing their management orientation. Indeed, Columbia/HCA's joint ventures generally included provisions under which it acts as day-to-day manager and is paid a management fee. The fact that the conversions were more than purchases of management fees suggests that there was more motivating the transaction than just potential efficiency gains.

2.3.3   Defensive Strategies

In the face of closure or a threatened takeover by a long-term not-for-profit competitor, directors of failing not-for-profit hospitals may view for-profit partners as their best hope for securing a continuing presence in a community. Neighboring not-for-profit hospitals often have a history of quasi-competitive interactions that make mergers and joining operations difficult.

For-profit buyers often promise to maintain operations at the acquired hospital, although many such promises are temporary or contingent on the good financial health of the hospital. In addition, conversion to for-profit status may release hospitals from cumbersome regulations, such as meeting mandatory community benefit measures, thus allowing them more flexibility to compete.

2.3.4   Self-Interest

Not-for-profit managers and directors may obtain job security and personal financial gain from their involvement in conversions. Physicians often favor conversions because the transactions include an opportunity for them to hold an ownership stake in the new entity—a benefit that cannot be offered legally by a not-for-profit corporation.

2.3.5   Culture

The individual and collective perspectives, beliefs, and values of hospital directors also influence decisions to sell or partner. For example, people from a business background may have different beliefs about the importance of for-profit and not-for-profit ownership in the medical sector.[16] Furthermore, culture may influence the choice of transaction partner. Local not-for-profit hospitals, for example, may have a long history of fierce competition that makes cooperation difficult. There are particular

---

16. Typically, economists treat "culture" as a residual explanation for firm behavior. Here, we have in mind a positive theory of why some managers would undertake actions different from other managers.

difficulties associated with merging institutions of various religious affiliations.

2.3.6   Mission Change

A conversion may help a not-for-profit hospital change or fulfill its health care mission. Board members may decide that resources that could be better used to improve public health are inappropriately tied to acute care services. Converting a hospital allows board members to liquidate their investment in the hospital and apply both their human efforts and the financial resources they oversee to non–acute care goals.

Since conversion transactions typically produce large foundations, a common trade-off cited by many not-for-profit hospital executives is that between having the not-for-profit hospital in the community or having a for-profit hospital and substantial cash for other purposes. Understanding what this means is somewhat difficult. One interpretation is that the hospital executives want to move forward future profits into current years, which they cannot do on their own. A fair-market sale to a for-profit hospital company would make future profits available immediately. Alternatively, it may be that the managers of the not-for-profits believe they can persuade for-profit hospitals to overpay for their assets. This view seems difficult to believe, however, since most people are on only one hospital board and for-profit hospital executives acquire many hospitals each year and have substantial expertise in negotiating deals. Finally, it may be that for-profit companies are better at managing hospitals than not-for-profit directors, and some of the overall profits from better management can be transferred to the community. What is interesting about this view, however, is how little attention is generally paid to *how* the for-profit company will run the hospital. In many cases, for example, selling board members assert that the buyer promised to keep essential services (such as emergency rooms) open, but such promises are not in writing or, when they are, the promises are insufficiently specified. The transfer of resources to the not-for-profit foundation may thus come at the expense of some valuable hospital services.

2.4   Case Studies—Why Convert?

Our case studies yielded two primary explanations regarding why hospitals convert; these findings are summarized in table 2.3. First, financial concerns are quite important in conversions, and these concerns are multifaceted. Expectations about future profits and anticipated problems in servicing debt played a key role in the conversions we studied. Second, board culture or the perceived mission of the board, particularly as generated by a board comprising mainly local business leaders, seems to influence decision making.

Table 2.3   **Rationales for Hospital Conversions**

| | | Presbyterian/St. Luke's | | |
Explanation	Wesley-HCA	Sale to AMI	Reconversion	Joint Venture with Columbia/HCA
Financial	***	**	***	***
Efficiency	*	*		*
Defensive strategy	*	*		***
Self-interest			?	?
Culture		***		
Mission change	***			

Source: Authors' opinions based on interviews, analysis, and newspaper reports.
Note: Stars indicate the importance of the explanation, as judged by the authors. More important explanations have more stars. Question marks indicate uncertainty, again as judged by the authors. Blanks indicate no evidence.

2.4.1   Wesley Medical Center

Three clusters of reasons motivated the Wesley sale to HCA. First, hospital directors and management decided the hospital's mission had been adequately met and that the money invested in the hospital could be better used to improve the health of Kansas's residents. Several of the former directors of Wesley Hospital indicated that they perceived that the choice was between having a hospital and having a hospital plus cash.

Second, culture drove this transaction in at least two distinct ways. Our interviewees characterized the directors as businessmen whose decision to sell was simply a financial decision. Once talks with HCA opened, some directors were attracted by the excitement of dealing with a powerful, for-profit corporation and felt an affinity with HCA's management. They had the opportunity to make a deal that would generate the highest price per bed paid at the time and would put them at the forefront of the conversion trend. Culture also affected the choice *not* to partner with other local not-for-profit hospitals. In Wichita, the most attractive potential not-for-profit partner was a Catholic hospital, a long-time competitor, with whom Wesley was unable to establish joint programs.

Third, while financial issues also motivated the sale, they played a smaller role in the decision than did reasons of mission and culture. While interviewees declared that the conversion was not about a need for money, some stressed the importance of HCA's promises to provide cash for capital development (discussed below). In addition, concerns relating to the viability of operating Wesley under the prospective payment system influenced decision makers. The sale could be understood as a way to transfer the risk of future financial difficulties to more experienced management.

2.4.2 Columbia-HealthOne

Different reasons motivated each transaction in HealthOne's corporate history.

Asset Sale to AMI

Two types of concerns motivated PSL Corporation's initial asset sale to AMI in 1985. One concern was the financial viability of the hospitals. The hospital's debt load, in particular, worried board members. Although the hospital only had approximately $45 million of outstanding debt, the managers and directors perceived constraints on their ability to access capital markets, and AMI promised access to capital. Indeed, AMI put nearly $100 million into the acquired hospital system within a five-year period.

The board was also afraid that the advent of PPS and state interest in reviving certificate-of-need requirements would lead to declines in the ability of the hospitals to compete, and it believed AMI could better handle the risk. Also, the board was uncertain about the future of hospitals in Denver.

In addition to financial concerns, culture played an important role in the initial sale. The board was heavily populated by businesspeople who saw the sale to AMI as an opportunity to place their hospital on the cutting edge of a coming health care trend.

Asset Sale to PSL Healthcare Systems

The reason for AMI's sale was clear—financial distress. AMI was heavily in debt by 1991, and work on a new hospital building had stopped. The construction and hospital management posed a heavy financial burden for AMI.

The reasons behind the not-for-profit buyback are somewhat less clear. Upset by AMI's poor management and history of draining capital from Colorado, old board members reactivated their lingering commitment to the hospital. In fact, the incomplete patient tower exercised a spectral influence over the old board members, many of whom were physicians. Newspaper reports, however, suggested that hospital insiders realized substantial gains from the transaction.[17] PSL, in addition, purchased consulting, financial, and legal services from firms at which the board members worked.[18] The significant overlap between the old hospital board, the local AMI advisory board, and the Colorado Trust board may have been the reason that concern for the hospital's demise was translated into action. But the role of these factors is not completely clear. AMI's advisory

---

17. "The [PSL-AMI] deal was marred by charges of self-dealing by board members, who allegedly pocketed large transaction fees" (Meyer 1996). PSL Healthcare Corporation denied these reports.
18. Specific examples were reported in the *Denver Post* (Graham 1995).

board had no governing power and interested Colorado Trust board members recused themselves from the decision to support the buyout.

Columbia-HealthOne Joint Venture

This joint venture is perhaps the most typical of all of the transactions we investigated for this paper. It was motivated primarily by financial problems, particularly debt overhang. Presbyterian/St. Luke's assumed a very high debt burden during the AMI buyback (reportedly as high as $216 million), and it assumed even more debt through subsequent mergers. Thus, HealthOne faced a bleak future, servicing approximately $360 million of system debt. Virtually everyone we spoke to stressed the importance of the debt overhang as instrumental in the decision to form a joint venture. The poverty of HealthOne might be somewhat overstated, however. While HealthOne was concerned about its bottom line, it significantly increased executive salaries (by 20–33 percent), which were already higher than national averages. Furthermore, it continued to pay board members until the summer of 1994, a controversial and rare practice in the not-for-profit world.[19]

Fears about how an uncertain industry and policy future would affect profits were also quelled by the idea of a joint venture with a wealthy for-profit that had a demonstrated history of generating high profits. In addition, merging with Columbia would bring access to managed care contracts that Presbyterian/St. Luke's wanted to guarantee. For example, Rose Hospital had contracts with two large managed care organizations that were seen as valuable sources of patients. Since Columbia-HealthOne was so big, managed care companies in the Denver area would virtually have to contract with the combined institution, whereas HealthOne on its own might be excluded from managed care contracts.

As in the other transactions, culture and momentum influenced this joint venture. Discussions with other hospitals (Lutheran Medical Center and St. Joseph's Hospital) proved unfruitful for both substantive and timing reasons. In early 1995, when Columbia/HCA bought one potential partner, Rose Hospital, timing pressed the board members. In addition, once the Presbyterian/St. Luke's board began exploring transaction options, it changed its focus from hospital operations to pursuing a reorganization. The momentum of the deal may have influenced the board to complete the transaction.

2.5   Case Studies—The Effects of Conversions

In this section, we consider the effects of hospital conversions on the market for medical care. We divide our discussion into two parts: the effect

19. The Colorado Trust pays its board members approximately $20,000 each.

of the conversion or joint venture (1) on the study hospital, and (2) on other hospitals and the community as a whole.

The data that we use come primarily from Medicare cost reports, annual reports of hospitals that are filed with Medicare administrators. The cost report data are the only public data source with information on revenues, expenses, and assets of hospitals. We form profits as earnings less patient care costs, excluding interest, taxes, depreciation, and assessments (EBITDA). This measure is standard in the literature; it avoids problems in the measurement of depreciation across institutions. The data may be subject to error. First, the amounts are self-reported and are only verified when Medicare conducts audits. Second, the reports filed during the first few years after a conversion may not accurately reflect financial status because converting entities are entitled to special deductions that obscure conventional profit measures. Finally, recent news reports suggest that Columbia/HCA routinely overestimated its costs to Medicare. If these reports are true, our conclusions regarding profits at the case-study hospitals are conservative since they reflect the enhanced cost estimates.

We focus our analysis on the financial health of the hospitals and the flow of patients to different hospitals. We would also like to examine measures of the quality of medical care, but the data to do this are not available.

Our results, summarized in table 2.4, address changes in the converting institution and other institutions in the market. For-profit buyers (and joint ventures) seem adept at increasing profit margins in converted hospitals—partly because they effectively manage billing to take advantage of reimbursement loopholes, and partly because they reduce staff as a method of reducing costs. Not-for-profit competitors of the converted (or joint-ventured) hospital react by consolidating and copying the billing practices of the new for-profit.

2.5.1 Wesley Medical Center

Direct Effects on the Converting Institution

We begin with the direct effects of the merger on Wesley Medical Center. One of the goals of the conversion was to raise money for capital improvements. Figure 2.4 shows the increase in fixed assets—plant and equipment—at Wesley. Fixed assets at not-for-profit Wesley hospital were about $80 million in 1985. In 1986, after HCA bought the hospital, fixed assets rose by about $50 million and remained at that higher level for the next decade. These additional assets were largely new centers for reproductive health and cardiac and pulmonary rehabilitation.

Perhaps more important, however, is the profitability of the resulting institution. Figure 2.5 shows the profit rate at Wesley Medical Center from

Table 2.4   **Effects of Hospital Conversions**

	Wesley		Presbyterian/St. Luke's		
	HCA	Columbia/HCA	AMI	Reconversion	Columbia/HCA
Own Institution					
Profits	∅	↑↑	↓	↑	↑↑
Costs	∅	↓↓	↑	↓	↓↓
Billing management	∅	↑↑↑	∅	∅	↑↑↑
Managed care contracts	∅	∅	∅	∅	↑↑↑
Staffing	∅	↓↓↓	∅	∅	↓↓
Infrastructure	↑↑	↑↑	↑↑	∅	↑↑
Physicians	∅	↓↓↓	∅	∅	∅
Other Institutions					
Patient shares	∅	∅	∅	∅	∅
Consolidation	∅	↑↑	∅	∅	↑↑

Source: Authors' opinions based on interviews, analysis, and newspaper reports.
Note: Up and down arrows indicate positive and negative findings, respectively. More arrows indicate stronger findings, as judged by the authors. Zeros indicate no effect.

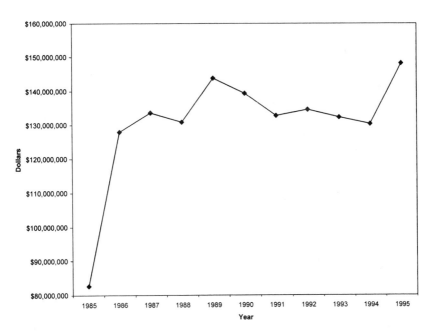

Fig. 2.4   Fixed assets at Wesley Hospital

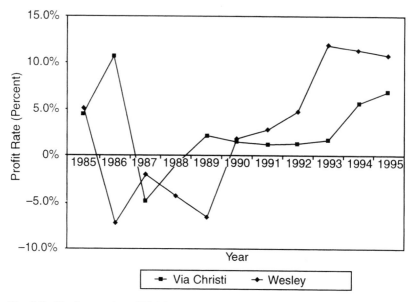

Fig. 2.5   Profit margin at Wichita hospitals

1985 through 1995.[20] Wesley's profits were about 5 percent in 1985. Between 1986 and 1990, under HCA's management, profit rates were negative. Although it appears that HCA was losing money on the hospital, two factors may explain the apparent losses. First, the increase in infrastructure noted above required substantial up-front costs, which reduced short-term profits. In addition, HCA charged the hospital with $12.4 million in interest expense and deferred loan cost transfers from the parent's $3.6 billion leveraged buyout by TF Investments, a corporation organized by HCA management. By the early 1990s, after these costs had been incurred, Wesley's profits were about 2–5 percent.

In 1993, Columbia/HCA began managing the hospital, and profits soared. In 1993, 1994, and 1995, Columbia/HCA's profit rates were about 10–15 percent annually.

To give some comparative analysis of profit rates in Wichita, we also show profit rates for Wesley's largest competitors—two Catholic hospitals, St. Francis Medical Center (587 beds) and St. Joseph's Medical Center (388 beds). In 1995, these two hospitals merged to create the Via Christi Medical Center. We form a simulated Via Christi system by combining the two institutions throughout the time period, which we then compare

20. The hospital reported only six months of information in 1985. This might affect profit rates if profits are different in the first and second halves of the year. This is unlikely to be very important, however.

to Wesley's operations. As figure 2.5 shows, profit rates for Via Christi con-
tinually averaged about 1–2 percent through 1993.

How could profits increase so dramatically under Columbia/HCA? Two
factors are at work. First, Medicare revenues increased. Figure 2.6 shows
real Medicare reimbursement per admission between 1985 and 1995. Beginning in 1992, Medicare reimbursement rose dramatically and remained
high. While we do not have definitive data on why this occurred, we suspect Columbia-Wesley increased reimbursements by effectively exploiting
common Medicare loopholes. To understand these loopholes, consider an
example of an elderly patient with a hip fracture. She needs some acute
services (e.g., setting the fracture or a hip replacement) and some rehabilitation services (e.g., help learning to walk). Since 1984, Medicare has paid
for inpatient admissions on a per-admission basis, paying a single amount
for each admission regardless of the services provided. Medicare, however,
pays separately for rehabilitation services that are provided independently
of a hospital admission. It is not difficult to see the revenue-maximizing
strategy. Where traditionally a hospital would provide acute and rehabilitation services in the same admission, the hospital exploiting the loophole
will provide the acute services only during the hospital admission and
move the patient for the rehabilitation services. For the same total costs,

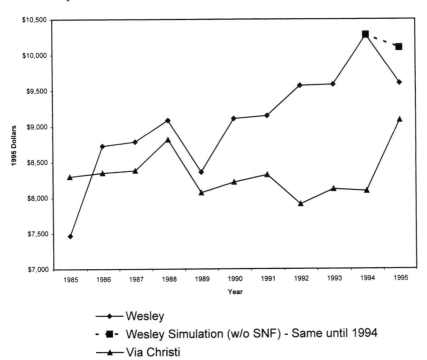

Fig. 2.6   Medicare reimbursement per admission

the hospital collects two payments. Indeed, in 1992 HCA opened its own rehabilitation hospital in Wichita (HCA/Wesley Rehabilitation Center), which could facilitate multiple reimbursements to the hospital for each Medicare recipient treated. We include the rehabilitation center's profits in our calculation of Columbia/Wesley's profits.

Similarly, Columbia opened a skilled nursing facility (SNF) at Wesley in 1995. These facilities provide another mechanism with which to unbundle hospital admissions (Newhouse and Byre 1988). Medicare admissions to Wesley—the hospital and nursing home combined—soared in 1995. It looks in figure 2.6 as if the opening of the SNF lowered Medicare reimbursement per patient. But if we assume that all of the Medicare admissions to the nursing facility were also admissions to the hospital (so that the appropriate denominator is the number of hospital admissions), we find no significant reduction in Medicare reimbursement in 1995.

There are other accounting changes Columbia/HCA might have made. For example, Medicare reimbursement is typically greater if the patient has "complications and/or comorbidities" than if the patient does not have complications or comorbidities. Hospitals will thus search for complications to maximize Medicare reimbursement, a process termed "DRG creep" (Carter, Newhouse, and Relles 1990). Without microdata, however, we do not know how much Columbia Wesley's number of complicated patients increased.

In addition to an increase in Medicare revenues, Columbia/HCA reduced costs. Figure 2.7 shows the growth in revenues and costs per admission between 1985 and 1995. Real costs actually fell in 1993 and 1994, before rising in 1995.[21] Figure 2.8 shows the source of some of this cost reduction. Length of stay in the hospital fell dramatically over this period. Among Medicare patients, for example, average hospital stays fell from 8.1 days in 1992 to 6.6 days in 1995, a 19 percent reduction. Somewhat surprisingly, nursing input did not fall. Licensed practical nurses (LPNs) per patient fell over this period, but registered nurses (RNs) per patient declined only slightly.

In our discussions at Wesley hospital, however, the reduction in nurses and nurses aides was described as a major source of tension between physicians and Columbia. The source of this tension appears to have risen

21. A word for researchers about sources of cost data. We have compared AHA data on costs for Wesley with Medicare cost report data. The AHA data are flawed in several important respects. HCA did not report all its costs when it was running the hospital, with the exception of one year. Thus, costs in AHA reports appeared to plummet when HCA bought the hospital and soared when Columbia began operating. Neither conclusion is true. But the cost report data are not entirely accurate either. In the cost report data, HCA appeared to count routine births (without complications) as discharges when hospitals generally do not do so. As a result, in the cost report data admissions soar under HCA and fall under Columbia. This is also not true. We use the admissions data from the AHA and cost data from the cost reports to adjust for these problems.

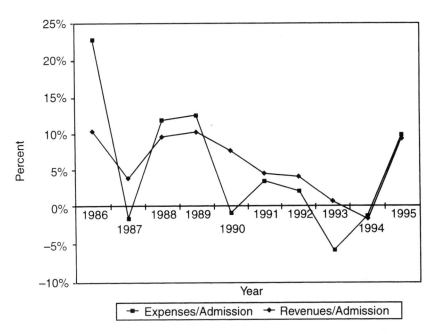

Fig. 2.7   Growth of revenues and expenses per admission at Wesley Hospital

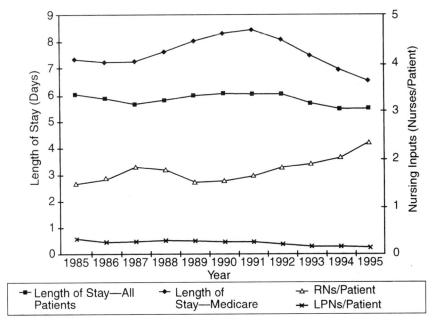

Fig. 2.8   Inputs at Wesley

after 1995. In January 1996, Wesley eliminated 204 positions (136 layoffs, 51 early retirements, and 17 voluntary departures). In January 1997, Wesley announced plans to eliminate 383 more jobs by the end of September 1997.

Indeed, the tension between the hospital and its physicians was sufficiently great that many physicians at Wesley sought alternative practice arrangements. Many moved some of their practice to Via Christi, a relatively simple move since Wichita doctors may easily garner admitting privileges at all of the Wichita hospitals. Some doctors took more drastic measures. In 1995, a group of orthopedic surgeons opened their own hospital, the 11-bed Kansas Surgery and Recovery Center. The Center treats routine, high-reimbursement orthopedic cases (particularly insured patients). The cardiovascular surgeons are building their own hospital as well.

Columbia wanted to entice the physicians to admit only at Wesley by offering them financial interests in the hospital, as it does in many places, but this strategy fared poorly. In fact, the failed negotiations between Columbia and the physicians of the Wichita Clinic—the largest primary care service in the area—have led to a lawsuit by the physicians charging antitrust violations on the part of Columbia.[22] When the negotiations fell through, Columbia hired about 20 percent of the physicians (13 people, including 40 percent of the family practice department). The remaining physicians claim that Columbia hired the physicians at excessive salaries and bonuses, and with promises to indemnify the doctors for damages resulting from breaches of noncompete clauses with the clinic as a predatory attempt to harm the clinic's business. The clinic also charged Columbia with misappropriating trade secrets such as internal operations information, fiscal performance data, and salary information. Finally, the clinic argued that Columbia tortiously interfered with the physician contracts and the clinic's business expectancy.

To discern how the change to for-profit form affected Wesley's ability to negotiate favorable contracts, we analyzed the hospital's contractual allowances and discounts. If Wesley's new corporate form helped it to exercise market power, this fact might be reflected in these data. This does not appear to be the case, however. Wesley's contractual allowances and discounts rose from 12 percent of charges in 1985 to 43 percent of charges in 1995, while Via Christi's rose from 9 percent of charges to 44 percent of charges in this same period. Contractual allowances and discounts are based on list prices instead of costs and, therefore, may mask some reduction in discounts. The similarity between the for-profit and the not-for-profit's trends is still noteworthy.

22. See *Wichita Clinic, P.A. v. Columbia/HCA Healthcare Corp.*, 1997 WL 225966 (D. Kan. 1997) (denying Columbia/HCA's motion to dismiss).

Effects on Competitors and the Wichita Market

The Wesley conversion not only affected Wesley hospital, it also affected the community as a whole. The Wesley conversion seems to have sparked increased consolidation in the hospital market more generally. As noted earlier, St. Francis and St. Joseph's merged in 1995 to form Via Christi Medical Center. Several people speculated that fear of Wesley's success as a for-profit drove the merger between these two institutions. The Catholic hospitals, however, explained that they merged because it was wrong for two Catholic hospitals to compete.

As figure 2.5 shows, the combined institutions have done very well financially. Where the two hospitals forming Via Christi's had combined profits of about 1–2 percent in the late 1980s and early 1990s, the profit rate rose to 7 percent in 1995. The reasons for this increase in profits appear to be similar to those for Columbia/Wesley. St. Francis, for example, opened a rehabilitation unit in 1994; Via Christi acquired a rehabilitation center in 1995; and in 1996, Via Christi planned to open a 36-bed continuing care subsidiary within the hospital, specifically to benefit from long-term acute care reimbursement. The increase in the number of rehabilitation beds in the Wichita area is astounding. In 1985, Wesley hospital had 18 rehabilitation beds and St. Joseph's had 31 rehabilitation beds. In 1991, HCA/Wesley had 26 rehabilitation beds and St. Joseph's had 37 beds. By 1995, Columbia-Wesley Rehabilitation Hospital had 50 rehabilitation beds; Via Christi Rehabilitation Center had 40 rehabilitation beds; St. Francis Hospital had 32 rehabilitation beds; and St. Joseph's Hospital had 38 rehabilitation beds. The number of rehabilitation beds more than tripled between 1985 and 1995.

Similarly, Via Christi also cut costs. As figure 2.9 shows, the average length of stay for all patients, and particularly Medicare patients, fell substantially after 1993. Between 1993 and 1995, for example, the average length of stay for Medicare patients at Via Christi declined by one day.

The experience of our case market offers a new understanding of how the presence of for-profit hospitals affect hospital markets—one that raises an "inverse-Hansmann problem." Hansmann (1980, 835) argued that the presence of not-for-profit hospitals in markets forces for-profit hospitals to keep quality high. Here, having for-profit hospitals in the market appears to cause not-for-profit hospitals to adopt the same money-making measures employed by for-profits. In this case, most of the measures come at the expense of the government.

Perhaps more important than the amount of rehabilitation care that patients receive is whether acute care patients have access to the most appropriate care. There has been particular concern that for-profit hospitals will shirk on care for the poor, leaving such patients to their not-for-

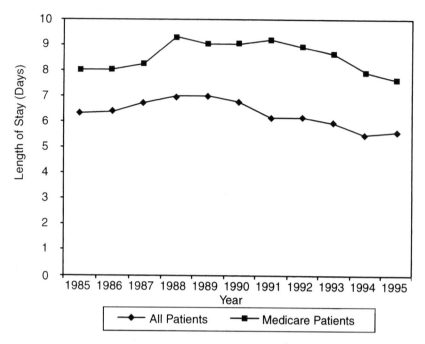

Fig. 2.9   Inputs at Via Christi

profit competitors. Our data do not indicate how much charity care different hospitals provide.[23] It does break out admissions for Medicare and Medicaid patients, however. Figure 2.10 shows the share of all patients, Medicare patients, and Medicaid patients in Wichita admitted to Wesley hospital.

These data do not suggest much cause for alarm. While Wesley's share of the overall Wichita market has been falling, its share of Medicaid patients has been constant or rising. Of course, different trends may be occurring for the uninsured relative to Medicaid patients, but our first pass evidence finds no adverse effect for the Medicaid group.

But some fragmentation of the medical care market is occurring. Wichita has seen an increase in surgi-centers and stand-alone clinics. The new orthopedic clinic, for example, saw no Medicaid patients in its first year of operation (108 patients in total), and one suspects the new cardiology center will also cater to the wealthy and well insured. In addition, the hospitals have attempted to attract low-risk patients to their facilities. In

23. As noted above, hospitals report contractual allowances and discounts on their Medicare cost reports, which include uncompensated care, but they also include discounts to managed care plans and unpaid coinsurance for insured patients.

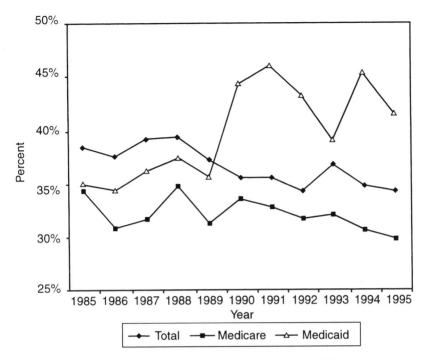

Fig. 2.10   Wesley Medical Center: Admissions as share of total Wichita market

1996, Wesley opened a free-standing birthing center that only admits low-risk patients. Soon thereafter, an independent obstetrics practice group approached Via Christi about opening a similar center on the Catholic campus. If these new ventures survive, there will be some segregation of the health system by class, propagated as much by doctors severing their hospital affiliations as by hospitals establishing independent clinics.

2.5.2   Presbyterian/St. Luke's-AMI

Direct Effects on Converting Institution

Once again, we start with the effect of the conversion on the converting institution. One of the rationales for the asset sale to AMI was to get more capital for Presbyterian/St. Luke's. Figure 2.11 shows the fixed assets of Presbyterian/St. Luke's from 1985 through 1994. From the pre-AMI period through 1990, assets nearly doubled.

To examine Presbyterian/St. Luke's financial performance before and after the sale to AMI, figure 2.12 shows the profit rate for Presbyterian/St. Luke's hospital from 1985 to 1994. We omit data for 1995 because there is no way to separate out profits for these hospitals from the other

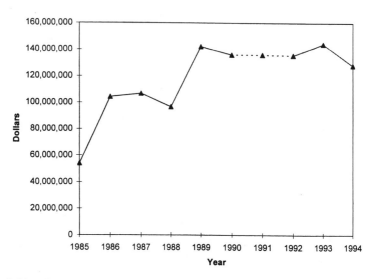

Fig. 2.11   Fixed assets at Presbyterian/St. Luke's

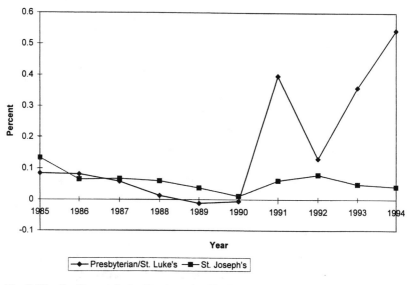

Fig. 2.12   Profit margin for Presbyterian/St. Luke's

parts of Columbia-HealthOne.[24] When Presbyterian/St. Luke's was sold to AMI in 1985, it had average profits of about 8 percent. During the AMI years, 1986 through 1990, profits steadily declined. In 1989 and 1990, the

24. We aggregate the two institutions to form profits prior to 1990, even though profits are reported separately.

hospital lost money. In the five months of 1991 that AMI owned the hospital, the hospital reported extremely large profits, but we suspect that this is an accounting anomaly rather than a true increase in profits. After AMI reconverted to not-for-profit form, reported profit rates increased dramatically. These data, based on Medicare cost reports, seem questionable, however, because the AHA data show much larger costs. We were unable to explain the variance.

As we observed in the Wesley case study, contractual allowances and discounts rose under AMI's for-profit ownership of Presbyterian and St. Luke's. Between 1987 and 1992, contractual discounts climbed from 27 percent to 46 percent of total patient charges. Presbyterian/St. Luke's closest competitor in the Denver market is St. Joseph's hospital (405 beds). Over the same time period, contractual discounts at St. Joseph's rose from 12 to 33 percent. Discounts at Presbyterian/St. Luke's rose somewhat less rapidly than at St. Joseph's, but we do not know if St. Joseph's rose more rapidly simply because it began at a lower base.

Under the control of not-for-profit Presbyterian/St. Luke's, contractual allowances and discounts fell. Between 1992 and 1994, contractual allowances and discounts fell from 46 to 37 percent. At St. Joseph's, in contrast, contractual allowances and discounts rose from 33 to 41 percent of charges between 1992 and 1994.

Given the lack of any discernible increase in profits under AMI, we do not report a detailed analysis of changes in revenues or expenses.

Effects on Competitors and Market

Denver is a bigger market than Wichita, so the effects of the conversion on the market as a whole were necessarily smaller. As figure 2.12 shows, profit margins at St. Joseph's fell in the late 1980s but then rebounded in the early 1990s.

We also examined the share of Medicare and Medicaid patients going to Presbyterian/St. Luke's. Figure 2.13 shows changes in Presbyterian/St. Luke's share of the patient market before and after the sale. Presbyterian/St. Luke's share of the hospital market was falling over this time period, but it fell disproportionately more for the non-Medicaid population compared to the Medicaid population. After 1991, Presbyterian/St. Luke's share of the market rose among both Medicaid and non-Medicaid patients. The evidence in figure 2.13 does not suggest that care to the poor was cut particularly heavily under for-profit management.

On the whole, the evidence thus suggests relatively small effects of the sale to AMI on operations of Presbyterian/St. Luke's hospital or the Denver market as a whole. Indeed, profits, if anything, fell under AMI's management. This is consistent with the financial difficulties that AMI found itself in by 1991.

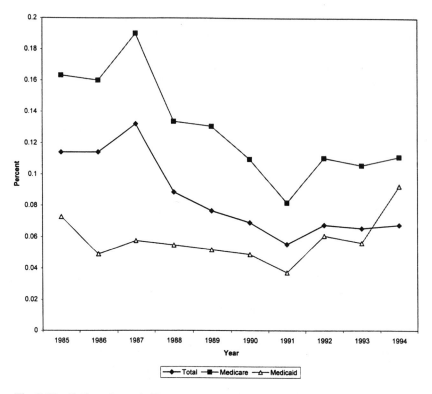

Fig. 2.13   Patient shares in Denver

2.5.3   Columbia/HealthOne

Because the Columbia-HealthOne joint venture occurred so recently, we were unable to obtain reliable data regarding the effects of that transaction. But some preliminary information about the effects of the joint venture is available. In 1996 Columbia-HealthOne reported profits similar to those of its not-for-profit competitors. Hospital profits in the Denver area increased an average of 7.2 percent in 1996, and Columbia-HealthOne's profits increased by 7.2 percent as well. For the Columbia-HealthOne system as a whole, reported profits were 3 percent in 1996.

We suspect that Columbia-HealthOne, like Wesley, has attempted to raise profits by aggressively managing government billings. According to the Colorado Hospital Association, Medicare inpatient charges per patient rose by 16 percent in Presbyterian/St. Luke's in 1996, while they had fallen by nearly one-quarter (in nominal terms) in the previous three years. Unfortunately, we do not know about Medicare revenues, so we cannot determine whether the increased charges resulted from higher list prices or increased billable services. Columbia-HealthOne also appears to have cut costs substantially. Between 1994 and 1996, inpatient costs per admission fell by 3 percent in nominal terms and Medicare average length of stay fell by 1.3 days. The number of full-time equivalent employees per occupied bed fell by 15 percent.

There is some indication that some of these changes were illegal. In October 1997, federal investigators asked two Columbia-HealthOne hospitals to turn over some patient records as part of an investigation of Columbia's billing practices. Columbia-HealthOne has begun to change its management practices. According to one report, 125 Columbia-HealthOne managers who were eligible for bonuses based on 1996 job performance will not be eligible for such bonuses in the future.

The controversy surrounding Columbia/HCA has led some members of the public and some members of the HealthOne board to question aspects of the joint venture. In the fall of 1997, the HealthOne representatives launched efforts to renegotiate the $370 million loan assumed by the LLC. Although the HealthOne board representatives perceived the approximately 17.5 percent interest rate to be the best they could negotiate at the time of the joint venture, there has been some speculation that the deal might not be renegotiated. The HealthOne faction has also exercised its power to block Columbia-inspired initiatives. For example, newspaper reports indicate that when the Columbia management told the board that it planned to lay off employees, the HealthOne faction voted against the proposal and forced Columbia to recalculate the budget.[25]

One of the striking features of this joint venture is how much of the Denver hospital market it encompasses. In 1996, Columbia-HealthOne accounted for 37 percent of all admissions to Denver hospitals. The Federal Trade Commission reviewed the joint venture but never filed objections to it. Allowing such a large percentage of a market's hospitals to be controlled by one entity raises ordinary monopoly-related concerns as well as the risk that the entity's policies may have negative and particularly widespread effects.

2.6 Conclusions

Our case studies suggest two primary explanations why hospitals convert from not-for-profit to for-profit form—(1) financial concerns and (2) board culture and perceived mission. Although we expected to find that financial concerns were important, we learned that such concerns are multifaceted. Expectations about future profits and anticipated problems servicing debt were central to selling directors, as were pessimistic views of government reimbursement policies.

Our results suggest a mixed view of the effects of hospital conversions.

---

25. The reduction in employment noted above resulted from attrition.

On the one hand, we find some efficiencies associated with conversion to for-profit form. For-profit hospitals cut costs when not-for-profit hospitals cannot do so.[26] For-profits also provide capital or relieve debt burdens, which not-for-profit hospitals could not otherwise do. And we find no evidence that for-profit hospitals reduce quality or cut back on access to the poor, although our measures of these effects are admittedly crude.

But the implications of for-profit organization are not entirely beneficial. For-profit hospitals make money in part by increasing reimbursement from the public sector. This is a gain for the hospital but a loss for society as a whole.[27] And having more for-profit hospitals leads to some fragmentation of the market between rich and poor, although this occurs as much from physician actions as from hospital actions.

Perhaps the most important issue raised by our results is the symbiosis between for-profit and not-for-profit hospitals. Our results show that for-profit and not-for-profit hospitals both influence and are influenced by each other's actions. Years ago, these actions were seen as beneficial; if not-for-profit hospitals maintained high-quality care, for-profit hospitals might have to do the same. But our results highlight the other side of this coin. When for-profit hospitals exploit Medicare loopholes, not-for-profit hospitals learn to do the same, or believe they must copy for-profits to compete. If for-profit hospitals skimp on the quality of care, not-for-profit hospitals might follow suit. The influence of for-profits will only grow as they become a larger part of hospital markets, such as Columbia-HealthOne in Denver. The possibility that for-profit hospitals will encourage not-for-profit hospitals to reduce their public goods provision is a substantial concern as the health care marketplace changes.

References

Barro, Jason, and David M. Cutler. 1997. Consolidation in the Medicare Care Marketplace: A Case Study from Massachusetts. NBER Working Paper no. 5957. Cambridge, Mass.: National Bureau of Economic Research, March.

Carter, G. M., J. P. Newhouse, and D. A. Relles. 1990. How Much Change in the Case Mix Index Is DRG Creep? *Journal of Health Economics* 9 (4): 411–28.

Claxton, Gary, Judith Feder, David Shactman, and Stuart Altman. 1997. Public Policy Issues in Nonprofit Conversions: An Overview. *Health Affairs* 16 (2): 9–28.

26. These results are somewhat at odds with those of Sloan, Taylor, and Conover (chap. 1 in this volume). Jim Rebitzer's comment on our papers (Rebitzer, in this volume) presents several potential sources of difference. Future research should explore these differences in more detail.

27. It is a loss, rather than a transfer, because raising the money for the payment involves some deadweight loss.

Frank, Richard G., and David S. Salkever. 1994. Nonprofit Organizations in the Health Sector. *Journal of Economic Perspectives* 8 (4): 129–44.

Graham, Judith. 1995. Will Sale of Rose Make Care Cost More? 1985 P/SL Buyout May Hold Lessons. *The Denver Post,* 12 February, G-01.

Hansmann, Henry. 1980. The Role of Nonprofit Enterprise. *Yale Law Journal* 89: 835–901.

Hollis, Steve. 1996. Remarks at Changes in the Not-for-Profit Status of Health Care Organizations conference, Georgetown University, Washington, D.C., October.

Horwitz, Jill R. 1998. State Oversight of Hospital Conversions: Preserving Trust or Protecting Health? Wiener Center for Social Policy Working Paper no. H-98-03. Cambridge, Mass.: Kennedy School of Government, Harvard University.

Jensen, Michael C., and William H. Meckling. 1976. Theory of the Firm: Managerial Behavior, Agency Costs, and Ownership Structure. *Journal of Financial Economics* 3:305–60.

Meyer, Harris. 1996. The Lure. *Hospitals and Health Networks* 70 (11): 28.

Newhouse, J. P., and D. Byre. 1988. Did Medicare's Prospective Payment System Cause Length of Stay to Fall? *Journal of Health Economics* 7:413.

Patel, Jayendu, Jack Needleman, and Richard Zeckhauser. 1994. Changing Fortunes, Hospital Behaviors, and Ownership Forms. John F. Kennedy Faculty Research Working Paper Series no. R94017. Cambridge, Mass.: John F. Kennedy School of Government, Harvard University.

Reinhardt, Uwe. 1996. Remarks at Changes in the Not-for-Profit Status of Health Care Organizations conference, Georgetown University, Washington, D.C., October.

Comment on Chapters 1 and 2   M. Kathleen Kenyon

Introduction

I have been asked to comment on two papers on hospital conversions, the first by Sloan, Taylor, and Conover and the second by Cutler and Horwitz. From my perspective,[1] both of these excellent papers touch on the truth and point to a bigger picture that needs to be addressed much more explicitly. Cutler and Horwitz's in-depth case studies of two conversions of large hospitals, now owned by Columbia, have an almost scene-of-the-crime interest, given Columbia's recent troubles with the Department of Justice. Their conclusions suggest that for-profits are bad role

M. Kathleen Kenyon, J.D., is general counsel of Deaconess Billings Clinic, a tax-exempt integrated health care organization in Billings, Montana.

1. Commenting on two papers on hospital conversions, by economists of this stature, has me somewhat out of my natural habitat. My perspective comes from having investigated and defended hospital mergers (as an antitrust lawyer), watched the industry from a policy perspective (as a Capitol Hill staffer and legislative counsel for a trade association), and served as general counsel to an integrated, not-for-profit health system that owns a hospital and physician group practice.

models, leading not-for-profits that share their markets to follow them in reimbursement maximization, with the federal Medicare coffers as the prime victim. On the other hand, Sloan, Taylor, and Conover, in a disciplined, methodologically complex investigation of a variety of relatively small conversions, come to conclusions that appear to go in the opposition direction. Their conclusions could be seen as a defense of for-profit conversions: For-profits pay (perhaps overpay) a fair price for the hospitals they acquire, invest in much-needed facility improvements, and continue to provide comparable levels of charity care and other services. In contrast to the possible benefits of conversion to for-profit ownership, Sloan, Taylor, and Conover find that, in two instances, conversions of small not-for-profits into larger not-for-profit systems are something of a steal by the larger not-for-profits.

Both studies advance the intelligent discussion of an important policy question that is also politically charged (and, for that reason, resists intelligent discussion). What are the social implications of the growth of the for-profit sector in health care, and, especially, the implications of the conversions of hospitals from not-for-profit to for-profit status?

Three Overarching Issues

Need for Political Economic Context

I have three overarching gripes about these papers. Both papers cry out for placing the conversions they investigate into the larger political economic context of the health care industry. Hospitals are only one segment of the health care industry (and an increasingly less powerful one). It isn't just hospitals that have been converting to for-profit status and becoming part of large, publicly traded systems; insurers/HMOs and physicians have as well. At one time, all Blue Cross Blue Shield plans were not-for-profit; today many are not, and more are looking toward for-profit conversion. Many of the not-for-profit HMOs formed in the 1970s in the wake of the HMO Act have converted to for-profit status and been merged into large, publicly traded corporations. For-profit insurers have expanded dramatically into managed care products.

Similarly, physicians are consolidating dramatically into ever larger groups. These groups are not, by and large, Mayo Clinic–like foundations (which are not-for-profit, tax-exempt, and dedicated to teaching and research as well as provision of health care); rather, they are managed by multi-billion-dollar physician practice management companies traded on Wall Street.

Furthermore, your local physicians and hospitals have less control over decisions about how and where health care dollars are spent than they did in the past. Health care is becoming like the rest of the economy, with the purchasers (especially the better informed, larger purchasers—large employers, unions, and government) demanding value and accountability from both the insurance companies (especially managed care companies) and the providers they turn to with their health care dollars. The payers, rather than hospitals and physicians, increasingly hold economic power.

That is the context (dramatically abbreviated and simplified) in which to view hospital conversions and to question their social significance. Placed in that context, it becomes clear that you cannot understand hospital conversions by looking only at hospitals pre- and postmerger. And you cannot understand the social implications of for-profit conversions without looking at the whole industry.

Need for a More Critical View of Medicare

My second gripe, really a subcategory of the first, is directed primarily toward the paper by Cutler and Horwitz. Their paper is not sufficiently critical of the role of Medicare in health care markets. Medicare is wonderful for at least one reason: It guarantees health care (except outpatient pharmaceuticals, certain preventive services, and a few other important health care benefits) to older Americans. Beyond that, Medicare's method of paying for health care services and the legal barriers to provider integration posed by some Medicare laws and regulations have created or worsened much of the inefficiency in health care, especially for providers trying to provide the full continuum of health care services in order to be able to deliver quality care while controlling costs.

It is a mistake to condemn behavior that appears calculated to increase Medicare reimbursements without a very careful look at whether the behavior being condemned makes sense viewed from other perspectives, such as the perspective of physicians committed to quality care or of commercial payers (the second largest source of hospital revenues, after Medicare). Cutler and Horwitz, for instance, criticize Columbia, and the not-for-profits that arguably follow in Columbia's tracks, for building rehabilitation units and adding transitional care beds, skilled nursing facilities, and home health in order to maximize Medicare reimbursement. The criticism should only be justified if, in a quality-driven, efficient health care system, you would not have, in the numbers you have today, these less-intense alternatives to medical surgical inpatient beds. Based upon conversations with physicians and representatives of well-regarded health plans, I suspect that if you removed Medicare from the picture entirely, and simply had enlightened geriatricians and caring payers designing high-quality, cost-effective health care for older Americans, you would find a heavy reliance on these less-intense, specialized health care alternatives to acute care hospitals. Furthermore, one wonders whether patients would prefer to recuperate in an acute care hospital bed when other less medically intense environments are available.

That stated, it may well be that Columbia built all of those rehab beds, as Cutler and Horwitz suggest, primarily to take advantage of Medicare reimbursement "loopholes." That subjective intent should not be imputed as the primary motive to others, including other hospitals in Denver and Wichita. If the move toward providing the full continuum of care is good for patients and makes sense as a possible cost saver to more enlightened payers than Medicare, maybe the other hospitals that have added such units are doing so not because of the corrosive influence of the for-profits. Obviously, however, the fact that Medicare has created economic incentives to reduce hospital length of stay, while making another payment for rehab and other step-down units, has undoubtedly made it economically more feasible to build such units. That such building has occurred should not surprise economists or Medicare.

Ask the Question Differently and Suggest a Better Explanatory Framework

My third gripe, which follows from the first, is that these papers should have viewed conversions as simply one response to current pressures facing all providers and payers in health care. The bigger question is, How do not-for-profits differ from for-profits, if at all, in their response to economically driven changes in health care? While both papers provide valuable evidence for an explanation, neither takes the step of explicitly suggesting an explanatory framework for future researchers to pursue to answer that question.

Whatever that explanatory framework might be, these papers suggest that it would look at legal, cultural, and contextual factors.

Legally, not-for-profit, tax-exempt hospitals differ from for-profits because they must be organized ("the organizational test") and operated ("the operational test") to benefit the community ("the community benefit standard"), and they are prohibited from operating to benefit insiders (private inurement) or other individuals, except incidentally (private benefit). If they abandon any of these basics, they cannot be tax-exempt not-for-profits. These legal requirements have real effects for the daily operations of not-for-profit hospitals and limit their ability to respond to external demands for change in ways that for-profits can.

It is clear from these papers, however, that while all tax-exempt hospitals operate under similar legal constraints, they do not all respond to them in the same way in difficult economic times. Apparently, culture and context matters. Researchers need to come up with a typology of not-for-profit hospitals that captures the cultural variables that matter. They need to identify contextual factors that might explain why culturally similar not-for-profits make different decisions in response to similar economic pressure—factors like the HHI analysis in Sloan, Taylor, and Conover; excess beds in the market; the relative financial size and strength of providers in the market; the presence of effective employer purchasing coalitions; and how concentrated and entrenched the managed care health plans are in the market.

My guess (supported by some evidence from these papers) would be that not-for-profit hospitals that convert are different from those not-for-profits that do not convert, since hospitals everywhere are, in one way or another, facing increased financial pressures, and most do not convert. I also believe that most, but certainly not all, not-for-profit hospitals are different from for-profit hospitals in measurable ways and that the dramatic expansion of the for-profit sector in health care will have significant social implications that research will eventually identify.

Evidence on the Implications of Conversions

Do we find in these papers evidence that not-for-profit ownership (especially private, not-for-profit ownership), rather than for-profit ownership, makes any difference in responding to increasingly intense financial pressures?

If the only thing you worry about is the dollar value dedicated to charity care (which tax-exempt hospitals are not legally required to provide), the answer is no (and the researchers giving that answer could form a chorus at this point). The research by Sloan, Taylor, and Conover also suggests that the type of services do not, in the exceedingly short time frame they observed, vary significantly between not-for-profits and for-profits, nor do they change significantly postconversion, at least in any direction that would suggest that not-for-profits are more willing to support needed but unprofitable services. I look forward to more long-term data on these matters, but I also believe a more nuanced look is needed. (Sloan, Taylor, and Conover, by dividing services into three categories, including services that are likely to be unprofitable but are important in the community, take a good step toward a more nuanced look.) For instance, timing of entry and exit for important services, where the profitability is unclear, may differ between not-for-profit and for-profit hospitals, at least if you control on the financial depth of the institutions. The dollar value of charity care may not vary based on ownership, but how those dollars are targeted may. Efforts to facilitate and establish connections with outside service providers when the local hospital cannot afford to provide an essential service itself may differ.

In general, I would expect many of the benefits of the not-for-profit organizational form to be hidden in staff time devoted to particular community needs or to involvement in community efforts to address social problems with health consequences. These differences are difficult, but not impossible, to measure. In the long run, communities may find that those differences matter. A board composed of members genuinely motivated by a mission and committed by law to the community benefit legal standard are simply more likely to look at the long-term interests of their community and to get engaged.

The most interesting evidence from these papers addresses why not-for-profit hospitals that turn to conversion as a solution to their problems do so. (In the next round of research, evidence from those not-for-profits that faced economic challenges and did not convert would be useful.) The answer both papers suggest is "cultural." Cutler and Horwitz tell us that boards dominated by businesspeople may be more willing to convert to for-profit status and less committed to a not-for-profit, tax-exempt structure. This may be especially so if they can come out of the deal with what they regard as a mission intact at the hospital, in the form of a continuing commitment to charity care by the resulting for-profit hospital, and with money for a foundation that continues to serve the community. If the evidence were stronger that the resulting foundations did a great deal more for the health of the community than pay for unprofitable services and teaching in the now for-profit hospital that the foundation board members used to direct, this mission-plus-money argument might be more convincing. More research is needed on the role of foundations in continuing and expanding their health care missions beyond the bricks and mortar of hospital services.

Both papers suggest that conversions take place in part because the not-for-profit board worries about an uncertain future or is facing community, tax, cultural, regulatory, or political pressures that make it difficult for those hospitals to respond to external financial pressures. Anyone who has been through the pain of changing a long-standing community hospital (which is probably also one of the largest employers in town), on matters as simple as who runs the food service or as difficult as reducing nursing staff as patient length of stay drops, can understand the attraction of putting such matters in the hands of experienced for-profit hospital managers they believe will be less constrained by local pressures. Local not-for-profit boards unable to act and ineffective hospital management, after all, are not likely to have much benefit for the community. On the other hand, does the community lose something when the local hospital (or health plan or physician group) is run day-to-day by corporate managers whose fiduciary obligations run through Wall Street to shareholders who cannot possibly understand the role of that hospital in the community, except as it affects profitability?

We do find some rather intriguing evidence in these papers that conversions worry people. Sloan, Taylor, and Conover, despite finding no significant negative effects of conversions with regard to the general fairness of the deal or loss of services, report communities worrying about a loss of community control when their hospitals converted to either for-profit or larger not-for-profit form. They also report two instances where community boards turned to large, nearby not-for-profit hospital systems for help out of their financial difficulties, rather than rely upon for-profits—one assumes despite the likelihood that they could have gotten more money out of for-profit conversion. These communities effectively put a very large price tag on the importance of staying not-for-profit, even when doing so still meant a loss of community control. As I write this, there are reports of fierce opposition to a Catholic hospital sale to Tenet, despite Tenet's willingness to pay tens of millions more than another potential purchaser from a Catholic system.

Why are some local and religious communities willing to pay such a high price in order to keep their hospitals not-for-profit? These papers put researchers in a better position to try to build a framework for answering that question, which is just another form of the question of how not-for-profits respond differently than for-profits to the economic pressures in health care. Answering that question will help us struggle politically with the question being asked with increasing frequency and concern: What are the social implications of the growth of the for-profit sector in health care?

Comment on Chapters 1 and 2   James B. Rebitzer

Nobody knows what really happens when hospitals convert from not-for-profit to for-profit status. Do not-for-profit hospitals offer important medical services to the indigent that for-profit institutions do not adequately provide? Do hard-nosed, for-profit managers impose the organizational discipline needed to control rising health costs? Do hospital conversions transfer the accumulated value of public subsidies to private hospitals at less than market rates? These questions make hospital conversions a lightning rod in the ongoing debate over the role of profits in health care.

The degree of public disquiet over hospital conversions is neatly illustrated by excerpts from magazines at opposite ends of the political spectrum. At one pole, the conservative *Economist* writes:

> The travails of America's largest for-profit hospital chain do not prove that profits are bad for health care. It seems only yesterday that Columbia/HCA Healthcare was acclaimed as a model of how a for-profit company could revolutionize health care. Its hard-driving boss, Richard Scott, enriched his investors by buying hundreds of hospitals, closing lots down and making the remainder far more efficient. Now the firm is in the dog house. It denies any wrong-doing, but Mr. Scott has resigned while a posse of investigators looks into allegations that, among

James B. Rebitzer is the Frank Tracy Carlton Professor of Economics at the Weatherhead School of Management, Case Western Reserve University.

other abuses, the company has been overbilling the Federal Government. Could there be clearer evidence, many people are asking, that health care and the profit motive do not mix? (*Economist*, 2 August 1997)

The *Economist*, true to form, answers this last question in the negative. At the other pole, the liberal, market-skeptical *American Prospect* writes

First it was hospitals and nursing homes, ambulatory care centers and health maintenance organizations. Now it is Blue Cross plans and major teaching institutions. In an accelerating rush to the marketplace, many of America's largest health care nonprofits are being converted into profit-making organizations. . . . if regulators fail to act, the charitable legacy will be lost and more executives of non-profits will become overnight millionaires by capturing the assets for themselves and their investors. (Bell 1996)

The papers by Sloan, Taylor, and Conover and by Cutler and Horwitz are important because they offer some of the first dispassionate and careful assessments of the consequences of hospital conversions. The papers also illustrate the power of well-executed case studies to illuminate issues relating to organizational governance.

Cutler and Horwitz examine two hospital conversions. The first conversion involved Wesley Medical Center in Wichita, and the second involved Columbia/HealthOne in Denver. In the Wesley conversion, Wesley's assets were sold to HCA in 1985, and HCA merged with Columbia to form Columbia/HCA in 1993. The Wesley conversion was accompanied by an increase in fixed assets due largely to new centers for reproductive health, and cardiac and pulmonary rehabilitation. In 1985, Wesley profits were about 5 percent. From 1986 to 1990, profits were negative. In 1993, Columbia/HCA began managing the hospital, and profits in 1993, 1994, and 1995 were 10–15 percent annually (compared to 1–2 percent at Wesley's two biggest competitors in Wichita). This excellent performance was due to an increase in Medicare revenues and a decrease in costs. Columbia/HCA managed to increase Medicare reimbursement by "unbundling" rehabilitation and nursing home services, a practice that may have contributed to Columbia's problems with the federal government. Costs also fell because of a 19 percent reduction in length of stay. There is no compelling evidence that the for-profit Columbia Wesley Medical Center provided fewer services to the poor than not-for-profit Wesley Medical Center.

The second conversion studied by Cutler and Horwitz is Columbia/HealthOne in Denver. The changes in ownership in this conversion are complex. In 1985, Presbyterian/St. Luke's sold its assets to for-profit AMI. Profits declined consequent to this conversion. The hospital reconverted to a not-for-profit in 1991 and merged with another not-for-profit to form HealthOne in 1993. Columbia/HCA and HealthOne formed a joint, for-profit venture in 1993, Columbia-HealthOne. In 1996, Columbia-HealthOne profits were 7.2 percent, similar to other hospitals in Denver. There is some indication in the paper that Columbia improved profits by aggressively increasing revenues from the government (although some of these tactics may not have been legal), by shortening the length of hospital stays, and by cutting staffing and other costs.[1]

Sloan, Taylor, and Conover ask whether hospital conversions were a good bargain for the private purchasers. This ambitious paper calculated the return on investment and cost of capital for 10 hospital conversions in North Carolina and South Carolina. The profitability of conversions was estimated using a pooled time-series, cross-section regression with data from hospitals in Tennessee. The Tennessee data suggest that hospitals converting from not-for-profit to for-profit status had low profits both before and after conversion. Furthermore, profit margins did not improve much after conversion. Assuming that these Tennessee results also hold for North Carolina and South Carolina, the rate of return to conversions appears to be low. These researchers conclude that, contrary to the concerns expressed in the *American Prospect,* the acquiring organizations likely paid too much for their not-for-profit hospitals. From the Tennessee data, Sloan, Taylor, and Conover also conclude that conversion to for-profit status had no discernable effect on the provision of uncompensated care.

Put side-by-side, the Cutler and Horwitz report appears inconsistent with the findings of Sloan, Taylor, and Conover. The message I take away from Cutler and Horwitz is that of savvy Columbia/HCA acquiring not-for-profits and increasing their value by introducing new managerial practices. The additional profits, however, may be partly the result of transferring value from taxpayers to Columbia shareholders by a clever "gaming" of Medicare. In contrast, the message I take away from Sloan, Taylor, and Conover is that of witless for-profits purchasing poorly performing hospitals at inflated prices. The taxpayers, in other words, are taking the shareholders and their managers to the cleaners.

Can the results of these two studies be reconciled? Perhaps. It is possible that the profit regressions by Sloan, Taylor, and Conover understate the true effect of conversions on profits. Both common sense and the qualitative case studies reported in these papers indicate that it takes time for conversions to substantially influence hospital management. Unfortunately, the Tennessee data do not have a long time-series on most conversions. This problem is confounded by the specification in Sloan, Taylor, and Conover's regressions. They use a single pre/post dummy variable to identify the effect of conversions. This specification averages early and

---

1. For a recent analysis of Columbia/HCA's methods in securing Medicare revenues, see Eichenwald (1997).

later effects and may therefore lead to an underestimate of the true effect of conversions on profits.

One way around the problems posed by the short time-series in Tennessee would be to consider different scenarios about the likely long-term effect of conversion on profits. In making their purchase, investors must have had expectations regarding the level of profitability needed to make money on the new for-profit hospital. For example, most conversions involved hospitals with below-average profits. Would the conversions look like good investments if investors believed that their hospital would eventually attain average industry profit rates? We might learn more about these expectations if Sloan, Taylor, and Conover used their simulations to evaluate a variety of counterfactual assumptions about long-term profit performance. What is the most conservative set of assumptions about future profits required to make the conversion look like a good deal? Do these conservative profit assumptions entail reasonable or unreasonable expectations?

Sloan, Taylor, and Conover's profit estimates may also understate the true return on a conversion investment if the market value of the investment is not reflected in current profits. For example, of all the conversions these researchers studied, the Hilton Head conversion lost the most money, but as they note, Hilton Head was located next door to a large, yet-to-be built, retirement community. The prospective value of this locational advantage is not captured in the profit projections of Sloan, Taylor, and Conover, but it surely should play a role in determining the hospital's purchase price.

Another way to reconcile Cutler and Horwitz with Sloan, Taylor, and Conover is to argue that Columbia/HCA is not representative of the for-profit hospital industry. There is some support for this in Sloan, Taylor, and Conover's sample. The Columbia/HCA conversion involving Providence hospital was the only not-for-profit conversion in the North Carolina and South Carolina sample with a positive rate of return. If Columbia/HCA is special, we cannot at present tell whether it is because they are especially good at managing costs or especially good at gaming the reimbursement system. Either way, the hypothesis that Columbia/HCA performance is unique is worth further investigation.

If the conclusions drawn by Sloan, Taylor, and Conover are correct and for-profit hospitals do overpay for not-for-profits, we need to know why. One explanation might be a "winner's curse." This term describes a competitive environment in which the winning bidders are those that systematically overestimate the value of the assets they are purchasing. A closely related phenomenon of "self-serving biases" has been observed to take place in negotiations. Even experienced lawyers have a tendency to interpret the facts of a case in a light most favorable to their interests (Babcock et al. 1995). If hospitals do not learn to overcome the asymmetric information and perceptual biases that sustain a "winner's curse," then we can anticipate that the market for not-for-profits will eventually disappear.

Alternatively, it may be that for-profit hospitals made bad purchases because those making the purchasing decisions were otherwise compensated for agreeing to the deal. Although this sort of private inurement is illegal, there is some scattered evidence that it does play a role in some hospital conversions (Kuttner 1996). For example, in Dickson, Tennessee, where Goodlark Hospital was sold in 1995, a local state representative was both the lawyer for Goodlark, a trustee of Goodlark, and the head of the new foundation created with the proceeds of the hospital's sale (Kuttner 1996).

The opportunity for private inurement as well as the possibility of uncompensated transfers of wealth from public charities to private investors has caused some states to examine hospital conversions closely. In Massachusetts and California, for example, the public and the state attorneys general are very involved in overseeing hospital conversions. In other states, however, conversions take place with much less public scrutiny (Kuttner 1996). We might learn a good deal more about conversions by investigating how different regulatory environments influence the terms of the deals that emerge. In the process, we would also learn valuable lessons about the role that profits play in the delivery of health care services.

References

Babcock, L., G. Lowenstein, Samuel Issacharoff, and Colin Camerer. 1995. Biased Judgements of Fairness in Bargaining. *American Economic Review* 85 (5): 1337–43.
Bell, Judith E. 1996. Saving Their Assets: How to Stop the Plunder at Blue Cross and Other Nonprofits. *American Prospect,* no. 26, 60–66.
Eichenwald, Kurt. 1997. Hospital Chain Cheated U.S. on Expenses, Documents Show. *New York Times,* 18 December, A1.
For-Profit Medicine. 1997. *Economist,* 2 August.
Kuttner, Robert. 1996. Columbia/HCA and the Resurgence of the For-Profit Hospital Business. *New England Journal of Medicine* 335:362.

II

Medical Care Quality in For-Profit and Not-for-Profit Organizations

3

Comparing Hospital Quality at For-Profit and Not-for-Profit Hospitals

Mark McClellan and Douglas Staiger

3.1 Introduction

Do not-for-profit hospitals provide better care than for-profit hospitals? While many studies have compared care delivered by for-profit and not-for-profit hospitals, these studies have provided relatively little empirical evidence on the performance of not-for-profits and for-profits.[1] The ultimate measure of hospital performance is the impact of its care on important patient outcomes, such as death or the development of serious complications that compromise quality of life. Assessing this impact is very difficult. First, collecting reliable long-term outcome data can be challenging. Second, without comprehensive controls for differences in patient case mix, such measures leave open the possibility that differences between hospitals reflect differences in patient disease severity and comorbidity rather than differences in quality of care. Finally, measures of important patient outcomes are notoriously noisy, due to the small numbers of patients on which they are based and the relative rarity of serious adverse outcomes for most patients. Thus, many policymakers and health care managers have expressed reservations about whether measures of se-

Mark McClellan is assistant professor of economics at Stanford University and a faculty research fellow of the National Bureau of Economic Research. Douglas Staiger is associate professor of public policy at the Kennedy School of Government, Harvard University, and a faculty research fellow of the National Bureau of Economic Research.

The authors thank David Cutler, Karen Norberg, Catherine Wolfram, and seminar participants at the NBER and various universities for their helpful comments. They also thank Dhara Shah and Yu-Chu Shen for outstanding research assistance, and the Health Care Financing Administration and the National Institute on Aging for financial support. All errors are the authors' own.

1. E.g., see Gaumer (1986), Gray (1986), Hartz et al. (1989), Keeler et al. (1992), and Staiger and Gaumer (1995).

rious outcomes are informative enough to identify useful differences in quality of care among hospitals.[2] The problem is particularly onerous for comparisons of quality of care between individual hospitals (e.g., for choosing among hospitals in a given market area).

We readdress the question of assessing hospital quality using longitudinal data sources and methods that we have recently developed (McClellan and Staiger 1997). We discuss the data and methods below. We study important health outcomes—all-cause mortality and major cardiac complications—for all elderly Medicare beneficiaries hospitalized with heart disease in the past decade. Our measures optimally combine information on patient outcomes from multiple years, multiple diagnoses, and multiple outcomes (e.g., death and readmission with various types of complications). As a result, we are able to develop measures that are far more accurate indicators of hospital quality than those previously used in hospital outcome studies. In our previous work, we have shown that these measures far outperform previously used methods in terms of forecasting hospital mortality rates in future years, and in terms of signal-to-noise ratios. Thus, we can expect these measures to enhance our ability to determine whether quality of care differs across hospitals.

After we introduce our data and methods, we present two sets of results. First, we examine how these new hospital quality measures vary across for-profit and not-for-profit hospitals, controlling for other characteristics of the hospital. In addition, we examine how these relationships have changed over our study period. We then examine the experience of three market areas closely: (1) a city in which a few large for-profit and not-for-profit hospitals have coexisted with stable ownership, (2) a city in which a large not-for-profit hospital was purchased by a for-profit chain, and later by another for-profit chain, and (3) a city in which the only for-profit hospital was converted to not-for-profit status.

Based on these new measures of hospital quality, our analysis uncovers a number of interesting differences between for-profit and not-for-profit hospitals. On average, we find that for-profit hospitals have higher mortality among elderly patients with heart disease, and that this difference has grown over the last decade. However, much of the difference appears to be associated with the location of for-profit hospitals: When we compare hospital quality within specific markets, for-profit ownership appears, if anything, to be associated with better quality care. Moreover, the small average difference in mortality between for-profit and not-for-profit hospitals masks an enormous amount of variation in mortality within each of these ownership types. Overall, these results suggest that factors other

---

2. E.g., see Ash (1996), Hofer and Hayward (1996), Luft and Romano (1993), McNeil et al. (1992), Park et al. (1990), and the sources cited in n. 1.

than for-profit status per se may be the main determinants of quality of care in hospitals.

3.2   Background

Comparisons of hospital quality, and of provider quality more generally in health care and other industries, must address three crucial problems: measurement, noise, and bias.

The first problem involves measurement. Without measures of performance, there is no basis for comparing quality of care. One of the major obstacles to research on provider performance is the development of reliable data on important medical processes and health outcomes. For example, a major obstacle to comparisons of different managed care plans today, including for-profit and not-for-profit comparisons, is that many plans simply do not have reliable mechanisms in place for collecting data on the care and outcomes of their patients, especially for outpatient care. While the problem is somewhat less severe for care during an inpatient admission, many hospitals do not have reliable methods for collecting follow-up data on their patients, and health plans do not have mechanisms for tracking patients across hospitals. For example, until several years ago, the Health Care Financing Administration (HCFA) published diagnosis-specific mortality rates for Medicare patients. But because these outcome measures were admission based, they could be favorably affected by hospital decisions about discharging or transferring patients, even though such actions may have no effect or adverse effects on meaningful patient outcomes. We use longitudinal data from the Medicare program linked to complete records of death dates to address the problem of collecting follow-up data on important outcomes for patients. But data limitations exist here as well: Medicare collects no reliable information on the care or outcomes of their rapidly growing managed care population.

The second problem involves noise. Important health outcomes are determined by an enormous number of patient and environmental factors; differences in the quality of medical care delivered by hospitals are only one component. Moreover, most of these outcomes are relatively rare. For example, even for a common serious health problem such as heart attacks, most hospitals treat fewer than 100 cases per year, and death within a year occurs in fewer than one-fourth of these patients. Even though a one or two percentage point difference in mortality may be very important to patients, few hospitals treat enough patients with heart disease in a year to detect such differences in outcomes. While data on other related health outcomes or on multiple years of outcomes might help reduce the noise problem, combining multiple outcome measures raises further complications. Hospital quality may improve or worsen from year to year, and the extent to which different outcomes are related to each other may not be obvious. We develop a general framework for integrating a potentially large number of outcomes over long time periods to address the noise problem. Our methods are designed to distinguish the signal of hospital quality from a potentially large number of noisy outcome measures.

The third problem involves bias. Patient selection may result in differences in outcomes across hospitals for reasons unrelated to quality. In particular, higher quality hospitals are likely to attract more difficult cases. A range of methods, including multivariate case-mix adjustment, propensity scores, and instrumental variables, have been developed to address the selection problem. In this paper, we address the problem by focusing on an illness—heart attacks, and heart disease more generally—for which urgency limits the opportunities for selection across hospitals. A more comprehensive analysis of the selection problem is beyond the scope of this paper. In section 3.6, we discuss some of the further evidence we have developed on the magnitude of the selection bias in our outcome measures.

In the next section, we outline our steps for addressing the measurement problems and noise problems that have complicated comparisons between for-profit and not-for-profit hospitals. Our results follow.

3.3   Data and Methods

3.3.1   Data

We use the same data as in McClellan and Staiger (1997) for this analysis. Our hospital performance measures include serious outcomes—mortality and cardiac complications requiring rehospitalization—for all elderly Medicare beneficiaries hospitalized with new occurrences of acute myocardial infarction (AMI, or heart attacks) from 1984 through 1994, as well as for all elderly beneficiaries hospitalized for ischemic heart disease (IHD) from 1984 through 1991. To evaluate quality of care from the standpoint of a person in the community experiencing heart disease, we assign each patient to the hospital to which he or she was first admitted with that diagnosis. Our population includes over 200,000 AMI patients and over 350,000 IHD patients per year. We limit our analysis of hospital performance to U.S. general short-term hospitals with at least two admissions in each year, a total of 3,991 hospitals that collectively treated over 92 percent of these patients. In this paper, we focus exclusively on outcome differences for AMI patients, but we use information on IHD patient outcomes to help improve our estimates of hospital quality for AMI treatment.

For each AMI and IHD patient, our mortality measure is whether the patient died within 90 days of admission. In principle, we could use other patient outcomes as well (e.g., death at other time periods or readmission for a cardiac complication). We focus on these two outcomes, and AMI patients in particular, for a number of reasons. First, death is an easily measured, relatively common adverse outcome for AMI, and many acute medical treatments have been shown to have a significant impact on mortality following AMI. Second, AMI cases that are not immediately fatal generally result in rapid admission to a nearby hospital, so that questions of hospital selection of patients are less of a problem for AMI. Finally, we found in a previous study (McClellan and Staiger 1997) that measures of hospital quality based on AMI have a relatively high signal-to-noise ratio and are strong predictors of hospital quality for other outcomes and diagnoses.[3]

For each hospital, we construct risk-adjusted mortality rates (RAMRs) for each year and each diagnosis. These are the estimated hospital-specific intercepts from a patient-level regression (run separately by year and by diagnosis) that estimates average all-cause mortality rates with fully interacted controls for age, gender, black or nonblack race, and rural location. These RAMRs provide the outcome measures on which our hospital comparisons are based.

To describe hospital ownership status and other characteristics, we use data on hospital and area characteristics from the annual American Hospital Association (AHA) survey of hospitals. We use data from the 1985, 1991, and 1994 surveys in this analysis. AHA data are not available for some hospitals, limiting our final sample to 3,718 hospitals.

3.3.2   Empirical Methods

Past work comparing quality of care in hospitals has generally relied on a single hospital outcome measure in a given year. For example, to compare quality of care at two hospitals, one would simply calculate the estimated RAMR and the precision of the estimate for each hospital, and assess whether the difference in the RAMRs is statistically significant. The limitation of this approach is that the standard errors are often quite large.

Alternatively, one can combine information from all the outcome measures available for a given hospital (e.g., other years, other patients, other outcomes for the same patients) in order to more precisely estimate a hospital's current quality. This is the approach taken in McClellan and Staiger (1997). We briefly outline the method below.

Suppose we observe AMI_DTH90 and IHD_DTH90. These are noisy estimates of the true hospital intercepts that are of interest:

$$\text{AMI\_DTH90}_{it} = \mu_{it}^1 + \varepsilon_{it}^1,$$

---

3. In particular, McClellan and Staiger (1997) also consider performance measures for ischemic heart disease and for a patient's quality of life following a heart attack (the occurrence of hospital readmission with congestive heart failure, ischemic heart disease symptoms, and recurrent heart attack).

$$\text{IHD\_DTH90}_{it} = \mu_{it}^2 + \varepsilon_{it}^2,$$

where μ is the true parameter of interest (the hospital-specific intercept in the 90-day mortality equations), ε is the estimation error, and we observe each outcome for T years. Note that $\text{Var}(\varepsilon_{it}^1 \ \varepsilon_{it}^2)$ can be estimated, since this is simply the variance of regression estimates.

Let $M_i \equiv \{\text{AMI\_DTH90}_i, \text{IHD\_DTH90}_i\}$ be a $1 \times (2T)$ vector of the T years of data on each outcome, and let $\mu_i \equiv \{\mu_i^1, \mu_i^2\}$ be a $1 \times (2T)$ vector of the true hospital intercepts. Our problem is how to use M_i to predict μ_i. More specifically, we wish to create a linear combination of each hospital's observed outcomes data in such a way that it minimizes the mean square error of our predictions. In other words, we would like to run the following hypothetical regression:

(1) $\mu_{it} = \{\text{AMI\_DTH90}_i, \text{IHD\_DTH90}_i\} \beta_{it} + \upsilon_{it} \equiv M_i \beta_{it} + \upsilon_{it},$

but cannot, since μ_i is unobserved and β will vary by hospital and time.

Equation (1) helps to highlight the problem with using a single year's RAMR as a prediction of the true hospital-level intercept. Since the RAMR is estimated with error, we can improve the mean square error of the prediction by attenuating the coefficient toward zero, and this attenuation should be greater for hospitals in which the RAMR is not precisely estimated. Moreover, if the true hospital-specific intercepts from other outcomes' equations (e.g., other years, other patients) are correlated with the intercept we are trying to predict, then using their estimated values can further improve prediction ability.

In McClellan and Staiger (1997), we developed a simple method for creating estimates of μ_i based on equation (1). The key to the solution is noting that to estimate this hypothetical regression (e.g., get coefficients, predicted values, R^2) we only need three moment matrices:

(i) $E(M_i' M_i) = E(\mu_i' \mu_i) + E(\varepsilon_i' \varepsilon_i),$

(ii) $E(M_i' \mu_i) = E(\mu_i' \mu_i),$

(iii) $E(\mu_i' \mu_i).$

We *can* estimate the required moment matrices directly as follows:

1. We can estimate $E(\varepsilon_i' \varepsilon_i)$ with the patient-level ordinary least squares (OLS) estimate of the variance-covariance for the parameter estimates M_{it}. Call this estimate S_i.
2. We can estimate $E(\mu_i' \mu_i)$ by noting that $E(M_i' M_i - S_i) = E(\mu_i' \mu_i)$. If we assume that $E(\mu_i' \mu_i)$ is the same for all hospitals, then it can be estimated by the sample average of $M_i' M_i - S_i$.

Finally, it helps to impose some structure on $E(\mu_i' \mu_i)$ for two reasons. First, this improves the precision of the estimated moments by limiting the number of parameters that need to be estimated. Second, a time series structure allows for out-of-sample forecasts. Thus, we assume a nonstationary first-order vector autoregression (VAR) structure for μ_{it} (1×2). This VAR structure implies that $E(\mu_i'\mu_i) = f(\Gamma)$, where Γ are the parameters of the VAR. These parameters can be estimated by generalized method of moments (GMM); that is, by setting the theoretical moment matrix, $f(\Gamma)$, as close as possible to its sample analog, the sample average of $M_i'M_i - S_i$. For details, see McClellan and Staiger (1997).

With estimates of $E(\mu_i'\mu_i)$ and $E(\varepsilon_i'\varepsilon_i)$, we can form estimates of the moments (i)–(iii) needed to run the hypothetical regression in equation (1). By analogy to simple regression, our predictions of a hospitals true intercept are given by:

$$(2) \quad \hat{\mu}_j = M_i E(M_i'M_i)^{-1} E(M_i'\mu_i) = M_i[E(\mu_i'\mu_i) + E(\varepsilon_i'\varepsilon_i)]^{-1} E(\mu_i'\mu_i),$$

where we use our estimates of $E(\mu_i'\mu_i)$ and $E(\varepsilon_i'\varepsilon_i)$ in place of their true values. We refer to estimates based on equation (2) as "filtered RAMR" estimates, since these estimates are attempting to filter out the estimation error in the raw data (and because our method is closely related to the idea of filtering in time series).

3.4 National Estimates

One common method of comparing quality of care across hospitals is to run cross-section regressions using a quality measure such as RAMR as the dependent variable and using hospital characteristics such as patient volume, ownership, and teaching status as independent variables. In this section, we investigate the extent to which using a filtered RAMR as the dependent variable affects the inferences that can be drawn from such regressions. A priori, we would expect that using the filtered RAMR (as opposed to the actual RAMR in a given year) would improve the precision of such regression estimates because the dependent variable is measured with less noise. The gain in efficiency is likely to be particularly large for smaller hospitals, since the RAMR estimates in any single year for these hospitals have the lowest signal-to-noise ratio.

Figure 3.1 illustrates this difference between filtered and actual RAMRs by plotting each against volume using data from 1991. Throughout the remainder of the paper we focus on RAMRs based on 90-day mortality among Medicare AMI admissions (although the filtered estimates incorporate the information from 90-day mortality among IHD admissions as well). Keep in mind that the unit for the RAMR measures is the probability of death, so that a RAMR of 0.1 means that the hospital had a mortality rate that was 10 percentage points higher than expected (e.g., 30 percent rather than 20 percent).

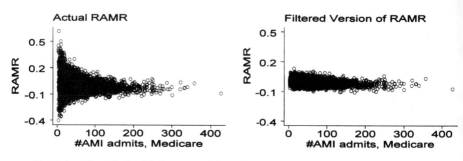

Fig. 3.1   The relationship between risk-adjusted mortality rates (RAMRs) and patient volume using actual versus filtered RAMR
Note: Based on 90-day mortality for Medicare AMI admits.

There are two interesting features of figure 3.1. First, the filtered RAMR estimates have much less variance than the actual RAMR estimates, particularly for smaller hospitals. This is the result of two distinct effects. Most importantly, the filtered estimates for small hospitals are relying more heavily on data from other years and other diagnoses, and this improves their precision. In addition, the filtered estimates assume the actual RAMR estimates for small hospitals have a very low signal-to-noise ratio, and therefore attenuate them back toward the average (similar to shrinkage estimators).

A second interesting feature of figure 3.1 is that the relationship between outcomes and volume is much more apparent in the filtered data. High-volume hospitals clearly seem to have lower mortality. Thus, these filtered RAMRs appear to be a useful tool for uncovering quality differences across hospitals.

Table 3.1 provides regression estimates that further suggest that these filtered RAMR estimates improve our ability to uncover differences in quality across hospitals. This table contains coefficient estimates from regressions of RAMR estimates (either actual or filtered) on dummies for ownership (for-profit and government, with not-for-profit the reference group), a dummy for being a teaching hospital, and the number of Medicare AMI admissions in the given year (in hundreds). Since volume is potentially endogenous (and since Medicare volume is a crude proxy for total volume), we also report estimates from regressions that do not control for volume. The table contains estimates for 1985, 1991, and 1994. The regressions using actual RAMRs are weighted by the number of Medicare admissions, while the regressions using filtered RAMRs are weighted by the inverse of the estimated variance of each hospital's filtered RAMR estimate.

As one would expect, the regressions based on the filtered RAMR yield much more precise coefficient estimates. The standard errors in regres-

Table 3.1   **Regression Estimates of the Relationship between Hospital Characteristics and the Risk-Adjusted Mortality Rate (RAMR) Based on 90-Day Mortality for AMI Admits (3,718 hospitals)**

	1985		1991		1994	
	Actual RAMR	Filtered Version of RAMR	Actual RAMR	Filtered Version of RAMR	Actual RAMR	Filtered Version of RAMR
Number of Medicare admits in AMI (100s)	−0.0178 (0.0022)	−0.0153 (0.0010)	−0.0148 (0.0018)	−0.0143 (0.0009)	−0.0093 (0.0014)	−0.0110 (0.0007)
Government	0.0151 (0.0033)	0.0104 (0.0012)	0.0219 (0.0033)	0.0120 (0.0013)	0.0169 (0.0033)	0.0109 (0.0012)
For-profit	0.0016 (0.0043)	0.0030 (0.0016)	0.0115 (0.0038)	0.0071 (0.0016)	0.0102 (0.0038)	0.0087 (0.0015)
Teaching	−0.0031 (0.0033)	0.0022 (0.0014)	−0.0047 (0.0030)	−0.0039 (0.0014)	−0.0083 (0.0028)	−0.0047 (0.0013)

Note: Standard errors are given in parentheses. Regressions using the actual RAMR weight by the number of AMI admits. Regressions using the filtered RAMR weight by $1/\sigma^2$, where σ is the standard error of the estimated RAMR.

sions using the actual RAMRs are two to three times larger than the corresponding standard errors from regressions using the filtered RAMR. For example, using actual RAMR estimates in 1985, mortality in for-profit hospitals is estimated to be 0.16 percentage points higher than in not-for-profit hospitals. But the standard error for this estimate is so large (0.43 percentage points) that the difference would have to be near a full percentage point before we could be confident of a real difference in mortality. In contrast, using filtered RAMR estimates in 1985, mortality in for-profit hospitals is estimated to be 0.30 percentage points higher than in not-for-profit hospitals and this difference is borderline significant because of the much smaller standard error.

More generally, the coefficients in the regressions using filtered RAMRs are precise enough to uncover a number of interesting facts. For-profit hospitals have higher mortality than do not-for-profits (by 0.30 to 1.15 percentage points depending on the year and specification). Government hospitals have higher mortality and teaching hospitals lower mortality than do not-for-profit hospitals. These differences are larger in specifications that do not control for volume, because (1) government and for-profit hospitals tend to be smaller than average, while teaching hospitals tend to be larger than average, and (2) there is a strong negative relationship between volume and mortality. For example, in 1985 we estimate that an additional 100 Medicare AMI admissions was associated with 1.5 percentage points lower mortality.

The most striking finding in table 3.1 is the apparent change in the coefficients between 1985 and 1994. In the specifications using the filtered RAMR, the coefficient estimates for for-profit and teaching hospitals rise by roughly half of a percentage point in absolute value between 1985 and 1994. At the same time, the coefficient on volume fell in absolute value by about half a percentage point.

These regression estimates suggest that the filtered RAMR can be a useful tool for uncovering general relationships between mortality and hospital characteristics. Based on the filtered data, three facts are clear: (1) there is a negative relationship between volume and mortality, (2) for-profit hospitals and government hospitals have higher mortality than not-for-profit hospitals, while teaching hospitals have lower mortality, and (3) between 1985 and 1994, mortality differences increased between for-profit and not-for-profit hospitals, and between teaching and nonteaching hospitals.

These findings are generally consistent with the existing literature, although our estimates tend to be more precise. Studies examining a variety of patient populations and outcomes measures have found that higher volume is associated with better patient outcomes.[4] Comparisons by ownership and teaching status, to the extent they have found any differences,

---

4. See Luft et al. (1990) for a fairly comprehensive study of the volume-outcome relationship.

have found not-for-profit and teaching hospitals to have better patient outcomes.[5] The most novel of our findings is that these differences have widened over the last decade. This decade has been a period of rapid change in hospitals, spurred by dramatic changes in the way that both government and private insurers pay for hospital care. The extent to which these market changes might explain the growing differences in hospital mortality is an important area for future research.

3.5 A Tale of Three Counties

3.5.1 The Sample

If the filtered RAMR helps to compare hospitals at the national level, can it also help at a more micro level? One important use for any measure of hospital quality is to compare individual hospitals within a given market. In this section, we look more closely at the mortality performance of particular hospitals in three counties. Our goals are (1) to learn whether these quality measures are able to identify meaningful differences (and changes over time) in mortality among hospitals in a given city; and (2) to explore whether these patterns in mortality could be attributed to for-profit ownership or other factors affecting the market. At the same time, by going to the county level and focusing on a fixed group of hospitals, we are able to address some of the general results discussed in section 3.4 from a "case study" perspective.

The three counties were chosen on the following basis. First, since we wanted to compare individual hospitals (but not too many hospitals) we limited our search to counties with 2–10 hospitals in our sample. In order to focus on for-profit hospitals, the county had to have at least one for-profit hospital and one other hospital with an average of at least 50 Medicare AMI admissions per year from 1984 to 1994. Within this subset we considered three categories of counties:

Case 1: No change in for-profit ownership over the study period
Case 2: At least one hospital converted into for-profit over the study period
Case 3: At least one hospital converted away from for-profit over the study period

Within each category we eliminated counties that were obviously not distinct markets (e.g., the suburbs of Miami). Finally, we chose the county that had the highest average volume in its primary hospitals.

The resulting counties all contain relatively isolated midsized cities. To preserve the confidentiality of individual hospitals, we refer to each hospital according to its rank in terms of AMI volume between 1984 and 1994.

---

5. See the sources cited in nn. 1 and 2.

Case 1 contains a small southern city with four larger-than-average hospitals. The largest (hospital 1) and smallest (hospital 4) are for-profit hospitals, both affiliated with the same for-profit chain. Hospital 2 is government run, while hospital 3 is a not-for-profit. Relative to the other two cases, this city had experienced rapid growth in population and income during the 1980s and has a high number of hospital beds per capita. The population is somewhat older, less educated, and less likely to be white, with 10–20 percent enrolled in HMOs by 1994.[6]

Case 2 contains a midsized midwestern city with three larger-than-average hospitals and one very small hospital (hospital 4). Hospitals 1, 3, and 4 are not-for-profit. Hospital 2 was a not-for-profit until the mid 1980s, at which time it was purchased by a large for-profit chain. The ownership of hospital 2 was transferred to a different for-profit chain in the early 1990s. Relative to the other two cases, this city had average growth in population and income during the 1980s and has a low number of hospital beds per capita. The population has higher income and is somewhat younger, more educated, and more likely to be white, with 10–20 percent enrolled in HMOs by 1994.

Case 3 contains a midsized southern city with five larger-than-average hospitals. Hospitals 1, 2, and 4 are not-for-profit. Hospital 3 was initially government owned, and hospital 5 was initially for-profit. Both hospital 3 and hospital 5 converted to not-for-profit status in the late 1980s. Relative to the other two cases, this city had low population growth during the 1980s. Otherwise, this city has fairly average population characteristics with 10–20 percent enrolled in HMOs by 1994.

3.5.2   Evidence on Quality in Each County

In keeping with the exploratory nature of this analysis, figure 3.2 simply plots the RAMR (left panel) and filtered RAMR (right panel) annually from 1984 to 1994 for each hospital in case 1. Note that the vertical scale differs between the two plots (in order to preserve the detail of the filtered RAMR plot). Figure 3.3 plots this data slightly differently. Each panel corresponds to a hospital, and plots the actual RAMR along with the filtered RAMR and its 90 percent confidence band. Confidence bands for the actual RAMR are too large to fit on the figure. A horizontal line denoting the RAMR at the average hospital in our sample is added to each panel for reference. The data for case 2 are similarly plotted below in figures 3.4 and 3.5, and for case 3 in figures 3.6 and 3.7.

For case 1, it is impossible to detect quality differences across the hospitals or over time based on the actual RAMR (see the left panel of fig. 3.2).

---

6. Information on each city/county comes from the *County and City Data Book* for 1988 and 1994. Information on HMO penetration in each county was provided by Laurence Baker, based on his calculations using HMO enrollment data from InterStudy.

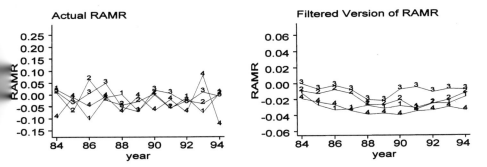

Fig. 3.2   Trends in risk-adjusted mortality rates (RAMRs) for case 1 (a mid-sized southern city)

Note: Left panel based on actual RAMR and right panel based on filtered RAMR. (Note that the vertical scale of the two panels differs.) The hospitals are ranked from largest (1) to smallest (4) according to their number of Medicare AMI admissions from 1984 to 1994. Hospitals 1 and 4 are for-profit hospitals and are affiliated with the same chain. Hospital 2 is government owned, while hospital 3 is not-for-profit.

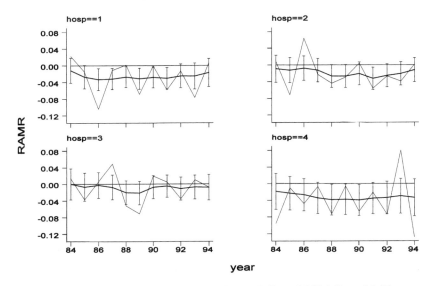

Fig. 3.3   Trends for case 1 in actual (*thin line*) and filtered (*thick line with 90 percent confidence bands*) RAMR by hospital

Note: The straight horizontal line denotes the RAMR at the average hospital in our national sample (RAMR = 0 by definition). For description of the hospitals, see the note to fig. 3.2.

Obviously, the problem is the variability in the actual RAMR: Even the largest hospital (1) experiences year-to-year changes in its actual RAMR of over five percentage points.

In contrast, the filtered RAMR is much more stable and displays three interesting features. First, the for-profit hospitals (1 and 4) have, if anything, lower mortality than the other hospitals in the market. The fact that the smallest hospital also has the lowest filtered RAMR seems surprising, but this may be the result of its affiliation with hospital 1 (recall that they are members of the same chain). A second interesting feature of the filtered data in figure 3.2 is that every hospital appears to experience an improvement in mortality of about one to two percentage points in the mid-1980s relative to other hospitals nationally. Although it is beyond the scope of this paper, an interesting topic for further research is the analysis of the cause of this general improvement in quality of care in this area.[7] Finally, it is notable that the range of filtered RAMR estimates, while much larger than the differences estimated between the average for-profit and not-for-profit in table 3.1, are still relatively compressed. Based on national data, we estimated (McClellan and Staiger 1997) that the standard deviation across hospitals is around four percentage points for the true hospital-specific intercepts for 90-day mortality.

Figure 3.3 plots each hospital's data separately and adds 90 percent confidence bands to the filtered RAMR (thick line with vertical bars). The horizontal line at RAMR = 0 represents the national average in that year, so when the confidence bands lie entirely below or above this line, it is likely that the hospital is, respectively, better or worse than average. Relative to the size of the confidence bands, there are not large differences either across these hospitals or over time. Hospital 1 (the large for-profit) is the only hospital that is consistently better than the national average, and this seems to be consistent with its general status in the community.

Thus, the overall picture for case 1 seems to be one of fairly homogeneous quality, perhaps slightly above the national average. There are hints of improvement over time and of better quality in the for-profit hospitals, but there are no dramatic differences.

As figure 3.4 illustrates, case 2 is quite different. The only similarity is that it is impossible to detect quality differences across hospitals or over time based on the actual RAMR data plotted in the left panel of the figure. Using the filtered RAMR, there is a clear ranking of quality across hospitals that roughly corresponds to size. The largest hospital (a not-for-profit) consistently has the lowest mortality, while hospital 4 (a very small hospital) has the highest mortality. The difference in mortality between the largest and smallest hospital is substantial, from six to over eight percentage points. These differences are large even relative to the 90 percent confidence bounds for the filtered RAMR (see fig. 3.5). As in case 1, the hospital that we identify as having the lowest mortality is recognized in the community as the leading hospital.

Hospital 2 is of particular interest because it was taken over by a for-

---

7. Recall that the RAMR measures mortality relative to the average hospital, so this improvement does not simply reflect the downward national trend in heart attack mortality rates. Mortality in these hospitals improved relative to the national average over this time.

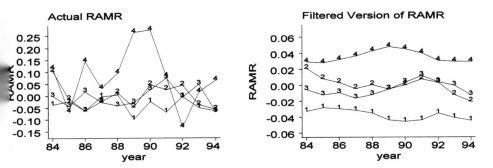

Fig. 3.4   **Trends in risk-adjusted mortality rates (RAMRs) for case 2 (a mid-sized midwestern city)**
Note: Left panel based on actual RAMR and right panel based on filtered RAMR. (Note that the vertical scale of the two panels differs.) The hospitals are ranked from largest (1) to smallest (4) according to their number of Medicare AMI admissions from 1984 to 1994. Hospital 4 is quite small. Hospitals 1, 3, and 4 are not-for-profit hospitals. Hospital 2 was a not-for-profit that was purchased by a for-profit chain in the mid-1980s, and then by a different for-profit chain in the early 1990s.

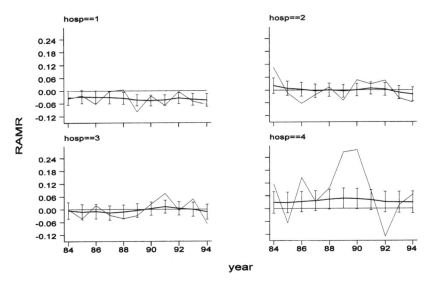

Fig. 3.5   **Trends for case 2 in actual (*thin line*) and filtered (*thick line with 90 percent confidence bands*) RAMR by hospital**
Note: The straight horizontal line denotes the RAMR at the average hospital in our national sample (RAMR = 0 by definition). For description of the hospitals, see the note to fig. 3.4.

profit chain in the mid-1980s and then became part of a different for-profit chain in the early 1990s. Around both of these ownership changes, there is a notable decline in the hospital's filtered RAMR of about two percentage points. In fact, it is the only hospital in case 2 that has an apparent trend (downward) in its mortality, going from being worse than average to better

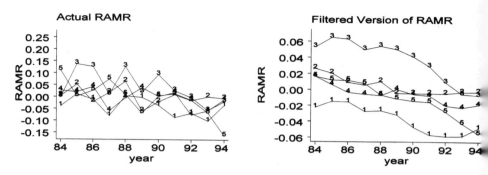

Fig. 3.6   Trends in risk-adjusted mortality rates (RAMRs) for case 3 (a mid-sized southern city)

Note: Left panel based on actual RAMR and right panel based on filtered RAMR. (Note that the vertical scale of the two panels differs.) The hospitals are ranked from largest (1) to smallest (5) according to their number of Medicare AMI admissions from 1984 to 1994. Hospitals 1, 2, and 4 are not-for-profit hospitals. Hospital 3 was initially government owned and then converted to not-for-profit status in the late 1980s. Similarly, hospital 5 converted from for-profit to not-for-profit status in the late 1980s.

than average. While it is not clear that the change in ownership per se led to these improvements, it is at least suggestive that this may be the case.

The overall picture for case 2 seems to be one of more diversity of quality, although fairly average quality overall. The purchase of a hospital first by one and then another for-profit chain seemed, if anything, to improve quality. However, the purchased hospital is still not clearly any better than the national average in terms of mortality.

Case 3 presents yet another situation (see figs. 3.6 and 3.7). Again, there is a wide range of quality across hospitals in this area, with the range in filtered RAMR of five to eight percentage points (see fig. 3.6). There is a clear downward trend in mortality occurring in this area, which is even seen in the actual RAMR (although the actual RAMR is still very noisy). Using the filtered RAMR, each of the hospitals in this area experienced a decline in mortality of between two and eight percentage points. Hospital 1, the largest not-for-profit, had the lowest mortality throughout almost the entire period. Hospital 3, which converted from government to not-for-profit in the late 1980s, clearly had the highest mortality initially but also experienced one of the largest declines by 1994. Hospital 5, which converted from for-profit to not-for-profit in the late 1980s, had the largest mortality decline of all five hospitals to the point where it had the lowest filtered RAMR in the area in 1994.

Thus, the overall picture for case 3 is one of rapidly improving quality in the area as a whole. At the same time, the for-profit and government hospitals converted to not-for-profit and had the most dramatic quality improvements in the area.

There are two common themes across all of these cases. First, filtered

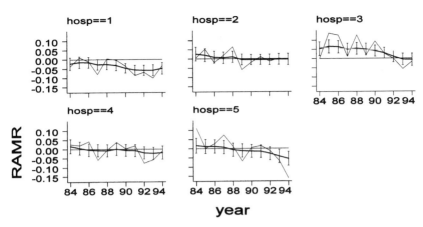

Fig. 3.7   **Trends for case 3 in actual (*thin line*) and filtered (*thick line with 90***
***percent confidence bands*) **RAMR by hospital**
Note: The straight horizontal line denotes the RAMR at the average hospital in our national sample (RAMR = 0 by definition). For description of the hospitals, see the note to fig. 3.6.

RAMRs appear to be a useful tool for analyzing quality of care differences across hospitals and over time. More importantly, our microlevel evidence from these specific cases is not consistent with the common belief (supported by our aggregate regressions) that for-profit hospitals provide lower quality of care. In two of our three markets, for-profits appeared to be associated with higher quality of care: Hospitals that were for-profit throughout our study period tended to have lower mortality rates, and changes to for-profit status were associated with mortality reductions.

What might explain this apparent conflict between the case-study evidence and the aggregate cross-section evidence, which showed a poorer performance overall for the for-profits? Some of the explanation may come from the way in which we chose our case studies, relying on areas with relatively large for-profit hospitals that were perhaps likely to represent "flagship" hospitals in their communities. These features may not be representative of the market status of a typical for-profit hospital.

One possible explanation for these results could be that for-profit hospitals selectively locate in areas with low quality (see, e.g., Norton and Staiger 1994). Thus, the aggregate evidence would tend to find that for-profit ownership was correlated with lower quality, while within their markets, the for-profit hospitals could provide higher quality (as in case 1) or at least improve quality in the hospitals they acquire (as in case 2). This explanation would also imply that for-profit hospitals would tend to leave markets in which the quality was rising (as in case 3). If the cross-section correlation is being generated by location, then we would expect within-county differences between for-profit and not-for-profit hospitals to be smaller than across-county differences. In fact, when we include county-level fixed-effects in the regressions from table 3.1, the estimated mortality difference between for-profit and not-for-profit hospitals falls by roughly half. Thus, it appears that at least some of the difference in quality is generated by the different location patterns of for-profit hospitals.

Why might for-profit hospitals tend to locate in areas with low hospital quality? One possible reason would be a relationship between poor hospital management and lower quality of care. Poorly managed hospitals might make attractive takeover targets for for-profit chains, but as a by-product, the for-profits would tend to enter markets with low quality of care. Alternatively, patients may demand high-quality care in some markets, either because of demographic factors such as high income or because of an existing high-quality hospital in the market (e.g., a teaching hospital). If providing such high-quality care results in lower patient margins, then for-profits would be less likely to locate in these areas.

These speculative explanations are based on the results of only a few market case studies. We will leave a more systematic exploration of this question to future work. Clearly, however, a final important conclusion of this research is that the "average" differences in mortality between for-profit and not-for-profit hospitals—or among any other general system for classifying hospitals, such as bed size—account for only a small share of the variation in outcomes across hospitals. Many not-for-profit hospitals are below average, many for-profit hospitals are above average, and these relationships vary enormously at the market level. More extensive market-level analyses using the methods we have developed to evaluate quality could yield new insights into these complex relationships.

3.6 Conclusion

In this paper, we have summarized new methods for evaluating the quality of care of for-profit and not-for-profit hospitals. These methods address two of the major problems that have limited the value of previous hospital quality assessments: measurement of important outcomes, and the high level of noise in these measures. In McClellan and Staiger (1997), where we describe these techniques in more detail, we also present evidence on a third major problem: bias in the hospital comparisons because of unmeasured differences in case mix across hospitals. We use detailed medical chart review data to show that hospital performance measures for heart attack care that account for patient disease severity and comorbidity in a much more extensive way are highly correlated with the measures we report in this research. In other words, our measures with limited case-mix adjustment provide reasonably good predictions of hospital performance in terms of measures based on detailed case-mix adjustment. Our results to date on the bias problem are by no means conclusive; hard-to-measure patient factors may differ systematically across hospitals, particularly for less acute conditions than heart attacks. At a minimum, however, by providing relatively precise measures of hospital performance for important dimensions of hospital quality of care, our approach allows further research to focus on this final key problem.

The results of our analysis provide a range of new insights for policy issues related to for-profit and not-for-profit hospital ownership. On average, the performance of not-for-profit hospitals in treating elderly patients with heart disease appears to be slightly better than that of for-profit hospitals, even after accounting for systematic differences in hospital size, teaching status, urbanization, and patient demographic characteristics. This average difference in mortality performance between for-profits and not-for-profits appears to be increasing over time. However, this small average difference masks an enormous amount of variation in hospital quality within the for-profit and not-for-profit hospital groups. Our case-study results also suggest that for-profits may provide the impetus for quality improvements in markets where, for various reasons, relatively poor quality of care is the norm. Understanding the many market- and hospital-specific factors that contribute to these variations in hospital quality is a crucial topic for further research. Using the methods and results developed here, such detailed market analyses can be based on rather precise assessments of differences in hospital performance, rather than on speculation necessitated by imprecise or absent outcome measures.

References

Ash, A. 1996. Identifying Poor-Quality Hospitals with Mortality Rates: Often There's More Noise Than Signal. *Medical Care* 34:735–36.

Gaumer, G. 1986. Medicare Patient Outcomes and Hospital Organizational Mission. In *For-Profit Enterprise in Health Care,* ed. B. H. Gray, 354–84. Washington, D.C.: National Academy Press.

Gray, B. H. 1986. *For-Profit Enterprise in Health Care.* Washington, D.C.: National Academy Press.

Hartz, A. J., H. Krakauer, E. M. Kuhn, M. Young, S. J. Jacobsen, G. Gay, L. Muenz, M. Katzoff, R. C. Bailey, and A. A. Rimm. 1989. Hospital Characteristics and Mortality Rates. *New England Journal of Medicine* 321:1720–25.

Hofer, T. P., and R. A. Hayward. 1996. Identifying Poor-Quality Hospitals: Can Hospital Mortality Rates Detect Quality Problems for Medical Diagnoses? *Medical Care* 34:737–53.

Keeler, E. B., L. V. Rubenstein, K. L. Kahn, D. Draper, E. R. Harrison, M. J. McGinty, W. H. Rogers, and R. H. Brook. 1992. Hospital Characteristics and Quality of Care. *Journal of the American Medical Association* 268:1709–14.

Luft, H. F., D. W. Garnick, D. H. Mark, and S. J. McPhee. 1990. *Hospital Volume,*

Physician Volume, and Patient Outcomes. Ann Arbor, Mich.: Health Administration Press Perspectives.

Luft, H. F., and P. S. Romano. 1993. Chance, Continuity, and Change in Hospital Mortality Rates. *Journal of the American Medical Association* 270:331–37.

McClellan, M., and D. Staiger. 1997. The Quality of Health Care Providers. Working paper. Stanford University, Stanford, Calif.

McNeil, B. J., S. H. Pedersen, and C. Gatsonis. 1992. Current Issues in Profiling Quality of Care. *Inquiry* 29:298–307.

Norton, E. C., and D. Staiger. 1994. How Hospital Ownership Affects Access to Care for the Uninsured. *RAND Journal of Economics* 25:171–85.

Park, R. E., R. H. Brook, J. Kosecoff, J. Keesey, L. Rubenstein, E. Keeler, K. L. Kahn, W. H. Rogers, and M. R. Chassin. 1990. Explaining Variations in Hospital Death Rates. *Journal of the American Medical Association* 264:484–90.

Staiger, D., and G. Gaumer. 1995. Price Regulation and Patient Mortality in Hospitals. Working paper. Harvard University, Cambridge, Mass.

U.S. Department of Commerce. Bureau of the Census. 1988. *County and City Data Book.* Washington, D.C.: U.S. Government Printing Office.

———. 1994. *County and City Data Book.* Washington, D.C.: U.S. Government Printing Office.

The Adoption and Impact
of Advanced Emergency
Response Services

Susan Athey and Scott Stern

4.1 Introduction

Emergency response services, provided through 911 calling and ambulance services, serve as the first line of contact between patients suffering from emergency conditions and the local health care infrastructure. Together with the emergency rooms in hospitals, emergency response services play an important role in the health care outcomes for a number of emergency indications. For example, in the case of out-of-hospital cardiac arrest, the time lapse between collapse and the initiation of cardiopulmonary resuscitation (CPR) and defibrillation is claimed to be an important determinant of the probability of survival.[1] In addition, the emergency response system plays a critical role in selecting which hospital receives each emergency patient, where hospitals may differ in their quality and in

Susan Athey is the Castle Krob Career Development Associate Professor in the Department of Economics, Massachusetts Institute of Technology, and a faculty research fellow of the National Bureau of Economic Research. Scott Stern is assistant professor at the Sloan School of Management, Massachusetts Institute of Technology, and a faculty research fellow of the National Bureau of Economic Research.

The authors are grateful to David Cutler, Catherine Wolfram, Karen Norberg, and conference participants for insightful discussions. John Kim, Irena Asmundson, Chris Bae, David Hellmuth, and Andres Nanneti provided exceptional research assistance. The authors are also grateful to the Pennsylvania Department of Health, and in particular Dr. Kum Ham, as well as the National Emergency Number Association, for providing the data, and to the numerous emergency response professionals who graciously provided their time and expertise. Generous financial support was provided by the Sloan School of Management at MIT and NSF grant SBR-9631760 (Athey).

1. The literature on this topic is large, but several relevant studies include Gibson (1977); Hoffer (1979); Siler (1975); Cummins et al. (1991); Bonnin, Pepe, and Clark (1993); Fischer, Fischer, and Schuttler (1997); Larsen et al. (1993); Tresch, Thakur, and Hoffman (1989); and Weston, Wilson, and Jones (1997).

the technologies available for emergency care. The patient benefits from emergency response services thus arise not only from the direct provision of medical and transportation services but also through the system's role in allocating patients to the hospital facilities that are most appropriate for their particular medical condition. Furthermore, emergency response systems may have indirect effects on patients through their influence on the choices made by hospitals. Emergency response systems affect the incentives of hospitals to adopt certain technologies, such as gaining "trauma center" certification and introducing capabilities for the provision of cardiac care, since these choices can potentially influence the allocation of emergency patients to hospitals.

There exists wide variation across communities within the United States in terms of the level of care provided through the emergency service system. For example, 911 services are publicly funded and are almost always operated by local government agencies such as police or fire departments. At one extreme, some communities have invested in "Enhanced 911" (E911) systems, which link digital information about the source of the call with a detailed address database maintained by the 911 center. The call takers see each caller's address and location on a computer screen almost instantaneously when the call is received. Even more advanced alternatives are available, including computer-aided ambulance dispatching. At the other extreme, there are many communities that have not invested even in a "Basic 911" capability. In these environments, individuals attempting to contact the local medical emergency infrastructure must locate and dial a seven-digit number. When the call is received, the call taker manually searches for and contacts the ambulance that is closest to the emergency and has the appropriate equipment. Likewise, we see substantial heterogeneity in the availability of in-hospital emergency services across communities. Although the American Heart Association has advocated the adoption of Enhanced 911 as the first step in a "chain of survival" for cardiac incidents (Cummins et al. 1991), there has been little systematic evidence presented about the benefits of 911 services.[2]

The principal aim of this paper is to evaluate the determinants and implications of differences in the prehospital and in-hospital emergency services adopted in a given community. To accomplish this goal, we evaluate the incentives to adopt emergency response systems and in-hospital technology, as well as the productivity gains from these investments. We focus in particular on the productivity and adoption of Basic and Enhanced 911 services, services that entail investments in information technology and telecommunications equipment.

---

2. For an exception, see Joslyn, Pomrehn, and Brown (1993), who find in a sample of 1,753 Iowa patients that 911 reduces response time, time to CPR, and time to defibrillation, as well as mortality. This study has a limited number of county-level covariates, however, leaving open issues of unobserved heterogeneity between counties.

As a service enabled by investment in information technology, emergency response systems belong to the substantial portion of the economy that has defied accurate productivity measurement (Griliches 1994; Bresnahan and Gordon 1997). For most services (including emergency response), it is difficult to measure quality. Each consumer's valuation can depend on several factors that are difficult to observe, such as timeliness and the location of service delivery as well as on the extent to which the product is customized to the individual. In the case of 911 services, however, we are able to address some of these challenges using a unique combination of data sources. The primary database is composed of a set of ambulance calls responding to reported cardiac incidents in Pennsylvania in 1995. These ambulance records have been linked with hospital billing records, hospital characteristics, and data about the level of 911 technology available in the county in which the call took place. We use this data to document how 911 is related to the benefits provided by the emergency response system, including its relationship to lower response times, more appropriate allocation of patients to hospitals, and reduced mortality of cardiac patients.

Our analysis focuses on relatively simple, reduced-form procedures. We begin by exploring the sources of heterogeneity in the allocation of 911 services to different localities. We find that 911 is allocated not only according to factors that might increase their technical efficiency (such as the number of residents per county) but also according to a county's political orientation. In particular, communities with more conservative voting patterns are less likely to adopt advanced 911 systems. Although we do not perform a formal cost-benefit analysis, these results suggest that public policies concerning 911 systems can potentially increase the efficiency of the diffusion process. For example, some of the barriers to adoption include the lack of incentives and information faced by county government officials, problems that could potentially be remedied at relatively low cost.

We then turn to analyze the productivity benefits from adopting Basic and Enhanced 911 systems, taking the patient as the unit of the analysis. We begin by studying the effects of the county-level 911 system on the time it takes to respond to cardiac emergencies and transport the patient to the hospital, factors that are an important component of the quality of emergency medical services. The detailed nature of the data set allows us to control for a variety of patient characteristics, as well as for features of the county, such as the hospital infrastructure and demographic characteristics.

We show that an ambulance arrives at the scene of a cardiac emergency 5 percent faster in counties with Enhanced 911 as opposed to no 911 or Basic 911. Even larger gains are measured when we restrict our sample solely to those counties that changed their level of 911 technology during our sample period. Moreover, patients are transported from the scene of an incident to the hospital approximately 10 percent faster in counties with Enhanced 911 as opposed to lower levels of 911.

Our findings regarding the relationship between 911 and mortality are more subtle. First, we are unable to establish a direct reduced-form statistical relationship between the level of 911 in a given county and patient mortality. Of course, this may be due to the fact that the overall mortality rate is relatively low (approximately 7 percent) and only a small portion of our sample resides in counties with no 911 technology (approximately 20 percent), making it difficult to infer the impact of the technology level on the mortality rate. However, our analysis of the impact of 911 on response time suggests an alternative strategy: We use the adoption of 911 as an instrument for an individual's response time in the patient mortality regressions. In particular, we show that 911 technology affects response time, and we can assume that 911 adoption is unrelated to the severity of a particular patient. Our preliminary instrumental variables analysis of the effect of response time on mortality finds that shorter response times do indeed reduce mortality. While this analysis is still exploratory, we believe that the use of county-level infrastructure as an instrument for individual-level services is a potentially fruitful approach for further exploration.

Beyond its direct effects on response time and mortality, a second role of the emergency response system is to allocate patients to hospitals. From a hospital's perspective, the emergency response system affects both the size and characteristics of its pool of emergency patients; the sensitivity of the allocation process to the hospital characteristics will also interact with the incentives of a hospital to adopt certain technologies. We thus take several preliminary steps toward exploring these effects.

Our first result about allocation is that patient severity affects the allocation of patients to high-technology hospitals. Our results about allocation have implications for our ability to draw inferences about the benefits of hospital technology through reduced-form analyses of the direct effect of technology on patient outcomes. This issue has been recognized by several authors, such as McClellan and Newhouse (1997), who argue that patient allocation to hospitals with different technologies is endogenous and so must be treated with an instrumental variables approach. Consistent with this view, our estimates provide *direct* evidence about the relationship between patient severity and allocation.

In addition, we document that in Pennsylvania, many patients reside in counties that do not include a hospital with certain high-level cardiac-specific technologies (such as a cardiac catheterization laboratory); as a consequence, these patients are not treated by hospitals with high-level cardiac technology in response to a cardiac emergency. It is interesting to observe that, in contrast to the general population, nearly all of the cardiac patients in our sample have some form of insurance (almost 99 percent). Instead, it seems to be the availability of medical technology in nearby hospitals that most significantly limits the access of patients to high levels of cardiac care in emergency situations.

Among the patients who do have access to high levels of cardiac care technology, we show that the allocation of patients to hospitals with cardiac catheterization laboratories depends on the presence of 911 services, where counties with higher levels of 911 technology are more likely to allocate patients to hospitals with higher levels of cardiac care technology. This can affect the incentives of hospitals to invest in high levels of technology. While these incentives can potentially lead to increased investment in technology by hospitals, we do not see strong evidence of strategic complementarity between 911 and hospital technology in our national sample. Despite the fact that the level of in-hospital emergency technology is positively correlated with the level of 911 technology at the national level, most of that positive interrelationship is accounted for by the fact that both in-hospital and prehospital care respond positively to the population and income of a county.

We further explore the salience of hospital incentives to adopt advanced technologies through a preliminary analysis of the determinants of a hospital's share of ambulance-transported cardiac patients in a given county. We find evidence that a hospital's "market share" is sensitive both to its overall level of emergency room technology as well as its level of cardiac-specific technology. In addition, increases in the level of technology by rival hospitals (other hospitals in the same county) have a negative impact on hospital market share.

The remainder of the paper is organized as follows. In section 4.2, we motivate our analysis more fully by introducing the institutional context of emergency response systems, outlining the principal technological choices faced by these systems and local hospitals, and suggesting the main economic issues that arise in the analysis of these systems. Section 4.3 presents the data that we will use to conduct the analysis. Sections 4.4, 4.5, and 4.6 consider the determinants of adoption of emergency response systems, our analysis of productivity, and the role of the emergency response system in allocating patients to hospitals. Our concluding remarks suggest a number of directions for future research.

4.2 Emergency Response Systems: Background and Motivation

The goal of this section is to motivate our empirical analysis of emergency response systems through a description of the background and institutions of prehospital care. To do so, we review the operation of the emergency medical response system (in most communities, a 911 system), focusing in particular on potential productivity benefits. We further discuss the interaction between prehospital and in-hospital emergency care.

Finally, we describe the factors that lead to heterogeneity in the adoption of 911.

Emergency response systems are a public service providing a standardized and integrated method for local communities to respond to emergencies. Until the late 1960s, emergencies were reported to a telephone operator (whose training and equipment usually did not accommodate the efficient handling of emergency) or by directly contacting a particular public service agency (requiring individuals to find the seven-digit phone number for a particular agency and precluding integration among agencies). Under this ad hoc system, emergency response was often inappropriate to the particular situation—overreaction to minor crises coexisted with frequent underreactions to critical emergencies (Gibson 1977; Siler 1975). Following a model developed in Europe after World War II (most particularly the 9-9-9 system in Great Britain), the first 911 systems were introduced into the United States in 1968 (in Haleyville, Alabama, and Nome, Alaska). Shortly thereafter, federal legislation explicitly encouraged the development of 911 systems in local communities and ensured that the Bell System would reserve 911 for emergency service use (Pivetta 1995).

While the scope and particular details of many systems vary, 911 systems operate according to the following standard procedure:

An individual in an emergency dials 911.
Call is answered by a Public Service Answering Point (PSAP) operator.
A trained 911 call taker evaluates the caller's emergency and gathers necessary information (location, severity, etc.).
Call taker communicates with the appropriate emergency service agencies for dispatch to the emergency.

While 911 calls can be routed to many different geographical locations, the adoption of 911 usually entails some increase in the centralization of call taking, to avoid duplication of fixed costs and adoption costs of the relevant telecommunications equipment. Even if centralization remains unchanged, 911 almost inevitably increases the degree of coordination between call centers.

From the perspective of the productivity analysis for cardiac patients, the most important benefit of 911 systems is to reduce response time. Our focus on cardiac care allows us to assess a particular medical condition for which outcomes have been closely linked (at least in the clinical emergency services literature) to the effectiveness of the emergency response system and ambulance technology. According to a variety of medical sources (see, e.g., Cummins et al. 1991; Bonnin, Pepe, and Clark 1993; and Tresch, Thakur, and Hoffman 1989), several medical procedures can contribute to survival in the case of a cardiac incident, including CPR and defibrillation. In particular, the medical literature has tied patients' survival probability to reductions in the time elapsed between initial collapse of a patient and the administration of CPR and defibrillation (Lewis et al. 1982; Larsen et al. 1993). While CPR can be in principle conducted by a non-professional bystander (perhaps with over-the-phone instructions from a trained call taker), it is typically best performed by paramedics. Furthermore, defibrillation—electrical shock therapy to "reset" the electrical activity of the heart in the case of ventricular fibrillation (irregularity)—requires equipment that is transported in ambulances or available in hospitals. As a result, correct administration of CPR and/or defibrillation are dependent on the time it takes for an ambulance (equipped with a defibrillator) to arrive at the scene of an emergency.

As a mechanism for reducing response times, 911 systems have several advantages. First, they save time in the placement of the telephone call, since citizens are unlikely to have memorized the telephone number for the relevant agency. Further, the personnel who receive the first telephone call are trained to handle emergencies, as opposed to standard telephone operators or directory assistance personnel. Even when the appropriate agency is reached, decentralized call centers without 911 tend to assign telephone duties to personnel who also have other responsibilities. Specialization might be important for learning the details of a geographical area as well as for developing the skills required to gather information from emergency callers. However, there is potentially a cost to centralization in the cases where 911 is provided at a central location without Enhanced 911 capabilities, since workers may not be as familiar with addresses and geography when they are responsible for larger areas.

As 911 systems have evolved and diffused over the past 30 years, there have been several important advancements in the technology utilized to implement these systems. One main area for advancement has been the development of Enhanced 911 systems (E911), which utilize caller identification together with databases of addresses. To implement this automatic location identification feature, counties must first develop a system of addressing that provides unique street addresses to every residence (which often do not exist in rural areas) and develop a map of the county with all of these addresses. This system allows call takers to pinpoint the location of a caller almost instantaneously (the databases may include very precise information about the location of a telephone in a building or public place, and they can also include special information about individual health issues or disabilities).

There are a number of benefits to E911 technology. Of course, even when the caller knows the location and directions precisely, it takes time to communicate this information, and mistakes are easy to make with callers who are experiencing panic or fear. For the frequent cases where people do not know their exact address (they are visiting a friend or experience an emergency incident in a public place), the location information is even more valuable. Likewise, the location information can be crucial for callers who are children and for adults who do not speak English or are unable to speak. Furthermore, once address information can be communicated instantaneously, the call taker has more time to gather information about the severity of the emergency, and the call taker can further provide prearrival instructions to the caller. Finally, this system mitigates some of the costs of centralizing the call centers, since detailed geographic knowledge of an area is not essential.

After a call taker receives and establishes the location and severity of an emergency call, the dispatcher directs an ambulance to the scene of the emergency. The ambulance provides three related services: provision of immediate emergency care, transportation service to a hospital, and the exercise of (limited) discretion over the allocation of patients to particular local hospitals. Counties differ in their provision of ambulance services.[3]

A potential benefit of specialized personnel and coordinated 911 services is that scarce resources for ambulance services can be more efficiently allocated.[4] The dispatcher might have to choose whether to dispatch an ambulance equipped with advanced life support (ALS) facilities, or, alternatively, a less technically sophisticated basic life support (BLS) unit. This decision can be made more efficient when the call taker gathers the relevant information about the nature of the emergency. When such decisions are made in the absence of appropriate information, ambulances may not be available to answer higher priority calls, and average response times for high-priority cases will rise. In fact, a number of studies document the fact that many ambulance systems service a large number of superfluous calls, where ambulance service was not the best method for providing care (Gibson 1977; Smith 1988; Brown and Sindelar 1993). This literature tends to strongly support the increased use of sophisticated prioritization and computerization in the dispatching process. Coordinated and trained call takers and dispatchers can better utilize the scarce ambulance resources, and the adoption of computer-aided dispatching and other such solutions are more easily accomplished in systems that have E911.

In addition to the direct effect of the 911 system on the productivity of the emergency health care system, the emergency response system also affects the allocation of patients to hospitals. The ambulance personnel are instructed to use a standard protocol for allocating patients to hospi-

3. However, we have not collected detailed data about the ambulance services in different counties for this paper.
4. While we focus in the current paper on the choice of technology for a community's 911 system, there are also important differences among counties in terms of the human resource practices employed. In the context of medical emergencies, there has been a diffusion of "emergency medical dispatch" (EMD) systems that provide a more systematic way of handling particular emergencies. EMD systems enable call takers to provide medical instructions over the phone to bystanders (such as instructions for CPR) to reduce the time until key medical procedures are performed (such as CPR) and to maintain calm at an emergency site until ambulance care arrives.

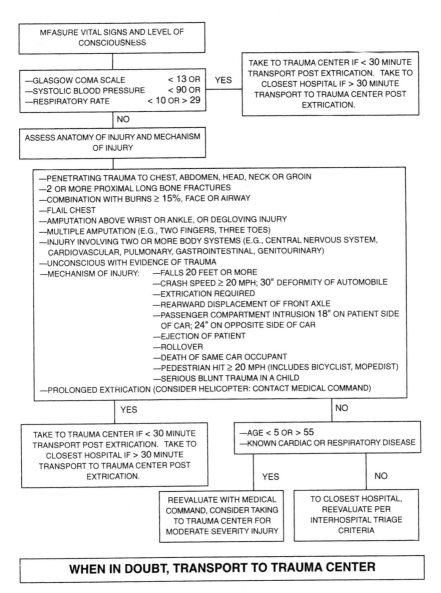

Fig. 4.1   County trauma protocol

tals (see fig. 4.1 for a representative county protocol). In figure 4.1, patients are allocated to hospitals according to a number of risk criteria, with more severe patients being allocated to the "trauma center" (which provides a certified level of emergency room services and technology) in most cases but to the geographically closest hospital if the nearest trauma center is greater than 30 minutes away from the site of the emergency. While the protocol provides "bright line" rules for most situations, ambulance personnel are given a limited amount of discretion about borderline cases and are also instructed to confirm some discretionary choices with "medical command." Thus, ambulance personnel, using agreed-upon protocols and their own judgment, resolve a trade-off between reduced transport time and allocating the patient to the hospital with the highest level of cardiac care facilities. By providing better dispatching, gathering more patient information prior to arrival, and shortening response time, higher levels of 911 service may allow the allocation of patients to hospitals to be more efficient. For example, when response time is shorter and dispatchers have more precise information about the patient's location, there will be more time to transport a cardiac patient to a hospital with specialized facilities.

The mechanism that allocates patients to hospitals can also have unintended consequences, in that it affects the incentives of hospitals to adopt various technologies. According to the triage protocols, certain patients should almost never be allocated to hospitals without a sufficient level of emergency services, and cardiac patients may tend to be allocated to hospitals known for cardiac care. Thus, hospitals may have a "business-stealing" incentive to increase the rating of their emergency room or their available technology (Vogt 1997). Anecdotal evidence suggests that hospitals are aware of the discretion of ambulance operators, although their response to this discretion is not always as sophisticated or expensive as increased technology adoption. In many localities, hospitals provide free supplies to the ambulances, as well as amenities for ambulance operators such as access to lounges supplied with food and beverages.

Empirically, there is wide variation across counties in the provision of 911 services. Some of the heterogeneity may be accounted for by efficiency considerations. For example, counties in which addresses are assigned systematically see lower benefits to E911. Differences in population may also account for differences in adoption across counties, since as a service with adoption costs and fixed costs, 911 should exhibit economies of scale, at least initially (systems that become too large may experience coordination costs). Further, the costs of adoption and implementation of 911 may vary across counties. Consider the nature of these costs. When adopting E911, it is necessary to assign new addresses, create new maps, and develop a computerized database, a process that is very labor-intensive and usually takes at least six months to a year to complete. Furthermore, the telephone equipment, caller identification database, and system of call-taker workstations must be procured and installed. While systematic data about the start-up costs of E911 is unavailable, based on several cases, we estimate that a typical county has a start-up cost of between $1 million and $4 million.

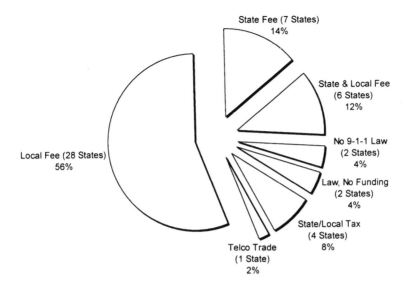

Fig. 4.2   911 Funding by state
Source: Adapted from Pivetta (1995, 135).

For example, consider Berks County, Pennsylvania, whose 1990 population was 336,000. Berks County reports that the capital start-up costs of its E911 system were approximately $3 million, while annual operating costs were over $2.3 million.[5] Its budget comes primarily from a tax on telephone lines ($0.97 per line each month) as authorized by state legislation. (Fig. 4.2 shows the national distribution of funding sources for 911 systems.) The Berks County 911 program employs nine call takers, two administrators, a programmer for its computer-aided dispatching software, and an administrative assistant.

In addition to capital costs, there are other factors that affect the adoption of 911 systems; we explored these motivations in informal interviews of administrators and regulators in several states. We found that in smaller counties, early adoption of E911 was often the result of the actions of a highly self-motivated and informed government employee. Because many different public and private agencies are involved in the implementation process (the post office, utility companies, and telephone companies), political factors and bureaucratic barriers may slow adoption. While in large counties there may be personnel assigned exclusively to this task, smaller counties tend to assign the same personnel to many different tasks, and the incentives as well as information required to organize an effort for

5. This number does not include overhead incurred by the Berks County Communication Center, which handles many calls in addition to 911 calls. For further information, see http://www.readingpa.com/911/.

adoption may be lacking. The adoption of a centralized 911 system may lead small, local police departments, as well as private ambulance dispatching services, to lose employment as well as local autonomy; these agencies may be able to block adoption. Finally, as a publicly provided service, public demand for the system will also play a role, where this demand depends not only on factors such as income but also on the political views of the citizens about government services.

4.3 The Data

As mentioned earlier, little previous empirical research has been done on the prehospital emergency system. Thus, in this paper we choose to conduct our analysis at several different levels of aggregation: individual, hospital, and county. Each of these sources of data allow us to address different questions about the adoption and productivity of elements of the emergency system. Tables 4.1, 4.2, and 4.3 provide definitions, sources, and means and standard deviations for all variables.

4.3.1 County-Level Variables

For the purposes of this paper, we characterize the prehospital emergency infrastructure and its determinants at the county level. Unfortunately, we are not aware of a comprehensive accounting of 911 practices in the United States. Within Pennsylvania, we gathered information about 911 provision through publicly available sources and telephone interviews. At the national level, we made use of a survey administered in 1995 by the National Emergency Number Association (NENA), a national advocacy organization for 911 systems. As a result, our national sample of counties is limited to 772 counties who completed the NENA survey and who provided answers that allowed us to characterize the 911 system at the county level.[6]

For each county, we organize our analysis around a three-tier characterization of the 911 system: whether there is a 911 system at all (NO 911) and whether it is a basic 911 (BASIC 911) or enhanced (ENHANCED 911) system. In the national sample, 75 percent of these counties have adopted the highest level of service (ENHANCED 911), illustrating that E911 has been diffused substantially (911_LEVEL is simply a variable that is 0, 1, or 2, depending on whether the system is NO 911, BASIC 911, or ENHANCED 911). However, the selection of counties who responded to NENA's survey is biased toward systems with higher levels of 911 service,

6. A large number of responses in fact reflected the technology and training choices of smaller 911 systems (e.g., townships or even university campuses). We selected out only those observations who reported that they were the PRIMARY PSAP center and who stated that their coverage was countywide. This selection process underrepresents counties for which there is no countywide 911 system.

Table 4.1 **Variables and Definitions**

	Definition	Source
Outcome measures		
DEAD	Dummy variable = 1 if spell outcome = dead	PA EMS
TIME_TO_SCENE	Time (mins) from dispatch to arrival at scene	PA EMS
TIME_AT_SCENE	Time (mins) of EMS unit at scene	PA EMS
TIME_TO_HOSP	Time (mins) from scene to hospital	PA EMS
911 level		
NO 911	No countywide 911 emergency response	NENA; telephone survey
BASIC 911	Countywide 911; no automatic location identification (ALI)	NENA; telephone survey
ENHANCED 911	Countywide 911 with ALI	NENA; telephone survey
911_LEVEL	No 911 = 0; Basic 911 = 1; Enhanced 911 = 2	NENA; telephone survey
Patient characteristics		
MALE	Dummy = 1 if sex = male	PA EMS
AGE	Patient age (years)	PA EMS
CARDIAC ARREST	Dummy = 1 if EMS unit records cardiac arrest incident	PA EMS
DEFIBRILLATE	Dummy = 1 if patient receives defibrillation prior to arrival at hospital	PA EMS
GLASGOW ##	Glasgow trauma score dummies (15 = Least Severe; 3 = Most Severe)	PA EMS
GLASGOW 0	Glasgow score = 0 (Unknown or Unrecorded)	PA EMS
Insurance status		
MEDICARE	Dummy = 1 if insurance status = Medicare	PA EMS
MEDICAID	Dummy = 1 if insurance status = Medicaid	PA EMS
PRIVATE	Dummy = 1 if insurance status = private or government	PA EMS
SELF PAY	Dummy = 1 if insurance status = self-pay	PA EMS
OTHER	Dummy = 1 if insurance status = other	PA EMS
Hospital characteristics		
URGENT CARE CENTER	Dummy = 1 if certified urgent care center	AHA
CATH LAB	Dummy = 1 if cardiac catheterization lab present	AHA
OPENHEART FAC	Dummy = 1 if open heart surgery facility	AHA
TRAUMA CNTR LEVEL	Dummy = 1 if clinic = 2 if emergency room = 3 if trauma facilities present = 4 if certified county trauma hospital	AHA

(*continued*)

Table 4.1   (continued)

	Definition	Source
EMERGENCY ROOM VOLUME	Total no. of emergency room visits in 1995 (in thousands)	AHA
HOSPITAL DOCTORS	No. of full-time doctors on staff in hospital	AHA
HOSPITAL RESIDENTS	No. of medical residents on staff in hospital	AHA
County hospital infrastructure		
CERTIFIED TRAUM CNTR	Dummy = 1 if county contains at least one hospital with TRAUMA CNTR LEVEL = 4	AHA
HOSP PER SQ. MILE	No. of hospitals in county/No. of square miles	AHA/CCDB
COUNTY CARDIAC PATIENTS	No. of recorded cardiac incidents in 1995	PA EMS
County demographics (reference year = 1992)		
POPULATION	County population/1,000	CCDB
DENSITY	Population/county square miles	CCDB
INCOME PER CAP	County-level income per capita/1,000	CCDB
CRIMERATE	Crime rate (incidents per 100,000 pop.)	CCDB
VCRIMERATE	Violent crime rate (incidents per 100,000 pop.)	CCDB
POLICE EXP	1992 level of police expenditures	COG
HEALTH EXP	1992 level of public health expenditures	COG
% REPUBLICAN	1992 Republican voter percentage (presidential)	CCDB
% PEROT	1992 Perot voter percentage (presidential)	CCDB
State legislation		
911_TRAIN_LAW	Legislation implemented for 911 Telecommunicator training requirements	NENA
911_TRAIN_PLAN	Legislation approved but not implemented for 911 Telecommunicator training requirements	NENA

Note: The natural logarithm of a variable will be denoted L VARIABLE NAME.

especially undercounting counties with no countywide 911 system; in Pennsylvania, where we have a comprehensive accounting of the counties, 30 of the 54 counties had E911 at the start of 1995 (see fig. 4.3).

In addition to the county-level variables, we include in our analysis two "911" variables drawn from NENA state-level surveys that indicate whether there is implemented legislation guiding the administration of 911 systems (in particular, governing training policies for workers using the systems) (911_TRAIN_LAW) or whether legislation has been passed but not yet implemented (911_TRAIN_PLAN). These variables are intended

Table 4.2   **Summary Statistics (county-level averages)**

	Pennsylvania Sample		National Sample	
	Mean	Standard Deviation	Mean	Standard Deviation
NO. OF COUNTY/SYSTEMS	58.000[a]		722.0000	
911 level				
NO 911	0.1897	0.3955	0.0692	0.2541
BASIC 911	0.2759	0.4509	0.1731	0.3786
ENHANCED 911	0.5345	0.5032	0.7576	0.4288
County hospital infrastructure				
CERTIFIED COUNTY TRAUMA CENTER	0.2586	0.4417	0.1898	0.3923
HOSP PER SQ. MILE	0.0072	0.0215		
COUNTY CARDIAC PATIENTS	1,264.8800	898.2086		
Demographics				
POPULATION	201.5020	280.0837	192.5940	370.3810
DENSITY	0.5084	1.5455	0.3331	0.7796
INCOME PER CAP	12.3244	2.6010	12.5994	2.9939
VCRIMERATE (CRIME RATE FOR NATIONAL SAMPLE)	0.0023	0.0021	0.0410	0.0234
POLICE EXP	16.1920	49.0941	15.4987	44.0724
HEALTH EXP	13.7416	40.4254	5.9974	14.4659
% REPUBLICAN	39.0000	7.6273	38.8680	7.8322
% PEROT	22.1622	3.3542	21.6440	6.1476
LAWSTRD	1.0000	0.0000	0.4626	0.4989
LAWPLAN	0.0000	0.0000	0.3518	0.4778

[a]Out of 54 Pennsylvania counties for which we observe the 911 level, 4 experienced midyear changes, yielding 58 "county system" observations.

to be proxies for the level of administrative information and assistance provided by the state.

We further gathered a variety of demographic, political, and economic data at the county level. In addition to a number of familiar demographic characteristics (POPULATION, DENSITY, INCOME PER CAPITA, CRIMERATE, POLICE EXP, HEALTH EXP, each drawn from the *City and County DataBook* or the *Census of Governments*), we also characterize the political climate of a community by the presidential voting shares from the 1992 election. This election is especially interesting because of the strong showing of Perot, allowing a somewhat more nuanced measure of a county's political demand for public expenditures (Perot voters were noted for their strong beliefs in limited government).

4.3.2 Hospital-Level Variables

Our information about hospitals is obtained from the American Hospital Association (AHA) annual hospital inventory survey. We use this infor-

Table 4.3   Patient-Level Summary Statistics (Pennsylvania sample only)

	Mean	Standard Deviation
NO. OF COUNTIES	54.0000	
NO. OF PATIENT OBS	24,664.0000	
Outcome measures		
DEAD	0.0711	0.2571
TIME_TO_SCENE	9.1251	6.0180
TIME_AT_SCENE	15.9059	7.6573
TIME_TO_HOSP	13.2354	9.6674
911 level		
NO 911	0.0827	0.2754
BASIC 911	0.1397	0.3467
ENHANCED 911	0.7777	0.4158
Patient characteristics		
MALE	0.4799	0.4996
AGE	69.8678	14.1957
CARDIAC ARREST	0.1043	0.3057
DEFIBRILLATE	0.3999	0.4899
Glasgow trauma score (15 = least severe; 3 = most severe; 0 = unknown)		
GLASGOW SCORE (EXCLUDING GLASGOW = 0)	14.2011	2.7239
GLASGOW 0	0.0442	0.2056
Insurance status		
MEDICARE	0.6627	0.4728
MEDICAID	0.0516	0.2212
PRIVATE	0.1885	0.3911
SELF PAY	0.0115	0.1067
OTHER	0.0358	0.1859
Hospital characteristics (based on patient allocation)		
URGENT CARE CENTER	0.2172	0.4123
CATH LAB	0.6703	0.4701
OPENHEART FAC	0.2940	0.4556
TRAUMA CNTR LEVEL	3.1670	0.4486
HOSPITAL DOCTORS	13.7234	19.3413
HOSPITAL RESIDENTS	27.2592	72.0307
EMERGENCY ROOM VOLUME	29.9091	12.7018

mation to provide information at three different levels of analysis. First, when we study the incentives of hospitals to adopt technology, we consider the availability of hospital technology at *any* hospital within a county. For example, CERTIFIED TRAUM CNTR represents the presence of a certified trauma center in a given county, while HOSP PER SQ. MILE represents the density of hospitals. We also consider the number of recorded cardiac incidents that required ambulance service in 1995 (COUNTY CARDIAC PATIENTS). Second, in our patient-level productivity analysis, we link hospital characteristics to our patient-level data-

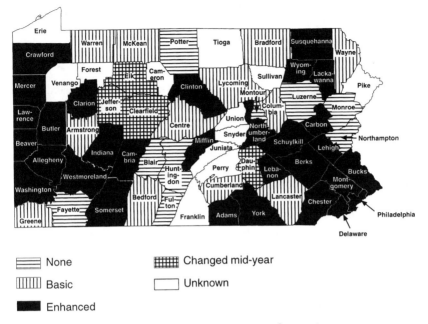

None

Basic

Enhanced

Changed mid-year

Unknown

Fig. 4.3   Distribution of emergency response systems, by county

base in order to control for hospital quality as well as to analyze the allocation process that assigns patients to hospitals. Third, we consider the hospital as the unit of analysis when we consider how technology investments interact with the share of cardiac patients who are treated in a given hospital.

For each hospital, we consider three main types of variables. First, we characterize the generic emergency infrastructure for a given hospital by identifying whether the hospital is an urgent care provider (URGENT) and by identifying the level of certified emergency care (TRAUMA CNTR LEVEL). In our analysis of individual data, we examine the case of cardiac care and we also look specifically at the cardiac care facilities provided by each hospital. In particular, we observe whether a hospital has a cardiac catheterization lab (CATHETER) and whether it has open heart surgery capability (OPENHEART). Finally, we characterize the overall features of each hospital, including its size (EMERGENCY ROOM VOLUME; HOSPITAL DOCTORS) and the number of residents (HOSPITAL RESIDENTS).

4.3.3   Patient-Level Variables

Our patient-level variables are drawn from a database of every ambulance ride in Pennsylvania that could be linked to a hospital discharge during 1995 (approximately 170,000 observations). This data set is gathered by the Pennsylvania Department of Health and has only recently been made available to a limited number of researchers; we are not aware of prior work on this database (or on a similar ambulance-level database) by health care economists.

The information provided in this patient-level data is unusually rich. First, there are several indicators associated with the responsiveness of the 911 system. We analyze three different measures of the timeliness of ambulance response: the amount of time it takes to get to the scene of an emergency (TIME_TO_SCENE), the amount of time spent at the scene (TIME_AT_SCENE), and the amount of time elapsed from when the ambulance leaves the scene to the time when the ambulance arrives at the hospital (TIME_TO_HOSP).

In the next sections, we will examine how the response time measures vary with other features of the medical care system. To better motivate that type of analysis, we restrict our analysis of the Pennsylvania data to the case of cardiac incidents. One of the main advantages of analyzing the case of cardiac incidents is that, in contrast to many data sets, there are in fact a number of quite precise indicators of the level of severity of each patient. In particular, each patient is assigned a Glasgow score, which is a number between 0 and 15 that indicates the severity of the heart attack (lower numbers imply higher severity, with 3 being the worst and 0 indicating "unknown" or "missing"). While the bulk of observations are coded with the weakest severity (GLASGOW = 15), there exists a substantial minority for which there is variation in the data. We are also able to observe whether the incident is believed to be a cardiac arrest or simply a cardiac incident (CARD_ARR = 1 or 0).

In addition to these measures of severity, the data includes relatively detailed information about each individual in the data set, including insurance status, age, and sex. We also observe some information about the types of procedures administered by the emergency response paramedics, including whether the patient received defibrillation treatment prior to arrival at the hospital. However, since the decision to defibrillate a patient is conditioned on patient characteristics that are unobserved to the econometrician, this variable serves mainly as a control in our analysis.

Finally, we are able to observe some concrete measures associated with patient outcomes. In our main analysis, we will focus on the most extreme of these measures, DEAD: whether or not the patient dies from the incident, either in the emergency room or in the hospital afterward.

4.4   The Determinants of the 911 System Adoption

Table 4.4 summarizes the characteristics of three groups of counties in Pennsylvania: those with no 911, Basic 911, and Enhanced 911. Because

Table 4.4   **County Characteristics by 911 Level (means of county-level averages)**

| | County 911 Level | | | |
	No 911	Basic 911	Enhanced 911	Enhanced 911 (Excluding 4 Largest Counties)
NO. OF COUNTIES	11.0000	16.0000	31.0000	27.0000
NO. OF CARDIAC OBS	2,039.0000	3,445.0000	19,180.0000	10,993.0000
Outcome measures				
DEAD	0.0567	0.0565	0.0680	0.0671
TIME_TO_SCENE	11.7469	11.2579	9.8656	10.1360
TIME_AT_SCENE	12.8364	14.3900	15.7645	15.5155
TIME_TO_HOSP	16.6352	15.2248	13.7586	14.2163
County hospital infrastructure				
CERTIFIED TRAUM CNTR	0.0000	0.1875	0.3871	0.2963
HOSP PER SQ. MILE	0.0032	0.0024	0.0111	0.0040
COUNTY CARDIAC PATIENTS	255.2500	267.3300	671.3667	421.8077
Demographics				
POPULATION	109.0007	106.6353	283.2884	172.4249
DENSITY	0.1756	0.1405	0.8164	0.2807
INCOME PER CAP	11.2406	11.6869	13.0380	12.5100
CRIMERATE	0.0018	0.0018	0.0026	0.0020
POLICE EXP	4.2037	4.3714	26.5468	7.9701
HEALTH EXP	2.3600	3.5011	23.0656	8.4577
% REPUBLICAN	39.9091	41.6875	37.2903	38.0741
% PEROT	23.6667	22.5455	21.7826	22.5500

four counties are significantly larger, more dense, and have more hospitals than the others, we also report the counties with E911 excluding the four largest counties (we will also report specifications that exclude these four counties in our subsequent regression analysis). There are some systematic differences between the demographic characteristics of the counties that have made different adoption decisions about 911. The largest and most densely populated counties, as well as those with the highest income and largest police and health budgets, tend to have adopted Enhanced 911.

When comparing the counties with no 911 to the counties with Basic 911, it is interesting to note that they are remarkably similar in terms of density, crime, income, and hospitals per mile. Figure 4.3 illustrates that many contiguous counties with similar geographic features have different levels of 911. The main differences are that the counties with Basic 911 have higher populations, higher expenditures, and more Perot voters. Since 911 systems involve fixed costs, the differences in adoption appear to be consistent with efficiency motivations on the part of the counties. However, since the county boundaries are purely political distinctions, this finding raises the question of whether between-county cooperation in the provision of 911 services might allow more citizens to be served by 911. The state of Vermont recently implemented a statewide 911 system, perhaps recognizing the economies of scale associated the provision of the service at the state level.

As described in section 4.2, we expect that the level of 911 technology will respond to political demand as well as demographic factors related to the efficiency of the service in a particular locality. While much of our productivity analysis will focus on a subset of cardiac patients in Pennsylvania, a within-state analysis can provide only limited insight as to the factors that determine the allocation of 911 services (and their productivity benefits) to different subsets of the population. Thus, in table 4.5, we consider the determinants of adoption of the level of 911 service in a national cross-section of counties. As expected, POPULATION is significantly correlated with adoption; politically, counties with a relatively high proportion of Perot voters tend to adopt lower levels of 911, consistent with the emphasis of the Perot movement on limited government expenditure. Also, counties in states with regulations about training had higher levels of 911 adoption. This legislation either requires or recommends standardized training programs in association with 911 programs, and may further proxy for the institutional support for 911 provided by the state boards that oversee 911 centers. We interpret this result to indicate that states that provide legislative support and guidance for 911 systems have a higher propensity to adopt 911 services. Thus, we conclude that 911 adoption responds to efficiency motivations as well as to political and regulatory factors that may be unrelated to efficiency.

The latter two specifications in table 4.5 include a variable that measures the highest level of in-hospital emergency care offered in the county (in addition to the controls described above). Even though the unconditional correlation between 911 and the level of in-hospital emergency care is positive (.19) and significantly different from zero, most of that positive relationship is accounted for by common factors that affect the adoption of both (e.g., population). Thus, despite the potential for strategic complementarities between hospital technology adoption and 911 services when higher levels of 911 better allocate patients to high-technology hospitals, we do not see strong evidence of this interaction in our national sample.

4.5   The Impact of 911 Systems and Hospital Choice on Ambulance Response Times and Mortality: The Case of Cardiac Arrest

We now turn to an analysis of individual cardiac incidents. We evaluate the effects of the 911 infrastructure on patient outcomes, as well as on several "intermediate inputs" to patient outcomes, in particular, several components of response time. We focus on intermediate inputs for several

Table 4.5   **911 Demand Regressions (national sample)**

	Base Regression (OLS)	Base Regression (Ordered Logit)	Include County Hospital Infrastructure	Include Hospital Infrastructure (Ordered Logit)
		Dependent Variable = 911 Level		
County hospital infrastructure				
CERT. TRAUMA CNTR.			−0.06458	−0.44596
			(0.06221)	(0.29835)
County demographic characteristics				
L POPULATION	0.11172	0.37180	0.11555	0.37754
	(0.02972)	(0.13783)	(0.02995)	(0.13877)
DENSITY	0.000004	0.00078	0.000008	0.00088
	(0.000037)	(0.00069)	(0.000037)	(0.00070)
INCOME PER CAP	0.01207	0.06675	0.01266	0.06894
	(0.00956)	(0.05483)	(0.00958)	(0.05516)
CRIMERATE	0.27501	4.34417	0.33910	4.77066
	(1.14780)	(5.69929)	(1.14940)	(5.74605)
POLICE EXP	−0.00108	−0.01212	−0.00104	−0.01176
	(0.00081)	(0.00747)	(0.00081)	(0.00781)
HEALTH EXP	0.00088	0.04322	0.00113	0.04601
	(0.00243)	(0.03065)	(0.00244)	(0.03077)
County political characteristics				
% REPUBLICAN	−0.00332	−0.01023	−0.00344	−0.01050
	(0.00284)	(0.01282)	(0.00285)	(0.01286)
% PEROT	−0.00854	−0.04217	−0.00873	−0.04301
	(0.00402)	(0.01774)	(0.00386)	(0.01781)
State legislation				
911_TRAIN_LAW	0.16148	0.47014	0.15724	0.46095
	(0.05926)	(0.23082)	(0.05940)	(0.23085)
911_TRAIN_PLAN	0.26570	1.04053	0.26365	1.04598
	(0.06372)	(0.27448)	(0.06375)	(0.27465)
Constant	0.41650		0.38349	
	(0.31374)		(0.31533)	
Ord. logit parameters		Insignificant		Insignificant
Observations	722	722	722	722
Log-likelihood		−444.51963		−443.44308
R-squared	0.1192		0.1206	

reasons. First, since 911 provides service benefits through an investment in information technology, we are inherently interested in disentangling the extent to which 911 provides services that are more timely and better respond to patient characteristics. Second, mortality is a very noisy measure of the productivity of the emergency response system, and even in our large data set, we see only a few thousand deaths from cardiac incidents, and only a few hundred in the counties without E911 systems.

Third, even in these cases, we expect that the policy variables will have a significant impact on outcomes in only a small subset of the cases. Many of the patients who die would die regardless of the response time; and many patients who survive did not rely heavily on the emergency response system. However, if we establish that 911 reduces response time, we can rely on a number of clinical studies that provide direct evidence about the benefits of faster response times for mortality.

Building on our analysis from section 4.2, we predict that the first component of response time, TIME_TO_SCENE, should be lower when counties are able to gather address and location information more rapidly and precisely, and when ambulance resources are allocated efficiently (recall cardiac emergencies are high-priority events). The second component, called TIME_AT_SCENE, should be longer when more treatment is given prior to moving a patient; it should also be longer when patients are located in high-rise buildings or large complexes. The final component, TIME_TO_HOSP, should be lower when dispatchers are able to provide better assistance to ambulance drivers in terms of routing and directions to hospitals from varied locations. On the other hand, TIME_TO_HOSP should reflect a trade-off between the benefits of arriving at a high-quality hospital and the benefits of receiving hospital attention as soon as possible. The impact of 911 on this trade-off might be to encourage ambulances to take somewhat longer rides, if time has been saved in other parts of the process.

Of course, both TIME_TO_SCENE and TIME_TO_HOSP will depend on the location of a given patient relative to the hospitals, and variation across counties in the average proximity of patients to hospitals is a potential source of unobserved heterogeneity that must be considered in interpreting our results. We partially alleviate this problem in several of our specifications by including controls for TIME_TO_HOSP in the regressions concerning TIME_TO_SCENE, and vice versa. For example, in the analysis of the determinants of TIME_TO_SCENE, the variable TIME_TO_HOSP acts as a control for the remoteness of the patient's location.

Table 4.6 reports the means of patient-level variables according to the level of 911 provided in a given county. Only 2,039 of the 24,664 cardiac incidents occurred in counties without 911. The mortality rates are very similar in counties with no 911 or Basic 911: Approximately 6.5 percent of cardiac emergencies result in death. In contrast, even excluding the largest four counties, the average mortality rate in counties with E911 is 7 percent (see fig. 4.4 for the distribution of county mortality rates). We further see that counties with higher levels of 911 have lower average TIME_TO_SCENE and TIME_TO_HOSP, while they have longer TIME_AT_SCENE. We will explore all of these relationships in more detail in our regression analysis.

The patient characteristics, trauma scores, and insurance status variables

Table 4.6   **Distribution of Pennsylvania 911 Level (patient-level averages)**

	No 911	Basic 911	Enhanced 911	Enhanced 911 (Excluding 4 Largest Counties)
		County 911 Level		
NO. OF COUNTIES	11.0000	16.0000	31.0000	27.0000
NO. OF CARDIAC OBS	2,039.0000	3,445.0000	19,180.0000	10,993.0000
Outcome measures				
DEAD	0.0652	0.0668	0.0726	0.0707
TIME_TO_SCENE	10.8759	10.1756	8.7503	9.2553
TIME_AT_SCENE	13.9897	14.2517	16.4068	15.4553
TIME_TO_HOSP	15.8141	15.5509	12.5453	13.8118
Patient characteristics				
MALE	0.4723	0.5013	0.4757	0.4825
AGE	70.0844	70.0673	69.8090	70.0183
CARDIAC ARREST	0.0510	0.0456	0.1205	0.0494
DEFIBRILLATE	0.5311	0.3358	0.3974	0.3879
Glasgow trauma score (15 = least severe; 3 = most severe; 0 = unknown)				
GLASGOW 0	0.0711	0.0761	0.0357	0.0259
GLASGOW 3	0.0436	0.0369	0.0455	0.0432
GLASGOW 4–9	0.0118	0.0134	0.0153	0.0121
GLASGOW 10–12	0.0098	0.0171	0.0171	0.0140
GLASGOW 13–14	0.0392	0.0360	0.0414	0.0388
GLASGOW 15	0.8244	0.8206	0.8450	0.8659
Insurance status				
MEDICARE	0.6714	0.6572	0.6628	0.6738
MEDICAID	0.0520	0.0453	0.0527	0.0505
PRIVATE	0.1751	0.1878	0.1900	0.1846
SELF PAY	0.0181	0.0125	0.0106	0.0142
OTHER	0.0451	0.0229	0.0372	0.0287
County hospital infrastructure				
CERTIFIED TRAUM CNTR	0.0000	0.0967	0.6380	0.3684
HOSP PER SQ. MILE	0.0040	0.0033	0.0284	0.0050
COUNTY CARDIAC PATIENTS	331.7543	687.1756	1,467.8430	778.5308
Demographics				
POPULATION	169.3076	226.2671	603.5968	261.0682
DENSITY	0.2812	0.2851	2.1253	0.3925
INCOME PER CAP	11.8924	13.3673	14.8970	14.0029
CRIMERATE	0.0020	0.0020	0.0045	0.0025
POLICE EXP	7.1510	10.4612	74.1042	13.4522
HEALTH EXP	3.9969	8.7517	61.2895	13.6651
% REPUBLICAN	36.9716	47.8389	35.3231	38.1708
% PEROT	21.9413	19.9428	19.9104	22.4042
Hospital characteristics				
URGENT CARE CENTER	0.0329	0.3759	0.2082	0.1957
CATH LAB	0.2398	0.6453	0.7205	0.6499
OPENHEART FAC	0.1525	0.3840	0.2929	0.2996
TRAUMA CNTR LEVEL	3.0000	3.0581	3.2049	3.2105
HOSPITAL DOCTORS	4.1187	9.6569	15.4748	14.7493
HOSPITAL RESIDENTS	5.3198	12.0136	32.3299	17.4391
EMERGENCY ROOM VOLUME	30.4250	27.0173	30.3736	31.0908

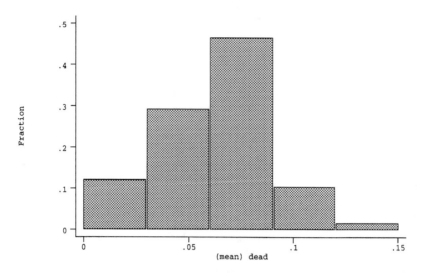

Fig. 4.4   County-level mortality distribution

have almost identical means across the no 911, Basic 911, and Enhanced 911 categories, with a few exceptions. First, the Glasgow score variables have different means in Enhanced 911 counties. Further, a much larger percentage of patients reported cardiac arrest in the Enhanced 911 group. Finally, many more patients reported defibrillation (before reaching the hospital) in the no 911 counties. This might be due to differences in scoring or poor recordkeeping in a few counties; it could also reflect real differences in the composition and treatment of emergencies, or differences in the availability of defibrillators in ambulances.

It is also worth noting the large differences between patients in no 911 counties and other counties in the level of technology possessed by the hospital that receives the patients. None of the no 911 patients received treatment in a certified trauma center, and only a quarter went to hospitals with cardiac catheterization laboratories. Likewise, the emergency room volume and size of hospitals is much lower in no 911 counties. There are also significant differences between Basic and Enhanced 911 counties in the provision of hospital care, but these differences are not as dramatic once the four largest counties are excluded.

Now consider the effects of 911 technology on the various components of response time, beginning with the time elapsed between the dispatch of a 911 call and the arrival at the emergency (TIME_TO_SCENE) (table 4.7). There are four specifications, which include a number of patient-level as well as county-level covariates (the results in tables 4.7–4.9 about the effects of patient-level characteristics are generally robust to specifications that include county fixed effects instead of county-level covariates). The

Table 4.7   **Time-to-Scene Equation**

	Dependent Variable = L TIME_TO_SCENE			
	Base Regression (OLS)	Time Controls (OLS)	Excluding 4 Largest Counties (OLS)	Only Counties with 911 Level Changes (Fixed Effects)
Time controls				
L TIME_AT_SCENE		−0.13163	−0.15461	−0.19951
		(0.00654)	(0.00763)	(0.02159)
L TIME_TO_HOSP		0.32575	0.3462	0.36371
		(0.00507)	(0.00607)	(0.02057)
911 level				
NO 911	0.09383	0.01831	0.05215	0.08953
	(0.01698)	(0.01557)	(0.01656)	(0.07063)
BASIC 911	0.07538	0.0222	0.00226	0.13546
	(0.01341)	(0.01228)	(0.01261)	(0.04305)
Patient characteristics				
MALE	0.03631	0.01558	0.01846	0.04848
	(0.0083)	(0.00759)	(0.00924)	(0.02857)
AGE	0.00745	0.00398	0.00197	0.01683
	(0.00205)	(0.00188)	(0.00252)	(0.0076)
AGE_SQUARED	−0.00006	−0.00002	−0.00001	−0.00011
	(0.00002)	(0.00001)	(0.00002)	(0.00006)
CARDIAC ARREST	−0.12503	−0.06098	0.05545	0.15153
	(0.01787)	(0.01635)	(0.03558)	(0.11695)
DEFIBRILLATE	0.03474	0.02764	0.02735	0.02532
	(0.00846)	(0.00773)	(0.0095)	(0.03216)
Glasgow trauma score (15 = least severe; 3 = most severe; 0 = unknown)				
GLASGOW 0	1.60486	1.33791	0.41029	−0.05927
	(0.20163)	(0.18496)	(0.22467)	(0.18582)
GLASGOW 3	1.63347	1.41933	0.41626	−0.10982
	(0.20315)	(0.18649)	(0.22637)	(0.18081)
GLASGOW 4–9	1.6558	1.4468	0.47398	
	(0.20322)	(0.18644)	(0.22688)	
GLASGOW 10–12	1.70663	1.43213	0.49918	−0.17747
	(0.20283)	(0.18607)	(0.22608)	(0.18852)
GLASGOW 13–14	1.6681	1.39132	0.45937	0.0092
	(0.20118)	(0.18456)	(0.22433)	(0.15863)
GLASGOW 15	1.6887	1.38023	0.47959	−0.08971
	(0.20057)	(0.18403)	(0.22347)	(0.1426)
Insurance status (excluded category = Medicare)				
MEDICAID	−0.08647	−0.0497	−0.02478	0.1198
	(0.02068)	(0.0189)	(0.02335)	(0.06903)
PRIVATE	−0.00113	−0.01811	−0.02074	−0.02352
	(0.01306)	(0.01193)	(0.01476)	(0.04388)
SELF-PAY	−0.00863	−0.0371	−0.0866	−0.27909
	(0.03815)	(0.03484)	(0.03826)	(0.20312)

(continued)

Table 4.7 (continued)

	Base Regression (OLS)	Time Controls (OLS)	Excluding 4 Largest Counties (OLS)	Only Counties with 911 Level Changes (Fixed Effects)
Dependent Variable = L TIME_TO_SCENE				

	Base Regression (OLS)	Time Controls (OLS)	Excluding 4 Largest Counties (OLS)	Only Counties with 911 Level Changes (Fixed Effects)
OTHER	−0.01691	−0.0206	−0.01409	0.10725
	(0.02288)	(0.0209)	(0.02733)	(0.06999)
County hospital infrastructure				
CERT. TRAUM CNTR	0.15789	0.09753	0.13947	
	(0.01474)	(0.01349)	(0.0196)	
L HOSP PER SQ. MILE	−0.12588	−0.04815	−0.00084	
	(0.01189)	(0.01092)	(0.01412)	
L COUNTY CARDIAC PATIENTS	−0.0567	−0.08468	−0.10222	
	(0.01177)	(0.01077)	(0.01176)	
County demographics				
L POPULATION	−0.09277	−0.03693	0.0374	
	(0.03064)	(0.02812)	(0.02924)	
DENSITY	0.0315	0.02544	−0.33748	
	(0.0055)	(0.00505)	(0.04916)	
L INCOME PER CAP	0.10874	0.22698	0.72577	
	(0.03698)	(0.03388)	(0.04689)	
VCRIMERATE	6.98859	9.77737	−6.69225	
	(4.24895)	(3.88727)	(4.69215)	
L POLICE EXP	0.06323	0.03356	−0.03753	
	(0.0224)	(0.02049)	(0.0219)	
L HEALTH EXP	−0.013	−0.02067	−0.01945	
	(0.00422)	(0.00386)	(0.00403)	
Hospital characteristics				
URGENT CARE CENTER	−0.03722	−0.04101	−0.03001	
	(0.01138)	(0.0104)	(0.01389)	
CATH LAB	−0.03328	−0.04442	−0.04749	0.20105
	(0.01185)	(0.01084)	(0.01375)	(0.04967)
OPENHEART FAC	0.02769	0.0203	0.02798	
	(0.01243)	(0.01137)	(0.01865)	
TRAUMA CNTR LEVEL	−0.06379	−0.04453	−0.04719	
	(0.01181)	(0.01079)	(0.01872)	
EMERGENCY ROOM VOLUME	−0.00031	0.00046	−0.00073	0.00614
	(0.00025)	(0.00039)	(0.00054)	(0.05292)
HOSPITAL DOCTORS	0.00023	−0.00075	−0.00039	−0.01573
	(0.00007)	(0.00023)	(0.00052)	(0.04498)
HOSPITAL RESIDENTS	0.00043	0.00003	0.00102	
	(0.00043)	(0.00007)	(0.00036)	
Constant				1.241
				(0.31835)
Observations	24,664.0000	24,664.0000	16,477.0000	1,635.0000
R-squared	0.7040	0.7170	0.7170	0.2774

base regression includes 911 dummies, patient-level variables, county-level demographics, and hospital infrastructure variables, as well as characteristics of the receiving hospital. Since the hospital allocation is conditioned on patient severity, it is difficult to interpret the coefficients for characteristics of the receiving hospitals. One interpretation is that they are simply controls for the patient's county and severity.

The next specification includes controls for TIME_AT_SCENE and TIME_TO_HOSP. The TIME_TO_HOSP variable can be thought of as a control for the distance from the patient to the hospital, although we show later that the hospital allocation (and thus expected travel time) are conditioned on the patient's severity. The TIME_AT_SCENE is more difficult to interpret. It might represent the extra time required to administer treatments that are only available on some ambulances, in which case longer TIME_AT_SCENE should be associated with longer TIME_TO_SCENE, since we expect a longer wait for the scarce resource of a better ambulance. It might also represent some features of the patient's location, such as the presence of elevators or stairs in a high-rise building. High-rises might be located closer to hospitals. However, when the largest counties are excluded, there are probably fewer high-rises in the data set.

The last specification considers only counties who changed their 911 system during the year. Since a fixed effect is included for each county, the coefficients on the 911 dummies can be interpreted as differences in the mean response time as a result of the change. Of course, all time-invariant variables are dropped from this regression, and in addition, several other control variables were dropped due to the small number of observations. Since an alternative explanation for any findings in the first three specifications is that unobserved differences in counties drive the results, our findings for within-county changes are particularly interesting despite the limited size of the data set that considers such changes.

Consider now the results of our analysis. The first result is that TIME_TO_SCENE is lower in counties with no 911 or Basic 911 than counties with E911. In the base specification, counties with no 911 are about 10 percent slower than counties with E911, while counties with Basic are approximately 8 percent slower than counties with E911. The magnitudes vary somewhat in different specifications, and the result for no 911 is not always significantly different from zero. Nonetheless, the signs of the coefficients are robust to a variety of specifications. When interpreting these results, it is of course important to observe the caveat that results may be driven by unobserved differences between counties, such as the distribution of residences relative to hospitals. However, as shown earlier in figure 4.3, many adjacent counties in similar geographical areas have different 911 systems, and further, when the four largest counties are excluded, the counties are fairly comparable in terms of demographics. Of course, controls are included for several important demographic variables as well as the number of hospitals per mile in the county (which decreases response time, as expected).

In order to provide further evidence about the robustness of the results, we consider the final specification, which includes only counties that changed during the year. The county that changed from Basic to Enhanced 911 saw a 14 percent decrease in its TIME_TO_SCENE, while the counties that changed from no 911 to Basic saw a decrease that is not statistically significant. The weaker results about changes from no 911 to Basic 911 may reflect the fact that moving to a centralized 911 system *without* automated address-finding technology may have ambiguous results, especially in the short run. At a minimum, the system may require some learning-by-doing before call takers in a new 911 system are able to gather correct address information for a large area.

We also find that the emergency response system appears to respond to the severity of the patient's symptoms: patients with a higher Glasgow score have somewhat higher TIME_TO_SCENE, although this result is not statistically significant. We do not, however, see differences in the TIME_TO_SCENE for different categories of insurance (Medicare is the comparison group) or for different ages, with the exceptions that Medicaid patients and younger patients tend to have faster response times.

County-level demographics are also correlated with TIME_TO_SCENE. When the largest counties are included, counties with large populations and high densities have faster response times; once the large counties are excluded, the results are reversed. In all cases, higher income is associated with faster response times.

Table 4.8 analyzes the determinants of TIME_AT_SCENE, following the same set of specifications as in table 4.7. TIME_AT_SCENE is negatively related to both TIME_TO_SCENE and TIME_TO_HOSP. It is increasing in the level of 911, and it is longer for more severe patients. TIME_AT_SCENE is also longer for highly populated counties and especially in those with high crime rates, while it is lower in densely populated, high-income, and high-expenditure counties. A full interpretation of these results would require further investigation into the services provided by ambulances and how they vary with TIME_AT_SCENE. For example, if longer TIME_AT_SCENE is positively correlated with more services, we can interpret the results as saying that more ambulance services are provided in counties with higher levels of 911. This interpretation seems inconsistent with the results on income and expenditures, however.

Table 4.9 considers the determinants of TIME_TO_HOSP. Again, the specifications parallel tables 4.7 and 4.8. We find that, in all specifications, counties with higher levels of 911 have shorter TIME_TO_HOSP. Again, this result holds controlling for demographic factors as well as for the number of hospitals per mile (which decreases TIME_TO_HOSP

Table 4.8   **Time-at-Scene Equation**

	Base Regression (OLS)	Time Controls (OLS)	Excluding 4 Largest Counties (OLS)	Only Counties with 911 Level Changes (Fixed Effects)
		Dependent Variable = L TIME_AT_SCENE		

Time controls | | | | |
L TIME_TO_SCENE		−0.12301	−0.1574	−0.25261
		(0.00611)	(0.00777)	(0.02734)
L TIME_TO_HOSP		−0.04943	−0.05542	−0.10568
		(0.00529)	(0.00669)	(0.02515)
911 level				
NO 911	−0.18644	−0.16716	−0.18038	−0.0343
	(0.01522)	(0.01501)	(0.01665)	(0.07951)
BASIC 911	−0.09558	−0.08014	−0.07043	0.11722
	(0.01202)	(0.01186)	(0.01271)	(0.0485)
Patient characteristics				
MALE	−0.03912	−0.03228	−0.03712	−0.03224
	(0.00744)	(0.00733)	(0.00932)	(0.03216)
AGE	0.00536	0.00691	0.00397	0.00001
	(0.00184)	(0.00181)	(0.00254)	(0.00857)
AGE_SQUARED	−0.00001	−0.00003	−0.00001	0.00002
	(0.00001)	(0.00001)	(0.00002)	(0.00007)
CARDIAC ARREST	0.02266	−0.00199	0.06571	0.13014
	(0.01602)	(0.01581)	(0.0359)	(0.13162)
DEFIBRILLATE	0.03347	0.03949	0.0247	0.06299
	(0.00758)	(0.00747)	(0.00959)	(0.03616)
Glasgow trauma score (15 = least severe; 3 = most severe; 0 = unknown)				
GLASGOW 0	2.17322	2.45456	2.54128	
	(0.1807)	(0.1783)	(0.22585)	
GLASGOW 3	2.45973	2.74229	2.75759	0.17614
	(0.18206)	(0.17964)	(0.22742)	(0.19364)
GLASGOW 4–9	2.30703	2.58851	2.60049	−0.26967
	(0.18212)	(0.1797)	(0.22805)	(0.20899)
GLASGOW 10–12	2.20594	2.5016	2.55148	−0.03566
	(0.18177)	(0.17938)	(0.22728)	(0.19633)
GLASGOW 13–14	2.19037	2.48132	2.54956	−0.15936
	(0.18029)	(0.17792)	(0.2255)	(0.1574)
GLASGOW 15	2.17405	2.47202	2.51962	−0.10864
	(0.17975)	(0.17741)	(0.22466)	(0.13614)
Insurance status (excluded category = Medicare)				
MEDICAID	0.00908	−0.00695	0.00054	−0.00165
	(0.01854)	(0.01827)	(0.02357)	(0.07775)
PRIVATE	−0.02495	−0.023	−0.0457	−0.10748
	(0.01171)	(0.01153)	(0.01489)	(0.04931)
SELF PAY	−0.00607	−0.00293	−0.01054	−0.51433
	(0.03419)	(0.03368)	(0.03861)	(0.22833)

(continued)

Table 4.8   (continued)

	Base Regression (OLS)	Time Controls (OLS)	Excluding 4 Largest Counties (OLS)	Only Counties with 911 Level Changes (Fixed Effects)
		Dependent Variable = L TIME_AT_SCENE		
OTHER	0.01131	0.01001	−0.00877	−0.10236
	(0.02051)	(0.0202)	(0.02758)	(0.07877)
County hospital infrastructure				
CERT. TRAUM CENTER	−0.08111	−0.05414	−0.11849	
	(0.01321)	(0.01305)	(0.01979)	
L HOSP PER SQ. MILE	0.12706	0.10232	0.08358	
	(0.01066)	(0.01054)	(0.01423)	
L COUNTY CARDIAC PATIENTS	−0.10168	−0.10644	−0.104	
	(0.01055)	(0.0104)	(0.01187)	
County demographics				
L POPULATION	0.43383	0.42261	0.37463	
	(0.02746)	(0.02706)	(0.02935)	
DENSITY	−0.07099	−0.06761	−0.03212	
	(0.00493)	(0.00486)	(0.04967)	
L INCOME PER CAP	−0.19859	−0.20712	−0.13367	
	(0.03314)	(0.03275)	(0.04764)	
VCRIMERATE	35.18246	36.32172	52.4423	
	(3.80783)	(3.75116)	(4.71698)	
L POLICE EXP	−0.17784	−0.16911	−0.18477	
	(0.02007)	(0.01978)	(0.02205)	
L HEALTH EXP	−0.01733	−0.01811	−0.01583	
	(0.00378)	(0.00373)	(0.00406)	
Hospital characteristics				
URGENT CARE CENTER	−0.03078	−0.0354	−0.07251	
	(0.0102)	(0.01005)	(0.014)	
CATH LAB	0.0825	0.08175	0.09871	0.13936
	(0.01062)	(0.01047)	(0.01386)	(0.05607)
OPENHEART FAC	−0.07375	−0.0707	−0.11318	
	(0.01114)	(0.01098)	(0.0188)	
TRAUMA CENTER LEVEL	0.0035	−0.0072	−0.00458	
	(0.01059)	(0.01044)	(0.01889)	
EMERGENCY ROOM VOLUME	0.0008	0.00087	0.00174	0.13112
	(0.00038)	(0.00038)	(0.00054)	(0.05946)
HOSPITAL DOCTORS	−0.00019	−0.00017	−0.00113	−0.12205
	(0.00023)	(0.00022)	(0.00052)	(0.05052)
HOSPITAL RESIDENTS	0.00027	0.00033	0.00167	−0.02503
	(0.00006)	(0.00006)	(0.00037)	(0.00954)
Constant				3.20254
				(0.33705)
Observations	24,664.0000	24,664.0000	16,477.0000	1,635.0000
R-squared	0.7040	0.7170	0.7170	

Table 4.9   **Time-to-Hospital Equation**

		Dependent Variable = L TIME_TO_HOSPITAL		
	Base Regression (OLS)	Time Controls (OLS)	Excluding 4 Largest Counties (OLS)	Only Counties with 911 Level Changes (Fixed Effects)
Time controls				
L TIME_TO_SCENE		0.44086	0.47724	0.44745
		(0.00686)	(0.00837)	(0.0253)
L TIME_AT_SCENE		−0.07159	−0.07504	−0.10268
		(0.00765)	(0.00906)	(0.02444)
911 level				
NO 911	0.15649	0.10178	0.10605	0.09964
	(0.01963)	(0.0181)	(0.01943)	(0.07834)
BASIC 911	0.12466	0.08459	0.08718	0.07311
	(0.01551)	(0.01427)	(0.01479)	(0.04786)
Patient characteristics				
MALE	0.04784	0.02903	0.02066	0.03623
	(0.00959)	(0.00882)	(0.01085)	(0.0317)
AGE	0.01282	0.00992	0.00874	0.00106
	(0.00237)	(0.00218)	(0.00295)	(0.00845)
AGE_SQUARED	−0.00011	−0.00009	−0.00008	−0.00002
	(0.00002)	(0.00002)	(0.00002)	(0.00006)
CARDIAC ARREST	−0.18747	−0.13073	−0.13198	−0.00151
	(0.02066)	(0.019)	(0.04177)	(0.03567)
DEFIBRILLATE	0.03532	0.0224	0.03799	−0.21201
	(0.00978)	(0.009)	(0.01115)	(0.07646)
Glasgow trauma score (15 = least severe; 3 = most severe; 0 = unknown)				
GLASGOW 0	1.6977	1.14576	1.15614	−0.34525
	(0.23308)	(0.21527)	(0.26366)	(0.19073)
GLASGOW 3	1.65137	1.10733	1.11887	−0.41187
	(0.23483)	(0.21709)	(0.26567)	(0.20586)
GLASGOW 4–9	1.57387	1.00906	1.07255	−0.0466
	(0.23491)	(0.21707)	(0.26628)	(0.19352)
GLASGOW 10–12	1.73412	1.13965	1.14773	−0.30685
	(0.23446)	(0.2166)	(0.26532)	(0.15502)
GLASGOW 13–14	1.73479	1.1562	1.16163	−0.04845
	(0.23255)	(0.21483)	(0.26326)	(0.13422)
GLASGOW 15	1.8255	1.23666	1.2426	−0.10085
	(0.23185)	(0.21419)	(0.26224)	(0.12976)
Insurance status (excluded category = Medicare)				
MEDICAID	−0.1092	−0.07043	−0.07683	−0.07046
	(0.02391)	(0.02198)	(0.02741)	(0.04865)
PRIVATE	0.04206	0.04077	0.04224	0.27275
	(0.0151)	(0.01388)	(0.01732)	(0.22532)
SELF PAY	0.08497	0.08834	0.11029	−0.08129
	(0.04409)	(0.04053)	(0.04492)	(0.07766)

(continued)

Table 4.9 (continued)

	Base Regression (OLS)	Time Controls (OLS)	Excluding 4 Largest Counties (OLS)	Only Counties with 911 Level Changes (Fixed Effects)
		Dependent Variable = L TIME_TO_HOSPITAL		
OTHER	0.01589	0.02416	−0.00221	
	(0.02645)	(0.02431)	(0.03209)	
County hospital infrastructure				
CERT. TRAUM CENTER	0.15252	0.07711	0.05555	
	(0.01704)	(0.0157)	(0.02305)	
L HOSP PER SQ. MILE	−0.18727	−0.12268	−0.09829	
	(0.01374)	(0.01269)	(0.01656)	
L COUNTY CARDIAC PATIENTS	0.0448	0.06252	0.09978	
	(0.01361)	(0.01254)	(0.01382)	
County demographics				
L POPULATION	0.00389	0.07585	0.06252	
	(0.03542)	(0.03272)	(0.03432)	
DENSITY	−0.01008	−0.02905	0.18259	
	(0.00636)	(0.00587)	(0.05779)	
L INCOME PER CAP	−0.44325	−0.5054	−0.46603	
	(0.04275)	(0.03932)	(0.05533)	
VCRIMERATE	5.65587	5.09363	2.34351	
	(4.91153)	(4.52272)	(5.50937)	
L POLICE EXP	0.01922	−0.02139	−0.08667	
	(0.02589)	(0.02383)	(0.0257)	
L HEALTH EXP	0.01653	0.02102	0.02104	
	(0.00488)	(0.00449)	(0.00473)	
Hospital characteristics				
URGENT CARE CENTER	−0.00081	0.0134	0.00072	0.16509
	(0.01316)	(0.0121)	(0.01631)	(0.05522)
CATH LAB	0.06756	0.08813	0.10653	
	(0.0137)	(0.01261)	(0.01613)	
OPENHEART FAC	−0.00712	−0.02461	−0.01003	
	(0.01437)	(0.01322)	(0.0219)	
TRAUMA CENTER LEVEL	−0.05772	−0.02935	−0.05217	−0.02545
	(0.01366)	(0.01256)	(0.02198)	(0.0587)
EMERGENCY ROOM VOLUME	0.00025	0.00012	−0.00144	0.02418
	(0.00049)	(0.00045)	(0.00063)	(0.04989)
HOSPITAL DOCTORS	0.00126	0.00138	0.00244	0.01174
	(0.00029)	(0.00027)	(0.00061)	(0.00942)
HOSPITAL RESIDENTS	0.00073	0.00065	0.00135	1.67951
	(0.00008)	(0.00008)	(0.00043)	(0.33885)
Constant				3.20254
				(0.33705)
Observations	24,664.000	24,664.000	16,477.000	1,635.000
R-squared	0.704	0.717	0.717	

sharply), and also when large counties are excluded and when only within-county changes are considered (although the result for changes from no 911 to Basic 911 are weakened substantially in the within-county specification). In future work, we hope to consider interactions between Enhanced 911 and other allocation variables.

We find that travel times are longer for patients allocated to hospitals with a large number of doctors, residents (indicating teaching hospitals), and with cardiac catheterization laboratories. Thus, we have some evidence that patients with more severe indications are transported to higher quality, but more distant, hospitals. This is consistent with the official protocols for patient allocation for Pennsylvania counties: According to the protocols, the most severe indications are to be transported to hospitals with appropriate capabilities, while less severe indications are to be transported to the nearest hospital.

Also in contrast to the results on TIME_TO_SCENE, we see that the patient insurance mix affects the time it takes to transport patients to the hospital. Relative to Medicare patients (the majority of our sample), Medicaid patients have shorter transport times. This may partly reflect the fact that Medicaid patients are more likely to reside in the urban areas of their counties (though rural areas of Pennsylvania have Medicaid patients as well). It may also reflect a lack of patient choice: Better-insured patients may travel longer to get to a better hospital. Privately insured patients tend to travel longer, although this result is somewhat weaker. In addition to the possibility that these patients choose to travel to better hospitals, an alternative explanation is that their insurance policies make some hospitals more desirable than others. For example, patients may anticipate financial penalties from receiving treatment from a hospital that is not affiliated with their health plan.

Having characterized the "intermediate inputs" to patient outcomes, we can now turn to assess the impact of 911 and hospital type on the probability of dying from a cardiac incident requiring ambulance transportation (fig. 4.4 and table 4.10). We begin with a simple reduced-form regression of mortality on 911 as well as the controls from tables 4.7–4.9. We do not find strong effects of 911 on mortality. There are several potential explanations for this result. One is that mortality rates are fairly low, and there are simply not enough deaths in the no 911 and Basic 911 counties to uncover the effects. Another possibility is that unobserved heterogeneity across counties confounds the effects of response time (although our results are robust to a variety of county-level control variables). We do see that mortality is decreasing in the number of hospitals per mile and the income of a county, while it is increasing in the crime rate and police expenditures.

In all of the specifications, we find that older patients are less likely to die (they may also be more likely to use ambulance services in less severe

Table 4.10   **Mortality Equation**

	Dependent Variable = Death Outcome Dummy		
	Reduced Form (OLS)	Base Regression (OLS)	Base Regression (IV)[a]
Time outcomes			
L TIME_TO_SCENE		0.00535	0.03122
		(0.00268)	(0.01974)
L TIME_AT_SCENE		0.01266	0.04073
		(0.00275)	(0.01434)
L TIME_TO_HOSP		−0.00690	0.01896
		(0.00228)	(0.01187)
911 level			
NO 911	−0.00104		
	(0.00658)		
BASIC 911	0.00030		
	(0.00520)		
Patient characteristics			
MALE	0.00529	0.00591	0.00479
	(0.00322)	(0.00322)	(0.00329)
AGE	−0.00281	−0.00276	−0.00352
	(0.00080)	(0.00080)	(0.00083)
AGE_SQUARED	0.00003	0.00003	0.00004
	(6.06 e-6)	(6.05 e-6)	(6.26 e-6)
CARDIAC ARREST	0.01709	0.01271	0.02566
	(0.00693)	(0.00627)	(0.00718)
DEFIBRILLATE	0.02500	0.02441	0.02149
	(0.00328)	(0.00326)	(0.00342)
Glasgow trauma score (15 = least severe; 3 = most severe; 0 = unknown and default)			
GLASGOW 3	0.31672	0.31605	0.30487
	(0.01177)	(0.01146)	(0.01249)
GLASGOW 4–9	0.19542	0.19380	0.19219
	(0.01485)	(0.01419)	(0.01536)
GLASGOW 10–12	0.11793	0.11838	0.11426
	(0.01423)	(0.01419)	(0.01449)
GLASGOW 13–14	0.02183	0.02261	0.01969
	(0.01077)	(0.01071)	(0.01090)
GLASGOW 15	−0.01625	−0.01459	−0.02021
	(0.00769)	(0.00762)	(0.00783)
Insurance status (excluded category = Medicare)			
MEDICAID	0.00943	0.00782	0.01291
	(0.00802)	(0.00800)	(0.00818)
PRIVATE	0.01071	0.01128	0.01137
	(0.00507)	(0.00505)	(0.00513)
SELF PAY	0.01425	0.01500	0.01194
	(0.01479)	(0.01473)	(0.01498)
OTHER	0.00219	−0.00022	0.00156
	(0.00887)	(0.00877)	(0.00886)

Table 4.10 (continued)

	Dependent Variable = Death Outcome Dummy		
	Reduced Form (OLS)	Base Regression (OLS)	Base Regression (IV)[a]
County hospital infrastructure			
CERT. TRAUM CNTR	0.00378		
	(0.00572)		
L HOSP PER SQ. MILE	−0.00729		
	(0.00461)		
L COUNTY CARDIAC PATIENTS	0.00499		
	(0.00457)		
County demographics			
L POPULATION	−0.00905		
	(0.01188)		
DENSITY	−0.00348		
	(0.00213)		
L INCOME PER CAP	−0.22546		
	(0.01434)		
VCRIMERATE	2.12906		
	(1.64770)		
L POLICE EXP	0.01159		
	(0.00869)		
L HEALTH EXP	−0.00039		
	(0.00164)		
Hospital characteristics			
URGENT CARE CENTER	0.01411	0.01818	0.01782
	(0.00441)	(0.00399)	(0.00428)
CATH LAB	−0.00171	−0.00118	−0.00071
	(0.00460)	(0.00394)	(0.00441)
OPENHEART FAC	−0.00320	0.01818	0.00157
	(0.00482)	(0.00443)	(0.00469)
TRAUMA CENTER LEVEL	0.00726	0.00872	0.01215
	(0.00458)	(0.00399)	(0.00404)
EMERGENCY ROOM VOLUME	0.00023	0.00033	0.00447
	(0.00458)	(0.00015)	(0.00404)
HOSPITAL DOCTORS	−3.46 E-06	0.00003	0.00003
	(0.00098)	(0.00009)	(0.00009)
HOSPITAL RESIDENTS	−0.00005	−0.00008	−0.00010
	(0.00003)	(0.00003)	(0.00002)
Constant	0.04104	−0.00302	−0.20416
	(0.07819)	(0.03106)	(0.07180)
Observations	24,664.000	24,664.000	16,477.000
R-squared	0.107	0.092	

[a]Instruments: NO 911, BASIC 911, CERT. TRAUM CNTR, HOSP PER SQ. MILE, L POPULATION, DENSITY, L INCOME PER CAP, VCRIMERATE, POLICE EXP, AND HEALTH EXP.

situations), while patients for whom cardiac arrest and defibrillation are reported are more likely to die. Likewise, we see a very strong effect of severity as measured by the Glasgow score: Sicker patients are significantly more likely to die than patients with less severe symptoms. Privately insured patients are more likely to die than Medicare patients.

The second and third specifications consider the effects of response time and patient characteristics on mortality. We have already shown that response time varies with the severity of the patient as well as with the kind of hospital to which the patient will eventually be admitted. Thus, it will be somewhat difficult to interpret the effects of the response time variables in the reduced-form mortality regression. We then propose a preliminary strategy for instrumental variables: We use county-level characteristics, and in particular the level of 911, as instruments for response time. We have already established that such characteristics affect the response time; it remains to argue that the level of 911 is uncorrelated with the unexplained variation in patient mortality (when patient-specific variables are included as controls in the regression). Our approach excludes all county-level demographic information from the regression; in future work, it may be possible to include zip-code-level demographic data to capture any heterogeneity that might have been correlated with excluded county-level demographics.

Our instrumental variables results, while preliminary in nature, are suggestive. They show that shorter response times reduce the probability of death. The main coefficient that changes in sign as a result of the instrumental variables approach is the coefficient on TIME_TO_HOSP. It is not surprising that the coefficient changes in sign, since it is most sensitive to the severity of individual patients (in particular, patients with nonurgent symptoms are transported to the hospital without lights and sirens). It is interesting to note that the instrumental variables strategy is successful despite the fact that higher levels of 911 are (unconditionally) correlated with both lower response times and higher average mortality rates.

We do not attempt an instrumental variables strategy for the technology of the hospital, though this is a potential area for future work. In our reduced-form specification, it is difficult to separate out the potentially beneficial effect of going to a better hospital from the effect due to the differential allocation of more severely ill patients and nonemergency patients to better hospitals.

4.6   The Role of Emergency Response Systems in Allocating Patients to Hospitals

As described in sections 4.1 and 4.2, the prehospital system plays an important role in allocating patients to hospitals. However, one of the most critical factors in determining a patient's allocation is the simple

Table 4.11   **Distribution of In-Hospital Emergency and Cardiac Technologies**

	In-Hospital Technology			Certified County Trauma Center
	Cath Lab	Open Heart Surgery Facility	Urgent Care Center	
Total share of patients allocated to hospital with technology	0.6703	0.2940	0.2170	0.1983
Share of patients living in counties with at least one hospital with technology	0.8243	0.6141	0.6055	0.5097
Conditional share of patients allocated to hospitals with technology	0.8131	0.4787	0.3586	0.3892

availability of a hospital with advanced technologies in his or her county. Table 4.11 shows that 80 percent of patients in our data set had within-county access to hospitals with cardiac catheterization laboratories, while only half had access to a certified county trauma center. Conditional on access to a hospital with a cardiac catheterization laboratory, approximately 80 percent of patients were allocated to such a hospital. The conditional probabilities of being allocated to hospitals with other features is substantially lower for the cardiac patients in our data set. Table 4.11 illustrates that, as opposed to the more common situation where the primary barrier to access derives from a patient's insurance status, a patient's geographical location may be the main determinant of whether a patient receives treatment in a hospital with specialized cardiac care or emergency services. Patients in poorer and less-populated regions may not receive access to such care.

In table 4.12, we explore further the factors that affect allocation of patients to hospitals, conditional on availability of the technology. The main result in this table is that for cardiac catheterization laboratories, the level of 911 significantly increases the probability of being admitted to a high-technology hospital (this result is robust to including controls for the *number* of hospitals in the county with cardiac catheterization laboratories). This is consistent with an important allocative role played by 911 centers.

We further find that, excluding the largest counties, patients with very severe and very mild indications were most likely to go to hospitals with high levels of technology. The result for less-severe patients could be due to the use of ambulances for cases that are more elective in nature, since patients may be reporting emergencies in order to have access to the ambulances for basic transportation. Patient insurance status further affects the hospital allocation decision. We find that privately insured patients are

Table 4.12   Patient Allocation Equation

	Dependent Variable = Allocated to Hospital with Cath Lab (Conditional on at Least One Cath Lab Hospital within County)	
	Cath Lab (Probit)	Excluding 4 Largest Counties
911 level		
NO 911	−1.00733	−1.16728
	(0.06863)	(0.07387)
BASIC 911	−0.28051	−0.46803
	(0.03050)	(0.03800)
Patient characteristics		
MALE	−0.03312	−0.00646
	(0.02189)	(0.02860)
AGE	−0.00412	0.00091
	(0.00562)	(0.00795)
AGE_SQUARED	−1.85 E-06	−0.00005
	(0.00004)	(0.00006)
CARDIAC ARREST	0.58741	−0.08791
	(0.05086)	(0.10797)
DEFIBRILLATE	−0.01392	0.01356
	(0.02256)	(0.03001)
Glasgow trauma score (15 = least severe; 3 = most severe; 0 = unknown and default)		
GLASGOW 3	−0.84533	−0.37461
	(0.08582)	(0.13860)
GLASGOW 4–9	−0.47575	−0.67050
	(0.10140)	(0.14290)
GLASGOW 10–12	−0.32729	−0.53630
	(0.10122)	(0.13994)
GLASGOW 13–14	−0.37244	−0.41117
	(0.07923)	(0.10938)
GLASGOW 15	−0.32983	−0.38695
	(0.06085)	(0.08417)
Insurance status (excluded category = Medicare)		
MEDICAID	0.18089	0.171265
	(0.05760)	(0.07802)
PRIVATE	0.04216	−0.00565
	(0.03485)	(0.04621)
SELF PAY	0.11544	0.27962
	(0.09776)	(0.10839)
OTHER	−0.22751	−0.26058
	(0.05842)	(0.08373)
County hospital infrastructure		
CERT. TRAUM CENTER	−0.19506	−0.66830
	(0.04109)	(0.05677)
L HOSP PER SQ. MILE	−0.15402	−1.15404
	(0.03673)	(0.06159)
L COUNTY CARDIAC PATIENTS	−0.09191	−0.13927
	(0.04060)	(0.05710)

Table 4.12 (continued)

| | Dependent Variable = Allocated to Hospital with Cath Lab (Conditional on at Least One Cath Lab Hospital Within County) | |
	Cath Lab (Probit)	Excluding 4 Largest Counties
County demographics		
L POPULATION	−2.34760	−2.67815
	(0.13631)	(0.15202)
DENSITY	−0.04246	1.72541
	(0.01450)	(0.18301)
L INCOME PER CAP	−0.39597	0.15092
	(0.10642)	(0.15613)
VCRIMERATE	−134.69580	−105.51410
	(14.0461)	(15.50315)
L POLICE EXP	1.85107	2.08144
	(0.10056)	(0.10894)
Constant	11.41237	5.40536
	(0.74178)	(0.86296)
Observations	20,333.000	12,146.000
Log-likelihood	−9,089.698	−5,336.958

allocated in a similar fashion to Medicare patients. However, Medicaid and self-pay patients are more likely to be treated in high-tech hospitals. This result, which is somewhat puzzling, may be due to the fact that hospitals are often located in poor areas; further, this result may be spurious, as almost all patients are insured either privately or through Medicare.

Table 4.12 also shows that the probability of being admitted to a hospital with a cardiac catheterization laboratory is *decreasing* in the number of hospitals per square mile. We interpret this result as a consequence of the allocation protocols: Patients are generally taken to the closest hospital that meets general criteria, and areas with more hospitals per square mile may have a number of hospitals with low levels of technology. In contrast, many counties have only two or three hospitals, one of which has a cardiac catheterization laboratory.

Our final empirical exercise considers directly the incentives of hospitals to adopt higher levels of technology. Identifying the role that hospital characteristics play in determining the allocation of ambulance patients is in many ways similar to a study of a differentiated goods demand system, in which hospitals compete in the marketplace for patients on the basis of geography and characteristics. However, these two settings also differ in some respects; in particular, while hospitals will presumably have incentives to attract some ambulance patients, a given hospital may want to

Table 4.13   Hospital Market Share Equation (excludes four largest counties)

	Dependent Variable = L Hospital Market Share
Individual hospital characteristics	
URGENT CARE CENTER	0.6070
	(0.2911)
CATH LAB	0.5998
	(0.2717)
OPENHEART FAC	0.1522
	(0.3994)
TRAUMA CENTER LEVEL	0.6626
	(0.3233)
HOSPITAL DOCTORS	0.0163
	(0.0122)
HOSPITAL RESIDENTS	0.0008
	(0.0102)
Intensity of rival hospital competition	
NO. OF HOSPITALS	−1.0527
	(0.1432)
AVERAGE URGENT CARE CENTER	−0.3947
	(0.3850)
AVERAGE CATH LAB	−0.6712
	(0.3689)
AVERAGE OPENHEART FAC	−0.1427
	(0.5958)
AVERAGE TRAUMA CENTER LEVEL	−0.6226
	(0.3575)
AVERAGE HOSPITAL DOCTORS	−0.0213
	(0.0157)
AVERAGE HOSPITAL RESIDENTS	0.0084
	(0.0138)
Constant	−0.1513
	(0.7788)
Observations	101.0000
R-squared	0.5419

deter particular types of patients (the uninsured or patients who are hard-to-treat but do not generate significant income). While these distributional questions are extremely interesting, the present analysis will focus on the sensitivity of the overall patient share to particular hospital investments.

Table 4.13 presents results that relate the proportion of a county's patients in the data set who are allocated to a given hospital, SHARE, to the characteristics of that hospital as well as the characteristics of other hospitals in the county. First, and not surprisingly, the market share of a given hospital is declining in the total number of hospitals present in a given county. Our more interesting results are derived from our analysis of the specific features of hospitals that seem to affect this market share.

In particular, simple measures of the overall size of the hospital—the total number of physicians, the total number of hospital beds—are uncorrelated with the hospital market share. In contrast, specific technological investments (such as cardiac catheterization laboratories and the rating of the emergency room) are correlated with the overall market share. Since allocation does appear to respond to technology investment, we conclude that the interaction between the prehospital system and technology adoption should be considered in analyses of the incentives for investment by hospitals.

One important caveat to our interpretation of table 4.13 is that our results do not necessarily imply that if a given hospital increased its technology, it would increase its market share. If our sample contains a hospital characterized by higher than average quality, larger numbers of consumers would use that hospital. The large market share could increase the incentives of the hospital to adopt technology; or it could be that technology is an integral part of maintaining high overall quality. In either case, a low-quality hospital that adopted sophisticated technology would not necessarily increase its market share.

It is also possible to investigate how the sensitivity of market share to hospital characteristics might depend on the type of prehospital emergency response system available in a given county. However, in our preliminary analysis of this data set, we have not found a robust interaction effect.

4.7 Conclusions

From our analysis in this paper, we draw several conclusions that we hope will have an impact on future research. First, our results highlight that emergency response systems play two distinct roles: productive and allocative. It therefore seems important to consider the potential bias that arises in studies that take allocation as exogenous or that do not account for the heterogeneity in county mortality rates that are induced by higher levels of prehospital care (such as lower response times or on-the-scene defibrillation). Further, the incentives generated by the prehospital system need to be taken into account when regulators and insurance companies consider creating additional incentives for hospitals. Our analysis highlights one particularly important feature of the prehospital system: It interacts with the incentives of hospitals to adopt new technologies and maintain highly rated emergency facilities.

Our reduced-form results can be extended to provide a more structural understanding of the interaction between the prehospital infrastructure and hospital competition. For example, we find that patients are allocated by the prehospital system according to their severity and the technology that a hospital employs (see tables 4.12 and 4.13); it is left to future work to evaluate whether these allocative effects are reflected in terms of strategic investment behavior by hospitals.

Examining 911 services also provides a glimpse into the challenges (and types of data) that are necessary for accurate measurement of productivity in the service sector. In particular, service-sector productivity measurement must incorporate the quality of the activity (such as timeliness) as well as whether the services received by the customer are responsive to his or her idiosyncratic characteristics (in this case, different patients experience different diagnoses and different degrees of severity of illness). By developing and analyzing a novel data set, we are able to provide evidence about both of these factors (in this case, timely response and allocation of patients to appropriate hospitals). Of course, we are not the first to evaluate multiple attributes of a service provided. However, our analysis is further able to connect these measures of quality to a well-defined overall service outcome measure—mortality.

Finally, a more careful understanding of the production structure of services is an important first step toward analyzing the nature of strategic interactions between service providers. For example, the extent to which firms can influence their market share through overinvestment in technology and wasteful business-stealing activities will depend in part on the importance of customized service and the quality of the match between consumer characteristics and firm investments. These considerations might have implications for the regulation and management of service industries.

References

Bonnin, M. J., P. E. Pepe, and P. S. Clark. 1993. Survival in the Elderly after Out-of-Hospital Cardiac Arrest. *Critical Care Medicine* 21 (11): 1645–51.

Bresnahan, Timothy F., and Robert J. Gordon, eds. 1997. *The Economics of New Goods*. NBER Studies in Income and Wealth, vol. 58. Chicago: University of Chicago Press.

Brown, E., and J. Sindelar. 1993. The Emergent Problem of Ambulance Misuse. *Annals of Emergency Medicine* 22 (4): 646–50.

Cummins, R. O., J. P. Ornato, W. H. Thies, and P. E. Pepe. 1991. Improving Survival from Sudden Cardiac Arrest: The "Chain of Survival" Approach. *Circulation* 83 (5): 1832–47.

Fischer, M., N. J. Fischer, and J. Schuttler. 1997. One-Year Survival after Out-of-Hospital Cardiac Arrest in Bonn City: Outcome Report According to the "Utstein Style." *Resuscitation* 33 (3): 233–43.

Gibson, G. 1977. Measures of Emergency Ambulance Effectiveness: Unmet Need and Inappropriate Use. *Journal of the American College of Emergency Physicians* 6 (9): 389–92.

Griliches, Z. 1994. Productivity, R&D, and the Data Constraint. *American Economic Review* 84 (1): 1–23.

Hoffer, E. 1979. Emergency Medical Services 1979. *New England Journal of Medicine* 301 (20): 1118–21.

Joslyn, S. A., P. R. Pomrehn, and D. D. Brown. 1993. Survival from Out-of-Hospital Cardiac Arrest: Effects of Patient Age and Presence of 911 Emergency Medical Services Phone Access. *American Journal of Emergency Medicine* 11 (3): 200–206.

Larsen, M. P., M. S. Eisenberg, R. O. Cummins, and A. P. Hallstrom. 1993. Predicting Survival from Out-of-Hospital Cardiac Arrest: A Graphic Model. *Annals of Emergency Medicine* 22 (11): 1652–58.

Lewis, R. P., R. R. Lanese, J. M. Stang, T. N. Chirikos, M. D. Keller, and J. V. Warren. 1982. Reduction of Mortality from Prehospital Myocardial Infarction by Prudent Patient Activation of Mobile Coronary Care System. *American Heart Journal* 103 (1): 123–29.

McClellan, M., and J. Newhouse. 1997. The Marginal Cost-Effectiveness of Medical Technology: A Panel Instrumental-Variables Approach. *Journal of Econometrics* 77 (1): 39–64.

Pivetta, Sue. 1995. *The 911 Puzzle: Putting All of the Pieces Together.* Cleveland, Ohio: National Emergency Number Association.

Siler, Kenneth P. 1975. Predicting Demand for Publicly Dispatched Ambulances in a Metropolitan Area. *Health Services Research* 10 (3): 254–63.

Smith, Ken. 1988. The Ambulance Service: Past, Present, and Future. *Practitioner* 232:879–82.

Tresch, D. D., R. Thakur, and R. Hoffman. 1989. Should the Elderly Be Resuscitated Following Out-of-Hospital Cardiac Arrest? *American Journal of Medicine* 86:145–50.

Vogt, W. 1997. Detecting Strategic Behavior in Technology Adoption: The Example of Magnetic Resonance Imaging. Carnegie Mellon University, Pittsburgh, Penn. Mimeograph.

Weston, C. F., R. J. Wilson, and S. D. Jones. 1997. Predicting Survival from Out-of-Hospital Cardiac Arrest: A Multivariate Analysis. *Resuscitation* 34 (1): 27–34.

Comment on Chapters 3 and 4   Catherine Wolfram

McClellan and Staiger

Mark McClellan and Douglas Staiger present a new method for measuring hospital quality and then use their approach to consider quality differences across hospital types. Using information from nearly 4,000 hospitals nationwide, they find that government and for-profit hospitals are lower quality than not-for-profit (heart patients at these hospitals are more likely to die within 90 days of treatment) and that high volume hospitals are higher quality than smaller hospitals. They also perform a more detailed case study of a handful of hospitals in three distinct markets, and they uncover an interesting correlate to their aggregate results. At least in

Catherine Wolfram is assistant professor of economics at Harvard University and a faculty research fellow of the National Bureau of Economic Research.

the three markets they consider, for-profit hospitals did not have higher mortality rates than their not-for-profit competitors, and in one market, a for-profit firm entered by taking over a low-quality hospital, but then raised the hospital's quality level. Their findings could imply that for-profit hospitals are not lower quality (as the national results suggest), but that they selectively enter markets (that is, take over hospitals) where quality is low. Perhaps they even subsequently improve quality levels.

Before discussing McClellan and Staiger's findings, I will comment on their approach to measuring quality differences, as it is novel and affects their results. The authors identify three issues confronted by researchers attempting to assess hospital quality—data availability, the ability to control for the selection of patients across hospitals, and noise. Their study improves on past quality measures but addresses two of the three issues (data and noise) more thoroughly than the third (selection).

The authors point out two shortcomings in the data currently collected by hospitals and health care providers for use in comparing hospital quality. For one thing, many institutions do not systematically collect and disseminate measures of patient outcomes. Secondly, the data that are collected often cannot be used to make meaningful comparisons across organizations, and worse, the convenient comparisons can be grossly misleading. In a particularly poignant example, the authors consider data that records each patient's status at the time he or she is discharged from the hospital. If we assume (for expositional purposes) that all patients undergoing a procedure performed in a hospital get worse over time, then hospitals or insurance plans that discharge their patients *earlier* would look *better* (i.e., they would report data on fewer sick patients) even if being discharged early reduced the patient's chances of surviving 90 days after the procedure.

McClellan and Staiger use Medicare records on all patients hospitalized for one of two heart-related illnesses between 1984 and 1991. Overall, their data include over one-half million observations. They avoid biases based on the length of a patient's hospital stay because their data set follows every patient through the 90th day following the *initial* hospitalization and records whether or not the patient dies. They then aggregate observations on patients to develop hospital-level mortality rates.

One advantage to using mortality rates as a measure of quality is that deaths are easy outcomes to measure consistently across hospitals. Also, if mortality rates are systematically different across hospitals, presumably few people would willingly choose a low-quality hospital that was equivalent to other hospitals on other dimensions (e.g., cost or proximity). Nonetheless, by comparing hospitals only based on mortality rates, the authors do not capture the full range of attributes patients and their families are likely to value. For instance, McClellan and Staiger find that smaller hospitals generally have higher mortality rates (confirming previous research).

If smaller hospitals provide other attributes that patients and their families value, such as more provider time, it is reasonable to think that rational, fully informed patients would choose a hospital with "lower quality" as measured by McClellan and Staiger. Since the authors are only capturing one dimension of quality, it may be unwise to use their results to make policy prescriptions, for instance, about the optimal hospital size.

A second problem confronting most hospital quality measures that rely on patient outcomes is that the initial allocation of patients to hospitals is not random. In particular, measured quality differences are likely to underrepresent true differences if sicker patients tend to go to (or be taken to) better hospitals. McClellan and Staiger argue that by considering heart disease, they are minimizing the problem since "urgency limits the opportunities for selection across hospitals." Compared to studies of other illnesses, this argument seems valid, though the paper by Athey and Stern in this volume suggests that some selection occurs even among heart patients brought to the hospital in an ambulance. Athey and Stern find evidence suggesting that sicker patients are more likely to be taken to hospitals with cardiac catheterization laboratories or trauma centers. In fact, ambulance operators follow strict protocols when they make decisions on allocating patients and are only allowed to take patients to a hospital other than the nearest one under prespecified conditions. As a result, selection is most likely limited to observables on the hospital type, for instance, whether or not it has a trauma center. Since McClellan and Staiger's main focus is on comparing hospitals by type, any such selection will only be problematic to the extent that, for instance, not-for-profit hospitals are more likely to have trauma centers and so are allocated the sicker patients. Controlling for technological differences across hospitals is probably feasible, particularly in the case studies performed by the authors.

In addition to explicit selection based on a patient's status at hospitalization, different hospitals may be located near patients with different demographic characteristics. In developing their risk-adjusted mortality measures (RAMRs), the authors control for several patient characteristics, including age and gender. Still, it is possible that other attributes of the patients, related to their ability to survive a heart incident, could differ systematically across hospital types. For instance, if government hospitals are more likely to treat veterans and veterans are more likely to smoke than other men of similar ages, McClellan and Staiger's methodology would assign government hospitals higher RAMR measures. It is important to note that the adjustments that McClellan and Staiger make to develop the filtered RAMR will not account for systematic differences across hospitals. In fact, by combining information from different years, they will tend to exacerbate them (by making the differences appear more precisely estimated). Though their measure seems a marked improvement over existing measures in the literature, we should still be a little wary about interpreting differences across their mortality measures as differences in hospital "quality" since hospital selection is still an issue.

The likelihood that a patient survives a heart attack is a function of a number of factors, including the treatment he or she receives at the hospital, his or her age, gender, overall health status, and simple luck. Assuming that the authors could control for all meaningful differences across patients (in other words, leaving the issues addressed in the last paragraph aside), it is still difficult to disentangle the extent to which one hospital provides better care than another from the different patients' luck. For instance, if one hospital admitted 10 heart attack patients over the course of a year and 4 of them died within 90 days and another hospital admitted 10 and 3 of them died, can we conclude that the second hospital provides superior care, or are we simply observing that one more patient at that hospital was lucky? Similarly, if one hospital had 3 out of 10 die and one had 31 out of 100, how do we compare the two hospitals?

The methodology that McClellan and Staiger present in section 3.3 of their paper is designed to minimize the noise in the quality measures (i.e., minimize the role played by luck) and distill information on persistent differences across hospitals. Two main features of their methodology are to adjust for the degrees of freedom by weighting measures by their precision, (so that 31 out of 100 is given more emphasis than 3 out of 10) and to use information from adjoining years and a related illness.

The implications of McClellan and Staiger's case studies—that for-profit hospitals may appear lower quality than not-for-profit because they are choosing to convert low-quality hospitals—is certainly a topic worthy of further research. At times the authors place a very strict interpretation of quality on their filtered RAMR measure as something that is completely under the control of hospital managers and is, for instance, unaffected by local demographics. Taking this interpretation, we would need to look for evidence that for-profit managers choose to convert low-quality hospitals in order to support the implications of their case studies. If we use a less strict interpretation of their quality measures, we could confirm their case study results by finding evidence that for-profit hospitals tend to locate in regions where (age- and gender-adjusted) mortality rates are higher.

It might also be interesting to consider the competitive dynamics between hospitals of different quality levels. For instance, if for-profit hospitals improve the quality of the hospitals they take over, do other hospitals in the local market become better? Along those lines, it would be interesting to see if further research could explain McClellan and Staiger's findings that mortality rates have fallen over time.

Athey and Stern

Susan Athey and Scott Stern have gathered an extensive new data set on 911 systems across the United States and, containing more detail, within

Pennsylvania. In the paper included in this volume, they lay out some of the basic relationships between the level of 911 service a county adopts, ambulance response times within the county, the technology available at the hospitals to which ambulances bring patients, and patients' eventual outcomes. They uncover a number of intriguing patterns, and their results touch on many issues of interest to health care economists, including the role of technology in health outcomes and the extent to which similar patients are allocated to hospitals with different technological capabilities. In these comments, I first give an overview of the paper and discuss some of the individual results, and then I comment on the implications the results have for some broader health care policy and economic questions. While the authors show responsible restraint in drawing conclusions from their results, I will suggest ways in which the results can be pushed to answer relevant policy questions.

At a fundamental level, the authors are concerned with the effect that 911 technologies have on the likelihood that a patient suffering cardiac arrest survives. There are a number of different reasons to believe that 911 would impact patient outcomes, and there are a number of factors potentially at play. For example, the authors point out that the local 911 infrastructure may affect local hospitals' decisions about the type of cardiac care technology in which to invest. Though the possible links between 911 technology levels and patient outcomes are complex, Athey and Stern have gathered enough information to disentangle much of what is going on. Table 4C.1 provides a schematic guide to the types of outcomes and decisions the authors consider. The columns of the table indicate the successive decisions that are made affecting a cardiac patient's chances of survival after calling 911. Each step is delineated in the row labeled "Outcome," the potential outcomes are listed in the row labeled "Possibilities" and several representative factors affecting the possibility that is realized are listed in the row labeled "Factors Affecting Outcome."

As column 1 of table 4C.1 depicts, all U.S. counties have adopted one of three levels of 911 technology (see their article for a description of the different choices). In tables 4.4 and 4.5, Athey and Stern consider covariates with county decisions in, respectively, Pennsylvania and the United States. As 911 service is a local public good, the framework they use is akin to median voter models that others have used to explore local heterogeneity in, for instance, education expenditures. They include factors likely to affect the relative prices of service from the different 911 technology levels (for example, population density, crime rate), income per capita and various demographic factors essentially as proxies for the median voters' tastes (for example, percent of Perot voters in the 1992 election). Their results are not that surprising—indicating, for instance, that more populous, richer counties are more likely to adopt more elaborate 911 systems. The results at the national level in table 4.5 should be interpreted with

Table 4C.1 Decisions Affecting the Treatment of a Cardiac Patient Who Calls 911

Outcome	911 Service Adopted by County (1)	Ambulance Response to Initial Call (2)	Treatment on Premises (3)	Transport to Hospital (4)	Treatment at Hospital (5)
Possibilities	Nothing; basic; E911	Slow to fast	None to defibrillators	Slow (better hospital), fast (closest hospital)	Patient lives or dies
Factors affecting outcomes	County geography; demographics; politics	911 service; county geography	Severity of patient illness	Severity of patient illness; county geography	Type of hospital; prior defibrillation

caution since the authors only have data from 772 counties (out of the universe of 3,000+ counties in the United States), all of which have self-selected by responding to a survey on the local 911 capabilities. The authors point out that the counties that responded to the national survey were more likely to have E911 than the counties in Pennsylvania (where the authors observe the universe of counties), and that selection could be biasing the coefficients reported in table 4.5. For instance, while most counties with E911 respond to the survey, it seems plausible that only counties with high levels of local services (potentially proxied by police expenditures in table 4.5) would have staff with time to respond. Consistent with that, the negative relationship between police expenditures and 911 service level found in table 4.5 is reversed in table 4.4 when the authors consider Pennsylvania.

Next, the authors consider the impact of the level of 911 service on the time it takes an ambulance to reach a patient, the time the ambulance team stays at the scene, and the time it takes the ambulance to drive the patient to the hospital (the relationships represented in table 4C.1 in columns 2, 3, and 4). Regression results are presented in tables 4.7, 4.8, and 4.9, and variable means by county technology level are presented in table 4.6. Consider first the relationship between the county's 911 service level and the time to scene. Here, the direct effect is relatively uncomplicated: All else equal, we would expect that higher levels of 911 technology will permit ambulances to reach patients sooner,[1] so we expect the coefficient on the variable "no 911" to be positive and larger than the positive coefficient on "Basic 911," suggesting that Enhanced 911 is generally quicker. Table 4C.1 indicates one potential problem with uncovering such a relationship across counties. Factors such as the county geography or population density may be correlated both with the benefits of better 911 service and with the speed it would take any ambulance (dispatched from a sophisticated 911 center or not) to reach a patient. That could create a spurious correlation (positive in the example given) between the 911 technology level and the time to scene.

The authors control for some unobserved county heterogeneity by including county-level controls. They also devise individual-level controls by including the variables "time at scene" and "time to hospital" in some specifications in table 4.7. They reason that if it initially takes an ambulance longer to reach a person in a remote location, it would also take longer to get the person to the hospital. The second solution is clever and basically sound, though it could be problematic if, for instance, decisions

---

1. The authors do point out one complication to the direct effects as I have stated them, suggesting that the ambulances carrying defibrillators may be more common in counties with E911 and that the 911 dispatcher may sacrifice time getting the ambulance to scene in order to find such a vehicle. Such countervailing effects seem much more important in the "time to hospital" and "time at scene" results.

about whether to bring the patient to the closest hospital are affected by the time it takes the ambulance to arrive on the scene. (For instance, if the ambulance gets lost and so takes a long time to arrive at the scene, it might choose to bring the patient to the nearest hospital rather than spending time to drive to a better equipped but more distant hospital.)[2]

The relationship between 911 and both the time the paramedics spend at the scene and the time to hospital are complicated both because the types of omitted variable biases described above might exist and also because there are factors pushing the direct relationship in both directions. For one thing, ambulances often face a trade-off between bringing the patient to the closest hospital and bringing him or her to a more distant but better-equipped facility. If E911 allows ambulances to reach patients quicker initially, the time saved may permit more trips to distant (but better-equipped) hospitals. Such an effect would cause E911 to look less efficient. The coefficients on the 911 service level variables in tables 4.8 and 4.9 do give an indication of the net effect of all factors. So, for instance, the positive coefficients on "no 911" and "Basic 911" suggest that the above-mentioned effect is less important than the fact that E911 helps ambulances navigate more efficiently to the nearest hospital.

Interestingly, the results in table 4.9 suggest that patients transported to better-equipped hospitals (e.g., with cardiac catheterization laboratories) have longer travel times, suggesting that patients are not simply taken to the nearest hospital and that better-equipped hospitals may be receiving sicker patients.[3] Taking off on this result, Athey and Stern analyze the probability that a patient is allocated to a hospital with a cardiac catheterization laboratory as a function of the 911 service level in table 4.12. They document a strong relationship between enhanced 911 and a patient's chances of going to a hospital with a catheterization laboratory (conditional on the county having at least one such hospital). Again, however, those results may reflect unobserved heterogeneity across counties, for example, in the proximity of such labs to the average cardiac patient. Confirming the pattern, though, the authors find that a hospital's level of technological sophistication (for heart patient treatment) affects its share of cardiac care patients brought to it by ambulances.

Athey and Stern note the possibility that 911 technology affects a hospital's decisions about the level of technology in which to invest, but they do not consider it empirically. (This decision is not reflected in table 4C.1,

---

2. The authors also examine the relationship between 911 level and time to scene using county fixed effects, so that their results are identified off of changes in the time-to-scene in counties that changed the level of 911 service they provide. These results should be interpreted with extreme caution since it appears that only one county changed from Basic 911 to Enhanced 911 and fewer than five changed from no 911 to the basic service.

3. The coefficients on the Glasgow scores—providing direct measures of a patient's sickness—suggest that sicker patients have longer travel times over a certain score range, though the standard errors on the coefficients are bigger than the differences between them.

though would impact the possibilities listed in column 4.) To the extent that 911 service levels have important implications for the way in which patients are allocated to hospitals, this promises to be a fruitful path for future research.

The authors also consider the overall impact of the level of 911 technology on patient mortality rates (see table 4.10). The overall relationship between 911 technology and mortality will reflect the balance of all of the factors documented in columns 2 through 5 of table 4C.1. Unfortunately, they are unable to discern a strong effect of 911 service level on mortality and offer several plausible explanations for that result (among them that mortality rates are extremely noisy, an issue addressed in the McClellan and Staiger paper in this volume). Taking the analysis one step forward (to column 2 in table 4C.1), however, they find that slower ambulance responses are associated with higher mortality rates. In a clever use of their previous findings, they also use the county's 911 service level as an instrument for ambulance transportation times and confirm the relationship between time and mortality that has been documented by previous researchers. (The instrumental variables specifications in table 4.10 also use dummy variables indicating whether or not the county has a catheterization laboratory or a trauma center as instruments. The argument for excluding these from the mortality equation is less clear.) Comparing the two sets of results, it is somewhat puzzling that the timing results are so much stronger than the 911 service levels.

Athey and Stern's work provides new insights on several issues. The authors have pulled together a rich data set with uncommonly detailed measures of the productivity of a particular health care technology. The level of detail they are working with permits them to show that while the relationship between 911 and mortality is muddied by a number of factors, there is a clear relationship between investment in 911 technology and the time to the scene. Their coefficients suggest that having enhanced 911 services reduces the average response times by 5 percent, or at the mean response time, by about 30 seconds. With such direct evidence on the benefits provided by a technology, it is hard to pass up the opportunity to compare the benefits to the costs. Rapidly increasing investments in technology have been blamed for the increase in health care costs over the past several decades (see, e.g., Newhouse 1992). While 911 is just one technology and it is difficult to draw any general conclusions (in all probability, county-level governments face different incentives to invest in technology and encourage its use than, for instance, hospitals), it would be interesting to see what the implicit cost of the new technology is per life saved. Table 4.10 provides estimates of the effect a reduction in the time to scene has on the probability a patient dies (and the authors cite clinical studies that give similar measures), and table 4.7 documents the effect of 911 service level on the time to scene. With more information like that provided for

Berks County on the cost of 911 systems, one could estimate the implicit cost per life saved. (Such a calculation could almost be done based on the information provided in the paper currently. One important missing factor is the number of ambulance trips in Berks County.)

To complete the accounting of the impact of 911 investments on patient lives saved, one would need to account for the authors' results on technology adoption by hospitals. For instance, if elaborate and highly productive 911 systems cause hospitals to engage in technology races and overinvest in catheterization laboratories, the overall benefits would be reduced.

A second notable result in this paper is the concrete evidence it provides on the extent to which different patients are allocated to hospitals with different technology levels. For instance, the results in table 4.9 suggest that patients that are brought to hospitals with better facilities are more likely to have longer ambulance rides to the hospital, and table 4.12 suggests that patients have a better chance of getting to a hospital with higher technological capabilities if the local county has E911. Both results suggests that even with a life-threatening, time-sensitive disease, patients with different unconditional probabilities of survival are allocated to different hospitals. That result suggests that any attempts to compare outcomes across hospitals that do not control for patient selection issues should be viewed with caution. It also emphasizes the value of efforts to control for initial allocation of patients (e.g., McClellan and Newhouse 1997).

References

McClellan, M., and J. P. Newhouse. 1997. The Marginal Cost-Effectiveness of Medical Technology: A Panel Instrumental-Variables Approach. *Journal of Econometrics* 77 (March): 39–64.
Newhouse, J. P. 1992. Medical Care Costs: How Much Welfare Loss? *Journal of Economic Perspectives* 6 (summer): 3–21.

Comment on Chapters 3 and 4   Karen Norberg

In a way, the two papers in this section are both concerned with the adoption of new information technologies: Athey and Stern have studied the adoption of an enhanced 911 technology that changes the delivery of ambulance-based emergency care and transport, and McClellan and Staiger have introduced a new statistical method that may improve the comparison of quality among hospitals.

Karen Norberg is assistant professor of psychiatry at Boston University Medical School and a clinical associate of the National Bureau of Economic Research.

Athey and Stern

In out-of-hospital cardiac arrest, the time between collapse and initiation of CPR is an important determinant of the likelihood of survival (Berek et al. 1997). There is wide variation across the United States in the level of 911 emergency services provided within the community. The most recent advance, known as Enhanced 911, involves the automatic identification of the address from which a call is made, and a database of information about the location of all addresses in the community. Athey and Stern find that an ambulance arrives at the scene of a cardiac arrest about 5 percent faster, and the patient is transported from the scene to the hospital about 10 percent faster, in Pennsylvania counties with Enhanced 911 compared to other levels of service. Protocols for 911 services specify that sicker patients are taken to hospitals with higher levels of specialization, and higher levels of 911 technology resulted in more discrimination about which patient is taken to which hospital.

Why do some communities adopt Basic or Enhanced 911 technology while some do not? Presumably, the counties that have adopted enhanced 911 are those that could afford the investment, and whose public officials believed that the technology would significantly benefit the county. Although a community's demand for Enhanced 911 services may be driven by the desire for crime or fire protection as well as by a demand for emergency medical service, the most significant predictors of level of 911 adoption appear to be county population, per capita income, and general political orientation toward government services.

McClellan and Staiger

Different hospital markets may be characterized by different levels of emergency medical service infrastructure, different community standards of care, different degrees of competition, different demographics, and different prevalence of illness. Such community differences may confound efforts to study the effects of hospital quality in a national sample. McClellan and Staiger introduce the use of a "filtered" risk-adjusted mortality rate (RAMR) to compare the outcomes of patients admitted with acute myocardial infarction. This filtered RAMR yields a much higher signal-to-noise ratio than ordinary methods, and makes it possible to compare individual hospitals within the same market with much greater confidence in the meaningfulness of the comparisons that are made.

Like other investigators, McClellan and Staiger find that for-profit and government hospitals have higher mortality than not-for-profit in their national sample. Their three case studies suggest a more complicated picture. In case 1, the two for-profit hospitals had lower mortality than the others in the community. In case 2, there were improvements in the mortality rates of hospital 2 at the times of two different purchases by two different for-profit chains; and in case 3, the two hospitals that changed ownership also showed the greatest improvements in mortality, but these changes in ownership involved a transition from government and for-profit to not-for-profit status.

Cases 1 and 2 are consistent with the hypothesis that for-profit hospitals may be more likely to enter markets where lower quality management has created attractive takeover opportunities; although they may, on average, be functioning in markets with lower average quality, some for-profit hospitals could provide higher than average services within their markets. Case 3 reminds us that any change in hospital ownership could be associated with improvement in productivity in the short run; the fact of a change in ownership implies that both buyer and seller foresaw an opportunity for benefit in the exchange. There are a great many public concerns about for-profit hospitals that are not explored in the present study; in any case, we cannot draw systematic conclusions about for-profit hospital ownership and quality of care from just three examples, but the case studies are enough to point out the hazard of oversimplified conclusions from aggregate national data.

McClellan and Staiger's filtered RAMR results in a dramatic reduction in the "noise" associated with mortality as a quality-of-care outcome measure. However, their method is subject to all of the other problems with risk adjustment, and a few caveats about generalizability. It is easy to imagine a study such as this one becoming the basis for a public quality-of-care "report card" in a particular hospital market. Clinicians, in particular, are notoriously skeptical of such report cards (Angell and Kassirer 1996; Chassin 1996; Epstein 1998). There are two principal reasons for this skepticism.

First, risk adjustment is hard to do well. In many clinical conditions, the patient's illness and other characteristics are much stronger predictors of outcome than are any nuances of medical intervention; differences in the case mix between hospitals may overshadow the effects of any true differences in the quality of care. However, the only risk factors that can be entered into a regression are those that have been measured. Administrative and clinical records may be sketchy about known clinical risk factors, and of course, they cannot account for risk factors that are still unknown. Instrumental variables are an alternative way around this problem; process measures, rather than mortality, may also be less confounded by problems of patient selection (Brook, McGlynn, and Cleary 1996; Chen et al. 1999).

Second, based on a study such as this one, it may be tempting to make generalizations about quality of care in for-profit hospitals. However, institutional quality in one outcome may or may not be correlated with institutional quality in another outcome. A hospital's neonatal mortality rate may be unrelated to its mortality rate from acute myocardial infarctions; its cardiac surgery service may have a different reputation from its orthopedics. Hospitals may offer high-quality care as a "loss leader" in services (such as cardiac care) where there may be significant market competition, and may provide lower quality care in services for which there is less competition. As Athey and Stern point out, hospitals may compete based on the criteria used by the emergency services that provide patient referrals. Regulators, of course, hope that the use of public report cards will lead to higher quality of care in the services reported, but this may be accomplished by lowering the quality of care in services that are not publicly reported. The qualities surveyed will depend on feasibility and on the priorities of the agency collecting the information; the feasibility of collecting certain information depends on existing administrative infrastructures, which themselves reflect the past priorities of the public and private institutions involved. For better or for worse, single-focus report cards may increase the influence of the targeted services within the hospitals in the community, as the general reputation of each institution may depend on the performance of its most visible department.

Most hospital quality information is collected by single entities, such as hospitals, insurers, or health maintenance organizations. Such information is usually treated as highly confidential, and it is unclear how often such agencies are able to use the information in a way that actually leads to quality improvement. Higher quality studies, with more sensitive and stable measures, may improve the credibility of internally collected data and may increase the acceptability of public reporting among clinicians and provider institutions.

References

Angell, M., and J. P. Kassirer. 1996. Quality and the Medical Marketplace—Following Elephants. *New England Journal of Medicine* 335 (12): 883–85.

Berek, K., A. Schinner, C. Traweger, P. Lechlietner, M. Baubin, and F. Aichner. 1997. The Prognostic Significance of Coma-Rating, Duration of Anoxia, and Cardiopulmonary Resuscitation in Out-of-Hospital Cardiac Arrest. *Journal of Neurology* 244: 556–61.

Blumenthal, D. 1996. Part 1: Quality of Care: What Is It? *New England Journal of Medicine* 335 (12): 891–94.

Brook, R. H., E. A. McGlynn, and P. D. Cleary. 1996. Part 2: Measuring Quality of Care. *New England Journal of Medicine* 335 (13): 966–70.

Chassin, M. R. 1996. Part 3: Improving the Quality of Care. *New England Journal of Medicine* 335 (14): 1060–63.

Chen, J., M. J. Radford, Y. Wang, T. Marciniak, and H. M. Krumholz. 1999. Do "America's Best Hospitals" Perform Better for Acute Myocardial Infarction? *New England Journal of Medicine* 340 (4): 286–92.

Epstein, A. 1998. Rolling Down the Runway: The Challenges Ahead for Quality Report Cards. *Journal of the American Medical Association* 279 (21): 1691–96.

Kassirer, J. 1999. Hospitals, Heal Yourself. *New England Journal of Medicine* 340 (4): 309–10.

Schneider, E. C., and A. M. Epstein. 1998. Use of Public Performance Reports: A Survey of Patients Undergoing Cardiac Surgery. *Journal of the American Medical Association* 279 (20): 1638–42.

How Much Is Enough?
Efficiency and Medicare Spending
in the Last Six Months of Life

Jonathan Skinner and John E. Wennberg

5.1 Introduction

Thinking about efficiency in health care is straightforward in theory but quite difficult in practice. Health economists have struggled for years to measure efficiency in hospital and health care more generally. One branch of the literature has concentrated on an objective measure of cost, typically the cost of a hospital bed or a hospital bed-day. Thus the question is, to what extent is a hospital bed-day produced at minimum cost?[1] Another branch of the literature has addressed a more general question: What is the least costly method of improving some dimension of health by a given amount?[2] We follow McEachern (1994) in defining this measure of cost minimization to be *productive efficiency*.

In practice, we observe widely divergent patterns of care for patients

Jonathan Skinner is the John French Professor of Economics at Dartmouth College, adjunct professor at Dartmouth Medical School, and a research associate of the National Bureau of Economic Research. John E. Wennberg is director of the Center for the Evaluative Clinical Sciences at the Dartmouth Medical School. He has been a professor in the Department of Community and Family Medicine since 1980 and in the Department of Medicine since 1989, and currently holds the Peggy Y. Thomson Chair for the Evaluative Clinical Sciences.

The authors are grateful to Frank Lichtenberg, David Cutler, and conference participants for very helpful comments. They are particularly indebted to Sandra Sharp for invaluable data analysis; to Therese Stukel, Elliott Fisher, and Thomas Bubolz for allowing them to use their cohort data; and to Derek Chau for excellent research assistance. Funding by the Robert Wood Johnson Foundation and the National Institute on Aging is gratefully acknowledged.

1. See Gaynor and Anderson (1995); Friedman and Pauly (1981); and Breyer (1987). See also Rosko and Broyles (1988, chap. 7); the more recent literature on hospital costs is concerned with stochastic demand for hospital beds.

2. For an excellent introduction to the enormous literature on cost effectiveness analysis, see Gold et al. (1996).

and for populations. For example, the underlying rate of surgery for men with enlarged prostates, a benign (noncancerous) condition that interferes with urination, varies more than fourfold among geographic regions in the United States. Revascularization procedures (bypass surgery and angioplasty) vary more than threefold (Wennberg and Cooper 1997). The intensity of care delivered to the seriously ill, measured as the amount of care delivered during the last six months of life, varies fivefold. These patterns raise a question not only about productive efficiency but also about *allocative* efficiency. Even if surgical procedures for enlarged prostates or heart disease are productively efficient, in the sense of minimizing average costs, perhaps these procedures are being allocated across regions—and people—in a decidedly inefficient way.[3]

In this paper, we consider these issues of productive and allocative efficiency in health care. We begin by considering Medicare expenditures and physician visits in the last six months of life for two communities, Miami and Minneapolis. People who are in their last six months of life are generally quite sick, regardless of where they live. Thus, we believe that how such patients are treated provides a good indicator of the local pattern of practice with respect to the chronically ill. And we find substantial differences in how people in their last six months of life are treated in the two cities. In Minneapolis, the average number of days spent during the last six months of life in an intensive care unit (ICU) is 1.3, in Miami, 4.8. On average, Medicare patients in their final six months in Miami can expect 76 percent more primary care physician visits, and 440 percent more specialist visits, than Medicare patients in Minneapolis. In turn, these indicators of the intensity of care are closely correlated with the overall intensity of Medicare spending on the entire elderly population.

How to interpret such differences? Perhaps people who live in regions like Miami that provide more intensive health care to all patients (as well as those near death) also experience improved life expectancy. In this case, such regions could be productively efficient in the sense of providing better quality health care albeit at higher cost. We address this question by considering prospective samples of elderly people, and we use our information about regional treatment patterns to "mark" individuals in regions where aggressive treatment is provided for *all* patients. The question is then whether regions with intensive health care treatment experience reduced mortality, after controlling for a variety of age, sex, race, and illness factors that might exert independent influences on mortality. Briefly, we find no evidence that improved survival outcomes are associated with increased levels of spending. In other words, hospitals may be at the minimum point

---

3. Again, we follow the McEachern (1994, 550) terminology; allocative efficiency is "the condition that exists when firms produce the output that is most preferred by consumers. . . ."

of their long-run average total cost curve in producing hospital bed-days, but stray far from a productively efficient level in terms of producing survival years.

While mortality may be the appropriate outcome variable to assess, say, the effectiveness of intensive care units, there is more to efficiency than life expectancy. Individuals seek to maximize utility, and there are costly procedures offering improved health functioning at the cost of increased mortality risk. Other expensive procedures may have no impact on survival rates, but do affect different aspects of health status. For example, surgical treatment for an enlarged prostate improves urinary flow, but it can adversely affect sexual functioning. There is no best treatment for enlarged prostates; some men prefer surgical treatment and others prefer drug treatment or watchful waiting. Thus, allocative efficiency means that the people are treated in the way that they would prefer, generally by being able to choose from the menu of productively efficient procedures.[4]

It is important to consider preferences for different types of treatment because it *could* be the case that people in Miami prefer the more intensive health care services because they prefer such treatment, even if there is no measurable difference in survival. We examine the importance of heterogeneity in preferences in light of the results from recent experiments in informed patient decision making for patients with enlarged prostates and with angina due to coronary artery disease. And while these studies are not specific to Miami, they do suggest that while some preferred the more intensive treatment options, on average patients preferred rates of surgery lower than the level prescribed by most physicians. Thus, the allocative costs of increased levels of surgical intervention could be even larger than those considered in standard cost-benefit trade-off comparisons.

5.2   A Look at Miami and Minneapolis

The hospital referral regions for Miami and Minneapolis include a larger area than just the cities themselves. They were determined as part of an effort by the *Dartmouth Atlas of Health Care* (Wennberg and Cooper 1997) to map the entire United States into 306 regions, each of which has one or more hospitals offering cardiovascular or neurosurgical services. Thus, the Minneapolis hospital referral region (HRR) comprises zip codes whose residents tend to be admitted, or referred to, the major hospitals in Minneapolis, even though the actual region extends well beyond the city limits (see fig. 5.1).[5] Individuals (and their utilization records) are allocated

---

4. A more difficult question is whether, at the margin, (productive) medical spending is worth what must be given up in terms of other nonmedical goods.

5. The geographical boundaries of the Miami and Minneapolis areas are defined using methods in the *Dartmouth Atlas of Health Care* (Wennberg and Cooper 1997). In the atlas, every zip code in the United States was allocated to a hospital service area (HSA); a local

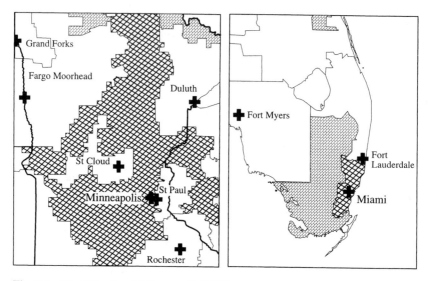

Fig. 5.1   The Miami and Minneapolis HRRs

Note: Because hospitals in Miami, and particularly Minneapolis, are magnets for surrounding areas, the actual HRRs for the two cities are quite a bit larger than the actual city boundaries. Note that even if a citizen of Miami, for example, received treatment in Fort Lauderdale, the utilization data is counted in Miami.

to Miami or Minneapolis not because they go to those hospitals, but because they live in zip codes where (typically) the majority of patients do go to such hospitals.

These two regions have been shown in prior research to have vastly different patterns of health care spending on a per capita basis. One problem inherent in comparing different regions is that they do in fact differ with regard to community-level disease patterns such as acute myocardial infarction (AMI) and stroke rates. However, even after correcting for such differences, there are still substantial differences in *per enrollee* rates of utilization (Wennberg and Cooper 1997; Skinner and Fisher 1997). For example, figure 5.2 summarizes data on differences in all per capita Medicare reimbursements, inpatient services, professional and laboratory services, and home health care (Wennberg and Cooper 1997). As the left-hand panel shows, the two cities are clearly at opposite ends of the spectrum in terms of overall Medicare spending. (Each of the fainter dots in

hospital (or more than one hospital in the same city or town) that served as a primary source of hospital care. The allocation of zip codes was done on the basis of a 100 percent sample of Medicare hospital discharges. In total, there were 3,436 HSAs in the United States. However, many of these HSAs were small in size, with low-volume local hospitals sending their patients to larger hospitals for complicated procedures. The atlas therefore allocated each of these HSAs to a hospital referral region (HRR); each HRR has at least one hospital that provides major cardiovascular and neurosurgical procedures.

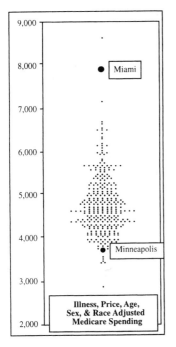

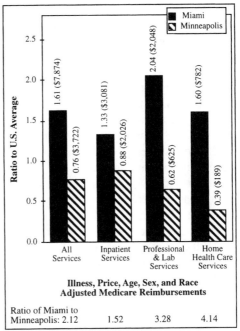

Fig. 5.2   Medicare reimbursements per enrollee, Miami and Minneapolis

Note: The left-hand panel gives the age, sex, race, price, and illness adjusted per person spending by the Medicare program in 1995 for the 306 hospital referral regions studied in the *Dartmouth Atlas of Health Care.* Spending varies nearly threefold from the lowest to the highest region. Total spending for residents of Miami is 2.1 times greater than Minneapolis on a per person basis. Inpatient reimbursements are 52 percent higher; those for professional and laboratory services are more than 3.2 times greater; home health spending is more than four times greater.

the diagram represents one of the other 306 hospital referral regions in the United States.)

In the right-hand panel, the height of the bars shows the ratio of price-illness-age-sex-race-adjusted levels of services to the United States. In Minneapolis, home health services are 39 percent of the national average, while in Miami they are 60 percent above average, meaning their ratio is roughly 4 to 1. By contrast, the ratio between Miami and Minneapolis for inpatient services is just 1.5 to 1, suggesting that services with the greatest discretionary (and profitability) component—home health and laboratory services—are the ones most sensitive to geographic location.

A different way of comparing spending is to look at expenditures and utilization during the last six months of life, a period of time when many Medicare enrollees are quite ill. Comparing spending in the last six months of life is useful for three reasons. First, it is more difficult to invoke plausible clinical scenarios that would explain the observed differences on the basis of difference in level of illness. Second, this spending has been shown elsewhere to account for a large fraction of total Medicare spending; thus, how people are treated near death has an important impact on the overall Medicare budget (Lubitz and Prihoda 1984). And third, spending levels among this group are probably particularly good markers of how intensely a region's medical system treats the very sickest, reflecting a sometimes unstated concern that too much is done for people who are going to die anyway.

Figure 5.3 shows that the Miami and Minneapolis regions are again at the opposite ends of the national distribution in the intensity of care during the last six months of life. Inpatient Medicare expenditures differ by about 2 to 1 ($14,212 in Miami versus $7,246 in Minneapolis), with an even greater divergence in the average number of ICU days per person in their last six months of life (the right-hand panel).

These are indicators of inpatient hospital use. A more telling comparison is the average number of physician visits billed to Medicare for those in their last six months of life. In Miami, the number of primary physician visits is certainly higher, 12.5 visits versus 7.1 visits, or a difference of 76 percent (fig. 5.4). The differences between the two regions, however, are

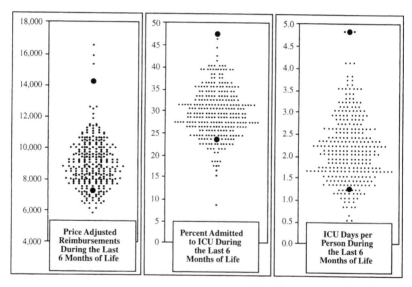

Fig. 5.3   Intensity of care in the last six months of life in Miami and Minneapolis
Note: Miami is the higher dot; Minneapolis is the lower dot. Among the regions, reimbursements for inpatient care varied more than 2.8-fold, from $5,831 to $16,571. Reimbursements for residents of Miami are about two times greater than Minneapolis (*left-hand panel*). The percentage of enrollees spending one or more days in intensive care varied from a low of about 9 percent to more than 45 percent. Miami is 2.1 times greater than Minneapolis (*center panel*). The numbers of days spent in intensive care varied more than ninefold. Miami enrollees spent 3.7 times more days in the ICU than Minneapolis enrollees (*right-hand panel*).

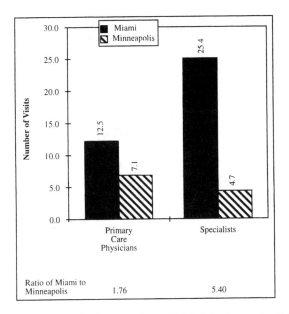

Fig. 5.4   Average number of primary and specialist visits (per patient) in the last six months of life, Minneapolis and Miami
Note: The average number of primary care physician visits is higher in Miami than in Minneapolis (12.5 visits versus 7.1), a difference of 76 percent. The average number of specialist visits is substantially higher in Miami (25.4 visits versus 4.7), a difference of 440 percent. Note that these averages are for the non-HMO population only, and a larger fraction of Miami residents are in HMOs.

most apparent in the average number of specialist visits during the last six months of life: 25.4 in Miami versus 4.7 in Minneapolis, a nearly fivefold difference. Some of this difference could be explained by the greater HMO penetration in Miami, meaning those people who remain in our Medicare claims data (the fee-for-service patients) are sicker. But even if we include the HMO patients in the denominator, thereby assuming they experience *no* visits to the doctor, the ratio of specialists visits in the region is still about 3 to 1. Thus we believe that the proliferation of specialist visits in Miami is central to the story of why these communities differ so much.

It is important to emphasize that the differences in indicators shown above largely reflect a different approach to the treatment of the chronically ill. For some surgical procedures, such as knee replacements and back surgery, rates of surgery are actually lower in Miami.

5.3   How to Interpret Population-Based Differences in Utilization

It is important to note that the mere existence of geographical variations does not imply the existence of either productive or allocative inefficiency.

One interpretation of variations across areas (theory 1) is they are simply the consequences of underlying differences in illness rates or in patient preferences for treatment. In this view, variations in surgical treatment for enlarged prostates are the consequence in part of mismeasurement; health care researchers are simply misled by geographic variations because they are unable to control for confounding factors. And what variation remains reflects geographical differences in preferences.

The second interpretation (theory 2) is that different hospitals and health care systems have very different protocols and standards for conducting surgery and treating illness. In some regions, many more men with enlarged prostates will end up having surgery or many more seriously ill patients will be treated in the ICU than their counterparts—with equivalent preferences and health status—living elsewhere. In this view, "location is destiny," or in the language of econometrics, location is an instrument.

Theory 1 and theory 2 have very different implications. In theory 1, the health care system is productively and allocatively efficient, at least in the sense that all American citizens are receiving treatment consistent with their preferences, and according to a well-established body of scientific evidence and knowledge. Not every hospital will be hugging the productively efficient production "envelope," of course, because of economies of scale and volume in the treatment of common diseases (e.g., McClellan and Staiger, chap. 3 in this volume). But the important policy issues are not whether the intensity of services in a community such as Miami is much different from that in Minneapolis, but instead whether these regions (together with other regions in the United States) lead to marginal benefits that exceed marginal costs at the national level. Not surprisingly, then, an important policy debate under theory 1 is whether rationing health care on a national level is the appropriate policy to contain potential overproduction in medical technology and services.[6]

According to theory 2, it is difficult to address national priorities in health care spending if in fact different communities are following such widely different treatment patterns. Instead, the immediate question is, Which community's rate is right? Theory 2 thus points to exploiting empirically the natural experiments afforded by the geographic variation phenomenon by measuring the correlation between inputs of resources and outputs of health. As we discuss below, the implications of theory 2 are not simply about allocative efficiency (Which rate is right?) but productive efficiency broadly defined (Are some rates always wrong?).

In figure 5.5 (upper panel), we consider one way to characterize these differences, where we summarize the intensity of care, Z, on the horizontal

---

6. For a discussion of global budget caps, see Aaron (1992). A uniform percentage decrease in health care costs will have a much different impact than setting a fixed per capita level of spending across regions.

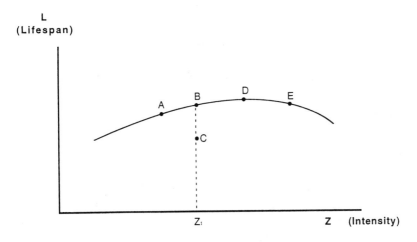

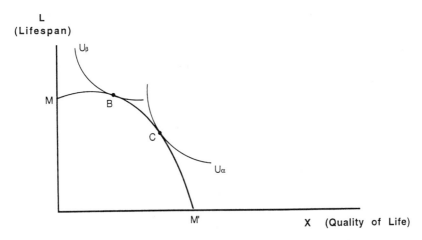

Fig. 5.5   A diagrammatic representation of efficiency in health care
Note: In the upper panel, the trade-off between the (dollar) intensity of inputs into health care is contrasted with community-level expected lifespan. Point D, for example, corresponds to the maximal level of lifespan given existing medical technology. In the lower panel, a trade-off is shown between lifespan and quality of life.

axis (measured in dollars) and life-year extension on the vertical axis. According to theory 1, most hospitals experience similar intensities of service. Not all health care systems are at the production possibility frontier, but they do not vary significantly in terms of their intensity of care, and any variation that does occur is primarily because of differences in patient health or patient preferences. For example, more people may die in hospital in Miami, but it is because of a lack of family support (or even available nursing home beds) rather than differences in the underlying approach to treating sick patients.[7] According to this theory, we would describe hospitals as clustering around one of the points (perhaps point A), or if differences in preferences lead to differences in intensity of care, along a continuum between points A and B. Thus, it makes sense to talk about national standards of care, because most hospitals are delivering about the same level of intensity.

According to theory 2, however, there exist wide variations in how a given disease is treated, leading to much more variable levels of intensity, perhaps ranging from points A to E or beyond, with additional dispersion below the production frontier, as represented perhaps by point C. These exogenous variations, however, can be used to gain information about the nature and shape of the production function. By comparing outcomes between high-intensity and low-intensity areas, one can begin to answer the question of whether the health care system is described best by clusters around point A or at the flat of the curve (point D), where more health spending yields nothing in expected lifespan. Or are some regions on the wrong side of the curve, point E, where the iatrogenic costs of health interventions actually lead to worse outcomes (Fisher et al. 1999)? For hospital procedures devoted simply to helping people to survive, such as ICU facilities, risk-adjusted survival rates are a good measure of outcomes.

The analysis becomes more complex once one recognizes the essential multidimensionality of outcomes. For many procedures, the objective is not to maximize lifespan but to improve the overall quality of life. Chemotherapy may have proven benefits in extending survival rates for breast cancer, but it can come at a large cost to the patient. Furthermore, there is tremendous heterogeneity across patients in the trade-off; in one recent study, 12 percent of the sample would undergo standard chemotherapy for metastatic breast cancer in return for an expected additional lifespan of just one week. By contrast, 28 percent of the sample would not undergo standard chemotherapy in return for increased longevity of 18 months (McQuellon et al. 1995). Similarly, there is wide variation in preferences for chemotherapy to treat advanced-stage non–small cell lung cancer (Brundage, Davidson, and Mackillop 1997; Silvestri, Pritchard, and Welch 1998; McNeil et al. 1982). For example, in the Silvestri, Pritchard, and Welch study, all respondents had been treated with chemotherapy previously for advanced non–small cell lung cancer. The authors write about the patients' response to a hypothetical case involving the decision of whether to elect chemotherapy: "In the setting of severe toxicity, for example, 5 (6%) patients would choose chemotherapy for only 1 week of additional survival while 9 (11%) others would not choose the therapy even when offered 24 months of additional survival. In both scenarios, however, less than half the patients would choose chemotherapy given the

7. Although Miami does not lack for home health care services on a per capita basis.

'best guess' of the actual average benefit—a 3 month difference in median survival." This heterogeneity in preferences makes it very hard to calculate a single "quality-adjusted life year" (QALY). For the average person, the loss in functioning and pain is not worth the extra life years; thus, the QALY associated with chemotherapy would probably be negative. But clearly, the average QALY is relevant only for the average person. For some people, the QALY associated with chemotherapy is positive; for others, clearly negative. Thus the upper panel of figure 5.5 is not an adequate representation of the types of trade-offs facing individual patients.

The lower panel in figure 5.5 demonstrates the problem of treatment choice when preferences are heterogeneous. For simplicity, we consider just the trade-off between lifespan and a generic quality of life measure X, shown on the horizontal axis. Thus we are implicitly considering a three-good utility function that depends on nonmedical consumption $Y - Z$, where Y is income and Z (as before) is health care resources, lifespan L, and quality of life X. Medical technology provides a trade-off between X and L; the opportunity set MM' is shown for a given level of Z equal to Z_1. This represents the possible trade-offs between lifespan and quality of life given the current state of medical technology. (A similar trade-off curve exists for lower or higher levels of Z; one hopes that more Z yields a trade-off curve to the northeast of MM'.) In this case, the point C, which appears to be productively inefficient in the upper panel, is actually preferred by some patients, shown by the α preference ordering, while point B is preferred by a different group of patients with preference orderings β. This is why we cannot simply "quality adjust" those life years; the different groups α and β disagree over the relative weights placed on lifespan extension versus quality of life.

The problem becomes more complicated once one accounts for a third class of medical procedures that are unlikely to have much impact on life expectancy but that will have a larger effect on different aspects of the quality of life. For example, it is unlikely that surgical treatment for an enlarged prostate will have a large impact on expected lifespan, but it might be expected to affect symptoms (positively) and sexual functioning or incontinence (adversely). Thus, the decision to choose surgical treatment of enlarged prostates is taken along the flat of the survival curve (point D), where increased spending will yield no benefit in terms of lifespan but will affect different dimensions of one's quality of life, X.

There are two points here. The first is that "best practice" medical care does not guarantee allocative efficiency. There is often a wide range of treatments available for a given problem, and which treatment is chosen should depend on the preferences of the individual patient (i.e., whether he or she is an α or β type). If an α type receives treatment option B (perhaps because the alternative, C, was not offered or was downplayed by the physician), then allocative inefficiency would result. And second, it seems unlikely that preferences among the various choices could vary systematically across regions in a way to generate such large differences in treatment patterns, particularly if the regions are (on average) in the vicinity of point D. Of course, without further research on actual preferences in the two regions, we cannot *prove* that preferences do not differ to the degree suggested by treatment variation, but the evidence (discussed below) suggests that, if anything, individuals prefer the less-intensive options when given the choice.[8]

5.4   Do Health Differences Explain Variation in End-of-Life Expenditures?

We return to asking whether theory 1 might explain the dramatic differences in health care spending in the last six months of life. This question is best seen as part of the very large and sometimes contentious debate over "small area variations." It is well established that differences in per capita medical utilization across the United States and other countries exists. Typically, researchers include as many "supply-" and "demand-" related measures as can be mustered, but there is still a large residual that remains. The battle is over the residual: Does it represent exogenous differences in practice patterns (theory 2), or does it represent preference or health-related factors that are simply not measured by the researcher (theory 1)? Without delving into details, we simply note that most research is unable to explain the variations using conventional measures of health needs (e.g., Wennberg and Fowler 1977; Henke and Epstein 1991; Wennberg and Cooper 1997; Fisher et al. 1994; Wennberg et al. 1989; Gruber and Owings 1996; Skinner and Fisher 1997; although see Green and Becker 1994).[9] Thus, under theory 1, regional variation is explained more by tastes (or unmeasured health needs), perhaps reflected in the decision of individuals to initiate contact with physicians (e.g., Escarce 1993; Folland and Stano 1989). The issue of whether to initiate contact with physicians, however, is not likely to be as important among this sample of Medicare enrollees in the last six months of life. Instead, the observed differences most likely reflect the *intensity* of care.

Still, it may be the case that the intensity of medical spending in the last

8. A final issue is whether people choosing between more- and less-intensive treatment on the basis of quality of life, as in the prostate example above, should face copayments for the more-intensive treatment. If, in fact, survival rates are not affected by the decision to treat enlarged prostates surgically, then might not patients be required to face some fraction of the extra resource cost?

9. There is also a literature suggesting that small area variations can be explained simply by random variation in averages of regions with small sample sizes (Diehr et al. 1990). However, the research using often 100 percent samples of Medicare data (e.g., Wennberg and Cooper 1997) shows that the regional variation is not due to small sample problems.

Table 5.1   **Regression Explaining Medicare Part A Reimbursements in the Last Six Months of Life, by Hospital Referral Region**

	Regression Excluding Health Resource Variables		Regression Including Health Resource Variables	
	Coefficient	t-Statistic	Coefficient	t-Statistic
AMI	−170.8	2.9	−93.0	2.0
Stroke (CVA)	53.9	0.6	83.4	1.2
GI bleeding	770.2	5.1	341.9	2.8
Lung cancer	1,185.4	4.1	−23.9	0.1
Hip fractures	−514.1	3.8	−343.9	3.1
Hospital beds			1,146.2	8.8
Specialist MD			38.4	7.2
Primary MD			−8.0	0.7
Family practice MD			14.26	3.5
Constant	4,505.6	3.2	1,609.5	1.4

Note: The dependent variable is the price-adjusted average Medicare reimbursements per person in their last six months of life. In the first regression, $R^2 = 0.18$; in the second $R^2 = 0.54$. Each observation corresponds to a hospital referral region (HRR), of which there are 306. All regressions are weighted by the number of Medicare enrollees in the HRR. All of these variables (except the percent not-for-profit) have been adjusted for age, sex, and race differences; thus, we do not include these variables into the regression.

six months of life is the consequence of patients in some regions dying of diseases requiring more costly palliative care. Thus, we would like to test the hypothesis of whether end-of-life expenditures are related to the mix of diseases in the hospital referral region (HRR). To do this, we regress the HRR-level measures of average inpatient spending in the last six months of life as a function of Medicare hospital admissions in 1994–95 for a set of common diseases that are reasonable measures of underlying community health levels: AMI, stroke, gastrointestinal (GI) bleeding, hip fractures, and lung and colon cancer (see Wennberg and Cooper 1997 for details). All regressions were weighted by the Medicare population in each of the 306 HRRs.

Table 5.1 displays coefficients from this first regression correlating just health indicators with spending near the end of life. There are generally significant effects, and the adjusted R^2 is 0.18. The coefficient on AMI, for example, is negative; this suggests that people with AMI are more likely to die quicker, and at lower cost, than people with other diseases such as lung or colon cancer.[10] While these diseases account for a large fraction of overall mortality, they explain only a small fraction of the variance in spending near the end of life.

10. We have included both types of cancer in one category because of relatively small sample sizes, particularly in later regressions.

A more general regression model is also presented in table 5.1 that includes resource levels: hospital beds per thousand, specialist MDs per 100,000, primary care MDs per 100,000, and family practitioners per 100,000. The adjusted R^2 rises to 0.54, and the age-sex-race-adjusted bed capacity is highly significant. The impact of primary care physicians on Medicare end-of-life spending is not significant (and is, in fact, negative), although the effect of family practitioners—holding constant the number of overall primary care physicians—is positive with a modest coefficient. However, the impact of specialists is of the greatest magnitude and significance. One could argue, of course, that in the long term, the supply of physicians in Miami and Minneapolis is not random; perhaps physicians (or specialists) are attracted to Miami because of the heavy volume of practice. The point remains that the characteristics of the regions that should matter most under theory 1 for end-of-life spending—disease burdens—explain less than 7 percent of the overall difference between Miami ($14,212) and Minneapolis ($7,246). In sum, we find it plausible to adopt, as a working hypothesis, that Medicare spending in the last six months of life contains a strong degree of exogeneity across regions.[11]

5.5 Does the Higher Spending Lead to Better Outcomes?

Even if there are real differences in how people get treated among areas, it still may be the case that people in regions with high levels of health care do better; thus, the extra expenditures in Miami could be justified by the improved health status of its population.[12]

We address this question in two ways, both using data from the entire United States. First, we consider whether differences in end-of-life spending have an impact on the overall age-sex-race-adjusted mortality rates in the United States. Using the statistical methods developed in Fisher et al. (1999), we perform a logistic regression on life expectancy for a 20 percent sample of the Medicare population (more than 5 million individuals), controlling for a wide battery of possible confounding factors such as levels of disability, poverty rates, and underlying levels of the five types of diseases noted above. Table 5.2 provides estimates of the coefficient of interest—the partial impact of spending in the last six months of life on mor-

11. Given that these two cities were chosen on the basis of their extreme differences in treatment patterns, it might be expected that they would exhibit the greatest deviation from the norm. The point holds, however, for other regions also. Note also that our claim to exogeneity with respect to spending patterns on patients near death does not require that one accept a "supplier-induced demand" view of the health care system, only that variations in medical spending on patients near death is not simply the consequence of health differences.

12. Thus our approach is similar to those comparing intensity of care and outcomes in New Haven and Boston; see Fisher et al. (1994) and Wennberg et al. (1989).

Table 5.2   Logistic Regression of Mortality in the Medicare Population

Variable	Odds Ratio	95% Lower Boundary	95% Upper Boundary	Significance
Spending in last 6 months	1.001	0.999	1.003	0.408
ICU days in last 6 months	1.008	1.003	1.014	0.002

Note: In the table above, the dependent variable is whether the individual lived or died in the benchmark year of 1990. The logistics odds ratio is shown for price-adjusted expenditures in the last six months of life, or for the average number of days spent in an ICU in the last six months of life. These variables (for 1994–95) are calculated for each hospital service area, of which there are 3,436 in the United States. Thus, the level of analysis is at a finer level of geography than for the standard hospital referral region used in most of the other statistical analyses. There are more than 5 million observations in the regression. This regression is adopted from Fisher et al. (1999). Covariates include age-sex-race-specific cells, and from the census: median family income (for blacks and whites separately) in the population over 65, percent of population 65+ below the poverty level, education (less than grade 12, high school graduates, and college graduates), percent in rural areas, percent in urbanized areas, percent with work disabilities, self-care limitations, and mobility limitations (all 65+).

tality—along with a description of the additional variables; also see the appendix for a full set of regression results.

Briefly, there appears to be little correlation between the intensity of care near the end of life and mortality rates, whether intensity is measured by spending, days in the hospital, or ICU days near the end of life. If anything, there is a slight positive (and highly significant) correlation between ICU days and mortality rates; an increase of 1.0 in the average number of ICU days in the last six months of life is predicted to increase mortality rates by 0.8 percent.

One objection to this analysis is that there may be reverse causation; sicker regions would tend to have higher spending near the end of life, and hence generate a spurious correlation between the two variables (possibly masking the true negative correlation). This objection, however, carries less weight given that we are restricting our measure of spending to the universe of people near death. Sicker communities might well spend more per Medicare enrollee and experience a higher mortality rate, but it is not clear that sicker communities would spend more *per person* for the set of people who die. Still, it is useful to consider this question using a different approach that focuses on disease-specific mortality rates.

We selected a 5 percent sample of Medicare enrollees who were diagnosed with diseases that almost surely caused admission to the hospital—AMI, stroke, GI bleeding, hip fractures, and lung/colon cancer—for the two-year period 1992–93. Conditional on having an AMI or stroke, one might expect that the underlying health status, and survival probabilities should be similar across areas, thus potentially correcting for the reverse causality problem. As our marker for the intensity of health care in the

Table 5.3   Logistic Regressions of Mortality in the Medicare Population for Five Specific Health Conditions

Mortality Variable	Odds Ratio	95% Lower Boundary	95% Upper Boundary	Significance (p Value)
6-month (full sample)	0.998	0.986	1.010	0.762
6-month (full sample)[a]	1.015	0.986	1.045	0.321
90-day (full sample)	0.994	0.981	1.007	0.348
6-month (AMI)	0.989	0.968	1.011	0.333
6-month (stroke)	0.994	0.974	1.015	0.566
6-month (hip fracture)	1.019	0.991	1.048	0.187
6-month (GI bleed)	1.003	0.972	1.034	0.173
6-month (cancer)	0.997	0.949	1.047	0.892

Note: The dependent variable is whether the individual lived or died within the 6-month (or 90-day) period, conditional on having been admitted to hospital for one of the five initiating conditions during the years 1992–93. The logistic odds ratio is shown for price-adjusted expenditures in the last six months of life (in units of $1,000) by HRR or (as in row 2) the average number of ICU days by HRR, again in the last six months of life. The overall sample size is 53,564. Average 6-month mortality rates are 22.6 percent; average 90-day rates are 18.7 percent.

[a]This logistics odds ratio is shown for the average number of ICU days in the last six months, by HRR.

region (or HRR), we also include the average Medicare spending and average number of ICU days for each HRR during the last six months of life (for all residents in 1994–95).[13]

We also include as independent variables controls for age, sex, and race; details of the logistic analysis are reported in table 5.3, with the full results from one regression shown in the appendix. Once again, there does not appear to be any positive impact on mortality of the region-level intensity of care for enrollees in the last six months of life (either measured in dollar terms or in ICU days).

One might object to this analysis because end-of-life spending is probably accounted for largely by treatment for chronic diseases, not for sudden medical emergencies such as AMI and stroke; thus, our indicator may not summarize well how a given AMI or stroke would be treated. Another way to approach this problem is to calculate the *disease-specific* levels of health care spending by HRR. We do this by first regressing Medicare reimbursements, at the individual level, on age, sex, race, and illness dummy variables. This regression reflects possible differences in Medicare spending as the consequence of demographic or illness variation across regions. We then average the residuals in each region (after controlling for these demographic and illness factors); these HRR-level constructed

---

13. While these data are from the period 1992–93 and the end of life data are from the period 1994–95, the temporal mismatch is not likely to bias our results substantially, given the secular stability in spending patterns of HRRs.

residuals were highly correlated with HRR-level spending in the last six months of life.[14] We then used the HRR-level residuals in a second-stage regression seeking to explain mortality rates, with insignificant results (regressions not reported). We regard these results as preliminary, however, given the larger sample sizes necessary for statistical power.

Of course, it could be that our measure of outcome, survival, does not adequately reflect the true underlying quality of life enjoyed by patients in Miami over those in Minneapolis. While we have no direct evidence on quality-of-life outcomes in the two regions, we can turn to more general evidence from research on whether patients in fact prefer these more intensive forms of treatment.

5.6   Do Patients Prefer More Intensive Levels of Health Care? The Case of Surgery

In this section, we return to the issue of preferences in health care and to the notion that specific surgical procedures could improve the quality of life even if survival rates are not improved (or worsened). Thus, we seek to address whether, in fact, patients *prefer* the more intensive patterns of health care. In contrast to treatment intensity during the last six months of life, the goal of surgery is often to increase the quality of life, not the length of life. In fact, the risks inherent in surgery often mean that improvements in the quality of life come at the cost of a small increase in the chance of early death. But length of life versus quality of life is not the only trade-off. For example, most patients who undergo surgery for an enlarged prostate gland experience a change in sexual function (retrograde ejaculation), and there is a risk of incontinence and impotence. Men with enlarged prostates thus face a dilemma: Although surgery provides the best option for reducing symptoms, it involves trade-offs with tangible risks. Men and women with stable angina benefit more in terms of immediate reduction in symptoms by undergoing coronary artery revascularization. But again, there are trade-offs. For example, among the Medicare population, mortality from bypass surgery is about 2 percent; a substantial number of those who undergo this operation experience a loss in short-term memory and other impairments of cognition.

Research shows that men, when fully informed about the options and their possible consequences, differ substantially in their preferences for surgery. For the case of enlarged prostates, the objective of the surgery is to improve the *symptoms,* including difficulty or strain in urination. In one study, a sample of men with prostate symptoms was presented with

---

14. In other words, there is a strong HRR-level correlation between the intensity of spending in the last six months of life and the intensity of spending more generally for these common acute conditions.

Table 5.4   Factors Predicting Choice of Surgery for Enlarged Prostate Gland

Variable	Odds Ratio	95% Confidence Interval
Symptom score		
Mild	0.09	0.01, 0.72
Moderate		
Severe	1.48	0.6, 3.6
Rating of symptoms		
Positive/mixed		
Negative	7.0	2.9, 16.6
Rating of impotence		
Positive/mixed		
Negative	0.20	0.08, 0.48

Source: Barry et al. (1995).

Note: $N = 347$; 32 of these men underwent a prostatectomy. The table presents the results of a logistic regression model to predict choice of surgery. Symptoms are whether the patient experiences difficulty with urinating. Although in the univariate model patients with severe symptoms were 2.4 times more likely to choose surgery than those who were moderately symptomatic, only 21 percent of those with severe symptoms actually choose surgery. In the multivariate model, the odds ratio dropped to 1.48 and was no longer significant. By contrast, the ratings patients gave to their symptoms (i.e., how much they were bothered by them) and concern about impotence were strong predictors of choice.

information about the risks and benefits of surgery, and then asked about their own preferences (Barry et al. 1995); a summary of results from a logistic regression is shown in table 5.4. The partial effect of severe (rather than moderate) symptoms is to raise the chance of choosing surgery (odds ratio of 1.48, or an increase of 48 percent), but the results are not significant.[15] By contrast, two much better (and significant) predictors of whether the patient chooses surgery were (1) if the given symptoms bothered the patient (odds ratio of 7.0) and (2) the degree of concern about the chance of impotence (odds ratio of 0.2). In other words, the most important predictors of whether the men chose surgery was less the severity of the symptoms, and more the degree to which the symptoms bothered the patient and their concerns about the possibility of impotence. Thus, geographical regions have the potential for significant allocative inefficiency, even if their average rates are "right." The necessary condition for efficiency is that the patients desiring surgery are the ones that get it and the patients who *don't* want surgery don't get it.

Two experiments designed to study the effects of shared decision making on the rates of surgery provide an insight into the extent that surgery may be misallocated in the United States. The first, conducted in two staff model HMOs, implemented a change in the way clinical decisions were

15. A mild symptom score reduced (significantly) the odds of having surgery. However, mildly symptomatic men generally do worse after surgery and probably should not be offered the option.

made for prostate surgery. After viewing an interactive video that informed patients about the risks and benefits of alternative treatment, patients were encouraged to choose the treatment they would prefer. Surgery rates were measured before and after the video was introduced, and also with reference to a control population. In each HMO, rates dropped about 40 percent, suggesting that the amount of surgery formally "prescribed" by the HMO exceeded the amount that informed patients wanted (Wagner et al. 1995). The resulting demand for prostate surgery is shown in figure 5.6; interestingly, this benchmark was less than virtually every region in the United States. Similarly, a randomized trial of a shared decision making program for treatment of coronary artery disease suggests that patient demand for revascularization (at least in Canada) may be lower than the rate of revascularization in nearly every HRR in the United States; see figure 5.6 (Morgan et al. 1997).

These findings suggest a point that should be easily absorbed by econo-

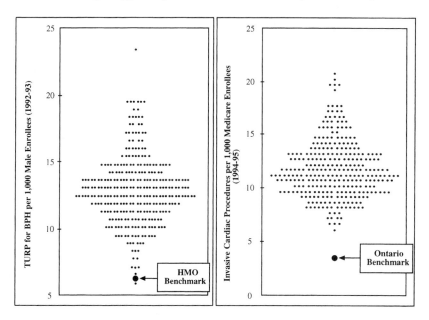

Fig. 5.6   Actual and desired rates of surgery for enlarged prostate and angina
Source: Wagner et al. (1995); Morgan et al. (1997).
Note: The distribution of rates in the left-hand panel is for surgery for enlarged prostate gland (benign prostatic hyperplasia [BPH]) among Medicare enrollees living in the nation's 306 hospital referral regions. The distribution in the right-hand panel is for coronary artery revascularization. A study of the effects of involving patients directly in their choice of surgery was conducted among patients with enlarged prostates in two staff model HMOs and among patients with angina in Toronto, Canada. In the prostate study, when patients were fully informed about the risk and benefits of alternative treatments and encouraged to participate actively in the choice of treatment, the population-based rate of surgery dropped 40 percent compared to controls. In the Ontario study, the rate dropped about 24 percent, even though the baseline rate in Ontario was substantially less than any rate observed in the United States.

mists. If patients are both less enthusiastic about surgery than the national averages would suggest, and show heterogeneity in their underlying preferences toward outcomes from surgery, there is a potential Pareto improvement by allowing them to make their own choice, even if the choice is ultimately to defer to the physician's choice. In the cases considered above, society gains: Patient welfare is improved, and expenditures on health care are reduced.

5.7 Discussion and Conclusion

Regions across the United States appear to have adopted much different strategies for treating Medicare patients. In this paper, we compare expenditures and ICU utilization across these hospital referral regions for elderly people in their last six months. We choose people in the last six months of life because they are all quite sick, and thus we can partially control for geographical differences in the underlying levels of disease. Medicare expenditures in the last six months of life are twice as high in Miami as in Minneapolis, and the average number of specialist visits is nearly five times higher. We have argued that these differences are unlikely to be explained simply on the basis of differences in health status or even preferences. In sum, we find little support for our theory 1 (that variation in health care treatment simply reflects differences in preferences or in underlying health status) and much more support for the notion that the variation in health status is to some extent exogenous (theory 2).

Variation in Medicare spending alone does not necessarily imply inefficiency in the distribution of health care. After all, sick people in regions with more intensive treatment patterns may survive longer, thus (possibly) justifying the extra expenses. However, using two much larger samples of individuals—one a 20 percent sample of all Medicare enrollees and the other a 5 percent sample of Medicare patients hospitalized with AMI, stroke, GI bleeding, and cancer—we find no evidence that higher levels of spending translate into extended survival. But it may still be the case that people in the high-intensity areas prefer the more intensive treatment. And while we do not know conclusively that people in such regions would prefer more intensive health care, we do know that patients living in other areas, if provided with information to make their own choices, generally prefer less, not more, intensive health care. Thus, we conjecture that on the basis of economic efficiency, Miami may fall short of Minneapolis.

Our results may appear inconsistent with recent evidence documenting the striking secular gains in survival rates following heart attacks (e.g., Cutler et al. 1996).[16] However, our test for the effectiveness of health care relates solely to regional differences in the intensity of care in a given year, and hence for a given body of medical knowledge.

16. We are grateful to Frank Lichtenberg for pointing this out to us.

One question we are not yet able to answer is, Why do physicians and hospitals in Miami adopt such an intensive strategy for health care, and in Minneapolis, a much less intensive approach? One reason could be the sheer amount of resources in Miami: more hospital beds per thousand (3.2 versus 2.6) and more specialists (146 per 100,000 versus 100).[17] Another explanation could be the much higher ratio of for-profit hospital beds in Miami: 56 percent versus less than 2 percent in Minneapolis. But there is still a substantial residual left unexplained even after accounting for supply factors. And even these "causal" factors are suspect, since for-profit hospital chains or physicians may be most likely to locate where practice styles are most aggressive.[18]

Perhaps the for-profit hospitals in Miami exerted a larger impact on the not-for-profits because of more dense markets in Miami causing the not-for-profits to imitate the behavior of the for-profits, in the sense of Cutler and Horwitz (chap. 2 in this volume). Alternatively, the key to explaining why Miami is so different could be in the structure of physician groups rather than the hospitals.[19] The interaction between patient demand and physician behavior is also important in understanding the practice of medicine in Miami; perhaps elderly patients come to expect numerous referrals as the norm, and would suspect physicians who do *not* refer them to other physicians.

The differences in practice patterns between these two cities (and across the United States more generally) appear to be real, but they are somewhat resistant to an entirely economic structural explanation. Ultimately, some part of the story may be the (random) emergence of small groups of entrepreneurial physicians who set the practice style for the entire area. A recent *Wall Street Journal* article, for example, identified a single aggressive cardiology physicians group as the reason for why Lubbock, Texas, had one of the highest per capita rates of angioplasty in the country (Anders 1996).[20] Whether regional differences in Medicare utilization can ultimately be explained in a structural model of medical practice, or whether these regional differences are the outcome of a "path-dependent" process originating with a few entrepreneurial physicians, is a topic for future research.

17. There are also more primary care physicians in Miami (83 versus 68 per 100,000), although as noted above, primary care physicians are not correlated with Medicare spending in the last six months of life.

18. Even if physician supply, for example, is increased in Miami because of the more intensive practice style, we can still view the resulting treatment intensity as exogenous from the point of view of a production function.

19. One conference participant suggested that fraud could also play a part in the high number of physician visits in Miami. Ironically, were the difference attributed to fraud, the efficiency considerations would be much more benign. Fraud is simply transfers from the government to physicians without any real resource cost except the effort of signing forms and filing them. There is a real resource cost, the alternative activities of the physician, if the doctor is actually visiting the patient.

20. The group expanded by advertising in the *New England Journal of Medicine* for cardiologists seeking potential incomes in excess of $1 million.

Appendix

Table 5A.1   Logit Regression Explaining Mortality (from All Causes) in the Medicare Population

	Coefficient (95% Confidence Interval)		Coefficient (95% Confidence Interval)
Medicare spending in the last 6 months of life ($ thousands per capita)	.0015 (−.001, .004)	Percent in nursing home	.0540 (.048, .060)
AMI/100	.0347 (.021, .048)	Percent Hispanic	−.0126 (−.017, −.008)
CVA (stroke)/100	.0345 (.021, .048)	Percent single	.0218 (.0159, .0277)
Hip fracture/100	.0296 (.012, .047)	Percent high school dropout	.0440 (.037, .051)
Colon cancer/100	−.0128 (−.043, .018)	Percent high school graduate	.0386 (.033, .044)
Lung cancer/100	−.0364 (−.098, .026)	Medicare HMO percentage	.0016 (.001, .002)
Percent with income $15,000–$20,000	−.0240 (−.035, −.012)	Percent employed (> age 16)	.0531 (.048, .059)
Percent with income > $20,000	−.0265 (−.042, −.011)	Percent with working disability	.0352 (.027, .044)
Percent in poverty	−.0041 (−.011, .003)	Percent with self-care limitation	−.0083 (−.022, .005)
Percent moved	−.0010 (−.006, .004)	Percent with mobility limitation	.0213 (.007, .035)
Percent rural	−.002 (−.004, −.000)	Per capita MDs 150–200 per 100,000	.0123 (.001, .023)
Percent in city	.0052 (.004, .007)	Per capita MDs > 150–200 per 100,000	.004 (−.009, .017)

Note: The reported coefficients are for the logit regression index and are not odds ratios. These results control for age-sex-race dummy variables (i.e., a dummy variable for a nonblack female age 70–74) and regional dummy variables (coefficients not reported). The number of age-sex-race-zip-code cells is 311,146.

Table 5A.2   Logit Regression Explaining Mortality for a Cohort in the Medicare Population with Specific Diseases

	Coefficient (95% Confidence Interval)		Coefficient (95% Confidence Interval)
Medicare spending in the last 6 months of life ($ thousands per capita)	.0998 (0.986, 1.010)	Male age 75–79	1.802 (1.608, 2.021)
AMI/1,000	2.474 (2.314, 2.645)	Male age 80–84	2.475 (2.204, 2.778)
CVA (stroke)/1,000	2.323 (2.179, 2.476)	Male age 85–90	3.533 (3.106, 4.019)
GI bleeding/1,000	1.077 (0.999, 1.161)	Male age 90+	6.039 (5.168, 7.056)
Lung and colon cancer/1,000	1.014 (0.914, 1.125)	Female age 70–74	1.176 (1.044, 1.324)
For-profit ratio	1.094 (0.984, 1.217)	Female age 75–79	1.483 (1.325, 1.659)
Male age 65–69	0.964 (0.852, 1.092)	Female age 80–84	1.922 (1.723, 2.144)
Male age 70–74	1.311 (1.167, 1.474)	Female age 85–89	2.576 (2.305, 2.879)
		Female age 90+	3.829 (3.407, 4.302)

Note: Reported coefficients are the logistic odds ratios. Sample size = 53,564. Excluded categories are female age 70–74 and hip fracture.

References

Aaron, Henry J. 1992. Health Care Financing. In *Setting Domestic Priorities: What Can Government Do?* ed. Henry J. Aaron and Charles L. Schultze. Washington, D.C.: The Brookings Institution.

Anders, George. 1996. In Lubbock, Texas, a Weak Heart Gets the Full Treatment. *The Wall Street Journal,* 16 July, A1, A5.

Barry, Michael J., Floyd J. Fowler, Jr., Albert G. Mulley, Jr., Joseph V. Henderson, Jr., and John E. Wennberg. 1995. Patient Reaction to a Program Designed to Facilitate Patient Participation in Treatment Decisions for Benign Prostatic Hyperplasia. *Medical Care* 33 (8): 771–82.

Breyer, F. 1987. The Specification of a Hospital Cost Function: A Comment on the Recent Literature. *Journal of Health Economics* 6:147–58.

Brundage, M. D., J. R. Davidson, and W. J. Mackillop. 1997. Trading Treatment Toxicity for Survival in Locally Advanced Non-Small Cell Lung Cancer. *Journal of Clinical Oncology* 15:330–40.

Cutler, David M., Mark McClellan, Joseph P. Newhouse, and Dahlia Remler. 1996. Are Medical Prices Declining? NBER Working Paper no. 5750. Cambridge, Mass.: National Bureau of Economic Research.

Diehr, P., K. Cain, F. Connell, and E. Volinn. 1990. What Is Too Much Variation? The Null Hypothesis in Small Area Variation. *Health Services Research* 24: 741–71.

Escarce, Jose J. 1993. Would Eliminating Differences in Physician Practice Style Reduce Geographic Variations in Cataract Surgery Rates? *Medical Care* 31: 1106–18.

Fisher, Elliott S., John E. Wennberg, Therese A. Stukel, and Sandra M. Sharp. 1994. Hospital Readmission Rates for Cohorts of Medicare Beneficiaries in Boston and New Haven. *New England Journal of Medicine* 331:989–95.

Fisher, Elliott, John E. Wennberg, Therese A. Stukel, Jonathan Skinner, Sandra M. Sharp, Jean L. Freeman, and Alan M. Gittelsohn. 1999. Associations among Hospital Capacity, Utilization, and Mortality of U.S. Medicare Benificiaries. United States: Might More Be Worse? *Health Services Research.* Forthcoming.

Folland, S., and M. Stano. 1989. Sources of Small Area Variation in the Use of Medical Care. *Journal of Health Economics* 8:85–107.

Friedman, B. and M. V. Pauly. 1981. Cost Functions for a Service Firm with Variable Quality and Stochastic Demand: The Case of Hospitals. *Review of Economics and Statistics* 63:610–24.

Gaynor, M., and G. F. Anderson. 1995. Uncertain Demand, the Structure of Hospital Costs, and the Cost of Empty Hospital Beds. *Journal of Health Economics* 14 (3): 291–318.

Gold, Marthe R., Louise B. Russell, Joanna E. Siegel, and Milton C. Weinstein, eds. 1996. *Cost-Effectiveness in Health and Medicine.* New York: Oxford University Press.

Green, Lee A., and Mark P. Becker. 1994. Physician Decision Making and Variation in Hospital Admission Rates for Suspected Acute Cardiac Ischemia: A Tale of Two Cities. *Medical Care* 32 (11): 1086–97.

Gruber, Jonathan, and Maria Owings. 1996. Physician Financial Incentives and Cesarean Section Delivery. *Rand Journal of Economics* 27 (1): 99–123.

Henke, Curtis J., and Wallace V. Epstein. 1991. Practice Variation in Rheumatologists' Encounters with Their Patients Who Have Rheumatoid Arthritis. *Medical Care* 29 (8): 799–812.

Lubitz, James, and Ronald Prihoda. 1984. The Use and Costs of Medicare Expenditures in the Last 2 Years of Life. *Health Care Financing Review* 5 (3): 117–31.

McEachern, William A. 1994. *Economics: A Contemporary Introduction.* Cincinnati, Ohio: South-Western Publishing Co.

McNeil, Barbara, Stephen G. Pauker, Harold S. Sox, Jr., and Amos Tversky. 1982. On the Elicitation of Preferences for Alternative Therapies. *New England Journal of Medicine* 306 (21): 1259–62.

McQuellon, Richard P., Hyman B. Muss, Sara L. Hoffman, Greg Russell, Brenda Craven, and Suzanne B. Yellen. 1995. Patient Preferences for Treatment of Metastatic Breast Cancer: A Study of Women with Early-Stage Breast Cancer. *Journal of Clinical Oncology* 13 (4): 858–68.

Morgan, M. W., R. B. Deber, H. A. Llewellyn-Thomas, P. Gladstone, R. J. Cusimano, K. O'Rourke, and A. S. Detsky. 1997. A Randomized Trial of the Ischemic Heart Disease Shared Decision Making Program: An Evaluation of a Decision Aid. *Journal of General Internal Medicine* 12, no. 1 (April supp.): 62.

Rosko, Michael D., and Robert W. Broyles. 1988. *The Economics of Health Care: A Reference Handbook.* New York: Greenwood Press.

Silvestri, Gerard, Robert Pritchard, and H. Gilbert Welch. 1998. Preferences for Chemotherapy in Patients with Advanced Non-Small Cell Lung Cancer: Descriptive Study Based on Scripted Interviews. *British Medical Journal* 317 (7161): 771–75.

Skinner, Jonathan, and Elliott Fisher. 1997. Regional Disparities in Medicare Expenditures: An Opportunity for Reform. *National Tax Journal* 50 (3): 413–25.

Wagner, E. H., P. Barrett, M. J. Barry, W. Barlow, and F. J. Fowler. 1995. A Randomized Trial of a Multimedia Shared Decision-Making Program for Men Facing a Treatment Decision for Benign Prostatic Hyperplasia. *Medical Care* 33: 765–70.

Wennberg, John E., and Megan M. Cooper, eds. 1997. *The Dartmouth Atlas of Health Care 1998.* Chicago: American Hospital Publishing.

Wennberg, John E., and Floyd J. Fowler, Jr. 1977. A Test of Consumer Contribution to Small Area Variations in Health Care Delivery. *Journal of the Maine Medical Association* 68 (8): 275–79.

Wennberg, John E., J. L. Freeman, R. M. Shelton, and T. A. Bubolz. 1989. Hospital Use and Mortality among Medicare Beneficiaries in Boston and New Haven. *New England Journal of Medicine* 321 (17): 1168–73.

Market Forces, Diversification of Activity, and the Mission of Not-for-Profit Hospitals

Richard G. Frank and David S. Salkever

6.1 Introduction

Bradford Gray, in his introduction to the report *The New Health Care for Profit,* observed that "Our dominant medical institutions—hospitals—have their origins in charity and local government and have long been seen as serving the public interest. Nonprofit hospitals benefited from tax exemptions and had public funds and charitable donations as the primary sources of money for construction. Hospitals were seen by many as serving a distinct ethic. . . . Its obligation to its community is not measured by its net earnings, but by the service it renders . . ." (Gray 1983, 7). Much of the implicit contract reflected in the above passage has changed. Hospitals are less dominant as medical care providers than they once were, as more and more services have been developed outside the hospitals' walls (e.g., freestanding ambulatory surgery centers, imaging centers). Direct public funds and charitable donations are now far less important for capital projects than is debt financing and retained earnings. The basic mission of not-for-profit hospitals is often unclear to policy makers, consumers, and even donors who question the degree to which "community benefit" is in fact funded by public monies (through tax preferences) or private donations.

The picture is further complicated by new trends that are appearing

Richard G. Frank is professor of health economics at Harvard Medical School and a research associate of the National Bureau of Economic Research. David S. Salkever is professor of health economics at Johns Hopkins University and a research associate of the National Bureau of Economic Research.

This research was supported in part by a grant from the Alfred P. Sloan Foundation. The authors are grateful to David Cutler, Brad Gray, Frank Lichtenberg, and conference participants for reactions to ideas used in preparing this paper.

in the medical care marketplace. Not-for-profit community hospitals are increasingly engaging in new activities that have been organized as profit-making operations. Home health care companies, nursing homes, wellness centers, durable medical equipment companies, real estate partnerships, and health clubs are among the for-profit enterprises that are commonly reported by not-for-profit hospitals. Accompanying the expansion of joint ventures and the creation of profit-making subsidiaries are a number of new service offerings aimed at augmenting revenues and retained earnings. These services include satellite clinics, urgent care centers, and industrial medicine centers. It appears that the rate of revenue growth for these new enterprises exceeds the rate of growth of "traditional" hospital revenue sources such as charitable giving and third-party payment for inpatient and outpatient care. The end result is a concern that the necessity of engaging in new revenue-generating activities that are not part of the traditional core services and populations of the hospital may compromise traditional notions of the not-for-profit hospital's mission, such as serving the medically indigent.[1]

In this paper we conduct an initial exploration of the links between some of the new developments in the health care marketplace and the adherence of not-for-profit hospitals to some of their traditional community-oriented services. The paper is organized into four sections. Following this introduction, we review some overall trends in the hospital market. Section 6.3 gives a very brief exposition, at a conceptual level, of some possible connections between diversification and supply of public goods or "community benefit." Section 6.4 is a detailed report on focus groups with hospital executives that explored possible links between not-for-profit status, diversification, and public goods. Finally, section 6.5 makes some observations on what has been learned and proposes direction for further investigation.

6.2   Trends in the Market for Hospital Services

The not-for-profit form remains dominant in the market for hospital services. Table 6.1 presents data from the American Hospital Association (AHA) on the numbers of community hospitals and beds by ownership category. Overall, the total number of community hospital beds has fallen by about 13 percent from the peak in 1985. The number of beds in not-for-profit hospitals has declined about 14 percent since the peak. The result, as indicated in the table, is great stability in the share of beds accounted for by not-for-profit community hospitals at 70 percent over the

1. Recent empirical support for this concern is reported by Young, Desai, and Lucas (1997) who find little evidence of declines in uncompensated care when not-for-profit community hospitals in California were acquired by for-profit corporations. The generalizability of this finding to other states has, however, been questioned (Shactman and Altman 1997).

Table 6.1   **Hospital Statistics**

	1970	1980	1985	1990	1995
No. not-for-profit	3,386	3,332	3,349	3,191	3,092
No. beds	592	692	707	657	610
No. for-profit	769	730	805	749	752
No. beds	53	87	104	101	106
No. public (nonfederal)	1,704	1,778	1,578	1,444	1,350
No. beds	204	209	189	169	157
No. combined	5,859	5,840	5,732	5,384	5,194
No. beds	849	988	1,000	927	873
Bed share (community hospitals, %)					
Not-for-profit	70.0	70.0	71.0	71.0	70.0
For-profit	6.2	8.8	10.4	10.9	12.1
Average bed size					
Not-for-profit	175	208	211	206	197
For-profit	69	119	129	135	141

Source: 1970 data from AHA (1987); data for 1980, 1985, 1990, and 1995 from AHA (1997).

past 25 years. It also suggests that the roughly doubling of the for-profit share of beds (from 6.2 percent to 12.1 percent) came almost entirely at the expense of the share accounted for by publicly owned community hospitals. Table 6.1 also points to the fact that while not-for-profit community hospitals are on average larger than their for-profit counterparts, the difference in size has been narrowing over time. This may be due in part to a convergence in the roles played by the two ownership forms (Sloan 1997).

During the 15 years reported, community hospitals have experienced substantial changes in their treatment patterns and revenues. This has, in part, been driven by changes in payment arrangements, such as Medicare's Prospective Payment System (PPS), more aggressive price negotiations with managed care organizations, and changes in community support. Admissions to community hospitals, overall, have declined by about 22 percent in the period from 1983 to 1995 (AHA 1997). Hospital stays have also declined, falling from an average of seven days in 1983 to slightly less than six days in 1995. Table 6.2 reports the annual average percentage growth in real community hospital revenues. The rate of growth in hospital revenues has dropped notably in real terms since the early 1980s. In 1996, for the first time, there was an actual fall in the level of hospital revenues as indicated by the negative rate of growth. Figure 6.1 shows the total (from all payers) payment-cost margins for various types of hospitals during the 1984–97 time period (PPS 1–14). Several trends are worth noting. The margins for both private for-profit and not-for-profit hospitals were at 8.75 percent and 7.75 percent, respectively, in 1984 and fell substantially during the mid-1980s. Not-for-profit hospital margins fell to about 4 per-

Table 6.2   Annual Percent Growth in Real Hospital Revenues

		Hospitals
Year	Overall	Outpatient
1981	7.5	9.8
1984	2.7	6.2
1988	5.1	6.4
1990	3.8	6.0
1996	−1.0	−0.5

Source: Prospective Payment Assessment Commission (1997).

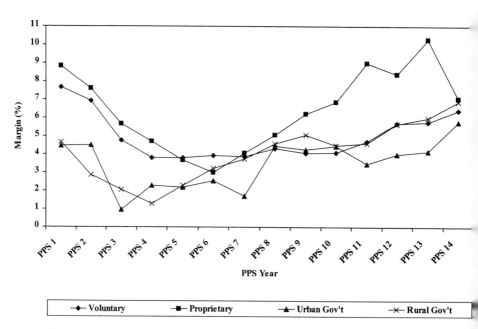

Fig. 6.1   Total margins by ownership category, first 14 years of PPS
Source: MedPac analysis of data from the Health Care Financing Administration.
Note: Data for PPS14 are partial and subject to revision.

cent by the latter part of the 1980s and have remained at a level of 4 to 4.5 percent since. For-profit hospital margins also fell sharply during the mid-1980s but have grown steadily since, returning to a 9 percent level in recent years. Public hospitals entered the PPS period at lower margin levels and experienced major reductions during the 1980s. They have returned to levels of 3 to 4.5 percent in recent years. Thus, while hospitals have generally faced increasingly tight revenues, both for-profit and not-for-profit entities have managed to reduce costs sufficiently to increase margins in recent years.

Table 6.3   **Not-for-Profit Revenue Shares and Philanthropy**

	1977	1982	1987	1992
Private contributions (%)	7.8	5.9	5.4	3.6
Private pay (%)	49.1	49.1	51.8	48.3
Government pay (%)	32.4	34.8	36.2	40.7
Other (%)	10.7	10.1	6.6	7.4
Contributions ($billions)	4.0	6.2	8.1	9.3
Real value of contributions ($billions)	4.00	3.89	4.33	4.00

Source: Independent Sector (1997).

Not-for-profit hospitals have traditionally relied on revenues from sales as well as revenues from charitable contributions. Researchers have pointed to the shifting roles of different sources of funds. Sloan et al. (1990) show that the reliance of not-for-profit hospitals on philanthropy has declined since the 1960s. They offer evidence suggesting that insurance coverage "crowds out" philanthropy. Frank, Salkever, and Mitchell (1990) provide evidence indicating that donations are negatively associated with hospital profits. Smith, Clement, and Wheeler (1995) estimate a positive association between "returns to the community" and donations to not-for-profit hospitals. One might therefore expect some increases in philanthropy in recent years when there was erosion of both insurance and hospital margins (during the middle part of the 1980s).[2]

Table 6.3 reports information on revenue shares of not-for-profit health care providers (predominantly hospitals) from different payer sources, and the nominal and real levels of philanthropy during the period 1977–92. Two important points emerge from the table. First, the share of revenues accounted for by private contributions to not-for-profit hospitals has continuously declined during the 15-year period observed, from 7.8 percent to 3.6 percent.[3] Second, even though the nominal value of contributions grew from $4 billion in 1977 to $9.3 billion in 1992 (a 133 percent increase), the real value of philanthropic contributions remained constant at $4 billion. Data on contributions to not-for-profit hospitals in California (table 6.4) mirrors this downward trend in the role of philanthropy. For the 174 hospitals reporting data in both 1990 and 1996, the size of contributions relative to gross patient revenues fell from 0.82 percent to 0.52 percent. (The much smaller percentage in the California data relative to the data in table 6.3 probably results from the fact that many contribu-

---

2. Sloan (1997) acknowledges that insurance has eroded in recent years. He argues that the erosion is quite small compared to the expansion in coverage that took place during the 1960s and 1970s.

3. The Independent Sector data have been criticized as being somewhat inaccurate. Thus, we direct the reader to the gross trend rather than a specific estimate of philanthropy.

Table 6.4   California Not-for-Profit Hospitals: Summary of Restricted and
                 Unrestricted Donations as a Share of Gross Patient Revenue

	1990	1996
Hospital mean	0.007	0.010
Median	0.0005	0.0004
Percentage > 0	65.52	62.64
Revenue weighted mean (mean donation/		
mean gross patient revenue)	0.0082	0.0052

Note: Data include only hospitals present as not-for-profit providers in 1990 and 1996;
$N = 174$.

tions are given to legally separate hospital foundations and, for accounting
reasons, are not captured on the state's hospital financial reports.)

These data notwithstanding, some observers of the industry have noted
an increased level of fundraising efforts by hospitals and particularly academic health centers (e.g., Ginzberg 1996, 72). There are several factors
that might explain why the aggregate donations data do not yet reflect a
corresponding increase: (1) lags in data collection, (2) incompleteness of
the available data on total donations, and (3) variability among nonprofit
hospitals, with increased fundraising efforts by academic health centers
and decreased efforts by other hospitals.

In addition to changing the level of fundraising effort, another possible
response by hospitals to constrained revenues from traditional sources is
to alter the composition of their products and activities toward more
profitable lines of business. Sloan (1997) notes that there is limited evidence on this point. Previous research noted that during the mid-1980s a
substantial portion of not-for-profit hospitals restructured (34 percent).
One common approach to restructuring was to create subsidiaries. Among
the central motivations for diversification by creation of subsidiaries is to
increase market share and to generate new sources of revenues (Clement,
D'Aunno, and Poyzer 1993). The evidence on the consequences of diversification is limited. Shortell, Morrison, and Hughes (1989) found that only
about 30 percent of the diversified services offered by eight multihospital
systems were profitable. Clement et al. (1993) examined diversification of
hospital activities in Virginia in 1987; they found that 62 percent of all the
hospitals were engaged in some type of nonhospital subsidiary. The key
results regarding the consequences of diversification suggest that older
subsidiaries and those that are directly engaged in health care services
tended to be the most profitable.

Other suggestive information from a recent study by the General Accounting Office (GAO) and from the American Hospital Association's annual survey points to an emerging trend toward diversification of both

for-profit and not-for-profit hospitals into for-profit joint ventures with various classes of business partners.[4] The GAO (1993) reported significant increases in the number of both not-for-profit and for-profit hospitals entering into joint ventures between 1984 and 1991. The GAO found a doubling of the percentage of not-for-profit hospitals engaged in joint ventures, from 9 to 18 percent. The corresponding change observed in for-profit hospitals was from 14 to 20 percent. Among the most commonly cited joint ventures were primary care clinics, imaging centers, and home health care companies. The GAO also noted that the joint ventures pursued by not-for-profits were less oriented toward serving those that cannot pay for their care than was the not-for-profit parent hospital. For example, 2.8 percent of spending by the joint ventures were devoted to care of the poor compared to 11.4 percent of spending by the parent hospital.

The diversification of activities by not-for-profit hospitals is also reflected by the results of the 1995 American Hospital Association's annual survey. Urban hospitals in particular are engaged in for-profit joint ventures. The AHA reports that 48 percent of urban hospitals are engaged in for-profit joint ventures. In addition, about 25 percent of all not-for-profit hospitals were part of a physician-hospital organization (PHO) and 18.6 percent participated in an independent practice association (IPA).

The trend toward diversification in response to financial pressure raises social concerns primarily because these new activities may divert hospitals from some of their traditional roles and social responsibilities. Students of hospital management have also questioned the wisdom of diversification because of the potential distraction created for management away from the core business of the hospital. Recent evidence on the supply of social goods offers little indication that there have been major shifts in the supply of hospital care to medically indigent populations. Mann et al. (1997) examined trends in uncompensated care based on national surveys for the period 1983–95. In the aggregate, the growth in value of uncompensated care, as reported by Mann et al., has been substantial, expanding by nearly 50 percent in real terms between 1983 and 1995. Since 1993 the rate of growth in uncompensated care has slowed. When viewed relative to either hospital spending or the number of uninsured people, the picture of uncompensated care changes. Hospital spending has grown more rapidly in recent years than has the value of uncompensated care. Uncompensated care accounted for 5.2 percent of hospital spending in 1983, 6.2 percent in 1987, and 6.1 percent in 1995. The value of uncompensated care per uninsured individual ranged from $401 in 1983, to $488 in 1988, to $431 in 1995, indicating that the number of uninsured people grew more quickly

---

4. Partners include groups of physicians, real estate developers, for-profit health care providers, and private investors.

during the 1990s than did the supply of uncompensated care.[5] The data on the share of uncompensated care provided by for-profit and not-for-profit hospitals show that the not-for-profit share has remained fixed at about 56 percent, while the for-profit share has grown from 4.1 percent to 5.3 percent. This compares to their shares of total spending in 1995 of 73 percent for not-for-profits and 8.2 percent for for-profits.

In summary, the evidence suggests that hospitals have experienced a period of tighter revenues and reduced demand for their traditional inpatient care services. Both not-for-profit and for-profit hospitals have recently experienced growth in their price-cost margins that appears to be explainable by efforts to reduce costs and by hospitals shifting the supply of services in the direction of more profitable services. Both the available statistics and the results of interviews suggest that the shift to more profitable lines of business by not-for-profit hospitals has been accomplished by the development of new products within the traditional hospital structure as well as creation of for-profit subsidiaries and joint ventures with for-profit organizations.

6.3   Conceptualizing the Relationship of Diversification to Community Benefit

In this section, we begin by sketching a conceptual model of the not-for-profit hospital that builds on our previous work and that of others (Frank and Salkever 1991; Gruber 1994; Thorpe and Phelps 1991) to characterize the potential issues relating to diversification. We begin with a hospital management objective function defined over net revenue (π), "public" goods (X), and the quantities of two services, H and Z, which are defined as "traditional" hospital services and new "diversified" services, respectively. Public goods may include, for example, participation in clinical research, education, or provision of care for the uninsured. We assume that the prices of H and Z services are set exogenously. The hospital may also receive revenue from the government as a subsidy for its provision of public goods; let r denote the exogenous per unit subsidy. The hospital also receives a flow of donations, D, which is assumed to depend upon the hospital's mix of services delivered; that is, $D = D(H, Z, X)$.[6] Costs incurred are based on the cost function $C(H, Z, X)$. Thus, the hospital manager's problem is

---

5. The estimates of the number of uninsured people must be interpreted with considerable caution because obtaining an accurate count for person years uninsured is quite difficult given the available data. It should also be noted that Mann et al. (1997) have made an effort to adjust the data based on the most recent methods for estimating the number of uninsured.

6. An alternative but equivalent formulation of the problem would make D depend explicitly on π. Thus, the above formulation might be most properly viewed as a reduced-form donation supply function.

(1) $$\underset{H,X,Z}{\text{Max}}\, U(\pi,\ H,\ X,\ Z),\ \text{subject to}$$

(2) $\pi = P_H H + P_Z Z + rX + D(H,\ Z,\ X) - C(H,\ Z,\ X).$[7]

First-order conditions for maximization imply the standard results that provision of H and Z should be pushed to the point where their price plus their direct marginal utility (relative to the marginal utility of net revenue) equals their "net" marginal cost, which includes both actual marginal production cost and any marginal impact of provision of H or Z on the flow of donations, D. (We assume that $U\pi > 0$ at the optimum.) If the management derives utility directly from provision of H and Z (i.e., U_H, $U_Z > 0$), the optimal supply of H and Z will occur at a point where the net marginal cost exceeds price for both services.[8] This implies that an exogenous upward shift in the hospital's donation supply function will tend to increase H and Z if these are "normal" goods to the hospital management.[9] The first-order conditions for optimal choice of X are similar except that the "price" of X is the per unit subsidy r.

The focus of our inquiry in this paper is the implications of diversification for the behavior of the nonprofit hospital in supplying "public" goods. Diversification here means choosing to move Z from a zero to positive level; increasing the level of Z could be viewed as increasing diversification. The corresponding comparative statics question would be: How does, say, optimal X change when P_Z increases relative to P_H? (The increase in P_Z could be viewed as an exogenous increase in the profit opportunities from diversification.)

How does an increase in P_Z affect the optimal amount of X? As might be expected, an unambiguous direction of effect cannot be determined in general. If one makes the simplifying assumptions that the managerial preference function is additively separable in profit and linear in profit, the sign and magnitude of the effect depends upon (1) the sign (presumably positive) and size of the cross-partials of U with respect to X, H, and Z, and (2) the corresponding cross-partials of the donation supply and

7. The assumption that the hospital chooses H, X, and Z implies either perfect competition or price regulation with persistent excess demand. The model could be expanded to allow for choice of nonprice "quality" or "amenity" attributes, with fixed prices, which affect the quantities of H, X, and Z that are actually "sold."

8. Note that the formulation given here yields a similar reduced form to that employed by Sloan et al. (1990). The models are slightly different in that we allow for multiple outputs and we do not explicitly incorporate solicitation effort. The reduced forms are similar, however, in that the hospital is viewed as choosing its "policy variables" (in our case H, X, and Z) taking account of the implications for this choice on donor supply.

9. It may be helpful to conceive of this formulation as a single-period condensed function of a multiperiod model in which hospitals need to accumulate capital in the present period to invest and expand the supply of H and Z in future periods. From that perspective, the increase in donations in the current period would be used in part to fund investment in subsequent periods and thereby expand H and/or Z.

cost function. If the latter are all zero, an increase in P_Z results in a decline in the supply of X.

While the implications of nonzero cross-partials for the donation supply and cost function are complex and interrelated, we offer several hypotheses about the signs of these cross-partials. These hypotheses are informally tested against anecdotal evidence from the focus groups below.

With respect to cross-partials and second partials in the cost function, we expect that all marginal costs tend to increase beyond some point as total output of H, X, and Z expands. We further propose that economies of scope may exist between H and X. For example, a hospital that treats more patients is better able to produce clinical research because it has more patients as potential research subjects. Similarly, a hospital that treats a larger number of paying patients can presumably supply any given volume of charity care to uninsured persons at lower cost because the problem of finding and triaging these uninsured persons is less costly when the total patient flow is larger.

With regard to the cross-partials of the donation-supply function, we expect that Z will tend to reduce the marginal donation revenue from an additional unit of X. In other words, increasing diversification will tend to reduce the supply response of donors to provision of public goods. The fact that the hospital is in many lines of business increases the uncertainty among donors that contributions will in fact go to support the public goods (X) that they wish to subsidize. The fact that the hospital is treating paying patients (H) will create this uncertainty, but if H is viewed by donors as complementary in production to X, their donation to the hospital is likely to result in an increased supply of X even if some of it is also used to expand the volume of H. In contrast, if some donation funds are channeled to increased production of Z, and economies of scope do not exist between Z and X, the hospital's increased production of Z will create uncertainty on the part of donors that their donations will in fact be used to increase the volume of X supplied in the future.[10] This can be depicted as a general downward shift in the donation supply function and as a downward shift in the marginal donation revenue from increasing the supply of X.

6.4 Mission and Diversification: Findings from the Focus Groups

Three focus groups were conducted during October 1997, one in Boston and two in Chicago. Hospitals invited to participate were midsize (150–400 beds) not-for-profit community hospitals. Major academic medical centers were not invited. The 14 participating hospitals generally fit this

10. The notion that uncertainty about the ultimate use of funds diminishes donation supply has been recently advanced and explored in a general context by Bilodeau and Slivinski (1996).

profile, with three exceptions. Representatives from a not-for-profit rehabilitation hospital, an academic medical center, and a for-profit community hospital were included in the focus groups. Each participant filled out a brief survey prior to the meeting of the focus group that elicited information on the participants (title, years of experience, and percent of time spent on planning issues) and the hospitals (name, bed size, statement of mission, and who is responsible for preserving the mission of the hospital) (see the appendix). Two of the three groups consisted of three participants and the third included eight individuals.[11] A professional moderator led each focus group discussion and followed a relatively broad outline (see the appendix) supplemented by specific examples and probes to be used to advance the discussion.[12] Below we report on the major points made by participants that were broadly held.

The purpose of the focus group discussions was to elicit views of hospital executives on four main topics: (1) the hospital's objective function (i.e., mission), (2) the role of philanthropy and fund raising in hospital financing, (3) the causes of the trend toward diversification, and (4) how hospitals are altering their service mix in response to the changing payment system.

6.4.1 Diversification

All participating hospitals were engaged in at least one or two joint ventures. The hospital executives pointed to two types of activities that might be viewed in terms of diversification. One approach related to the development of new products within the confines of the traditional hospital organization (that is, without joint venture partners or subsidiaries). These included occupational medicine clinics, urgent care centers, and wellness clinics. In some cases, wholly owned for-profit subsidiaries were created; for example, one hospital entered the nursing home business through a wholly owned subsidiary. Home health programs and durable medical equipment companies were also organized in this way. Another approach to diversification involved joint ventures and creation of jointly owned for-profit subsidiaries. Commonly mentioned joint-venture enterprises were primary care clinics, medical office buildings, surgi-centers, imaging centers, and health clubs. Most indicated that the diversified activities were profitable. The nursing homes, home health care companies, and medical office buildings were most often pointed to as successful profit-making enterprises.

---

11. One group began with four participants but was reduced to three because of concerns that the individual had not received clearance from the hospital CEO to discuss the issues that were proposed.

12. Videotapes, audio tapes, and transcripts of the three focus groups were provided the authors and are available for review subject to the confidentiality rules established with the participants.

6.4.2 Not-for-Profit Hospital Objectives

Several themes emerged in the discussion regarding the mission of not-for-profit community hospitals and how it might differ from the mission of for-profit hospitals. In the general statements of mission by the participating hospitals, all refer to provision of high-quality, low-cost health care to the community. They also claim the promotion of health in the community to be a goal of the organization and a relatively new aspect of mission. The basis for pursuing this goal appears to lie in (1) an expanded view of health and health care among both professionals and the general public, and (2) an approach to marketing that establishes the hospital's identity as the place to go for health care. It was especially notable that the only for-profit hospital represented in the group was very active in prevention/screening programs and other outreach activities involving mobile vans. The representative of the for-profit stated the following: "With prevention . . . really . . . you're looking for market share, whether you charge or do it free . . . you want people to think of you when they think of health care." All of the participants were in basic agreement with this assessment. The literature has generally viewed the provision of health promotion as being a social good, but its supply also appears to be consistent with profit maximization.

The importance of strong financial performance was noted repeatedly by the participants. The increasing emphasis on financial performance, in the face of competitive pressures and constraints from payers, was viewed as affecting the priority placed on other aspects of the hospital's mission. As a further indication of the strength of competitive uncertainties, most of the participants characterized their institutions as exposed to substantial longer term risk.

The participants acknowledged the role of the hospital as a charitable institution. Some noted the role of the hospital as the "provider of last resort"; others pointed to a duty to attend to underserved populations. It was nevertheless striking that treating the underserved or the medically indigent was generally not mentioned in the basic statement of mission nor as a major concern of most of the participants. In fact, there was substantial agreement that a hospital's commitment to serving the poor and uninsured is largely a consequence of location decisions taken decades earlier.

In summary, while the objective function proposed in section 6.3 is broadly consistent with the discussion in the focus groups, we view much of the discussion as implying a large weight on current and future profits in the face of perceived financial and competitive risks.

6.4.3 The Role of Philanthropy

The aggregate national data from the early 1990s reported earlier suggests that 3.6 percent of revenues were philanthropic contributions. Several participants in the focus groups estimated their philanthropic contributions to be approximately 1 percent of revenues. The academic medical center and one hospital located in a very affluent suburb reported that they received substantial levels of philanthropy but noted that they were likely to be exceptional. In general, fund raising was either a small activity or was part of a larger effort aimed at marketing services to the community and public relations. Several participants noted that this was a very substantial change from earlier years, when much of the capital for the original building or new construction came from philanthropy. They generally agreed that philanthropy could serve to provide "add-ons" that might be valued by patients or families but could not be paid for directly through insurance funds. One specific example was overnight accommodations in the hospital for parents whose children were inpatients. These "add-ons" were seen as valued by the community, but they could also be viewed (a view not explicitly expressed by the participants) as enhancing market share.

The discussion of fund raising yielded a number of important impressions regarding the link between hospital financial performance and donations (which is tied to the cross-partial of X and Z in the donation supply function described earlier). The observations made suggest that there are two specific indicators of financial performance that tend to affect donations: overall hospital margins and investment income. Members of a hospital's board of trustees in particular are aware of the financial performance of the hospital and typically have a variety of competing demands for their financial support. Thus, in years where hospitals have strong financial performances (large or growing margins and significant investment income), board members tend to offer less financial support. Similarly, the larger community is less well informed, but its donations still appear to be sensitive to the financial performance of the hospital. A number of participants also pointed to a general public perception that hospitals are somewhat "bloated" organizations and are therefore less deserving of financial support. The construction of large office buildings and the continued rise of hospital prices serve to reinforce this general perception. The end result is that donations play a very small role in hospital strategic decision making, and a larger share of donations now have restrictions placed on their use than was once the case.[13]

---

13. The reduction in flexibility is in part due to donors' concerns about the use of their contributions (the agency problem) and because fund raising appears to focus more on specific projects than may have once been the case.

6.4.4   Explaining Diversification/Joint Venture

One simple explanation for diversification, noted earlier, is that increased financial pressure leads hospitals to seek new sources of revenues and funds. That observation would explain a desire by hospitals to seek new "products" but not necessarily to choose for-profit subsidiaries or joint ventures as the means for attracting the new revenues. The discussion in the focus groups pointed to another important explanation for a number of the joint ventures and subsidiary activities of not-for-profit hospitals. The explanation is summarized here.

Most hospital markets in the nation are characterized by excess capacity and relatively high levels of competition. Thus, retaining and expanding market share has gained an increasingly central place in hospital strategic planning since the risk of rapid declines in market share are much clearer than in the past. Competition stems primarily from other not-for-profit hospitals but also from for-profit hospitals and more specialized health care providers (niche players). This latter group might include free-standing clinics, surgi-centers, and urgent care centers. At the same time, traditional relationships with office-based physicians have been altered. Physicians, who typically have admitting privileges at several hospitals, have become more aggressive in negotiating terms for their appointments with hospitals. This is in part due to new constraints on physician earnings as well as the advent of for-profit physician management companies that are well informed and experienced in negotiation with hospitals. The result is that the demand for hospital services is becoming less predictable.

Hospitals can potentially gain market share and reduce the uncertainty in demand by pursuing strategies that (1) offer new products directly to consumers and (2) make their relationships with office-based physicians more exclusive. Sloan (1997) also notes that "product" innovations are important means for hospitals to expand into more-profitable services. He cites examples of hospitals adopting new technologies, including cardiac catheterization programs, inpatient mental health units following implementation of PPS, and expansion of rehabilitation units in more recent years. Participants in the focus groups identified wellness programs, primary care clinics, and urgent care centers as examples of new services that are profitable. The primary care clinics were pointed to as being particularly important. This was because, in these subsidiaries, the physicians are often employees of the clinic. Thus, the hospital begins to develop a direct relationship with an organization that will steer patients in its direction. It was noted that some hospitals make an effort not to publicly link the clinic and the hospital, thereby reinforcing the impression of patients that one's "doctor just refers most of his/her cases to one hospital." In this manner, the hospital reduces its dependence on private, office-based attending physicians.

Joint ventures offer some similar advantages in terms of generating new streams of revenues and stabilizing demand. A number of for-profit joint ventures involve enterprises such as primary care clinics, home health companies, health and fitness clubs, and physician office buildings where partners in the joint ventures are physicians.[14] By creating a for-profit joint venture that can pay partners (shareholders) a portion of the net revenues and is backed by hospital assets and access to capital, the hospital strengthens its ties with physicians, thereby strengthening incentives for physicians to want the hospital to prosper. These types of arrangements are an incomplete form of vertical integration.[15] Several participants cited the desire to develop greater physician loyalty and more exclusive relations with physicians as being important factors in choosing to enter into certain types of joint ventures. Several also had involvement in physician-hospital organizations, a strategy for alliance building between hospitals and staff physicians that may be particularly important for community hospitals in the coming years (Ginzberg 1996).

6.4.5   Reduction and Elimination of Services

In addition to looking for new opportunities to earn surpluses, hospitals also evaluate whether various traditional service operations need to be continued. All participants described strategic review of services. Some of the participating hospitals had eliminated obstetrics services, outsourced pathology services, or had changed the organization and management of the emergency department. Generally, they identified a set of conditions that led to elimination of services. They were: (1) the service was a money loser, (2) there were similar services available from nearby competitors, and (3) it was not considered fundamental to the hospital. We probed the focus group participants regarding whether emergency services might be eliminated if they lost money. All of the hospital representatives stated that they viewed the emergency department as a core feature of the hospital and therefore would not eliminate it under any conceivable circumstances. Several participants noted that they had changed the manner in which the emergency department operated. Specifically, one hospital jointly staffed the emergency department with an urgent care outpatient clinic that met the pricing standards for most HMOs. The effect was to reduce the role of the emergency department and presumably to offer more appropriate levels of care to patients.

The discussions with the representatives of not-for-profit hospitals participating in our focus group did not suggest that joint ventures and creation of subsidiaries were motivated primarily by seeking flexible revenues

---

14. The focus group discussions revealed that there were no meaningful joint ventures outside of the health arena.

15. It is interesting to note that these practices are quite similar to those that have created such intense scrutiny of Columbia/HCA and its relationship to physicians.

that could be used to maintain or expand charitable activities directed to care of the medically indigent. Nor did any participant identify the provision of uncompensated care in pursuit of serving the community as a source of financial stress on their hospitals. Discretionary funds appear to be primarily directed toward new product development, joint ventures, and investment in financial markets. Thus, beyond adding to the general financial health of the hospitals, returns from profit-making activities do not seem to be targeted specifically to increased supply of social goods.

6.5   Conclusions

It is logical to expect that the emergence of price competition in the market for hospital services will threaten the traditional funding of charity care and other public goods by not-for-profit hospitals through cross-subsidies. This expectation is also supported by research that links increases in competitive pressures to declines in the supply of uncompensated care. It is also logical to expect this trend to increase the importance of philanthropy as a source of support for supplying these public goods and to conclude that a reversal of the secular decline in philanthropic support will be needed to avoid a sharp reduction in the supply of public goods.

Against this background, we have examined the trend of hospitals to diversify into new lines of business. Our particular focus was on the notion that diversification could reduce the supply of public goods by either (1) adversely affecting the supply of philanthropy, or (2) increasing the cost of public goods via diseconomies of scope.

In our view, the focus group evidence reported here provides little support for the idea that diversification adversely affects the supply of public goods. They appear not to consider it at all in strategic diversification decisions. There is recognition that high profit margins may impact negatively on the supply of philanthropy, but diversification per se is not seen as a factor in philanthropy supply. (A minor qualification might be added for the preference of some hospitals to not use their own name on joint venture projects, but clearly this was mainly motivated by a reluctance to appear as infringing on the clinical independence of physician-partners.) Information from the focus groups was less clear on the question of diseconomies of scope and the effect of diversification on the incremental cost of public goods supply. Finally, offsetting any of these possible negative effects was the clear consensus that diversification efforts were profitable. Some discounting of this evidence may be in order because of the selected nature of our informants and their own personal involvement in diversification efforts, but their message seemed very clear. Diversification was a new source of profits that maintained the financial health of the hospital, including its ability to supply public goods.

These observations are also consistent with national trend data cited earlier. In the face of budgetary restraints from Medicare and Medicaid and the presumed rise in price competition in the private sector, hospital profit margins have not been shrinking and, in fact, have recently been rising. While we do not have information on operating margins for "traditional" lines of hospital business versus margins on joint ventures, some of the recent increase in hospital margins is presumably due to joint venture profits. In addition, it appears that margins on private sector patient care increased during the 1990s and have only recently started to decline but still remain strongly positive (Guterman, Ashby, and Greene 1996). Thus, our presumption that private sector margins are shrinking due to increased price competition may be at least premature if not incorrect. Managed care certainly appears to have an affect on the level of utilization and the rate of increase of total and unit revenues for hospital services, but hospitals' responses in containing costs have thus far been more than sufficient to maintain healthy profit levels on "traditional" lines of business.

In short, the initial presumption of our work—that the supply of public goods was being threatened by the disappearance of cross-subsidies—needs to be modified. The flow of profits that are the source of the cross-subsidies has not dried up. Accordingly, even though the role of philanthropy continues to diminish, the supply of some public goods (e.g., charity care) has not declined nationally. Additional funding sources have arisen, such as statewide indigent care pools, but profits continue to be an important funding source.

The short-run success of not-for-profit hospitals in maintaining their profit margins is, however, no guarantee of future survival under present circumstances. In the presence of substantial excess capacity, hospitals are financially vulnerable to price pressures, especially in the inpatient market (Ginzberg 1996); concerns for survival may dominate, and diversification decisions may be largely driven by these survival concerns. The motivation for diversification in the form of joint ventures with physicians appears to be greater forward integration with the physician practices that are an important component of the increasingly uncertain demand for "traditional" hospital services. Preserving the supply of such specific social goods as care for the indigent is a secondary factor in this consideration.

Appendix

BACKGROUND INFORMATION

Greenleaf Associates, Inc.

October, 1997

Name: _____ Hospital: _____

Title: _____ Years in Current Position: _____

Previous position held, if any, in same hospital: _____

1. What do you feel is the most critical strategic planning issue currently facing your hospital? *(Please describe.)*

_____

_____

_____

2. About what percent of your professional time is spent on strategic planning issues for your hospital?
   (Write in %) _____

3. What members of the hospital community are most influential in strategic planning decisions? *(Please describe role/title; do not include names.)*

_____

_____

_____

4. How would you define the "mission" of your hospital? *(Please describe.)*

_____

_____

_____

5. Who do you feel are the people most invested in preserving this "mission"? *(Please describe.)*

_____

_____

_____

DISCUSSION GUIDE OUTLINE

Strategic Planning for Not-for-Profit Hospitals

Monday, October 20, 1997 *(Boston: 7:00 PM)*

Tuesday, October 28, 1997 *(Chicago: 6:30 PM)*

I. Introduction
   A. Procedures
   B. Participant introductions
II. Background Information
   A. Mission of Not-for-Profit Hospitals
      1. Definitions of mission, of community
      2. Importance of "mission"
         Probe: Perceptions from community, from donors, from medical staff
      3. Present commitment to mission: the entrenched vs. the drifting
   B. Mission "Gatekeepers"
      1. Principal gatekeepers and evolution of their roles
      2. Role of board
      3. Existence and membership of a Mission Affairs Committee
         Probe, as appropriate: Evolution of a committee's role
         Probe: Involvement, if any, in committee's balance of commercial and mission activities
   C. Pressures Affecting Pursuit of the Hospital's Mission
      1. Principal pressures and degrees/area of influence
         (Easel summary of spontaneous mentions prior to moderator's probes)
      2. Pressures from the "competition"
         Probe: Perceived need and ability to "compete"
         Probe: Descriptors of the principal "competition"
         Probe: Extent to which competing is bolstered versus hindered by commitment to mission
      3. Financial pressures
         Probe: To what extent, in what areas
      4. Pressures from the community
      5. Pressures from the medical staff
III. Strategic Planning
   A. Perceived Impact of Pressures on Not-for-Profit Hospitals
      1. Areas most influenced and reasons why
         Probe: extent to which new directions/strategies embrace/conflict with mission
         Probe, as appropriate: Degree of departmental integration (e.g., financial, medical education, etc.), if any, drawn upon to accomplish new direction/strategy

(Easel summary of spontaneous mentions prior to moderator's probes. Areas probed will include brief discussion of current involvement as well as anticipated future involvement)

2. Effect on fund raising efforts
   Probe: Motivating criteria for key donors and perceived points of conflict, if any
   Probe: Changes, if any, to volume and restricted/unrestricted donations and reasons why
3. Effect on involvement with profit-making activities (e.g., imaging centers, wellness and/or fitness centers, sleep centers)
   Probe: Effect of diversification into "high margin", non-traditional activities on "organizational" culture (to include process/cost/size/complexity of management)
4. Effect on involvement with subsidiaries/joint ventures (e.g., home health areas, MD partnerships, insurance) and/or mergers
5. Effect on staffing (e.g., quality of staffing, morale)
6. Effect on quality of care issues

B. Key Dilemmas Facing Not-for-Profit Hospitals
   1. Prioritization of principal issues: current and near future
      Probe: Relationship of key issues to mission
C. Key Influencers in Process of Strategic Planning
   1. Relationship of strategic planners and mission gatekeepers
D. Role of Marketing
   1. Strategic planning role/influence
   2. Changes, if any, in marketing emphasis and/or direction
      Probe: Introduction, growth, and role of marketing department
   3. Range of services marketed
      Probe: Services with the most impact (e.g., on needs of community, of hospital) and reasons why
E. Principal Strategic Planning Considerations
IV. Closing Remarks
A. Confidentiality Emphasized
B. Words of Appreciation

References

American Hospital Association (AHA). 1987. *Hospital Statistics, 1987 Edition.* Chicago, Ill.: American Hospital Association.
———. 1997. *Hospital Statistics, Emerging Trends in Hospitals, 1996–7 Edition.* Chicago, Ill.: American Hospital Association.
Bilodeau, Marc, and Al Slivinski. 1996. Rival Charities. Working paper. Department of Economics, University of Sherbrooke, Quebec, Canada.

Clement, J. P., T. D'Aunno, and B. L. M. Poyzer. 1993. The Financial Performance of Diversified Hospital Subsidiaries. *Health Services Research* 27 (6): 742–63.

Frank, R. G., and D. S. Salkever. 1991. The Supply of Charity Services by Nonprofit Hospitals: Motives and Market Structure. *RAND Journal of Economics* 22 (3): 43–55.

Frank, R. G., D. S. Salkever, and J. Mitchell. 1990. Market Forces and the Public Good: Competition among Hospitals and Provision of Indigent Care. In *Advances in Health Economics and Health Services Research,* ed. R. M. Scheffler and L. F. Rossiter, 159–84. Greenwich, Conn.: JAI Press.

Ginzberg, Eli. 1996. *Tomorrow's Hospital: A Look to the Twenty-First Century.* New Haven: Yale University Press.

Gray, B. H., ed. 1983. *The New Health Care for Profit.* Washington, D.C.: National Academy of Sciences Press.

Gruber, J. 1994. The Effect of Competitive Pressure on Charity: Hospital Responses to Price Shopping in California. *Journal of Health Economics* 13 (3): 183–212.

Guterman, S., J. Ashby, and T. Greene. 1996. Hospital Cost Growth Down. *Health Affairs* 15 (3): 134–39.

Independent Sector. 1997. *Nonprofit Almanac 1996–1997.* Washington, D.C.: Independent Sector.

Institute of Medicine. 1983. *The New Health Care for Profit.* Washington, D.C.: National Academy Press.

Mann, J. M., G. Melnick, A. Bamezai, and J. Zwanziger. 1997. A Profile of Uncompensated Hospital Care. *Health Affairs* 16 (3): 223–32.

Prospective Payment Assessment Commission (ProPAC). 1997. Report and Recommendations to the Congress. 1 March. Washington, D.C.: U.S. Government Printing Office.

Shactman, David, and Stuart Altman. 1997. Hospital Conversions and Uncompensated Care. *Health Affairs* 16 (3): 270–71.

Shortell, S. M., E. M. Morrison, and S. L. Hughes. 1989. The Keys to Successful Diversification from Leading Hospital Systems. *Hospital and Health Services Administration* 34 (4): 471–92.

Sloan, F. A. 1997. Commercialism in Nonprofit Hospitals. Working paper. Duke University, Durham, N.C.

Sloan, F. A., T. Hoerger, M. Morrissey, and A. Hassan. 1990. The Demise of Hospital Philanthropy. *Economic Inquiry* 28 (4): 725–43.

Smith, D., J. P. Clement, and J. R. C. Wheeler. 1995. Philanthropy and Hospital Financing. *Health Services Research* 30 (5): 615–36.

Thorpe, K., and C. C. Phelps. 1991. The Social Role of Not for Profit Organizations: Hospital Provision of Charity Care. *Economic Inquiry* 29 (3): 472–84.

U.S. General Accounting Office (GAO). 1993. Nonprofit Hospitals: For-Profit Ventures Pose Access and Capacity Problems. Washington, D.C.: U.S. Government Printing Office.

Young, G. J., K. R. Desai, and C. V. Lucas. 1997. Does the Sale of Nonprofit Hospitals Threaten Health Care for the Poor? *Health Affairs* 16 (1): 137–41.

Comment on Chapters 5 and 6   Bradford H. Gray

As a sociologist who has worked for many years on the question of ownership form in health care, I have found the papers and discussion at this conference to be enormously interesting and stimulating. Like the conference itself, the papers I've been asked to discuss have a strong interdisciplinary flavor—Frank and Salkever's paper because they use the focus group methodology that comes out of sociology (Merton and Kendall 1946), and Skinner and Wennberg's because it is a collaboration between an economist and an epidemiologist.

Theoretical work in both sociology and economics suggests why ownership form might or might not make a difference in the performance of organizations. In sociology, DiMaggio and Powell (1983) suggested that organizations in the same field will tend to look similar to each other because of coercive, imitative, and normative pressures toward isomorphism. That is, all organizations are subject to the same regulatory and market pressures, all notice each other and copy what seems to work, and all are subject to social expectations. In health care, an important source of normative pressure comes from the professional values of physicians to which hospitals, for example, must pay attention. It should be noted, however, that coercive and normative pressures are not identical for for-profits and not-for-profits in health care. Not-for-profits' tax exemptions as charitable organizations and their ability to obtain donated funds may create both resources and external expectations of charitable behavior and the provision of public goods, even though, as Frank and Salkever note, charitable contributions are now a very small part of the financial picture for most hospitals.

Economics—particularly in agency theory—has also suggested reasons why ownership form may have little effect on organizational behavior. But economic theory regarding property rights, public goods, and contract failure has also given us reasons to expect differences in behavior (Hansmann 1987). One implication of these ideas is that for-profit organizations might be more prone to exploit the informational asymmetries that typify health care—asymmetries that involve not only patients but also third-party payers (Steinberg and Gray 1993).

These various concepts do a pretty good job of accounting for the broad patterns that have been observed in the behavior of for-profits and not-for-profits in health care (see Gray 1991 for a summary). To broadly generalize across studies, there are similar costs in hospitals although for-profits charge higher prices. There are similar levels of uncompensated care where need is low, but different levels and different geographic patterns of owner-

Bradford H. Gray is the director of the Division of Health and Science Policy at the New York Academy of Medicine.

ship where the need is high. There are large sectoral differences in organizational involvement in educational and research activities, which contain an element of public good. There are similar levels of quality in hospitals (where normative pressures from physicians are strong), but there are differences in nursing homes (Marmor, Schlesinger, and Smithey 1987) and, perhaps, in HMOs (Gray 1997).

It is good that Frank and Salkever went beyond formulating a problem and positing the way they thought the world works to the collection of primary data and the modification of their initial presumptions on the basis of it. This particular set of focus groups, however, does not provide a strong basis for sweeping conclusions because of the small numbers, inclusion of some unintended hospital types, and limitation to two cities. Even with these limitations, Frank and Salkever found that the world is more complicated than they had expected, and they shared what they learned in an informative way.

Economists sometimes seem to presume that ownership form is an epiphenomenon and to expect, often implicitly, that behavior of not-for-profits and for-profits is essentially the same. Although Frank and Salkever's model does not assume that the objective function of not-for-profit hospitals is profit maximization, they still have their suspicions. Even after reporting that the not-for-profit hospital executives in the focus groups all said they would not eliminate their hospital's emergency room under "any conceivable circumstances," Frank and Salkever still concluded in their original version of their paper that "profit maximization may be a reasonable approximation of not-for-profit objectives." This formulation was changed in the final version of the paper to read that not-for-profit hospitals place "a large weight on current and future profits in the face of perceived financial and competitive risks" (section 6.4.2). Although their original formulation is a better illustration of how our disciplinary background shapes our perceptions (a phenomenon not peculiar to economists), even their second formulation goes beyond the evidence, I think.

As I read their evidence, not-for-profit hospitals engage in diversification activities in an attempt to allow themselves to continue to do what they have been doing. But they do not all define this identically. Frank and Salkever's surmise that diversification—and profits resulting therefrom—may help explain why hospitals have been able to maintain (or build) *both* their profit margins and their uncompensated care load in the face of an increasingly competitive health care system is plausible to me. The fact that the focus groups provided little evidence that enhanced charity or public goods was their goal is worth reporting, to be sure, and this points to an important issue regarding our expectations of not-for-profit hospitals. As the respondents suggested, a hospital's role in providing charity care may have been heavily influenced by decisions made decades earlier under different circumstances regarding where the hospital would be located. After all, not-for-profit hospitals vary with regard to their proximity to large numbers of poor and uninsured people, a fact that may relate to variations in their conceptions of their missions. Not-for-profits are not a homogeneous lot, a point that Weisbrod (1988) emphasizes in his analysis of the role of not-for-profits. They have considerable latitude in meeting community needs, as their trustees define them. Since neither the hospitals nor their administrators are a uniform lot, those who were selected to participate in a small number of focus groups are not necessarily representative. Overgeneralization is a danger.

The importance of not-for-profit hospitals' self-definitions of mission has received public policy support. In 1969, the Internal Revenue Service changed its interpretation of the meaning of "charitable" for purposes of hospital tax exemptions from a definition that emphasized service to the poor to a definition, thought to be more realistic, that emphasized service to the community at large—the so-called "community benefit" standard (Fox and Schaffer 1991). As trustee-governed institutions, hospitals define their missions for themselves, and as Frank and Salkever found, they do not necessarily do this in terms of service to the poor. Thus, there is little reason to expect that most hospitals' diversification efforts would be undertaken to support service to the poor. Nor does service to the poor necessarily lie behind the intentions of donors to hospitals—particularly large donors who contribute to capital projects. If, as has happened in a few states, not-for-profit hospitals come under increased pressure to demonstrate that their charitable or community benefit activities are commensurate with the value of their tax exemptions, fund raising and diversification activities may become more focused on generating revenues to support the activities that justify the tax exemption (Pauly 1996). Frank and Salkever's finding that this purpose receives little mention now is interesting in light of the fact that Massachusetts is one of the states that has begun to demand greater accountability regarding tax-exempt status.

As a final comment on Frank and Salkever's paper, I would note that diversification is not new among hospitals, even if it has increased in recent years. The phenomenon was attracting much attention when I first became involved in the for-profit/not-for-profit topic 15 years ago. Several points were then being made, including how common diversification was and how often it was connected with corporate restructuring, which itself was driven in part by the goal of generating revenues to support the hospital's activity. The creation of separate organizational structures was then—and I suspect is now—driven in part by tax rules and the need to separate out revenue streams that were subject to the unrelated business income tax. The fact that Frank and Salkever's respondents did not mention tax-related reasons for diversification suggests that the nature of the phenomenon has changed from the earlier period.

Turning to the Skinner and Wennberg paper, I will not repeat the pattern of findings that they have woven together to reach their conclusions, which I find convincing. They point us to a fundamental challenge in assessing the effects of a profit-maximizing orientation in health care, as well as the difficulty in measuring the efficiency of health services. These difficulties both result from our old friend—the information asymmetry problem. But the findings may also be due to differences in physician preferences regarding how to respond to given sets of clinical circumstances.

As with many earlier studies by Wennberg and his colleagues, Skinner and Wennberg find evidence that the volume of services in an area is directly related to the supply of physicians and appears unrelated to underlying medical needs in the population (although perhaps not unrelated to patients' preferences). An interesting aspect of this is their evidence that the extra services received by the Miami patients are not only costly but that they may actually detract from patients' well-being. This is extraordinarily important in this period in which managed care plans are being criticized for policies that result in reduced hospital usage.

Also important is their evidence that there are high-utilizing *places*. Skinner and Wennberg show that Miami has much higher use of *many* services than does Minneapolis—hospitals, ICUs, primary care visits, and, especially, specialist visits. What is it about a place like Miami that accounts for such patterns? The fact that some surgical procedures occurred at a higher rate in Minneapolis should warn us against simple explanations. Processes involving selection and patient preferences may be going on. However, the inclusion of this paper in this conference on for-profit and not-for-profit care suggests that the authors and conference organizers saw it as relevant to that topic. This view has considerable plausibility.

Why might Miami be a high-utilizing place? One way that Miami differs from Minneapolis is its very large Medicare population that attracts all kinds of profit-seeking organizations. About half of Florida hospitals are for-profit, and about half of those are owned by Columbia/HCA. This company, of course, has been charged with a wide variety of manipulations of payment systems, and it used a much-criticized strategy of joint ventures with physicians to encourage their use of Columbia/HCA hospitals in ways that would enhance their profitability (Kuttner 1996). One possible result would be elevated admission rates.

Fraud appears to be a major problem in Florida. In a presentation about Florida health care at the annual meeting of the American College of Medical Quality in Orlando in November 1997, James T. Howell, M.D., the secretary of the Florida Department of Health, described two recent interventions aimed at reducing fraudulent care in Florida. The first, undertaken because home care costs were wildly out of control, was to require that home care organizations reapply for certification. It was made known that there would be fingerprinting and background checks of owners. Of the existing 1,600 certified agencies, 1,200 did not reapply. Dr. Howell also described how new practice guidelines involving less-invasive care were implemented for low back pain in Florida's workers' compensation program; a 62 percent reduction in costs occurred in the first year. His conclusion was that cost containment is hopeless in a fee-for-service system.

Interestingly, the high rates of service utilization in Florida have made the state attractive for Medicare HMOs, since Medicare payment rates for HMOs are heavily influenced by costs within the fee-for-service system. (The 1997 average annual per capita cost (AAPCC) on which Medicare HMO costs are based was $748 per month in Dade county compared to $406 in Hennipin county.) Twelve of fifteen HMOs in Miami are for-profit. The largest most notorious case of HMO fraud in the Medicare program—the International Medical Centers scandal—occurred there a decade ago (see Gray 1991, chap. 6, for an account).

If Miami is indeed a place in which entrepreneurial providers have been actively exploiting the vulnerabilities of payment systems, an interesting question arises. What will be the effect of managed care and associated strategies in a situation in which most of the HMOs are themselves for-profit and most of the physicians that they attract are strongly responsive to economic incentives? It would be very interesting to see the results of a Skinner and Wennberg analysis comparing HMO enrollees and nonenrollees in the two cities. In Minneapolis, with its high HMO penetration, all health plans are not-for-profits as a result of state law; in Miami, the for-profits overwhelmingly dominate. (Interstudy reports HMO penetration rates of 44 percent in Minneapolis and 52 percent in Miami.) Economists have long noted that the health care market is influenced in important ways by the fact that the customers—the patients—do not know their own needs and must rely on the advice of others (Arrow 1963). Managed care does not eliminate the vulnerability of patients, and it introduces new ways that those vulnerabilities can be exploited by those who are inclined to do so (Gray 1997). The study of patterns of services across geographic areas and delivery systems can provide important clues regarding when that might be happening.

References

Arrow, Kenneth. 1963. Uncertainty and the Welfare Economics of Medical Care. *American Economic Review* 53:941–73.
DiMaggio, Paul, and Walter W. Powell. 1983. The Iron Cage Revisited: Institutional Isomorphism and Collective Rationality in Organizational Fields. *American Sociological Review* 82:147–60.
Fox, Daniel, and Daniel C. Schaffer. 1991. Tax Administration as Health Policy: Hospitals, the IRS and the Courts. *Journal of Health Politics and Law* 16 (2): 251–79.
Gray, Bradford H. 1991. *The Profit Motive and Patient Care: The Changing Ac-*

countability of Doctors and Hospitals. Cambridge, Mass.: Harvard University Press.

———. 1997. Trust and Trustworthy Care in the Managed Care Era. *Health Affairs* 16 (1): 29–47.

Hansmann, Henry. 1987. Economic Theories of Nonprofit Organization. In *The Nonprofit Sector: A Research Handbook,* ed. Walter Powell, 27–41. New Haven, Conn.: Yale University Press.

Kuttner, Robert. 1996. Columbia/HCA and the Resurgence of the For-Profit Hospital Business: Part 1. *New England Journal of Medicine* 335 (5): 362–67.

Marmor, Theodore R., Mark Schlesinger, and Richard W. Smithey. 1987. Nonprofit Organizations and Health Care. In *The Nonprofit Sector: A Research Handbook,* ed. Walter Powell, 221–39. New Haven, Conn.: Yale University Press.

Merton, Robert K., and Patricia L. Kendall. 1946. The Focused Interiew. *American Journal of Sociology* 51 (6): 541–57.

Pauly, Mark V. 1996. Health Systems Ownership: Can Regulation Preserve Community Benefits? *Frontiers of Health Services Management* 12 (3): 3–34.

Steinberg, Richard, and Bradford H. Gray. 1993. The Role of Nonprofit Enterprise in 1992: Hansmann Revisited. *Nonprofit and Voluntary Sector Quarterly* 22 (winter): 297–316.

Weisbrod, Burton A. 1988. *The Nonprofit Economy.* Cambridge, Mass.: Harvard University Press.

Comment on Chapters 5 and 6   Frank Lichtenberg

The fact that hospitals have experienced a period of tighter revenues and reduced demand for their traditional inpatient care services has raised concerns about their ability to provide traditional community-oriented services, such as hospital care to medically indigent populations. But the main conclusion of Richard Frank and David Salkever's interesting paper is that neither increased price competition nor diversification of hospitals into new activities necessarily threatens the supply of public goods.

Due to the hospital's budget constraint, the supply of "public goods" is limited by its net income

$$N = \pi + D = (R - C) + D,$$

where N = net income, R = revenue from traditional inpatient care services, C = cost of traditional inpatient care services, π = profit from traditional inpatient care services, and D = donations (charitable contributions). The "naive" hypothesis is that $dN/dR = 1$: A \$1 reduction in traditional revenue results in a \$1 reduction in net income available to support public good provision. However, Frank and Salkever's analysis and evidence suggests that this view is too pessimistic: dN/dR is much less

Frank Lichtenberg is the Courtney C. Brown Professor of Business at Columbia University and a research associate of the National Bureau of Economic Research.

than one (and may even be negative!), because both C and D do not remain constant when R changes. I would paraphrase their analysis as follows:

$$C = \theta R \quad (\theta > 0),$$

$$D = -\gamma\pi \quad (\gamma > 0).$$

The first equation embodies the notion that hospitals may operate with some degree of X-inefficiency,[1] and that they will reduce costs and inefficiency when revenues are declining. Hence, profits will not fall as much as revenue. Between 1985 and 1995, the number of not-for-profit hospitals declined from 3,349 to 3,092, and the number of beds declined from 707,000 to 610,000.[2] Presumably, the hospitals that closed had higher costs than those that remained open, so that this reduction of capacity contributed to cost reduction.

The second equation embodies the idea that the supply of charitable contributions is inversely related to profits: Donors are less inclined to contribute when the hospital is earning large profits. Hence, net income will not fall as much as profits. Substituting these two equations into the net income identity,

$$N = \pi - \gamma\pi = R(1 - \theta)(1 - \gamma).$$

Hence $dN/dR = (1 - \theta)(1 - \gamma)$, which is certainly less than one. At times Frank and Salkever seem to suggest that the cost-reduction efforts triggered by declining revenue were so intense and effective that the net effect has been an increase in profits: "While hospitals have generally faced increasingly tight revenues, both for-profit and not-for-profit entities have managed to reduce costs sufficiently to increase margins in recent years" (section 6.2). In other words, $\theta > 1$, so that $d\pi/dR = (1 - \theta) < 0$. Hospitals should have wished for a decline in revenues years ago! It is plausible to me that revenue decreases stimulate some cost reductions, but not that the latter are more than adequate to compensate for the former.[3] Of course, the apparent decline in costs may have been completely unrelated to the decline in revenue. In any case, one should not infer from the revenue numbers alone that the provision of public goods is or is not threatened.

The equation above reveals that even a decline in profit from traditional inpatient care services (π) does not necessarily spell trouble for community-oriented services. If donations are highly sensitive to hospital profitability

1. The term *X-inefficiency* was coined by Harvey Leibenstein (1966).
2. The increase in concentration may be partly responsible for the recent increase in hospital profitability noted by Frank and Salkever. See also Barro and Cutler's (1997) case study of consolidation in the Massachusetts medical care marketplace.
3. There is an obvious parallel in "supply-side economics": A reduction in the tax rate (t) will increase the tax base (Y), but will it increase it enough to increase total tax revenue (tY)?

($\gamma > 1$), resources available to provide those services would be inversely related to profitability. There is no evidence to support this extreme view. But the point that the marginal response of donations to profits (γ) acts like a "tax" on the supply of public goods is an important one.

For simplicity, the preceding analysis ignored a source of net income (and determinant of donations) that figures prominently in Frank and Salkever's analysis: diversification into nontraditional activities such as operation of primary care clinics, imaging centers, and home health care companies. They argue that this diversification was prompted by the decline in traditional revenue sources and was a new source of profits that maintained the financial health of the hospital, including its ability to supply public goods. (But diversification per se may reduce donations directly, as well as indirectly by increasing profits.) I am struck by the contrast between this sector and the world of business; the consensus seems to be that among corporations, *excess* profits ("free cash flow"), rather than declining revenues, triggers diversification, and that diversification destroys rather than creates shareholder value. I would also pose the question, If diversification was such a profitable strategy, why did hospitals have to be "forced" by declining traditional revenues to adopt it?

The paper by Jonathan Skinner and John Wennberg provides strong evidence for two puzzling facts. The first of these is that the intensity of medical resource use varies dramatically across regions of the United States (even after controlling for disease incidence). They report the following ratios of per capita utilization in Miami to per capita utilization in Minneapolis:

Home health services	4.1
Inpatient services	1.5
Inpatient Medicare expenditure (last 6 months of life)	2.0
Primary MD visits (last 6 months of life)	1.8
Specialist MD visits (last 6 months of life)	5.4

Such pronounced cross-sectional variation in medical resource use cries out for explanation. Skinner and Wennberg estimate regressions of average Medicare Part A reimbursements in the last six months of life on a number of health, resource, and financial variables, and find that average reimbursements are positively correlated with hospital beds and specialist MDs per capita and with the percent of nongovernment hospitals that are for-profit. They recognize, though, that one cannot necessarily infer from this that the presence of high medical resources *causes* high medical expenditure. The equation that they estimate bears some resemblance to the accounting identity between expenditure and the price-weighted sum of the quantities of each type of medical service consumed. Since specialist visits per capita are much higher in Miami than Minneapolis, the only reasons *not* to observe a positive correlation across regions between the number of specialists per capita and average reimbursement would be that Miami specialists see far fewer patients per year or charge much lower fees. The reduced-form expenditure equation they estimate does not enable us to identify, or test hypotheses about, the parameters of the medical input supply or demand functions.

The second important fact that they document is that health outcomes (mortality) are uncorrelated across regions with medical resource use. Often, there is reason to expect the cross-sectional correlation between inputs and outputs to *overstate* the marginal productivity (or output elasticity) of inputs. Suppose that we have data on output and employment for a cross-section of firms, and that the firms vary with respect to some unobservable characteristic (such as managerial ability) that influences productivity. In competitive equilibrium, the firms with greatest managerial ability should employ the most workers, and as a result, the coefficient on employment in the production function would be biased upward. In other words, a positive input coefficient indicates not only that inputs are productive, on average, but also that they are allocated to the places where they are most productive; failure to observe a positive relationship between medical resource use and outcomes suggests that neither of these is true.

I have also examined the relationship between real medical expenditure and a measure of mortality; my analysis is at the national level using longitudinal data for a sample of 17 countries from the Organization for Economic Cooperation and Development (OECD) health database. I distinguished three types of medical expenditure: inpatient care (INPAT), ambulatory care (AMBUL), and pharmaceuticals (PHARM), all measured in purchasing-power-parity-adjusted expenditure per capita. The average expenditure shares of these three inputs of the "health production function" are about 50 percent, 35 percent, and 15 percent, respectively. The mortality measure I used is potential life-years lost before age 65 per 100,000 population (PLYL). The model that I estimated was

$$\ln PLYL_{it} = \beta_1 \ln INPAT_{it} + \beta_2 \ln AMBUL_{it}$$

$$+ \beta_3 \ln PHARM_{it} + \alpha_i + \delta_t + u_{it},$$

where $i = 1, \ldots, 17$ OECD countries; and $t = 1960, 1965, \ldots, 1990$. Since the model includes fixed country and year effects, estimates of the β coefficients reveal whether or not countries with above-average increases in per capita medical expenditures experienced above-average reductions in per capita life-years lost. (I think it would be desirable for Skinner and Wennberg to add cross-region data for at least one additional year to their sample, so that they could include fixed-region effects to control for stable, unobserved determinants of expenditure and/or outcomes.) The estimated equation was (*t*-statistics in parentheses; $N = 80$):

$$\ln \text{PLYL}_{it} = -.038 \ \ln \text{INPAT}_{it} \ -.092 \ \ln \text{AMBUL}_{it} \ -.187 \ \ln \text{PHARM}_{it}$$
$$\phantom{\ln \text{PLYL}_{it} = }(0.51) \phantom{\ln \text{INPAT}_{it} \ } (1.79) \phantom{\ln \text{AMBUL}_{it} } (2.51)$$

$$+ \ \alpha_i + \delta_t + u_{it}.$$

Consistent with Skinner and Wennberg's findings, there is not a statistically significant relationship between inpatient expenditures—which account for about half of total health care costs—and this measure of premature mortality. The coefficient on ambulatory medical expenditure is only marginally statistically significant. Pharmaceutical expenditure, which accounts for a fairly small share of total health expenditures, is the only component that has a highly significant (and large) effect on mortality. (To assess the relative marginal productivity of the three inputs, one should divide the elasticities by their respective expenditure shares.) This finding is robust to changes in the mortality measure and the measure of pharmaceutical utilization. I also estimated models of the form

$$\ln X_{it} = \beta \ln \text{N\_DRUGS}_{it} + \alpha_i + \delta_t + u_{it},$$

where X is a mortality measure and N_DRUGS is annual per capita consumption of medicines (in defined daily dosages). The estimates of β are shown below:

X	β
Life expectancy of males at age 40 ($N = 63$)	.022 (2.55)
Potential life-years lost before age 65 per 100,000 males ($N = 83$)	$-.070$ (2.18)
Potential life-years lost before age 65 per 100,000 females ($N = 83$)	$-.129$ (2.81)

These estimates are consistent with the hypothesis that utilization of pharmaceuticals significantly reduces mortality. The positive relationship between life expectancy and pharmaceutical use may partly reflect reverse causality, however: Since pharmaceutical consumption tends to increase with age (beyond age 40), exogenous increases in life expectancy may lead to increased pharmaceutical use. Since reverse causality should also result in overstatement of the relationship between inpatient expenditure and mortality, the apparent absence of any relationship between the two is especially strong evidence that inpatient expenditure does not reduce mortality.

The puzzle amply documented by Skinner and Wennberg—failure to detect a relationship between expenditures (especially public expenditures) and outcomes—is not unique to this type of expenditure. As Machado (1997) observes, 30 years ago the Coleman Report concluded that expenditures per student and school inputs had no measurable impact on student performance; the latter depended primarily on student background. Such conclusions were so controversial that an avalanche of further studies emerged, but very little consensus has been reached among researchers about whether, or how much, "money matters" in education.

Machado attempted to determine the effect of public substance abuse treatment expenditures on outcomes (e.g., the number of abstinent discharged patients) using data from Maine's Office of Substance Abuse (OSA). She noted that a simple regression of treatment outcomes on expenditures per patient showed no positive relationship between these two variables. She recognized, however, that failure to observe a relationship might be attributable to the potential endogeneity of expenditures: OSA might allocate more funds per patient to programs that treat more difficult patients. Not controlling for patient and other characteristics would dampen the estimated impact of funds on outcomes. She pursued two different econometric strategies to attempt to address the endogeneity of funds per patient. But even after accounting for the potential endogeneity of expenditures, she concluded that "the marginal impact of expenditures per patient on the number of abstinent people in the state of Maine is so small that it is not economically significant."

The data presented by Skinner and Wennberg about the allocation of medical resources in the United States were prepared with great skill and are of considerable interest and importance. Explanation of these relationships (or lack of relationship!) should be a high priority in future research.

References

Barro, Jason, and David Cutler. 1997. Consolidation in the Medical Care Marketplace: A Case Study from Massachusetts. NBER Working Paper no. W5957. Cambridge, Mass.: National Bureau of Economic Research, March.
Leibenstein, Harvey. 1966. Allocative Inefficiency vs. X-Inefficiency. *American Economic Review* 56:392–415.
Machado, Matilde Pinto. 1997. Dollars and Performance: Cost Effectiveness of Substance Abuse Treatment in Maine. Instituto de Analisis Economico, CSIC Universidad Autonoma de Barcelona, Spain.

III

Managed Care and
Hospital Quality

7

Managed Care and Provider Volume

Sarah Feldman and David Scharfstein

7.1 Introduction

Between 1980 and 1995, the number of individuals covered by managed care plans grew more than fivefold. With this increase have come growing concerns about the quality of the care provided by managed care plans. There have been a number of responses to these concerns: the establishment of the National Committee on Quality Assurance (NCQA) to measure health care quality and provide accreditation of health plans; the attempt by some health care plans to create legally enforceable national standards for patient protection; and the formation of a presidential advisory committee on health care quality.

Despite the widespread interest in measuring health care quality, there is still limited understanding of the differences in the quality of managed care and more traditional fee-for-service (FFS) health plans. Indeed, in their survey of research on the topic, Miller and Luft (1997) concluded that it is difficult to draw definitive conclusions about the differences between the two types of coverage. Of the 15 studies they reviewed, some found evidence that managed care plans offer higher quality care than

Sarah Feldman is assistant professor of obstetrics, gynecology, and reproductive biology at Harvard Medical School; chief of obstetrics and gynecology and director of women's health at Cambridge Hospital; and an associate in gynecologic oncology at the Dana Farber Cancer Institute. David Scharfstein is the Dai-Ichi Kangyo Bank Professor of Management and professor of finance at the Sloan School of Management, Massachusetts Institute of Technology.

This research was supported by a grant from the National Institute on Aging. The authors are grateful for many helpful discussions with Judy Chevalier, David Cutler, Jennifer Haas, and Julio Rotemberg, as well as the comments of conference participants. Aileen Chen provided exceptional research assistance.

FFS plans; others found just the opposite; and still others found little difference between the two types of health plans.

Research on quality takes two approaches. In one approach, researchers examine the *process* of health care, comparing the ways in which health care providers treat disease.[1] In the second approach, researchers compare patients' health *outcomes*.

For example, Sheldon Retchin and coauthors (Retchin and Brown 1990, 1991; Retchin and Preston 1991; Retchin et al. 1992), taking the process approach to study the medical management of colorectal cancer, diabetes, and congestive heart failure, found no meaningful differences in the way patients in managed care plans are treated compared to patients in fee-for-service plans. In a more recent study, however, Retchin et al. (1997) found that stroke patients covered by managed care plans were less likely to be discharged to a rehabilitation center, suggesting that they received less comprehensive (and perhaps lower quality) therapy.

An example of the outcomes approach is Retchin et al. (1992), which found no differences in the health status of elderly patients under the two types of coverage. Similarly, Yelin, Criswell, and Feigenbaum (1996) found no outcome difference for patients suffering from rheumatoid arthritis. By contrast, Ware et al. (1996) did find differences between managed care and FFS plans. They found that, over a four-year period, chronically ill nonelderly patients fared better in managed care plans, while chronically ill elderly and poor patients fared better in the FFS plans. Exactly why they observed different patterns depending on age and income remains an open question.

There are a number of studies that combine the process and outcomes approaches to measure quality. Young and Cohen (1991) found that managed care patients were less likely to receive coronary artery bypass graft and arteriography following AMI, but there were no statistically significant differences in post-AMI mortality. Similarly, Cutler, McClellan, and Newhouse (1997) found lower resource utilization in managed care plans but no difference in AMI mortality rates. Carlisle et al. (1992) took a similar approach, although with a more in-depth analysis of the process of medical care for AMI patients. They found higher-quality processes and lower AMI mortality rates in managed care plans.[2]

In this paper, we take a different approach. In particular, we compare

1. The NCQA takes the process approach, collecting information, for example, on whether health plans screen for breast and cervical cancer, advise smokers to quit smoking, and prescribe appropriate medication for heart disease.

2. One limitation of this study, however, is that it covers only three HMOs. The three are among the most successful HMOs in the United States, whereas the patients in the FFS plans were drawn from a broader sample reflecting hospitals and health care providers of average quality. It is an open question whether one would continue to see differences in performance if one compared the FFS patients to patients in a broader cross-section of HMOs.

the hospitals and physicians that treat managed care patients and FFS patients. The starting point for our analysis is the large literature establishing that patients have better clinical outcomes when they are treated by physicians and hospitals with more experience treating the disease. For example, it has been shown that the patients of surgeons and hospitals that perform a larger number of coronary artery bypass grafts (CABGs) are less likely to die during or shortly after the procedure. The relationship between physician and hospital volume and outcomes has also been established for a wide range of surgical procedures and some medical treatments of chronic illness, including orthopedic surgery, angioplasty, organ transplantation, colorectal and breast cancer, hysterectomy, and AIDS.

The precise mechanism that links volume and outcome is unknown. It could be that experience makes physicians and hospitals better; that is, there is some sort of learning-by-doing.[3] Or it could be that higher-volume hospitals and physicians attract more patients because they are correctly perceived by patients to be better. For our purposes, the exact cause of the relationship between volume and outcome is less important than the fact that such a relationship exists.

Thus, our empirical goal is simply to examine whether patients in managed care plans tend to be treated by higher- or lower-volume physicians and hospitals. We analyze this question using data on all hospital discharges in Massachusetts in 1995. These data identify the physicians and hospitals providing the care, as well as the patient's insurance plan (e.g., Harvard Community Health Plan, HMO Blue, Blue Cross/Blue Shield, Medicare, etc.). The data set also provides fairly detailed clinical information—patient diagnoses and procedures performed—as well as some demographic information on the patients.

We examine the relationship between managed care and volume for surgeries related to three types of cancer: breast cancer, colorectal cancer, and gynecologic cancer. We chose these particular diseases because they are almost always treated surgically, and thus there are unlikely to be major differences in whether managed care patients or FFS patients are treated surgically. We find that, on average, and after controlling for demographic differences, patients with breast cancer who are covered by managed care plans are operated on by physicians who performed 22 percent fewer procedures than the physicians of FFS patients. Managed care patients with gynecologic cancers are operated on by physicians who perform 25 percent fewer surgeries. There is no appreciable difference between managed care and FFS plans in the volume of the physicians operating on patients with colorectal cancer.

---

3. Laffel et al. (1992) suggests that learning by doing is part of the explanation. They examined the performance of physicians and hospitals as they became more experienced performing heart transplantation.

These averages mask considerable heterogeneity across plans. Some managed care plans use physicians with volumes that are considerably lower than the average. For example, one of the plans used physicians performing 43 percent fewer breast surgeries and 68 percent fewer hysterectomies. By contrast, patients in another plan were treated by physicians who were slightly less experienced than the physicians of FFS patients, and the difference was statistically insignificant.

We also find that managed care patients tend to be treated at hospitals that perform fewer procedures. For example, in the case of breast cancer surgery, patients in five of the six largest plans are treated at hospitals with significantly lower volumes—hospitals with volume 35 percent below the average of FFS patients' hospitals. One finds similar results for colorectal cancer surgery, and statistically insignificant differences for gynecologic cancer surgery. However, one of the managed care plans sends patients to hospitals with 23–41 percent higher volume than the hospitals of FFS patients (depending on the procedure).

If one accepts the view that volume and quality are related, then these results indicate that, in many cases, managed care plans offer lower quality care than FFS plans. The results also indicate that not all managed care plans are alike; not surprisingly, some are better than others. Moreover, even the same managed care plans can offer different quality care for different diseases.

These results are consistent with Escarce, Shea, and Chen (1997), who find that managed care patients undergoing coronary artery bypass graft in southeastern Florida were more likely than FFS patients to be treated at lower-volume hospitals. By contrast, Chernew, Scanlon, and Hayward (1998) find that in 1991 in California, managed care patients were more likely to be treated at high-quality hospitals—those with low mortality rates (and probably high volume). The differences in the results across studies is consistent with our view that not all managed care plans are alike, and it also suggests that health care markets may differ. More research into understanding these differences would clearly be useful.

In the next section of the paper, we discuss the data used in this study and describe our empirical approach. Section 7.3 presents the basic empirical results. We discuss the implications of the results and suggest future research opportunities in section 7.4.

7.2   Data and Empirical Approach

We use the 1995 hospital case mix and charge data compiled by the Division of Health Care Finance and Policy of the Massachusetts Office of Health and Human Services. Like most states, Massachusetts requires hospitals to report detailed clinical and financial information on all hospital stays. However, Massachusetts is one of the few states that includes (encrypted) physician identifiers in the data set and identifies the health care plan by name and type.[4] We use 1995 data because it is the first full year with physician identifiers, and the 1996 data were not available when we began this study.

While, in principle, one could analyze all hospital admissions, we chose not to do so. The reason is that hospital admissions and surgeries may differ in the extent to which they are discretionary. For example, prostate cancer can be treated with surgery or by outpatient radiation therapy. Because we did not want our analysis to be confounded by the possibility that managed care plans and fee-for-service plans differ in the extent to which they treat patients on an inpatient or outpatient basis, we chose to focus on diagnoses and treatments where there is little discretion as to whether to perform inpatient surgery. While there are possibly many such diagnoses and treatments, we focus on the following three: (1) breast cancer treated with mastectomy or lumpectomy;[5] (2) gynecologic cancer (ovarian, uterine, cervical) treated with hysterectomy (total abdominal or radical);[6] and (3) colorectal cancer treated with resection of colon or rectum.[7]

For each of these procedures there is evidence that the patients of high-volume providers have better outcomes. As a measure of experience with one of the procedures, for each physician we calculate the total number of such procedures the physician performed during the year. This number includes procedures that were performed for diagnoses other than cancer, such as hysterectomy for nonmalignant uterine fibroids.[8] Of course, this measure—which we refer to as *physician volume*—is only an imperfect proxy for the physician's experience with the procedure, and an even more imperfect proxy for the physician's skill with the procedure. Unfortunately, we were unable to get further information on physicians such as years of practice, board certification, and subspecialty training. The analogous measure of a hospital's experience with one of the procedures is the total number of the procedures performed at the hospital for the relevant diagnoses, which we refer to as *hospital volume*.

Our focus is on the relationship between the patient's health plan and

4. Other states may indicate the type of health care coverage but not the actual name of the health plan.

5. Breast cancer is defined here as ICD9 hospital codes 1740–1749 inclusive. The surgical procedures are ICD9 hospital codes 8521–8523 inclusive, 8541, and 8543.

6. Gynecologic cancer is defined here as ICD9 hospital codes 179 and 1800–1839 inclusive; total abdominal hysterectomy is ICD9 code 6840, and radical abdominal hysterectomy is ICD9 code 6860.

7. Colorectal cancer is defined here as ICD9 hospital diagnoses codes 1530–1541 inclusive; the procedures are ICD9 hospital procedure codes 4573–4576 inclusive and 4863.

8. An alternative measure of physician experience with the procedure could include only the procedures performed to treat the cancer diagnoses. Although we do not report the results, the basic conclusions are unaffected by this alternative definition of physician experience.

the experience of the physicians treating the patient. There are several different categories of health plans recorded in the Massachusetts case mix data. Two are Medicaid and Free Care (a state-run program for the otherwise uninsured), which we exclude from the analysis because the indigent populations they serve are likely to be quite different from the population with private insurance and Medicare. There are four managed care plan categories: health maintenance organizations (HMOs), preferred provider organizations (PPOs), commercial managed care, and Medicare managed care. Because the differences among HMOs, PPOs, and commercial managed care are unclear—at least in the way they are coded in the data—we make no distinction among these types of plans.

In 1995, the managed care plans in Massachusetts with the largest number of hospital admissions were (1) HMO Blue (a managed care plan offered by Blue Cross/Blue Shield), with 35,949 admissions; (2) Harvard Community Health Plan (HCHP), with 30,621 admissions; (3) Tufts Associated Health Plan, with 24,584 admissions; (4) Pilgrim Health Care (since merged with HCHP), with 20,379 admissions; (5) Fallon, with 11,488 admissions; and (6) Bay State Health Care (another Blue Cross/Blue Shield managed care plan), with 9,997 admissions. In our analysis, we will break out the results for these large managed care plans, and group all other managed care plans together. Because of the possibly sensitive nature of our results, we will not identify these plans by name when we present the specific results.

There are also a number of different types of fee-for-service plans. The largest is Medicare, with 287,285 hospital admissions, and the largest private plan is Blue Cross/Blue Shield Indemnity, with 40,269 admissions. There are also 31 commercial plans identified by name, the largest of which is John Hancock Life Insurance, with 4,211 hospital admissions. In our analysis we separate out the results for Medicare fee-for-service, and we group Blue Cross/Blue Shield together with all commercial FFS plans.

In addition to the type of health insurance, there are other factors that can have an effect on physician and hospital choice. In particular, proximity to high-volume hospitals should increase the likelihood that patients are treated by high-volume providers. As a measure of proximity, we use the shortest distance from the zip code of the patient's residence to the 10 highest-volume hospitals for the procedure.[9] Income may also have an effect on provider choice since higher-income patients are likely to be more educated health care consumers. Although we do not have patient income data, we do have information on median income in the patient's zip code of residence. Age and race may also affect provider choice.

In the patient-level regression analysis for each procedure, we examine

---

9. One could also calculate distance to high-volume physicians, but it is highly correlated with distance to high-volume hospitals.

whether managed care patients are treated by higher- or lower-volume providers than are FFS patients, controlling for patient demographic characteristics. Thus, the regressions take the following form:

$$\text{Provider Volume}_i = \alpha_0 + \sum_j \alpha_j \text{Insurance Plan}_{ij} + \beta_1 \ln(\text{Age}_i)$$

$$+ \beta_2 \ln(\text{Income}_i) + \sum_k \beta_{3k} \text{Race Dummies}_i + \beta_4 \ln(\text{Distance}_i) + \varepsilon_i,$$

where Provider Volume refers to the number of procedures performed by the provider (hospital or physician) during the year, and i indexes patients.

Before presenting the results of the regression analysis, it is worth reviewing the characteristics of the sample. Table 7.1 provides summary statistics for each of the three cancer surgeries. The mean physician volumes

Table 7.1   **Sample Summary Statistics**

Variable	Breast Cancer Surgery	Colorectal Cancer Surgery	Gynecologic Cancer Surgery
Physician volume	15.6	18.4	21.0
	[11]	[17]	[5]
	(14.5)	(11.4)	(24.9)
Hospital volume	91.7	120.4	65.1
	[67]	[102]	[65]
	(81.3)	(79.1)	(56.7)
Age	63.3	72.5	62.6
	[66]	[73]	[65]
	(14.6)	(10.8)	(13.6)
Income (1990)	18,178.9	17,758.2	17,726.7
	[16,741]	[16,683]	[16,409]
	(6,138.8)	(5,797.4)	(5,499.2)
Distance (in miles) to	22.0	11.7	19.3
high-volume hospital	[11.3]	[9.9]	[11.9]
	(88.5)	(11.8)	(43.2)
% White	92.8	93.9	93.1
% Private fee-for-service	16.2	9.0	19.2
% Private managed care	30.4	13.2	29.7
% Medicare fee-for-service	52.2	75.3	48.9
% Medicare managed care	1.2	2.5	2.2
N	2,042	2,220	902

Note: The table records means of some of the variables in the data set broken out by breast cancer surgery, colorectal cancer surgery, and gynecologic cancer surgery. (See notes 5–7 for more precise definitions of the diseases and surgeries.) The number in brackets is the median of the variable, and the number in parentheses is the standard deviation. Physician volume is the number of procedures performed by the physicians, including those that were not performed for a cancer diagnosis. The sample includes only those patients covered by private insurance and Medicare, thus eliminating patients covered by Medicaid, Free Care, other government programs, and patients paying themselves.

for breast cancer surgery, colorectal cancer surgery, and gynecologic cancer surgery are 15.6, 18.4, and 21.0, respectively. There is substantial heterogeniety in the physician volumes for each of these procedures. For example, the standard deviation of physician volume for breast cancer surgery is 14.5, almost as large as the mean. The physician in the lowest 25th percentile performs 6 surgeries, while the physician in the 75th percentile performs 20.

These numbers count physicians each time they perform surgery, thus oversampling the high-volume physicians and understating the number of low-volume physicians. For example, of the 400 physicians performing at least 1 breast cancer surgery in the sample, 25 percent performed 3 or fewer, 75 percent performed 9 or fewer, and only 7.5 percent (30 physicians) performed 20 or more. For gynecologic cancer, the median physician performed only 1 hysterectomy, and there were only 14 out of 313 (4.5 percent) who performed 20 or more. For colon cancer, 451 physicians performed at least 1 surgery for the disease, the median performed 9 surgeries, and 58 (12.91 percent) performed 20 or more surgeries.

Table 7.1 shows that mean hospital volume is 91.9 for breast cancer surgery, 119.2 for colon cancer surgery, and 65.1 for gynecologic cancer surgery. Here, too, the variation across providers is very large. Of the 76 hospitals performing at least 1 surgery for breast cancer, 25 percent performed fewer than 15, 75 percent performed fewer than 52, and there were only 6 that performed more than 100 surgeries during the year. The volume numbers are even lower for gynecologic cancer: Of the 66 hospitals operating on women with gynecologic cancer, 25 percent performed fewer than 4 such procedures, 75 percent performed fewer than 17, 7 performed more than 60 procedures, and only 3 performed more than 100. In the case of colorectal cancer, the hospital volume numbers are considerable higher. Of the 73 hospitals, 25 percent performed fewer than 29, 50 percent performed fewer than 65, and 75 percent performed fewer than 100. There are 19 hospitals that performed 100 or more surgeries for colon cancer.

In addition to summary statistics on some of the demographic variables, table 7.1 provides information on patients' insurance. Given that cancer tends to be concentrated among the elderly, it is not surprising that most of the patients (51–78 percent depending on the cancer) have Medicare insurance. However, only a small fraction of these Medicare patients (3–4 percent) are covered by managed care. The non-Medicare patients are covered by private managed care plans or fee-for-service plans. Depending on the procedure, between 60 percent and 65 percent of these privately insured patients are covered by managed care plans.

7.3   Empirical Results

7.3.1   Physician Volume

For each of the three surgeries, table 7.2 lists the mean physician volumes for (1) all private fee-for-service plans; (2) the six largest private (non-Medicare, non-Medicaid) managed care plans; (3) all other private managed care plans grouped together; (4) standard Medicare fee-for-service; and (5) Medicare managed care plans grouped together. In all three cases, the mean physician volume of private FFS patients exceeds that of private managed care patients. We discuss the results for each of the three surgeries in turn.

Table 7.2   **Mean Physician Volume for Various Health Care Plans**

Type of Health Insurance Plan	Breast Cancer Surgery	Colorectal Cancer Surgery	Gynecologic Cancer Surgery
Private fee-for-service	20.8	18.0	23.9
Private managed care	16.4	17.3	18.3
Plan A	18.6	13.2	24.4
	(0.217)	(0.008)	(0.891)
Plan B	13.0	17.2	13.0
	(< 0.001)	(0.562)	(0.004)
Plan C	16.9	18.6	18.3
	(0.027)	(0.733)	(0.237)
Plan D	16.2	18.3	13.6
	(0.003)	(0.887)	(0.002)
Plan E	16.1	18.1	13.7
	(0.071)	(0.991)	(0.017)
Plan F	13.0	22.2	9.2
	(< 0.001)	(0.114)	(< 0.001)
Other	16.2	17.3	23.7
	(0.002)	(0.611)	(0.496)
Medicare			
Fee-for-service	14.0	18.6	22.0
	(< 0.001)	(0.486)	(0.406)
Managed care	14.9	23.1	8.4
	(0.007)	(0.004)	(< 0.001)
N	2,148	2,353	947

Note: The table records the mean physician volumes broken out by breast cancer surgery, colorectal cancer surgery, and gynecologic cancer surgery and type of health plan. (See notes 5–7 for more precise definitions of the diseases and surgeries.) The number in parentheses is the p-value of the difference with the private fee-for-service health plans, calculated using White's (1980) robust standard errors. Physician volume is the number of procedures performed by the physicians, including those that were not performed for a cancer diagnosis. The sample includes only those patients covered by private insurance and Medicare, thus eliminating patients covered by Medicaid, Free Care, other government programs, and patients paying themselves.

Breast Cancer Surgery

The mean physician volume for private FFS plans is 20.8, compared to 16.4 for private managed care patients; that is, FFS is 27 percent higher than managed care. For all of the large managed care plans except Plan A, the differential is statistically significant. In the case of Plan B and Plan F, the difference in physician volume is very large; physicians that treat private FFS patients perform 60 percent more surgeries than the physicians treating Plan B and Plan F patients (i.e., 20.5 versus 13.0 for Plans B and F).

Physicians treating patients covered by Medicare—both FFS and managed care—perform fewer surgeries than the physicians treating private FFS patients. The differences are large: The physician volume of private FFS patients is 49 percent higher than the physician volume of Medicare FFS patients (14.0) and 40 percent higher than the physician volume of Medicare managed care patients (14.9).

Table 7.3 indicates the predicted physician volumes for the various health care plans using the regression model described in section 7.2. The predicted values are based on the means of the demographic variables—age, income, distance to large hospitals, and race. The table indicates that there continue to be statistically significant differences in physician volumes between private managed care and FFS plans and that the magnitude of the differences is not changed much. The difference between Medicare and private FFS is reduced and is no longer statistically significant.

Colorectal Cancer Surgery

The mean volume of physicians treating private FFS patients with colorectal cancer is 18.0 as compared to 17.3 for private managed care patients. The overall difference is not statistically significant and only one of the seven private managed care plans, Plan A, exhibits a statistically significant difference in physician volume as compared to FFS plans. The regression analysis that controls for demographic variables does not change this conclusion. The mean physician volume of Medicare FFS patients is slightly higher (but insignificantly so) than FFS patients, while the mean physician volume of Medicare managed care patients is significantly higher than that of private FFS patients. In table 7.3, once demographic controls are included, the difference between Medicare FFS and private FFS becomes statistically significant and the difference between Medicare managed care and private FFS remains statistically significant.

Gynecologic Cancer Surgery

The average number of procedures performed by physicians treating private FFS patients for gynecologic cancer is 23.9 as compared to 18.3 for physicians treating patients in private managed care plans. Physicians

Table 7.3   **Mean Demographically Adjusted Physician Volume for Various Health Care Plans**

Type of Health Insurance Plan	Breast Cancer Surgery	Colorectal Cancer Surgery	Gynecologic Cancer Surgery
Private fee-for-service	17.9	16.4	21.7
Private managed care	14.0	15.7	16.2
Plan A	15.8	11.4	19.9
	(0.229)	(0.007)	(0.605)
Plan B	10.2	15.7	8.0
	(< 0.001)	(0.634)	(< 0.001)
Plan C	14.8	17.1	19.3
	(0.087)	(0.351)	(0.615)
Plan D	14.1	17.0	15.1
	(0.016)	(0.283)	(0.055)
Plan E	14.1	16.5	11.0
	(0.187)	(0.981)	(0.005)
Plan F	10.9	19.7	10.3
	(< 0.001)	(0.210)	(< 0.001)
Other	14.2	15.8	21.2
	(0.010)	(0.413)	(0.860)
Medicare			
Fee-for-service	15.8	19.0	24.0
	(0.094)	(0.016)	(0.396)
Managed care	16.8	21.7	9.8
	(0.634)	(0.009)	(0.001)
N	2,042	2,220	902

Note: The table records the predicted physician volumes broken out by breast cancer surgery, colorectal cancer surgery, and gynecologic cancer surgery and type of health plan. (See notes 5–7 for more precise definitions of the diseases and surgeries.) The number in parentheses is the *p*-value of the difference with the private fee-for-service health plans, calculated using White's (1980) robust standard errors. Physician volume is the number of procedures performed by the physicians, including those that were not performed for a cancer diagnosis. The sample includes only those patients covered by private insurance and Medicare, thus eliminating patients covered by Medicaid, Free Care, other government programs, and patients paying themselves. The demographic adjustments include race, log of age, log of median income in the patient's zip code, and the log distance to the closest of the 10 highest volume hospitals performing the procedure. The predicted physician volumes are derived from the regression model described in the text evaluated at the means of the demographic controls.

used by patients in four of the six largest managed care plans have statistically significant lower volume than physicians used by FFS patients. The magnitude of the differences are very large. In the case of Plan F, the average physician volume is 62 percent lower than the average volume of private FFS plans (9.2 versus 23.9). Physician volume in Medicare managed care plans (8.4 surgeries per year) is also significantly lower than physician volume in private FFS plans and Medicare FFS plans (22.0 surgeries per year). The differences continue to hold once demographic controls are included, as table 7.3 shows.

7.3.2 Hospital Volume

Tables 7.4 and 7.5 indicate that managed care and FFS patients are treated at hospitals with significant differences in the number of procedures they perform. Table 7.4 gives the raw means for the various plans, while table 7.5 adjusts the means for demographic factors.

Breast Cancer Surgery

The average private FFS patient is treated at a hospital that performs 120.9 surgeries per year, while the average managed care patient is treated at a hospital that performs 99.8 surgeries per year. However, patients in one of the managed care plans, Plan A, are treated by hospitals with significantly higher volume than the patients covered by private FFS plans—

Table 7.4	Mean Hospital Volume for Various Health Care Plans		
Type of Health Insurance Plan	Breast Cancer Surgery	Colorectal Cancer Surgery	Gynecologic Cancer Surgery
Private fee-for-service	120.9	134.7	67.1
Private managed care	99.8	121.2	63.4
Plan A	171.1	168.4	99.9
	(< 0.001)	(0.002)	(< 0.001)
Plan B	63.7	98.4	33.0
	(< 0.001)	(< 0.001)	(< 0.001)
Plan C	89.0	121.2	54.3
	(< 0.001)	(0.208)	(0.288)
Plan D	81	116.9	56.3
	(< 0.001)	(0.035)	(0.207)
Plan E	80.8	104.9	70.3
	(0.001)	(0.018)	(0.021)
Plan F	53.9	102.1	54.7
	(< 0.001)	(0.016)	(0.083)
Other	83.0	117.5	62.7
	(< 0.001)	(0.057)	(0.496)
Medicare			
Fee-for-service	80.9	119.2	65.6
	(< 0.001)	(0.015)	(0.761)
Managed care	73.9	156.7	63.2
	(< 0.001)	(0.007)	(0.696)
N	2,148	2,353	947

Note: The table records the mean hospital volumes broken out by breast cancer surgery, colorectal cancer surgery, and gynecologic cancer surgery. (See notes 5–7 for more precise definitions of the diseases and surgeries.) The number in parentheses is the p-value of the difference with the private fee-for-service health plans, calculated using White's (1980) robust standard errors. Physician volume is the number of procedures performed by the physicians, including those that were not performed for a cancer diagnosis. The sample includes only those patients covered by private insurance and Medicare, thus eliminating patients covered by Medicaid, Free Care, other government programs, and patients paying themselves.

Table 7.5   **Mean Demographically Adjusted Hospital Volume for Various Health Care Plans**

Type of Health Insurance Plan	Breast Cancer Surgery	Colorectal Cancer Surgery	Gynecologic Cancer Surgery
Private fee-for-service	106.5	120.4	63.5
Private managed care	87.1	107.1	58.3
Plan A	149.9	148.1	90.8
	(< 0.001)	(0.011)	(0.003)
Plan B	46.2	86.0	23.8
	(< 0.001)	(< 0.001)	(< 0.001)
Plan C	75.1	99.5	55.8
	(0.001)	(0.064)	(0.533)
Plan D	74.9	106.0	52.3
	(< 0.001)	(0.088)	(0.231)
Plan E	66.9	92.6	56.4
	(0.002)	(0.044)	(0.618)
Plan F	46.2	96.2	54.3
	(< 0.001)	(< 0.041)	(0.454)
Other	74.2	103.7	58.8
	(< 0.001)	(.053)	(.538)
Medicare			
Fee-for-service	89.9	121.4	69.6
	(0.013)	(0.873)	(0.324)
Managed care	85.7	159.7	70.1
	(0.130)	(< 0.001)	(0.625)
N	2,042	2,220	902

Note: The table records the predicted hospital volumes broken out by breast cancer surgery, colorectal cancer surgery, and gynecologic cancer surgery and type of health plan. (See notes 5–7 for more precise definitions of the diseases and surgeries.) The number in parentheses is the *p*-value of the difference with the private fee-for-service health plans, calculated using White's (1980) robust standard errors. Physician volume is the number of procedures performed by the physicians, including those that were not performed for a cancer diagnosis. The sample includes only those patients covered by private insurance and Medicare, thus eliminating patients covered by Medicaid, Free Care, other government programs, and patients paying themselves. The demographic adjustments include race, log of age, log of median income in the patient's zip code, and the log distance to the closest of the 10 highest volume hospitals performing the procedure. The predicted hospital volumes are derived from the regression model described in the text evaluated at the means of the demographic controls.

171.1 for Plan A versus 120.9 for the private FFS plans. As will be discussed shortly, this differential for Plan A is true of the other procedures as well. Interestingly though, while Plan A patients are treated at higher-volume hospitals than private FFS patients, table 7.2 indicates that they are not treated by higher-volume physicians. In fact, patients covered by Plan A are treated by relatively low-volume physicians at high-volume hospitals.

The patients covered by the other managed care plans are treated at significantly lower-volume hospitals—from 23 percent lower in the case of Plan C to as much as 56 percent lower in the case of Plan F. On average, patients in Plans B through F are treated at hospitals with volumes of 79.2, 34 percent below the average for FFS patients.

Finally, patients covered by both types of Medicare plans—FFS and managed care—are treated at lower-volume hospitals.

Table 7.5 presents the means once they are adjusted for demographic differences, and there is no appreciable difference in the results. Plan A patients are treated at higher-volume hospitals than FFS patients, and patients in Plans B through F are treated at hospitals with 35 percent lower volume.

Colon Cancer Surgery

The same pattern exists for colon cancer surgery, although the magnitude of the differences are somewhat smaller. On average, patients in private FFS plans are treated at hospitals with a volume of 134.7 colorectal surgeries, while the corresponding volume is 121.2 for private managed care plans. Here, too, Plan A patients are treated at higher-volume hospitals than FFS patients. As table 7.2 shows, they are treated by low-volume physicians at these high-volume hospitals. Patients in all other managed care plans are treated at lower-volume hospitals than patients in private FFS plans. On average, they are treated at hospitals with a volume of 110.2 as compared to 134.7 for FFS patients, an 18 percent differential.

The same pattern of results carry over to table 7.5, where demographic controls are included. Plan A patients are treated at higher-volume hospitals and patients in Plans B through F are treated at hospitals that perform an average of 22 percent fewer surgeries than the hospitals of FFS patients.

Gynecologic Cancer Surgery

The difference between private FFS and private managed care plans are somewhat less pronounced for gynecologic cancer surgery. The overall mean for private FFS patients is 67.1, while it is 63.4 for private managed care patients. Plan A patients are treated at hospitals with relatively high volumes, those with an average volume of 90.8. Patients in the other plans are treated at hospitals with lower volume, but the only plan where the difference is statistically significant is Plan B, with an average volume of 33.0 as compared to 67.1 for private FFS patients. Inclusion of demographic controls does not alter this basic conclusion.

7.3.3 Effect of Demographic Variables

Panels A and B of table 7.6 provide information on the effect of demographic variables on the choice of physician and hospital. The effects are estimated from the regression analysis described in section 7.2 and are evaluated at the means of all the other variables in the regression.

Table 7.6   **Effects of Demographic Variables on Physician Volume and Hospital Volume**

Demographic Variable	Breast Cancer Surgery	Colorectal Cancer Surgery	Gynecologic Cancer Surgery
A. Physician Volume			
Income			
1 st. dev. below mean	13.8	16.1	17.0
1 st. dev. above mean	16.9	17.9	25.0
	(< 0.001)	(< 0.001)	(< 0.001)
Age			
1 st. dev. below mean	17.8	17.9	22.3
1 st. dev. above mean	12.9	16.1	19.6
	(< 0.001)	(0.005)	(0.0189)
Race			
African American	14.2	14.8	30.1
White	15.5	18.3	19.2
	(0.557)	(0.007)	(0.049)
Distance to high-volume hospital			
1 st. dev. below mean	15.4	18.2	19.8
1 st. dev. above mean	15.3	15.8	22.2
	(0.824)	(0.001)	(0.265)
N	2,042	2,220	902
B. Hospital Volume			
Income			
1 st. dev. below mean	80.5	110.0	60.7
1 st. dev. above mean	103.3	128.4	69.5
	(< 0.001)	(< 0.001)	(0.024)
Age			
1 st. dev. below mean	102.5	127.4	70.4
1 st. dev. above mean	81.3	111.0	59.8
	(< 0.001)	(< 0.001)	(0.050)
Race			
African American	148.6	131.9	73.6
White	88.3	129.2	65.6
	(0.002)	(0.795)	(0.573)
Distance to high-volume hospital			
1 st. dev. below mean	98.0	137.3	68.6
1 st. dev. above mean	85.8	101.1	61.6
	(< 0.001)	(< 0.001)	(0.086)
N	2,042	2,220	902

Note: The table records the predicted physician volumes (panel A) and hospital volumes (panel B) broken out by breast cancer surgery, colorectal cancer surgery, and gynecologic cancer surgery for different values of the demographic control variables. (See notes 5–7 for more precise definitions of the diseases and surgeries.) The number in parentheses is the *p*-value of the coefficient of the demographic control in the regression analysis described in the text. Physician volume is the number of procedures performed by the physicians, including those that were not performed for a cancer diagnosis. The sample includes only those patients covered by private insurance and Medicare, thus eliminating patients covered by Medicaid, Free Care, other government programs, and patients paying themselves. The demographic controls are race, log of age, log of median income in the patient's zip code, and the log distance to the closest of the 10 highest volume hospitals performing the procedure.

The tables indicate that higher-income patients—or more precisely, patients living in higher-income zip codes—are more prone to go to higher-volume physicians (panel A) and higher-volume hospitals (panel B). For all the procedures, the effect of income on volume is highly statistically significant. In the case of breast cancer surgery, patients with income one standard deviation above the mean are treated by physicians with 22 percent higher volume than the physicians of patients with income one standard deviation below the mean (16.9 procedures versus 13.8). The higher-income breast cancer patients are treated at hospitals with 28 percent higher volume than the hospitals that treat lower income patients (103.3 versus 80.5).

The effects of income on physician and hospital volume are somewhat smaller for colorectal cancer surgery; higher-income patients are treated by physicians that perform 11 percent more surgeries and than the physicians of lower-income patients (17.9 versus 16.1) and at hospitals that perform 17 percent more surgeries (128.4 versus 110.0).[10] Finally, the effect of income on physician volume is quite large in the case of gynecologic cancer surgery, with higher-income patients being treated by physicians that perform 47 percent more surgeries than the physicians of lower-income patients (25.0 versus 17.0). The effect of income on hospital volume for this procedure is smaller; higher-income patients are treated at hospitals with only 11 percent higher volume than the hospitals of lower-income patients (69.5 versus 60.7).

These results are consistent with the findings of McClellan and Skinner (1997) that higher-income Medicare patients use more Medicare services, mostly physician and outpatient services. This suggests that higher-income patients are more aggressive in seeking high-quality health care. Thus, it is not surprising that they tend to seek care from higher-volume physicians and hospitals.

Age also has an effect on provider choice; older patients tend to be treated by lower-volume physicians and hospitals. For example, the average 84-year-old with breast cancer (one standard deviation above the mean) is treated by physicians who performed 12.9 breast cancer surgeries during the year, while the average 61-year-old with breast cancer (one standard deviation below the mean) was treated by a physician who performed 17.8 (38 percent more) breast cancer surgeries. The average 84-year-old is treated at hospitals that perform 81.3 breast cancer surgeries, while the average 61-year-old is treated at hospitals that perform 102.5 surgeries. There are similar effects of age for the other procedures, though the magnitudes of the effects are smaller. It is not completely clear how to

10. A small part of the difference in the effect of income for colorectal and breast cancer surgeries is attributable to the lower standard deviation of income for colorectal cancer patients.

interpret the results on age. One possible interpretation is that it is more difficult for elderly patients to find high-volume physicians or travel to high-volume hospitals.

Table 7.6 presents inconclusive evidence on the effects of race on provider choice. White patients tend to be treated by higher-volume physicians than African American patients for colorectal cancer, but the opposite is true for gynecologic cancer, and there is no significant difference for breast cancer. African American women are treated for breast cancer at hospitals with significantly higher volumes than white women, but there are no significant effects of race for colorectal cancer and gynecologic cancer.

Finally, table 7.6 presents evidence that proximity to high-volume hospitals increases the likelihood that patients will be treated at higher-volume hospitals. The effect is relatively small for breast cancer and gynecologic cancer and larger for colorectal cancer. Hospital proximity has no effect on physician choice for breast cancer and gynecologic cancer, but it does have an effect for colorectal cancer.

7.4   Discussion and Conclusion

The results of this paper indicate that patients covered by managed care plans tend to be treated by lower-volume physicians and at lower-volume hospitals than patients covered by FFS plans. Although this is the overall pattern, there is quite a bit of variation across health plans. The patients in one plan (Plan B) were treated by physicians who performed many fewer surgeries than physicians treating FFS patients, while there was little difference in physician volume for another plan (Plan C). One of the health plans (Plan A) treated their patients at hospitals with considerably higher volume than FFS patients, but Plan B patients were treated at hospitals with considerably lower volume. If volume is a valid indicator of quality, it suggests that there is substantial variation in health care quality across managed care plans.

Our results, at first glance, seem difficult to reconcile with the literature on managed care quality, which find little systematic differences in the health outcomes of managed care and FFS patients. If our results are valid—that is, if there are quality differences between the two types of coverage as a result of provider-volume differences—why don't we see these differences in the health outcomes of managed care and FFS patients? There are two possible answers. One is that the literature investigating quality differentials tends to focus on outcomes of chronic diseases that are generally managed through medical, rather than surgical, intervention. The quality of medical intervention may be harder to measure than the quality of the kinds of surgical interventions we are studying. The second answer may be that existing studies compare quality of FFS plans and the *average* managed care plan. As our study indicates, however, looking at averages may mask considerable heterogeneity across plans. Some managed care plans may be better than FFS plans, while others may be worse. Ultimately, to reconcile our results with the literature, it would be useful to more directly measure the health outcomes of patients in our sample.

One question that we have not addressed is exactly why it is that managed care patients tend to be treated by low-volume providers. One possibility is that managed care plans limit patients to using relatively low-volume providers. They might not be referred to specialists for their procedures, or their access to high-volume specialists may be restricted. In addition, managed care health plans may not send their patients to high-volume tertiary-care teaching hospitals because they only have contracts with low-volume community hospitals. This interpretation is plausible because lower-cost community hospitals and low-volume surgeons are likely to offer their services at more attractive rates to managed care health plans. To determine whether this is indeed the explanation, one could collect information on the hospitals and providers with whom the managed care plans have contracts.

An alternative interpretation of the findings is that managed care plans do not restrict patient choice, but rather that individuals who enroll in managed care plans are less-aggressive health care consumers. In this interpretation, even if they had enrolled in an FFS plan, they would choose to be treated by low-volume providers because they care less about the quality of their care. This leaves open the question of why managed care plans don't direct these patients to high-volume providers who offer higher-quality care. We suspect the answer again is that high-volume providers are more expensive.

This discussion raises the related question of why some managed care plans use high-volume providers and others do not. Ultimately, the negotiated prices between health care providers and insurers will depend on provider costs and the bargaining power of the two parties. It is likely that size gives providers and insurers bargaining power. Thus, one would expect the patients of larger insurance plans—those with more bargaining power vis-à-vis the hospitals—to be treated by higher-volume providers than the patients of smaller insurance plans. This implication is easy to analyze with our data. In addition, one could examine whether mergers between health plans—such as that between Harvard Community Health Plan and Pilgrim—affected the volume of the providers treating patients in these plans.

Another way to address this question is to analyze data from other states where managed care penetration levels differ. For example, in southern states where there is relatively little managed care penetration, high-volume physicians and hospitals are in better positions to turn away low-priced managed care contracts. As a result, one might expect to see bigger differences in the volume of physicians and hospitals treating managed care and fee-for-service patients in these states. By contrast, in California, the state with the largest managed care penetration, there may be little difference between managed care and fee-for-service plans, because all hospitals and physicians are reliant on managed care business. With a long enough time series, one could also examine how changes over time in managed care penetration affect the allocation of patients across low-volume and high-volume providers.

Finally, in order to draw more general conclusions about provider volume differences between managed care and FFS, one would have to analyze more procedures. Our preliminary analysis of other procedures—including those that are more elective in nature—indicates that the sort of effects we have identified are prevalent, at least in Massachusetts in 1995.

References

Carlisle, D. M., A. L. Siu, E. B. Keeler, E. A. McGlynn, K. L. Kahn, L. V. Rubenstein, and R. H. Brooks. 1992. HMO vs Fee-for-Service Care of Older Patients with Acute Myocardial Infarction. *American Journal of Public Health* 82 (12): 1626–30.

Chernew, M., D. Scanlon, and R. Hayward. 1998. Insurance Type and Choice of Hospital for Coronary Artery Bypass Graft Surgery. *Health Services Research* 33:447–66.

Cutler, D., M. McClellan, and J. Newhouse. 1997. Prices and Production in Managed Care Insurance. Working paper. Harvard University, Cambridge, Mass.

Escarce, J., J. Shea, and W. Chen. 1997. Segmentation of Hospital Markets: When Do HMO Enrollees Get Care? *Health Affairs* 16:181–92.

Feldman, S., B. Harlow, and D. Scharfstein. 1997. The Relationship between Surgical Volume and Complications, Length of Stay, and Inpatient Charges for Patients Undergoing Abdominal Hysterectomy. Brigham and Women's Hospital, Boston, Mass.

Hannan, E. L., M. Racz, T. J. Ryan, B. D. McCallister, L. W. Johnson, D. T. Arani, A. D. Guerci, J. Sosa, and E. J. Topol. 1997. Coronary Angioplasty Volume-Outcome Relationships for Hospitals and Cardiologists. *Journal of the American Medical Association* 277 (11): 892–98.

Laffel, G., A. Barnett, S. Finkelstein, and M. Kaye. 1992. The Relation Between Experience and Outcome in Heart Transplantation. *New England Journal of Medicine* 327 (17): 1220–25.

Luft, H. F., D. W. Garnick, D. H. Mark, and S. J. McPhee. 1990. *Hospital Volume, Physician Volume, and Patient Outcomes: Assessing the Evidence.* Ann Arbor, Mich.: Health Administration Press Perspectives.

McClellan, M., and J. Skinner. 1997. The Incidence of Medicare. NBER Working Paper no. 6013. Cambridge, Mass.: National Bureau of Economic Research.

Miller, R., and H. Luft. 1997. Does Managed Care Lead to Better or Worse Quality of Care? A Survey of Recent Studies Shows Mixed Results on Managed Care Plan Performance. *Health Affairs* 16 (5): 7–25.

Retchin, S. M., and B. Brown. 1990. Management of Colorectal Cancer in Medicare Health Maintenance Organizations. *Journal of General Internal Medicine* 5 (2): 110–14.

———. 1991. Elderly Patients with Congestive Heart Failure under Prepaid Care. *American Journal of Medicine* 90 (2): 236–42.

Retchin, S. M., R. Brown, S. C. J. Yeh, D. Chu, and L. Moreno. 1997. Outcomes for Patients with Stroke in Managed Care versus Fee-for-Service. *Journal of the American Medical Association* 278 (2): 119–24.

Retchin, S. M., D. G. Clement, L. F. Rossiter, B. Brown, R. Brown, and L. Nelson. 1992. How the Elderly Fare in HMOs: Outcomes from the Medicare Competition Demonstrations. *Health Services Research* 27 (5): 651–69.

Retchin, S. M., and J. Preston. 1991. The Effects of Cost Containment on the Care of Elderly Diabetics. *Archives of Internal Medicine* 151 (11): 2244–48.

Ware, J. E., Jr., M. S. Bayliss, W. H. Rogers, and A. R. Tarlov. 1996. Differences in 4-Year Health Outcomes for Elderly and Poor, Chronically Ill Patients Treated in HMO and Fee-for-Service Systems: Results from the Medical Outcomes Study. *Journal of the American Medical Association* 276 (13): 1039–47.

White, H. 1980. A Heteroskedasticity-Consistent Covariance Matrix Estimator and a Direct Test for Heteroskedasticity. *Econometrica* 48:817–30.

Yelin, E. H., L. A. Criswell, and P. G. Feigenbaum. 1996. Health Care Utilization and Outcomes among Persons with Rheumatoid Arthritis in Fee-for-Service and Prepaid Group Practices. *Journal of the American Medical Association* 276 (13): 1048–53.

Young, G., and B. Cohen. 1991. Inequities in Hospital Care, the Massachusetts Experience. *Inquiry* 28 (3): 255–62.

Implications of Managed Care for Teaching Hospitals
Comparisons of Traditional and Managed Care Medical Services within a Single Institution

David Meltzer, Frederick L. Hiltz, and David Bates

8.1 Introduction

The spread of managed care presents important challenges to teaching hospitals. Perhaps most importantly, the downward pressures on health care prices associated with the spread of managed care are forcing teaching hospitals to attempt to decrease their own costs. Yet the traditional independence of academic physicians and the rapid turnover of housestaff in teaching hospitals make many of the methods used by managed care to control costs—such as provider capitation, utilization review, and active management of care using critical pathways and other algorithms—especially difficult for teaching hospitals to implement.

The need to make these major changes in the operation of teaching hospitals comes at a time when changing physician workforce needs present a new set of educational challenges for teaching hospitals. Widespread belief that there is a growing surplus of physicians has led to national calls to decrease the number of physicians in training. Because of this belief that the numbers of physicians in training should be reduced, and because of the developing challenges to the solvency of the Medicare trust fund, the traditional revenue that academic medical centers have received from the federal government for graduate medical education is clearly in jeopardy. Moreover, at the same time, a growing demand for primary care

David Meltzer is assistant professor in the Section of General Internal Medicine, Department of Economics, and Harris Graduate School of Public Policy at the University of Chicago and a faculty research fellow of the National Bureau of Economic Research. Frederick L. Hiltz, Ph.D. is a software developer at Partners Healthcare System, Inc., in Boston, Massachusetts. David Bates is chief of the Division of General Medicine at Harvard Medical School and medical director of Clinical and Quality Analysis at Partners Healthcare System, Inc.

physicians, also driven by managed care, is forcing teaching hospitals to move housestaff from specialty and inpatient-oriented training to ambulatory and generalist training. Within residency programs in internal medicine, this is exemplified by the new Residency Review Commission requirement that at least 30 percent of training time being spent in the ambulatory setting (ACGME 1997).

With all of these challenges facing teaching hospitals, there are serious concerns about their ability to maintain their academic mission and financial viability. While prominent medical journals have devoted a great deal of attention to speculation concerning how teaching hospitals will and should meet these challenges related to the spread of managed care, there is surprisingly little empirical evidence about the effects of managed care on academic medical centers. In this paper we examine the experience of one large academic medical center and its relationship to a single large managed care organization. Although the institution in question represents, of course, only one institution, it is interesting to examine in some detail the role that managed care has come to play in that institution.

Section 8.2 describes the institutional context for this study, focusing on the different incentives of the traditional and managed medical services in the hospital. Section 8.3 provides some summary statistics that describe the populations in these two services, including data on the mix of patients by diagnosis and severity of illness. This provides preliminary data on costs and some insight into the ways in which a managed care service can affect the educational experience provided by the teaching hospital. Section 8.4 examines costs on the traditional and managed care services, including both differences in costs and causes of those differences. Although the ability to measure severity of illness with these data is limited, the results suggest that the managed care services do indeed have substantially lower costs than the traditional services, and that the lower costs are largely attributable to a decrease in length of stay. Section 8.5 examines this difference in length of stay within the context of house officer workload and summarizes results we have reported elsewhere concerning how differences in workload on the traditional and managed care services can affect length of stay and costs (Meltzer, Hiltz, and Bates 1997). A formal model of attending physician incentives and behavior that provides a potential mechanism for understanding these results is then presented in section 8.6. In focusing on the behavior of physicians as agents functioning within an incentive system structured by the hospital, the analysis is most similar in spirit to the work of Harris (1977) on the internal organization of hospitals. However, in emphasizing nonpecuniary incentives for physicians, and in suggesting that hospital production is inefficient, it has important connections to the broader literature on not-for-profit hospitals (i.e., Newhouse 1970, and Pauly and Redisch 1973). Section 8.7 concludes.

8.2   Institutional Context

The hospital we examine is one of the primary teaching hospitals of a major academic medical center (AMC). The managed care organization (MCO) is a local managed care organization with several hundred thousand covered lives. The two organizations have been closely linked since the establishment of the MCO approximately 30 years ago, with all of the faculty of the MCO holding faculty appointments at the academic medical center associated with the hospital. Nevertheless, until the 1980s, the MCO ran its own independent hospital. At that time, the MCO decided that it could decrease costs by closing its own hospital and contracting with the teaching hospital to provide inpatient care for its patients, with the physicians of the MCO maintaining primary control of those patients admitted to the hospital. The terms of this arrangement have varied over time. However, throughout the period covered by the data in this study (March 1994 to August 1995), the MCO compensated the hospital purely on a per diem rate independent of diagnosis or costs.

This study examines the 14,878 admissions to the internal medicine services during this period. Care on these services is divided among six services that constitute general internal medicine and subspecialty internal medicine care in the hospital (table 8.1). Physician staffing on these services generally follows a common pattern. Each service is divided into two teams, each of which is staffed by two interns, one resident, and one attending physician. On each service, each intern is on call every fourth night, so that one of the four interns from the two teams that constitute a service is on call every night. The on-call intern both admits new patients and provides "cross cover" for emergencies that arise among the patients usually cared for by the other three interns on the service. The residents across several services use a pooling arrangement so that the interns have supervision and assistance even when the usual resident from their team is not in the hospital.

Table 8.1   **Medicine Services**

Service	Description	No. of Patients during Study Period
Teams 1/2	Traditional general medicine service	2,519
Teams 3/4	Traditional hematology/oncology service	2,086
Teams 5/6	Managed care medicine service	2,472
Teams 7/8	Mixed traditional and managed care service	2,460
Teams 9/10	Traditional medicine service	2,455
Cards B1/B2	Traditional cardiology service	2,886
Total		14,878

Table 8.2   Distribution of Patients by Payer among Medicine Services

Service	Medicare	Other	Managed Care	Total
Teams 1/2	1,245	1,194	80	2,519
Teams 3/4	1,148	572	366	2,086
Teams 5/6	80	179	2,213	2,472
Teams 7/8	596	613	1,251	2,460
Teams 9/10	1,105	1,208	142	2,455
Cards B1/B2	1,338	1,541	7	2,886
Total	5,512	5,307	4,059	14,878

This basic model holds on all six services. However, the services also have important differences. Teams 1/2 and 9/10 are traditional general medicine services. As seen in table 8.2, a large portion of patients on these services are Medicare patients. The "other" category is diverse, including a mixture of patients with traditional indemnity insurance, insurance from smaller managed care plans, Medicaid, or no insurance. As in most teaching hospitals, care on the traditional services is supervised by academic medicine attendings employed by the teaching hospital. This is true on both the general medicine and specialty services. On those teams, the attending is responsible both for patient care and for teaching the housestaff and medical students. The majority of managed care patients are on teams 5/6. On those teams, teaching is provided by an attending employed by the managed care service who has no direct patient care responsibilities, while management of the patients remains under the control of attendings from the individual health centers of the managed care organization. A smaller number of managed care patients are cared for on the other services (especially teams 7/8, which later became a managed care service run along the model of teams 5/6). On these teams, patient care decisions for the managed care patients are made by the managed care attendings, while traditional attendings perform the majority of teaching.

There are important differences in the incentives of housestaff and attendings on the two services. While the analysis that follows will focus on financial incentives to minimize resource utilization, it should be noted that both attendings and housestaff have strong incentives to provide high-quality care. All are informally but closely evaluated by their peers for the quality of care they provide, and both the AMC and MCO have reputations for patient care of extremely high quality that they do not want to jeopardize. On the traditional services, the evaluation of housestaff is more formal, with a written evaluation prepared by the attending physician at the end of each month. While these evaluations generally will not have a large effect on a house officer, the opinions of attendings concerning a house officer may have important effects on their ability to obtain a desirable fellowship position or job following residency. Perhaps because patient care on the managed care service is divided among the attendings from the different health centers, evaluation on that service comes only from the teaching attending, who has relatively little opportunity to observe the house officer in direct patient care. Financial incentives play no significant role in determining the quality of care provided by the housestaff. They are paid a fixed salary for their work and are responsible for caring for all the patients who come onto their service on the days they admit until either the patients are discharged or the end of the month, at which time the house officer switches services and the care of the patient is passed on to the next house officer on the service.[1]

Attendings on both the traditional and managed care services also have important reputational concerns, but they may also face financial incentives to decrease resource utilization. Certainly this is true for their employers; the teaching hospital is paid a prospective rate per hospitalization for the majority of its patients (mostly by Medicare under the Prospective Payment System), and the MCO pays the teaching hospital a per diem rate. Thus, both organizations have strong incentives to accelerate the discharge of patients, while the teaching hospital may also have an incentive to decrease the total cost of hospitalization by decreasing other costs such as radiology, pharmacy, and so forth. The MCO may, in fact, have opposite incentives concerning some radiological procedures. If a patient requires a procedure that could be done on an inpatient or outpatient basis, the MCO may prefer to have it done as an inpatient when it will be included in the per diem, as long as it does not result in an increased length of stay.

While both the teaching hospital and MCO may wish to decrease length of stay, the attendings on the two services face very different incentives. On the traditional services, the incentives of attendings to decrease resource utilization are weak. Attendings are given no financial incentives to discharge patients sooner, and during the time period examined in this study, they did not even receive regular feedback concerning their length of stay or costs compared to those of other attendings. In contrast, on the managed care service services, the physicians from the individual health centers who are responsible for direct patient management receive direct feedback concerning length of stay. Moreover, their centers are partially compensated by the MCO based on their ability to control length of stay and costs. Therefore, as members of relatively small centers, the earnings of both the attendings and their colleagues are related to the resource utilization of the patients they have cared for. This can generate strong incentives for accelerated discharge on the managed care service. To rein-

---

1. The possibility of shirking work by leaving patients for the next house officer does not seem to be important in practice. In fact, there is extra work involved in signing out a patient to the incoming house officer and a strong set of social pressures not to sign out an unnecessarily large service to a colleague.

Table 8.3   **Characteristics of Traditional and Managed Care Patients**

	Traditional	Managed Care	Total
Number of patients	10,819	4,059	14,878
Age	58.4	56.5	57.9
Male (%)	46	52	48
DRG weight	1.50	1.26	1.43
Mortality (%)	2.8	2.5	2.7
Length of stay	6.54	4.54	6.00
Total charges	15,981	10,824	14,574
Admit day load	9.42	8.11	9.07

force these efforts to accelerate discharge, patients on the managed care service are assigned nurse managers who assist with efforts to muster the inpatient and outpatient resources required for discharge.

8.3 Patient Characteristics

Table 8.3 provides summary statistics for the differences in demographic characteristics, severity of illness, health outcomes, and costs between the traditional and managed care services. Patients on the managed care service are younger and more likely to be male. They are also less ill as measured by diagnosis-related group (DRG) weight. All of these differences are statistically significant ($p < 0.0001$). Although the managed care service has a lower crude mortality rate, this difference is not statistically significant even at $p < 0.1$.[2] Length of stay on the managed care service is substantially shorter than on the traditional service (4.54 versus 6.54 days), and charges per admission are approximately $5,000 lower ($10,824 versus $15,981), with these differences both significantly different from zero at $p < 0.0001$. The substantially shorter length of stay on managed care services may have negative effects on housestaff education, since evaluations for acute conditions are often completed on an outpatient basis. For example, a patient admitted with chest pain may be discharged prior to an exercise tolerance test so that the decision making that follows that test is now passed back to the referring physician and is not part of the educational experience of the housestaff.

One factor that may also affect the way the presence of the managed care organization influences the educational experience provided by the teaching hospital is the distribution of diagnoses among the patients. Table 8.4 describes this for the traditional and managed care service. Despite the breadth of these categories, it is interesting to note that many

2. It is also not statistically significant in a multivariate logistic regression that controls for patient age, sex, race, and DRG weight.

Table 8.4   Distribution of Diagnoses on Traditional and Managed Care Services

Diagnosis-Related Group Name	Traditional	Managed Care	Total
Acute & subacute endocarditis	27	7	34
Abortion w/ D&C, aspiration curettage, or hysterotomy	4	0	4
Acute adjustment reaction & disturbances of psychosocial dysfunction	16	5	21
Acute leukemia w/o major O.R. procedure age >17	45	5	50
Acute major eye infections	0	1	1
Admit for renal dialysis	4	0	4
Adrenal & pituitary procedures	2	0	2
Aftercare w/o history of malignancy as secondary diagnosis	16	3	19
Aftercare, musculoskeletal system & connective tissue	0	1	1
Alcohol/drug abuse or dependency, detoxification or other symptoms treated w/ cc	23	12	35
Alcohol/drug abuse or dependency, detoxification or other symptoms treated w/o cc	7	5	12
Alcohol/drug abuse or dependence, left against medical advice	3	0	3
Allergic reactions age >17	9	4	13
Amputation of lower limb for endocrine, nutritional, and metabolic disorders	1	0	1
Amputation for circulatory system disorders except upper limb & toe	3	1	4
Anal & stomal procedures w/ cc	3	1	4
Anal & stomal procedures w/o cc	0	1	1
Angina pectoris	151	75	226
Appendectomy w/ complicated principal diagnosis w/ cc	1	0	1
Arthroscopy	1	1	2
Atherosclerosis w/ cc	62	19	81
Atherosclerosis w/o cc	9	0	9
Back & neck procedures w/ cc	7	4	11
Back & neck procedures w/o cc	0	1	1
Benign prostatic hypertrophy w/ cc	4	0	4
Bilateral or multiple major joint procedures of lower extremity	1	0	1
Biliary tract procedure except only cholecystectomy w/ or w/o common duct exploration w/ cc	4	0	4
Biopsies of musculoskeletal system & connective tissue	4	3	7
Bone diseases & specific arthropathies w/ cc	12	0	12
Bone diseases & specific arthropathies w/o cc	2	2	4

(continued)

Table 8.4   (continued)

Diagnosis-Related Group Name	Traditional	Managed Care	Total
Bone marrow transplant	3	0	3
Breast biopsy & local excision for non-malignancy	1	0	1
Bronchitis & asthma age >17 w/ cc	125	46	171
Bronchitis & asthma age >17 w/o cc	152	87	239
Cardiac arrhythmia & conduction disorders w/ cc	256	71	327
Cardiac arrhythmia & conduction disorders w/o cc	126	68	194
Cardiac congenital & valvular disorders age >17 w/ cc	21	2	23
Cardiac congenital & valvular disorders age >17 w/o cc	6	2	8
Cardiac pacemaker device replacement	12	1	13
Cardiac pacemaker revision except device replacement	24	8	32
Cardiac valve procedures w/ cardiac cath	141	13	154
Cardiac valve procedures w/o cardiac cath	20	3	23
Cellulitis age >17 w/ cc	122	26	148
Cellulitis age >17 w/o cc	21	13	34
Cellulitis age 0–17	0	1	1
Cesarean section w/ cc	2	2	4
Chemotherapy w/acute leukemia as secondary diagnosis	47	4	51
Chemotherapy w/o acute leukemia as secondary diagnosis	457	86	543
Chest pain	547	294	841
Cholecystectomy except by laparoscope w/o common duct exploration w/ cc	12	2	14
Cholecystectomy except by laparoscope w/o common duct exploration w/o cc	2	2	4
Cholecystectomy w/common duct exploration w/ cc	0	1	1
Chronic obstructive pulmonary disease	183	123	306
Circulatory disorders except acute myocardial infarction, w/ cardiac catheterization & complex diagnosis	376	66	442
Circulatory disorders except acute myocardial infarction, w/ cardiac catheterization w/o complex diagnosis	255	69	324
Circulatory disorders w/ acute myocardial infarction & cardiovascular comp disch alive	80	35	115
Circulatory disorders w/ acute myocardial infarction w/o cardiovascular comp disch alive	105	66	171
Circulatory disorders w/ acute myocardial infarction; expired	11	3	14

Table 8.4 (continued)

Diagnosis-Related Group Name	Traditional	Managed Care	Total
Cirrhosis & alcoholic hepatitis	40	15	55
Coagulation disorders	46	3	49
Complicated peptic ulcer	13	4	17
Complications of treatment w/ cc	16	6	22
Complications of treatment w/o cc	4	0	4
Concussion age >17 w/ cc	1	0	1
Connective tissue disorders w/ cc	44	31	75
Connective tissue disorders w/o cc	37	8	45
Coronary bypass w/ cardiac catheterization	266	78	344
Coronary bypass w/o cardiac catheterization	33	10	43
Cranial & peripheral nerve disorders w/ cc	18	2	20
Cranial & peripheral nerve disorders w/o cc	3	1	4
Craniotomy age >17 except for trauma	11	6	17
Craniotomy for trauma age >17	1	2	3
D&C, conization & radio-implant, for malignancy	1	0	1
D&C, conization except for malignancy	1	0	1
Deep vein thrombophlebitis	10	9	19
Degenerative nervous sytem disorders	5	2	7
Dental & oral disorders except extractions & restorations, age >17	7	3	10
Dental extractions & restorations	3	1	4
Diabetes age >35	78	22	100
Diabetes age 0–35	26	13	39
Digestive malignancy w/ cc	46	17	63
Digestive malignancy w/o cc	3	1	4
Disequilibrium	26	12	38
Disorders of liver except malignancy; cirrhosis, alcoholic hepatitis w/ cc	51	22	73
Disorders of liver except malignancy, cirrhosis, alcoholic hepatitis w/o cc	6	1	7
Disorders of pancreas except malignancy	193	91	284
Disorders of personality & impulse control	1	0	1
Disorders of the biliary tract w/ cc	30	19	49
Disorders of the biliary tract w/o cc	10	9	19
Ear, nose, mouth, & throat malignancy	6	2	8
Endocrine disorders w/ cc	18	3	21
Endocrine disorders w/o cc	10	1	11
Epiglottitis	1	2	3
Epistaxis	8	3	11
Esophagitis, gastroenteritis, & misc. digestive disorders age >17 w/ cc	214	82	296
Esophagitis, gastroenteritis, & misc. digestive disorders age >17 w/o cc	80	21	101
Esophagitis, gastroenteritis, & misc. digestive disorders age 0–17	0	1	1

(*continued*)

Table 8.4   (continued)

Diagnosis-Related Group Name	Traditional	Managed Care	Total
Extensive O.R. procedure unrelated to principal diagnosis	45	12	57
Extracranial vascular procedures	7	3	10
Fever of unknown origin age >17 w/ cc	62	26	88
Fever of unknown origin age >17 w/o cc	5	3	8
Fractures of hip & pelvis	6	2	8
Fracture, sprain, strain, & dislocation of forearm, hand, foot age >17 w/ cc	0	1	1
Fracture, sprain, strain, & dislocation of forearm, hand, foot age >17 w/o cc	2	0	2
Fracture, sprain, strain, & dislocation of upper arm, lower leg except foot age >17 w/ cc	6	1	7
Gastrointestinal hemorrhage w/ cc	182	91	273
Gastrointestinal hemorrhage w/o cc	30	22	52
Gastrointestinal obstruction w/ cc	23	15	38
Gastrointestinal obstruction w/o cc	4	3	7
Hand procedures for injuries	2	0	2
Heart failure & shock	434	151	585
Heart transplant	15	0	15
Hepatobiliary diagnostic procedure for malignancy	2	0	2
Hepatobiliary diagnostic procedure for non-malignancy	2	0	2
Hernia procedures except inguinal & femoral age >17 w/ cc	1	1	2
Hip & femur procedures except major joint age >17 w/ cc	17	4	21
Hip & femur procedures except major joint age >17 w/o cc	1	0	1
HIV w/ extensive O.R. procedure	5	4	9
HIV w/ major related condition	160	129	289
HIV w/or w/o other related condition	37	31	68
Hypertension	25	14	39
Inborn errors of metabolism	9	0	9
Infections, female reproductive system	4	3	7
Inflammation of the male reproductive system	8	3	11
Inflammatory bowel disease	37	21	58
Inguinal & femoral hernia procedures age >17 w/ cc	1	0	1
Interstitial lung disease w/ cc	14	2	16
Interstitial lung disease w/o cc	7	2	9
Intraocular procedures except retina, iris, & lens	1	0	1
Kidney & urinary tract infections age >17 w/ cc	126	57	183

Table 8.4   (continued)

Diagnosis-Related Group Name	Traditional	Managed Care	Total
Kidney & urinary tract infections age >17 w/o cc	48	15	63
Kidney & urinary tract infections age 0–17	1	0	1
Kidney & urinary tract neoplasms w/ cc	1	1	2
Kidney & urinary tract signs & symptoms age >17 w/ cc	6	1	7
Kidney & urinary tract signs & symptoms age >17 w/o cc	3	0	3
Kidney, ureter, & major bladder procedure for non-neoplasm w/ cc	11	2	13
Kidney, ureter, & major bladder procedures for neoplasm	3	0	3
Knee procedures w/ cc	3	0	3
Laparoscopic cholecystectomy w/o common duct exploration w/ cc	10	0	10
Laparoscopic cholecystectomy w/o common duct exploration w/o cc	3	1	4
Lens procedures with or without vitrectomy	1	0	1
Local excision & removal of internal fixed devices except hip & femur	1	2	3
Local excision & removal of internal fixed devices of hip & femur	0	1	1
Lower extremity & humerus procedure except hip, foot, femur age >17 w/ cc	4	2	6
Lymphoma & leukemia w/ major O.R. procedure	14	8	22
Lymphoma & non-acute leukemia w/ cc	61	13	74
Lymphoma & non-acute leukemia w/ other O.R. procedure w/ cc	13	10	23
Lymphoma & non-acute leukemia w/ other O.R. procedure w/o cc	1	0	1
Lymphoma & non-acute leukemia w/o cc	24	6	30
Major cardiovascular procedures w/ cc	65	18	83
Major cardiovascular procedures w/o cc	11	5	16
Major chest procedures	27	12	39
Major joint & limb reattachment procedures of lower extremity	21	4	25
Major joint & limb reattachment procedures of upper extremity	1	0	1
Major shoulder/elbow procedure, or other upper extremity procedure w/ cc	0	1	1
Major skin disorders w/ cc	20	2	22
Major skin disorders w/o cc	1	1	2
Major small & large bowel procedures w/ cc	38	7	45
Major small & large bowel procedures w/o cc	3	1	4

(continued)

Table 8.4   (continued)

Diagnosis-Related Group Name	Traditional	Managed Care	Total
Malignancy of hepatobiliary system or pancrease	51	15	66
Malignancy, female reproductive system w/ cc	6	0	6
Malignancy, female reproductive system w/o cc	1	0	1
Medical back problems	34	8	42
Menstrual & other female reproductive system disorders	2	0	2
Minor bladder procedures w/ cc	1	1	2
Minor skin disorders w/ cc	11	5	16
Minor skin disorders w/o cc	10	4	14
Miscellaneous ear, nose, mouth, & throat procedures	0	1	1
Mouth procedures w/o cc	1	0	1
Multiple sclerosis & cerebellar ataxia	1	2	3
Myeloproliferative disorders or poorly differentiated neoplasms w/ major O.R. procedures w/ cc	4	1	5
Myeloproliferative disorders or poorly differentiated neoplasms w/ other O.R. procedures	6	1	7
Nervous system infection except viral meningitis	15	10	25
Nervous system neoplasms w/ cc	25	24	49
Nervous system neoplasms w/o cc	3	2	5
Neurological eye disorders	2	1	3
Neuroses except depressive	1	0	1
Non-extensive burns w/ skin graft	1	0	1
Non-extensive O.R. procedure unrelated to principal diagnosis	19	3	22
Non-specific arthropathies	3	2	5
Nonspecific cerebrovascular disorders w/ cc	3	3	6
Nonspecific cerebrovascular disorders w/o cc	1	0	1
Nontraumatic stupor & coma	4	2	6
Nutritional & misc. metabolic disorders age >17 w/ cc	159	60	219
Nutritional & misc. metabolic disorders age >17 w/o cc	32	12	44
O.R. procedure w/ diagnoses of other contact w/ health services	2	0	2
O.R. procedure for infectious & parasitic diseases	20	7	27
Orbital procedures	1	0	1
Organic disturbances & mental retardation	20	4	24
Osteomyelitis	9	6	15

Table 8.4   (continued)

Diagnosis-Related Group Name	Traditional	Managed Care	Total
Other permanent cardiac pacemaker implant or automatic implantable cardioverter defibrillator lead or generator procedure	134	33	167
Other antepartum diagnoses w/ medical complications	13	11	24
Other antepartum diagnoses w/o medical complications	1	2	3
Other cardiothoracic procedures	29	5	34
Other circulatory system diagnoses w/ cc	137	52	189
Other circulatory system diagnoses w/o cc	20	15	35
Other circulatory system O.R. procedures	16	5	21
Other digestive system diagnoses age >17 w/ cc	48	14	62
Other digestive system diagnoses age >17 w/o cc	1	4	5
Other digestive system O.R. procedures w/ cc	11	2	13
Other digestive system O.R. procedures w/o cc	1	2	3
Other disorders of nervous system w/ cc	18	8	26
Other disorders of nervous system w/o cc	5	1	6
Other disorders of the eye age >17 w/ cc	3	0	3
Other disorders of the eye age >17 w/o cc	3	0	3
Other ear, nose, mouth, & throat diagnoses age >17	9	6	15
Other ear, nose, mouth, & throat diagnoses age 0–17	1	0	1
Other ear, nose, mouth, & throat O.R. procedures	2	0	2
Other endocrine, nutritional, & metabolic O.R. procedure w/ cc	4	0	4
Other endocrine, nutritional, & metabolic O.R. procedure w/o cc	2	0	2
Other factors influencing health status	34	4	38
Other hepatobiliary or pancreas O.R. procedures	4	0	4
Other infectious & parasitic diseases diagnoses	28	4	32
Other injury, poisoning, & toxic effect diagnoses w/ cc	2	1	3
Other injury, poisoning, & toxic effect diagnoses w/o cc	4	0	4
Other kidney & urinary tract diagnoses age >17 w/ cc	64	7	71
Other kidney & urinary tract O.R. procedures	14	5	19

(continued)

Table 8.4   (continued)

Diagnosis-Related Group Name	Traditional	Managed Care	Total
Other kidney & urinary tract O.R. procedures	29	6	35
Other male reproductive system diagnoses	2	0	2
Other male reproductive system O.R. procedures except for malignancy	1	0	1
Other multiple significant trauma	2	1	3
Other musculoskeletal system & connective tissue O.R. procedure w/ cc	1	3	4
Other musculoskeletal system & connective tissue O.R. procedure procedure w/o cc	1	0	1
Other musculoskeletal system & connective tissue diagnoses	7	3	10
Other myeloproliferative disorder or poorly differentiated neoplasm diagnosis w/ cc	7	1	8
Other myeloproliferative disorder or poorly differentiated neoplasm diagnosis w/o cc	2	2	4
Other O.R. procedures for injuries w/ cc	5	3	8
Other O.R. procedures of the blood and blood forming organs	2	1	3
Other respiratory system O.R. procedures w/ cc	50	15	65
Other respiratory system O.R. procedures w/o cc	4	1	5
Other respiratory system diagnoses w/ cc	19	4	23
Other respiratory system diagnoses w/o cc	6	1	7
Other skin, subcutaneous tissue, & breast procedures w/ cc	5	1	6
Other skin, subcutaneous tissue, & breast procedures w/o cc	0	2	2
Other vascular procedures w/ cc	64	14	78
Other vascular procedures w/o cc	2	1	3
Otitis media & upper respiratory tract infection age >17 w/ cc	35	9	44
Otitis media & upper respiratory tract infection age >17 w/o cc	11	3	14
Pancreas, liver, & shunt procedures w/ cc	21	3	24
Pancreas, liver, & shunt procedures w/o cc	3	1	4
Pathological fractures & musculoskeletal & connective tissue malignancy	68	35	103
Percutaneous cardiovascular procedures	664	160	824
Peripheral & cranial nerve & other nervous system procedures w/ cc	1	3	4
Peripheral & cranial nerve & other nervous system procedures w/o cc	1	0	1
Peripheral vascular disorders w/ cc	99	44	143
Peripheral vascular disorders w/o cc	65	54	119
Peritoneal adhesiolysis w/ cc	1	1	2

Table 8.4   (continued)

Diagnosis-Related Group Name	Traditional	Managed Care	Total
Permanent cardiac pacemaker implant w/ acute myocardial infarction, heart failure, or shock	7	0	7
Pleural effusion w/ cc	20	5	25
Pleural effusion w/o cc	4	0	4
Pneumothorax w/ cc	4	5	9
Poisoning & toxic effects of drugs age >17 w/ cc	88	28	116
Poisoning & toxic effects of drugs age >17 w/o cc	36	17	53
Postoperative & post-traumatic infections	10	3	13
Postpartum & post abortion diagnoses w/o O.R. procedure	9	4	13
Primary iris procedures	1	1	2
Prostatic O.R. procedure unrelated to principal diagnosis	1	0	1
Psychoses	4	2	6
Pulmonary edema & respiratory failure	5	3	8
Pulmonary embolism	42	26	68
Radiotherapy	19	7	26
Red blood cell disorders age >17	196	44	240
Renal failure	70	20	90
Respiratory infections & inflammations age >17 w/ cc	120	58	178
Respiratory infections & inflammations age >17 w/o cc	15	6	21
Respiratory neoplasms	58	21	79
Respiratory signs & symptoms w/ cc	37	10	47
Respiratory signs & symptoms w/o cc	28	17	45
Respiratory system diagnosis with ventilator support	67	19	86
Reticuloendothelial & immunity disorders w/ cc	134	33	167
Reticuloendothelial & immunity disorders w/o cc	13	7	20
Retinal procedures	2	0	2
Seizure & headache age >17 w/ cc	32	19	51
Seizure & headache age >17 w/o cc	9	11	20
Septic arthritis	5	2	7
Septicemia age >17	98	33	131
Signs & symptoms of musculoskeletal system & connective tissue	23	9	32
Signs & symptoms w/ cc	22	10	32
Signs & symptoms w/o cc	6	4	10
Simple pneumonia & pleurisy age >17 w/ cc	330	145	475

(*continued*)

Table 8.4   (continued)

Diagnosis-Related Group Name	Traditional	Managed Care	Total
Simple pneumonia & pleurisy age >17 w/o cc	77	39	116
Skin graft &/or debridement for skin ulcer or cellulitis w/ cc	11	4	15
Skin graft &/or debridement for skin ulcer or cellulitis w/o cc	1	0	1
Skin grafts & wound debridement for endocrine, nutritional, & metabolic disorders	2	1	3
Skin ulcers	14	3	17
Soft tissue procedures w/ cc	4	2	6
Soft tissue procedures w/o cc	1	1	2
Specific cerebrovascular disorders except transient ischemic attack	42	88	130
Spinal procedures	5	0	5
Splenectomy age >17	4	0	4
Sprains, strains, & dislocations of hip, pelvis, & thigh	0	1	1
Stomach, esophageal, & duodenal procedures age >17 w/ cc	13	5	18
Stomach, esophageal, & duodenal procedures age >17 w/o cc	0	1	1
Subtotal mastectomy for malignancy w/ cc	2	1	3
Syncope & collapse w/ cc	77	43	120
Syncope & collapse w/o cc	56	33	89
Tonsil and adenoid procedure, except tonsillectomy &/or adenoidectomy only, age >17	2	1	3
Tendonitis, myositis, & bursitis	16	8	24
Testes procedures, for malignancy	1	0	1
Thyroid procedures	1	0	1
Total mastectomy for malignancy w/ cc	2	0	2
Tracheostomy except for face, mouth, & neck diagnoses	45	8	53
Tracheostomy for face, mouth, & neck diagnoses	4	2	6
Transient ischemic attack & precerebral occlusions	11	24	35
Transurethral procedures w/ cc	3	2	5
Transurethral prostatectomy w/ cc	2	0	2
Trauma to the skin, subcutaneous tissue, & breast age >17 w/ cc	6	0	6
Trauma to the skin, subcutaneous tissue, & breast age >17 w/o cc	1	0	1
Trauma injury age >17 w/ cc	4	0	4
Traumatic injury age >17 w/o cc	2	0	2
Traumatic stupor & coma, coma <1 hr age >17 w/ cc	2	2	4
Traumatic stupor & coma, coma >1 hr	1	0	1

Table 8.4   (continued)

Diagnosis-Related Group Name	Traditional	Managed Care	Total
Uncomplicated peptic ulcer w/ cc	2	0	2
Uncomplicated peptic ulcer w/o cc	3	2	5
Upper limb & toe amputation for circulatory system disorders	1	0	1
Urinary stones w/ cc, &/or extracorporeal shock wave lithotripsy	6	4	10
Urinary stones w/o cc	1	1	2
Uterine & adnexal procedure for non-malignancy w/ cc	6	1	7
Uterine, adnexal procedure for non-ovarian/adnexal malignancy w/ cc	1	0	1
Vagina, cervix, & vulva procedures	2	0	2
Vaginal delivery w/ complicating diagnoses	2	1	3
Vaginal delivery w/ sterilization &/or D&C	1	0	1
Viral illness & fever of unknown origin age 0–17	0	2	2
Viral illness age >17	32	10	42
Viral meningitis	15	8	23
Wound debridement & skin graft except hand, for musculoskeletal & connective tissue disorder	12	2	14
Wound debridements for injuries	4	1	5

Note: cc = Complicating conditions.

DRGs occur only a few times over the period of somewhat more than a year even in such a large teaching hospital. In this respect, the sheer volume of patients brought in by managed care may be its greatest contribution to the teaching experience available for housestaff. This might be less of a contribution, however, if the managed care services are more likely to admit patients with very common diagnoses than are the traditional services, where more rare conditions might be more frequently admitted as "teaching" cases. Figure 8.1 plots the fraction of patients in DRGs of varying frequency who come from managed care services, and finds no support for that hypothesis. Because we have not compared the frequency of admissions for the DRGs in this institution to those occurring nationwide, we cannot say that either service necessarily emphasizes common or rare diagnoses. Nevertheless, the managed care service does not seem to decrease the diversity of diagnoses.

Another commonly discussed set of hypotheses concerning managed care patients is that they are less ill on average when admitted because they tend to be drawn from a healthier population than traditional patients. This is consistent with the lower average DRG weight on the managed care service reported in table 8.3. Alternatively, others speculate that

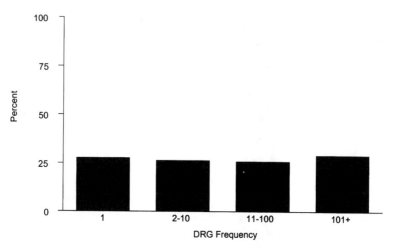

Fig. 8.1   **Percentage of managed care patients by DRG frequency**

the managed care patients admitted with a given diagnosis may be more ill on average than the traditional patients because there is a higher threshold for admission to the hospital. One way to examine this is to look at admissions for individual DRGs with and without complicating conditions. Though we found a slightly higher percentage of managed care patients in those DRGs without complications than we found in DRGs with complications (0.29 versus 0.23), this difference is not statistically different from zero.

8.4   Differences in Costs

This section examines the difference in costs on the traditional and managed care medical services. The data on costs are generated from a cost accounting system that imputes costs using cost-to-charge ratios. For those patients for whom no actual detailed bill is generated (i.e., Medicare or capitated or per diem managed care), charges are assigned based on utilization in the same way they would be for a patient billed under traditional insurance.

Table 8.5 reports regressions that examine the effect of managed care on costs controlling for managed care status, age, sex, race, and DRG weight (WT95). Regression 1 suggests that costs are approximately $2,800 lower per hospitalization for patients on the managed care service controlling for these covariates. Regression 2 suggests one major reason for this reduction in costs—namely, that length of stay is approximately 1.3 days shorter on the managed care service controlling for these same covariates. Regression 3 includes length of stay in the total cost regression. The partial effect of managed care now becomes insignificantly different from zero. This suggests that managed care exerts most or all of its effect on

Table 8.5   Cost and Length-of-Stay Regressions

Dependent Variable	1 Total Charge	2 Length of Stay	3 Total Charge	4 Pharmacy Charge	5 Pharmacy Charge	6 Lab Charge	7 Lab Charge	8 Radiology Charge	9 Radiology Charge	10 Room Charge	11 Room Charge
Managed care	-2,798***	-1.34***	233	-490***	-17	-609***	-223***	23	187***	-969***	284***
	(399)	(0.13)	(279)	(84)	(71)	(77)	(68)	(30)	(25)	(128)	(49)
Age	-37***	0.005	-48***	-34***	-35***	5***	-4**	-2***	-3***	5	1
	(10)	(0.003)	(7)	(2)	(2)	(2)	(2)	(2)	(1)	(3)	(1)
Male	-492	-0.32***	242	-245***	-130**	489***	583***	-100***	-60***	-340***	-36
	(356)	(0.11)	(248)	(75)	(63)	(69)	(61)	(26)	(23)	(115)	(44)
White	1,842***	-0.04	1,928***	633***	646***	485***	496***	23	28	-103	-67
	(391)	(0.12)	(272)	(82)	(70)	(76)	(67)	(29)	(25)	(126)	(48)
DRG weight	10,731***	2.71***	4,602***	1,234***	278***	2,155***	1,375***	432***	100***	3,461***	924***
	(113)	(0.04)	(92)	(24)	(24)	(22)	(23)	(8)	(8)	(36)	(16)
Length of stay			2,263***		353***		288***		123***		937***
			(18)		(5)		(4)		(2)		(18)
Constant	1,143*	2.39***	-4,263***	1,779*	935***	-381***	-1,070***	340***	47	338	-1,900***
	(661)	(0.21)	(462)	(139)	(118)	(128)	(113)	(49)	(42)	(213)	(82)
N	14,878	14,878	14,878	14,878	14,878	14,878	14,878	14,878	14,878	14,878	14,878
Adjusted R^2	0.39	0.29	0.70	0.17	0.40	0.41	0.55	0.15	0.38	0.39	0.91

$*p < 0.1$, $**p < 0.05$, $***p < 0.01$.

costs through a decrease in length of stay in this setting. Since the managed care organization compensates the hospital on a per diem rate, this is perhaps not surprising.

The remaining regressions examine specific components of costs. Regressions 4 and 5 show a similar story for pharmacy costs as for total cost: a decrease for managed care patients that is eliminated after controlling for length of stay. Regressions 6 and 7 show a decrease in lab charges under managed care that is substantially reduced to only about $200 by controlling for length of stay. Regressions 8 and 9 show no effect of managed care on radiology costs without controlling for length of stay. After controlling for length of stay, radiology costs are about $200 higher on the managed care service. Not surprisingly, regressions 10 and 11 show a large effect of managed care on room charges that is eliminated by controlling for length of stay. In fact, the difference reverses, with higher average costs for managed care controlling for length of stay, presumably because managed care patients spend a larger fraction of their days in intensive care for any length of stay for a diagnosis. This is consistent both with the incentives of the managed care organization, which pays a fixed rate per diem, and the MCO's relative expertise in moving patients from a nonintensive hospital bed to home.

Overall, the results of this section suggest that the managed care organization in this institution accomplishes the majority of its cost saving through a decrease in length of stay. This suggests that examining the effects of incentives on mechanisms that affect length of stay may be particularly fruitful. The following sections discuss a specific set of management decisions that have effects on length of stay.

8.5 Effects of Workload on Length of Stay

In previous work (Meltzer, Hiltz, and Bates 1997), we used discrete time logistic hazard models and Monte Carlo simulation to examine the effects of house officer workload on length of stay and found significant effects of workload on discharge probabilities over the hospital stay which differed between the traditional and managed care services. On both the traditional service and the managed care service, increased workload was found to decrease discharge probabilities during the first four days of a hospitalization. This is consistent with congestion effects when housestaff are simply too busy to complete their work quickly enough to permit the most rapid possible discharge of patients. From days 5 through 8, there is no effect of workload on length of stay. After day 8, however, there is a positive effect of workload on discharge probabilities on the traditional service, but not the managed care service. This is consistent with a dumping effect in which busy house officers discharge patients who are not necessarily in acute need of hospitalization in order to decrease their workload. It is possible that this is not evident on the managed care service because the strong incentive for attendings to discharge on that service implies that all of the patients on that service who remain in the hospital are there because they absolutely cannot be safely discharged.

On the traditional service, these two opposing effects of increased workload net out to suggest a very small decrease in length of stay with increased workload. On the managed care service, however, with a significant congestion effect and no dumping effect, the net effect of increased workload is to increase length of stay. Our estimates suggested an increase in costs of approximately $125,000 per year from a 20 percent decrease in housestaff, which would save less than $125,000 per year in salary.

8.6   Differences in Staffing on the Services

These differing effects of workload on length of stay on the traditional and managed care services suggest that there might be greater benefits to higher staffing on the managed care service. The average daily workload on the two services reported in table 8.3 confirms that there is indeed higher staffing on the managed care service. It seems, then, that the hospital is responding in some sense to the differing incentives with respect to housestaff workload on the two services. To understand better how it is that the differing incentives for staffing on the two services may exist, it is useful to examine the effects of attending incentives in the two services on the optimal house officer staffing decision.

To model the hospital's house officer staffing decision, we assume that hospitals choose staffing and attending salary to maximize profit (Π) subject to: (1) attending discharge incentives and (2) attending participation constraints.

In order to model attending discharge decisions, we assume that attendings care about quality of care (Q) and income (I), where $Q = Q(L,n)$, so quality depends on length of stay (L) and staffing level (n), where $Q_L > 0$, $Q_n > 0$. As described above, attending discharge incentives differ on the two services in that physician's pay rises with lower resources utilization, and especially length of stay on the managed care service. Thus, physician income can be modeled as $I = I_0 - iL$, so that income is a baseline level I_0 minus an incentive, i, to decrease length of stay.

Subject to these incentives, attendings choose L to maximize $Q(L,n) + I_0 - iL$ so that:

$$(1) \qquad\qquad Q_L(L,n) - i = 0.$$

This is the attending incentive compatibility constraint, and it describes how long an attending will choose to keep a patient in the hospital given staffing (n) and incentive (i).

To compete for attendings, hospitals must offer attendings a compensation package including quality of care and total income that is at least as good as the competitive level of utility for attendings at other hospitals (U_0). Specifically, assume that attendings choose a hospital based on financial compensation and quality to maximize their utility:

$$U_{attending} = Q(L,n) + I_0 - iL \geq U_0.$$

If this is the case, then hospitals must provide attendings a base compensation (I_0) of at least

(2) $I_0 = U_0 - Q(L,n) + iL.$

This is the attending participation constraint.

Given these constraints, hospitals choose staffing (n) to maximize profit (Π)

$$\Pi = P(Q(L,n)) - (I_0 - iL) - kn - cL,$$

where $P(Q(L,n))$ is the price received for care of quality Q, $I_0 - iL$ is total physician compensation, kn is the cost of staffing level n (k per staff position), and cL is the cost per day of hospitalization, subject to the attending incentive compatibility (1) and participation (2) constraints.

Substituting the participation constraint into the profit equation generates the LaGrangian:

$$L = P(Q(L,n)) + Q(L,n) - U_0 - kn - cL + \lambda[i - Q_L],$$

which is then maximized over n, L, and λ to yield:

FOC n: $[P_Q + 1]Q_n - k - \lambda \times Q_{Ln} = 0,$

FOC L: $[P_Q + 1]Q_L - c - \lambda \times Q_{LL} = 0,$

FOC λ: $Q_L(L,n) - i = 0.$

If $[P_Q + 1]Q_L - c < 0$ so that hospitals want to decrease length of stay at the margin and if $Q_{LL} < 0$ so that there are diminishing returns to length of stay, then $\lambda > 0$. If better staffing has a larger effect on quality when length of stay is shorter, so $Q_{Ln} < 0$, then $[P_Q + 1]Q_n - k > 0$, which implies that staffing (n) would be higher for any length of stay.

To be strict in determining the effect of incentives on staffing, we can totally differentiate and solve for

$$\frac{dn}{di} = \frac{\lambda[Q_{LLL}Q_{Ln} - Q_{LLn}Q_{LL}]}{[DET]}$$

the sign of which will be the same as the sign of the term in brackets in the numerator if $\lambda > 0$ and since the denominator is greater than zero by second-order conditions. The sign of this term cannot be determined in general, but if it is positive, optimal staffing would rise with attending discharge incentives. This will be the case if, as stated above, hospitals want to decrease length of stay at the margin, there are diminishing returns to length of stay, and better staffing has a larger effect on quality when length of stay is shorter.

8.7 Conclusion

This paper presents some preliminary observations concerning the role and functioning of a managed care medicine service in a single teaching hospital. Although the results are clearly preliminary, the suggestion is that the managed care service is able to decrease resource utilization compared to the traditional service, and to do so largely by achieving reductions in length of stay. It is possible that this is a peculiarity of the managed care service in this institution, particularly given the fact that it is rewarded for reductions in length of stay because it pays the hospital a per diem rate. However, the ease of monitoring length of stay and high cost associated with staffing a hospital bed make it likely that reductions in length of stay are a common mechanism for reducing costs under other payment systems as well.

With the ease of monitoring length of stay, it is interesting that the traditional service has not adopted mechanisms to provide attendings more powerful incentives to cut length of stay. Indeed, more powerful incentives for attendings are beginning to find their way into academic medical centers. For example, the desire to provide stronger incentives to control inpatient costs is probably an important reason for the strong interest in academic medical centers in shifting responsibility for inpatient care to "hospitalists"—physicians who specialize in inpatient care (Wachter and Goldman 1996). Because of their higher patient volume and greater responsibility for inpatient care, these hospitalists can presumably be compensated more directly for their success in controlling costs and may be in a better position to control costs.

In the absence of such innovative approaches, the lower staffing on the traditional service and the empirical and theoretical result that this lower staffing might be an alternative mechanism to encourage early discharge suggest that the teaching hospital may implicitly employ other methods to control length of stay. Similarly, the presence of higher staffing on the managed care service is accompanied by other efforts to decrease length of stay, such as the use of nurse managers. The presence of these multiple incentive mechanisms and other means of controlling resource use within the institution suggest a potential difficulty in studying the effects of incentives on behavior within organizations as complex as teaching hospitals. This may prove important as changing educational needs and financial realities tempt teaching hospitals and regulators to experiment with new financial arrangements.

As for the effects of managed care on the educational objectives of teaching hospitals, this paper has even more limited ability to draw conclusions. In this institution, the managed care service appears to admit a substantial number of patients with diagnoses that vary significantly in severity of illness and frequency. This suggests that the managed care service is making a positive educational contribution. Moreover, the experience of observing how physicians working under managed care are able to accelerate discharge may be a valuable lesson in its own right. While there may be truth in the frequently cited concern that with shorter lengths of stay, housestaff may not have as much opportunity to learn from their patients, examination of that hypothesis will require data on what housestaff learn from their training that we do not currently possess. In previous work (Meltzer, Hiltz, and Bates 1997), we have found some evidence that managed care also takes some of the decision making out of the hands of the housestaff, which may also compromise their educational experience. Examining this hypothesis will also require richer data than is currently available.

Though the spread of managed care presents challenges to teaching hospitals, it is clear that they cannot remain financially viable unless they learn to work with managed care. This will be an important challenge in the years ahead.

References

Accreditation Council for Graduate Medical Education (ACGME). 1997. ACGME Program Requirements for Residency Education in Internal Medicine—Not Yet in Effect. ACGME web site, http://www.acgme.org/acgme/progreq/nyie/im798.htm, accessed 23 December 1997.

Harris, Jeffrey. 1977. The Internal Organization of Hospitals: Some Economic Implications. *Bell Journal of Economics* 8 (2): 467–82.

Meltzer, David, Frederick L. Hiltz, and David Bates. 1997. Effect of House Officer Workload on Length of Stay on Traditional and Managed Care General Medical Services. University of Chicago, Chicago, Ill.

Newhouse, Joseph. 1970. Toward a Theory of Non-Profit Institutions: An Economic Model of a Hospital. *American Economic Review* 60 (1): 64–74.

Pauly, Mark, and Michael Redisch. 1973. The Non-Profit Hospital as a Physician Cooperative. *American Economic Review* 63:87–100.

Wachter, R. M., and L. Goldman. 1996. The Emerging Role of "Hospitalists" in the American Health Care System. *New England Journal of Medicine* 335 (7): 514–17.

Comment on Chapters 7 and 8   Laurence Baker

The growth of managed care over the past two decades has brought many new questions to the forefront of health policy research in the United States. Among the most fundamental is the effect that managed care has on the provision of medical care and, particularly, the quality of health care. Of course, managed care could influence health care provision and quality in a variety of ways. Perhaps the most important is through the financial incentives and central oversight imposed on providers, which can have strong impacts on the health care delivered to patients enrolled in managed care organizations. Patients and their advocates have long feared that financial incentives to treat less and the utilization of review processes that limit care would lead to the underprovision of quality in health care. As pressure from employers has grown and competition between plans has intensified, so have fears that managed care could compromise quality in pursuit of financial gain.

These fears have generated a strong demand for information about the quality of care in managed care plans, to which the research community has responded by generating a large and steadily increasing body of work examining the health care provided to patients enrolled in managed care plans. But because of the complexity of these questions, much remains to be understood about the care provided by managed care organizations. The papers by Sarah Feldman and David Scharfstein and by David Meltzer, Frederick L. Hiltz, and David Bates explore two of the areas in need of further research.

Questions about the quality of health care are at the forefront of many current health care policy discussions, but the available information about quality is far from complete. Even the concept of "quality" is difficult to define in practice. Beyond defining quality, the methodological hurdles to doing research on quality are formidable. The prototypical quality studies have compared patients with traditional indemnity insurance plans who receive (more or less) fee-for-service health care to managed care patients (Miller and Luft 1997). But these studies have suffered through imperfect measures of quality, data difficulties, and questions about the interpretation of differences in those things that can be measured.

Most attempts at quality measurement have tended to fall into three categories: measurement of health outcomes, analyses of the processes by which care is produced, and surveys of consumer satisfaction. Analyses of health outcomes, a common approach to studying quality in managed care plans, typically rely on large administrative databases like hospital discharge abstracts collected by state regulators or databases containing

Laurence Baker is assistant professor of health research and policy at Stanford University and a faculty research fellow of the National Bureau of Economic Research.

insurance claim records. These databases provide information on some baseline characteristics of the patients and basic information about their medical condition and the treatments they received. It is often possible to link these data to mortality records or other databases to provide information about the outcome of their care. But administrative databases often provide only a limited set of outcomes for analysis, and the available outcomes are often relatively rare events, leading to difficulties with small samples; for many health problems, studying differences in mortality rates can be difficult. Moreover, using nonrandomized data to study outcomes forces investigators to deal with variations in illness severity or health status across patients that can be difficult to observe. In many cases, sufficient data to fully control for severity differences across patients that influence their health outcomes as well as, say, their choice of insurance are not available, leaving results subject to substantial bias.

Other studies examine processes of care, such as determining whether patients with diabetes received appropriate follow-up care and periodic retinal examinations and asking whether the processes of care for managed care and non–managed care patients are similar. These studies are also potentially interesting, but they tend to require burdensome data collections, making it difficult to conduct broadly based process studies. As a practical matter, process measures can only focus on a relatively small number of items, which also limits their applicability—knowledge about vaccination rates for children may be of little use to an adult picking a health plan. The use of satisfaction surveys, while useful, captures information from the patient's perspective. While this information is often of crucial importance to patients, it is not clear that it always reflects the actual health outcomes of interest.

Against a backdrop of numerous helpful but imperfect attempts to study quality, Feldman and Scharfstein's focus on care volume offers a new perspective on quality measurement. The use of volume as a quality measure is based on the literature that reports a positive correlation between the number of procedures performed by health care providers and the outcomes for patients (the so-called volume-outcome relationship). Volume has also been used by other groups as an indicator of quality. For example, various specialty groups, state governments, and other accreditation agencies have considered the implementation of rules that would force providers offering some services to demonstrate that they have performed at least a minimum number of procedures per year, basing their argument on volume-outcome studies.

Feldman and Scharfstein's finding that there is wide variation in provider volumes between health plans and generally strong differences between managed care and fee-for-service plans signals the possibility of variations in the quality of care provided by managed care plans and, following the volume-outcome relationship, raises the possibility that outcomes for managed care patients may not be as good as outcomes for fee-for-service patients. The results also highlight the fact that quality may vary from service to service within a plan, something that could significantly complicate broad assessments of quality across plans. For physician volume, Feldman and Scharfstein find that plan A has the highest volumes for breast cancer surgery and for gynecologic cancer surgery but is among the plans with the lowest volumes for colorectal cancer surgery. Conversely, the surgeons used by plan F had the highest volumes for colorectal cancer surgery but were among the lowest for volume of breast and gynecologic cancer surgery. A goal of many quality-measurement efforts is the construction of a small number of measures that can be used to characterize quality across plans and can be made understandable to patients making complex choices across plans. But the large differences across plans suggests that a small set of indices may fail to capture important variations for individual procedures, or that the creation of a small set of indicators that are truly representative may be impossible.

In highlighting the provocative differences in volume across plans and between managed care and traditional insurers, this work also prompts a series of more detailed questions about the interpretation of volume differences and about the degree to which they could be more widely used as indicators of quality. First, additional attention to the shape of the relationship between volume and outcomes would strength the interpretation of these results. While studies of the relationship between volume and outcomes suggest that increases in volume go with improvements in outcomes, it is not clear that this relationship is linear. Many volume-outcome studies suggest that outcomes improve with volume over some range of volumes, but that once sufficiently high levels of volume have been reached, the benefits to additional increases in volume are limited. Feldman and Scharfstein make the case that the volumes of providers seen by managed care patients are often lower than volumes of providers seen by traditionally insured patients, but we must be somewhat cautious in inferring that outcomes are worse; if we are on a flat part of the volume-outcome curve, reductions in volume may have small or no impact on outcomes.

Second, it would be interesting to expand the analysis of the appropriate set of procedures to include when volumes are computed. In spirit, the question is, What makes a surgeon good at what she or he does? Is it the number of surgeries within a broad group of procedures that determine outcomes for a specific procedure? Or should we count only the specific instances of surgeries exactly like the one in question? Similar questions could be asked at the hospital level, where the crucial question is the ability of the hospital to take good care of patients after surgery, which may or may not depend on the specific procedures done for the patients.

A third set of questions begins with the mechanisms that drive the relationship between volume and outcomes. Do increases in volume bring about improvements in outcomes, say, through learning by doing? Or do higher volumes reflect the underlying skill or other attributes of providers—that is, do some surgeons have high volumes because they have good outcomes or other attributes that attract patients? In an environment where managed care plans can influence the volume of services performed by physicians, the answers to these questions will have a strong bearing on the usefulness of volume measures, particularly over time. Suppose, for example, that an HMO were to send all of its gynecologic cancer surgery cases to a surgeon with initially low volumes for these procedures, raising the volumes of the surgeon. If the initial low volume reflected an inherently lower level of skill, then the use of volume as an indicator of quality could be inaccurate. But if higher volumes created better outcomes, the measure would be better.

While Feldman and Scharfstein's work attempts to assess the quality of the providers seen by managed care patients, David Meltzer, Frederick L. Hiltz, and David Bates investigate the complex financial and other interactions between managed care organizations, physicians, and hospitals that also have a strong impact on the care received by patients enrolled in managed care organizations. One of the central questions raised by the growth of managed care is the impact of the new financial incentives (e.g., capitation) on the behavior of health care providers. In isolation, this question is not difficult; if physicians are paid more when they do less, they will have an incentive to do less. But in reality, the health care delivery system is a complex organism in which health care for any given individual is produced through numerous interactions between a variety of agents, each of whom may have differing financial and other incentives influencing his or her behavior. In this setting, gaining a full understanding of the impact of these incentives on the behavior of providers is not an easy task. Even the most straightforward HMO arrangements can impose a complicated set of incentives on interacting providers. It is not difficult, for example, to find HMOs that contract with groups of physicians using incentives to limit hospitalizations. The groups, in turn, often pay member physicians using salaries, so the incentives are not effectively passed on to the individual physicians. The same HMO may also have contracts with hospitals in which payment is based on the number of patient days, so that under some circumstances, the financial incentives would lead the hospital administrators to prefer to keep a patient in the hospital an extra day, while the physician group would rather discharge the patient, and the individual physician would find himself or herself more or less indifferent. Things only get more complex in teaching hospitals, where hospitals, attending physicians, and interns and residents may all have varying incentives. These difficulties may be among the reasons that many previous investigators have chosen to examine only ultimate outputs from hospital care, choosing to leave the lid on the black box that conceals the actual interaction of the incentives within the hospital.

Meltzer, Hiltz, and Bates lift the lid and allow us a glimpse inside. In explicitly describing the various levels of incentives and providing empirical evidence about the effects of managed care on the operation of a teaching hospital, this paper provides very valuable information that should fuel further work on these important questions. While we know that the overall effect of managed care is to reduce hospital utilization, we now find out some more about the complex interactions that generate this outcome. Their finding that the incentives of the managed care plans on attending physicians do have a strong influence on care provided in a teaching hospital is further indication of the power of managed care organizations in dictating the care that will be provided to their members.

In the end, both of these papers provide important evidence that both helps us understand the effects of managed care on the health care system and highlights the need for further work on these questions.

Reference

Miller, R. H., and H. S. Luft. 1997. Does Managed Care Lead to Better or Worse Quality of Care? *Health Affairs* 16:7–25.

Comment on Chapters 7 and 8   Alan Weil

The paper by Feldman and Scharfstein offers insight into an important and timely topic—how the growing reliance on managed care in the health care system may affect the quality of services people receive. The paper cites but does not discuss in detail the literature showing that higher-volume providers, both hospitals and physicians, tend to offer higher-quality care. The paper provides a quantitative analysis, using Massachusetts hospital discharge data, of the extent to which managed care organizations direct patients to higher- or lower-volume providers than patients in fee-for-service (FFS) plans select.

The findings are varied. For two of the three surgical procedures examined, after controlling for factors such as patient age, location, race, and income that might affect patients' choice of providers, patients enrolled in private managed care plans are found to receive services from lower-volume physician providers. For Medicare patients, managed care plans use higher-volume physicians than Medicare FFS patients for two of the

Alan Weil is director of the Assessing the New Federalism Project at The Urban Institute in Washington, D.C.

services, but much lower-volume physicians for the third. For all three procedures, private FFS patients tend to use higher-volume hospitals than patients in managed care plans. The comparison yields mixed results when looking at Medicare.

An important additional finding is that volume varies across managed care plans. The variation is limited when analyzing physician services. But when looking at hospital services, the variation is pronounced. Patients in one of the six health plans separately reported receive their services from high-volume hospitals at a far higher rate than that of any other plan or patients enrolled in fee-for-service plans.

These findings raise two sets of questions. First, How should we interpret the results that show a relationship between care delivery system and provider volume? Second, How do these findings help us understand the quality of care in different systems?

Given the varied results across plans, procedures, and payment sources, a finding of a relationship between delivery system and provider volume is difficult to interpret without a model of behavior by those systems that would suggest why volume might differ and vary across these parameters. One theory offered by the authors is that lower-volume hospitals are more likely to be community hospitals, which are lower cost. Price-sensitive managed care plans would rather contract with lower-cost providers, which results in a lower-volume network. This hypothesis prompts the reader to wonder what explains the other sources of variation in volume. Do Medicare plans face different incentives than private plans? Do plans use different contracting approaches for physicians than they do for hospitals? Do plans use different approaches for different sorts of physicians? Only when these issues are examined will it be possible to interpret the paper's finding that volume ratios differ by payer, provider, and procedure.

In addition, it is not clear that plans contract primarily or exclusively on the basis of price. Plans must amass a provider network that satisfies geographical and practice-breadth objectives. Plans may seek to build relationships with provider networks that rely on that plan for a large portion of their volume, thereby allowing the plan to have a greater say in the providers' actions. Provider arrangements may reflect historical alliances in a community more than they reflect an economic transaction on the basis of price.

The paper also examines variations in provider volume as a basis for understanding more about plan quality. This step in the analysis must be taken with great caution. The paper presents information that suggests an interesting hypothesis about health plan markets that the authors briefly explore. The data showing one plan with heavy reliance upon high-volume hospitals while other plans use lower-volume hospitals raises the possibility that the managed care market is segmented into high-quality and low-quality plans. High-quality plans compete for enrollees who are interested in savings as compared to fee for service, but who are willing to pay extra to retain a higher-cost and presumably higher-quality network. Low-quality plans compete for enrollees who are primarily interested in price and are less concerned or less willing or able to pay for a higher-quality network. If this market segmentation exists, comparing aggregate HMO and fee-for-service volumes does not yield valuable information. In this model, HMOs do not affect quality. Rather, they pick a level of quality and market and price themselves within a segment of the health plan market.

In this regard, it is worth considering the possibility that product identification operates in the same manner for HMOs as it does for hospitals. Utilization patterns in fee-for-service plans are driven entirely by choices made by individual enrollees. The plan is simply a payment mechanism. An alternative way of formulating the question asked by the authors is: What actions are taken by HMOs in their selection of providers that leads them to select lower-volume providers than individuals do when left to their own choice? If fee-for-service patients tend to select higher-volume providers solely on the basis of name recognition or brand identification, HMOs that select providers on any other basis, even random choice, will tend toward lower-volume providers. Again, in this scenario, quality and volume differences between types of delivery systems are artifacts of other market factors that cannot be ascribed to actions taken by the plans.

Even after exploring these issues, it is worth asking what decision-making model for managed care plans selecting providers would cause one to believe that quality should vary plan by plan. While higher-volume providers may, in general, provide higher-quality care, and certain types of plans may rely on higher-volume providers, the conclusion that certain types of health plans are higher quality is only valid if there is some theory of plan behavior that suggests those plans seek higher-quality providers. One possible way out of this analytical challenge is to posit that plans care about quality, but believing that they cannot measure it directly, they seek to use volume as a proxy, much as the authors have done. This is a plausible approach, but again, it can only be understood in the context of a description of actual plan behavior, not through analysis of hospital records of patients. The authors do not explore this question directly—an undertaking that would require investigating the provider-selection criteria for the plans.

While not the focus of the paper, the specification of the relationship between volume and quality seems important. Particularly, knowing whether there is a linear relationship between volume and quality or a threshold level of volume necessary before quality is likely to be high would help interpret the results. This topic is of particular importance as it applies to this paper because the authors note the skewed distribution of volume across providers. The vast majority of providers operate at very low volume as the term is defined in this paper. A comparison of mean values of volume by plan type, even when adjusted for patient factors, is meaningful if one assumes a linear relationship. If the relationship is more complex, a different comparison would be appropriate.

In sum, the paper begins to analyze a very complex and important subject. Any single analysis can only address one part of the complex relationship among plan type, provider volume, and quality of care. This paper offers information in one area that, in combination with a better understanding of the structure and dynamics of plan contracting behavior and the nature of the health plan market, helps us understand this relationship.

The Meltzer, Hiltz, and Bates paper examines utilization patterns inside a teaching hospital, comparing the practices of teams that serve a fee-for-service population with teams that serve managed care patients. The paper provides very valuable insight into how financial incentives and organizational design can affect the practice of medicine.

The setting examined in the paper offers almost ideal circumstances for an experimental design. Each of six practice services within the same hospital operates in largely the same way. In general, the attending physician who directs patient care is employed by the hospital. However, in the two services that serve the bulk of managed care patients, care is directed for managed care patients by attending physicians affiliated with the managed care organization. The authors show that the financial incentives differ for managed-care-oriented teams in very specific ways. They also show that physicians from the managed care plans receive feedback on the length of stay of their patients, while no similar feedback occurs for the housestaff.

The paper reaches a simple and strong conclusion. Managed care patients have lower costs in this hospital setting, and those lower costs are essentially entirely due to shorter lengths of stay. Since the analysis fits the behavioral model nicely, the clear implication is that financial incentives can and do affect physician behavior.

The paper creates an excellent foundation for additional analysis that could shed light on the behavioral effects of incentives. It would be interesting to know if similar behavioral results could be achieved for the hospital-based care managers if they were given feedback on the lengths of stay relative to those in the HMO-based team. That is, could information without a financial incentive affect behavior?

It would also be interesting to test the behavioral hypothesis in other areas where financial arrangements are relevant. Similar financial incentives have been established for primary care physicians in their decisions to refer patients to specialists. When referral patterns are compared across physicians with varying incentives, are behavioral differences found? The authors note the reputation that both the health plan and the hospital have for high quality. If quality were less of a behavioral constraint, would the effects of the financial incentives increase? And if so, are there other constraints that could be designed to assure that quality does not suffer when there are incentives to control utilization?

An interesting comparison point would be the hospital's actions with respect to its Medicare patients, where payments are made on the basis of diagnosis-related groups (DRGs), which create incentives for the hospital similar to those the HMO faces. According to the authors, the hospital does not translate this institutional incentive into an individual or team incentive for the physicians treating Medicare patients. Are there institutions where efforts have been made to do so? Have these efforts had a similar effect on lengths of stay? Are there institutional reasons for avoiding approaches such as this in-house?

The authors also examine how these incentives and practice models affect the educational mission of the institution. This is a complex matter. If patients can be treated effectively and with high quality using a shorter, more intensive hospital stay, then perhaps that is the care model physicians should be educated to pursue. The appropriate pedagogical response may be to determine how care can most effectively be organized during that limited stay and how systems can be developed to meet the needs of the patient before admission and after discharge. This is not to deny the relevance of changed inpatient models on education. It is simply to say that the sense of lost opportunity from a traditional training perspective should be balanced against the opportunity to reexamine what physicians need to know to provide the best quality of care.

The authors close with a note that teaching hospitals can only survive in the current health care market if they learn to work with managed care. The impression one gains from this analysis is that at least one such hospital has taken an approach that shifts the behavior of the institution to conform to the changing financial incentives in the health care system. The paper provides those concerned about the future of teaching hospitals with excellent information that will be useful in navigating and understanding these changes.

IV

Taxation and Information

The Tax Benefits of
Not-for-Profit Hospitals

William M. Gentry and John R. Penrod

9.1 Introduction

Not-for-profit (NFP) hospitals in the United States receive several tax advantages relative to for-profit (FP) hospitals. The major tax advantages are exemption from federal and state corporate income taxes, exemption from state and local property taxes, and access to tax-exempt bond financing. In addition, charitable contributions to NFP hospitals are tax deductible for the donor. The expansion of FP hospitals over the last 15 years has led to increased scrutiny of why NFP hospitals receive a tax preference. Our objective is to quantify the importance of this array of tax breaks for NFP hospitals, assuming that the behavior of hospitals is otherwise static. We are interested in both the magnitude of these benefits and the heterogeneity of these benefits across hospitals.

The concern over whether NFP hospitals provide enough social benefits to justify their tax exemption has led to research comparing the social benefits of NFP hospitals with the cost in terms of forgone tax revenue of the tax exemption. If, as managers of FP hospitals contend, the social benefits of NFP hospitals are less than this tax cost, then the tax exemptions seem difficult to justify. Clement, Smith, and Wheeler (1994) present

William M. Gentry is associate professor of economics and finance at the Graduate School of Business at Columbia University and a faculty research fellow of the National Bureau of Economic Research. John R. Penrod is an economist at the Centre for the Analysis of Cost-Effective Care at the Montreal General Hospital Research Institute and an assistant professor in the faculties of medicine and economics at McGill University.

The authors thank David Cutler, Judith Hellerstein, William Sage, William Vogt, NBER conference participants, and seminar participants at Columbia University and the University of Toronto for helpful comments. They also thank Marvin Schwartz of the Statistics of Income, Internal Revenue Service, and Bruce Davie of the U.S. Treasury Department for unpublished data. All remaining errors are the authors' responsibility.

a methodology for measuring community benefits from not-for-profit hospitals and the size of the tax benefits of NFP status; they apply their methodology to a sample of NFP hospitals in California. They find considerable heterogeneity in the level of community benefits provided by NFP hospitals; depending on their recommended community benefit standard, between 20 and 80 percent of NFP hospitals have benefits exceeding their costs. As emphasized by Sloan (1997), the trade-off between the benefits and costs of NFP status should be evaluated relative to what would be provided by FP hospitals. Sloan argues that the massive changes in the U.S. health care market have pushed NFP hospitals to become more similar to FP operations.

Rather than divide our attention between community benefits and tax benefits, we focus on the underlying determinants of the value of the tax benefits and estimate the magnitude and heterogeneity of each tax break throughout the United States. The level of tax benefits will vary substantially across NFP hospitals. For the income tax, this variation will arise mainly from differences in profitability, capital intensity, state corporate tax rates, and the types of investment undertaken by the hospital (since effective tax rates vary across types of assets). The value of property tax exemption varies because hospitals differ in their use of capital and because property tax rates, assessment practices, and the definition of the property tax base (e.g., the inclusion of different types of property) vary across locations.

While the property tax exemption applies across the whole spectrum of NFP hospitals and the income tax exemption is valuable for NFP hospitals with net income, the use of tax-exempt bonds and charitable contributions are concentrated in a subset of hospitals. The value of the access to tax-exempt bonds depends on how much tax-exempt debt a hospital has in its capital structure. While NFP hospitals benefit from the lower interest rate on tax-exempt debt relative to using taxable debt, FP hospitals might have a lower after-tax cost of borrowing since they can deduct their interest payments from their corporate income tax base. Tax-exempt bonds can also create opportunities for tax arbitrage. Hospitals differ in their reliance on charitable contributions depending on the mission of the hospital. The value of the tax benefit from the charitable contribution accrues directly to the donor and depends on the donor's marginal tax rate; however, this tax deduction can create an additional incentive for giving by changing the "price" of a donation.

In summary, we find that NFP hospitals receive substantial benefits from reduced capital taxes. For 1995, the aggregate value of the exemption from federal and state income taxes is $4.6 billion and the aggregate property tax exemption is $1.7 billion. For the median hospital, these tax exemptions are worth roughly 2.5 percent of the value of total assets each year.[1] The benefit of the exemption from income taxes varies widely across hospitals because it depends on the profitability of the hospital. In contrast, the variation in the benefits from the exemption from property taxes comes more from variation in state and local tax rules than from differences in hospital operating characteristics. We estimate that the aggregate benefits of the access to tax-exempt bond markets are $354 million per year and that donors received $1.1 billion of tax benefits from contributing to NFP hospitals in 1994. While these benefits are smaller than the benefits from the capital tax exemptions, they are highly concentrated among larger NFP hospitals. Our research provides a framework for discussing the tax benefits of NFP status and estimates of these benefits. However, future research is needed on how these tax advantages ultimately affect health care. Without examining hospital behavior, we cannot answer whether these tax advantages improve the quality of health care, redistribute resources toward the less advantaged, lead to less efficient choices in allocating resources, or accrue to providers of noncapital inputs.

The paper proceeds as follows. Section 9.2 reviews some of the justifications for special tax policies toward NFP hospitals. Section 9.3 compares some basic characteristics of NFP and FP hospitals in terms of size and outputs. Section 9.4 discusses and imputes the value of capital tax exemptions. In section 9.5, we examine NFP hospitals' use of tax-exempt bond financing. Section 9.6 discusses the tax benefits of tax-deductible charitable contributions. Section 9.7 links our results to dynamic considerations and the ultimate incidence of who benefits from the tax treatment of NFP hospitals. Section 9.8 concludes with suggestions for further research.

9.2 Justifications for Tax Policy toward Not-for-Profit Hospitals

This section briefly reviews the arguments used to justify tax exemptions for NFP hospitals. These justifications fall in three categories: historical, administrative, and theoretical.

9.2.1 Historical Perspective on the NFP Hospital Tax Exemption

Not-for-profit organizations have been exempt from the U.S. federal income tax since its inception early in the twentieth century.[2] At the time, NFP organizations accounted for a small portion of the economy and engaged mainly in charitable activities. In general, hospitals were organized as not-for-profit, affiliated with either religious groups or philan-

1. Since our estimates are based on observed levels of capital and profitability, they are likely to be a lower bound on the capital tax revenue that would be realized if these hospitals were converted to for-profit institutions.

2. See Hansmann (1981) for a review of the rationales on exempting NFP organizations from taxation, and see Sanders (1995) for a specific application to NFP hospitals.

thropic foundations, and served families that could not afford to pay the doctor to visit their home. These NFP hospitals provided public benefits, financed most of their investment through charitable gifts, and did not generate substantial "income" that would be subject to tax. Thus, historically, NFP hospitals received tax preferences because they provided public services and earned little profit.

As noted by Marmor, Schlesinger, and Smithey (1987), drastic changes in medical technology and financing changed the role of hospitals in society. Technological advances transformed hospitals from places for the poor to seek comfort to places for the sick, regardless of income, to get well. The growth in private health insurance and government funding of health care of the poor and elderly made it viable to finance investment with revenues from patients. Hence, the purely historical arguments for the tax exemptions have grown less relevant.

9.2.2 Administrative Perspective on the NFP Hospital Tax Exemption

In addition to the historical reasons for the tax exemption, administrative, or legal, issues also arise for taxing NFP organizations. For the income tax, NFP organizations present challenges for measuring income. As discussed by Bittker and Rahdert (1976), donations received by NFP hospitals could be designated either as taxable revenue (the donor has "purchased" a good) or as nontaxable gifts received; likewise, the charity provided to individuals could be classified as a deductible business expense or as a nondeductible gift. Hansmann (1981) argues that these measurement problems are overstated for "commercial" NFPs—organizations, such as hospitals, that rely heavily on revenues from goods and services rather than donations.

Attributing the "income" of a NFP organization to "owners" also creates administrative problems. For many NFPs, income is small; however, for commercial NFPs (rather than donative NFPs), income is the business equivalent of "retained earnings." Even though retained earnings cannot be distributed, they measure the capital income generated by the NFP. If a religious or charitable organization is the "owner" of the income, one could argue that the income should face a zero marginal tax rate. However, since the corporate-level tax is an entity-level tax, the counterargument is that the NFP should pay the entity-level tax but the tax-exempt owner should not pay taxes on distributions. These administrative concerns are much smaller for the property tax since ownership can be assigned to the NFP organization, which could be held liable for the tax payment.

To qualify for the income tax exemption, organizations face two tests: organizational and operational. The organizational test, also called the nondistribution constraint, requires that the NFP "own" itself; revenues in excess of expenses must be reinvested in the hospital's mission. The NFP cannot have shareholders who receive the residual claims on the firm's income and cannot operate for the private inurement of interested parties. This restriction implies that the NFP hospital cannot transfer the profits to physicians or directors through excessive compensation. The operational test requires the NFP hospital to have an exclusively charitable purpose. If a NFP hospital engages in profit-making activities unrelated to its primary mission, it faces an unrelated business income tax that is equivalent to the income tax that would have been paid on the earnings from these activities. The requirement of being exclusively charitable has raised both federal and state policy concerns regarding what constitutes charitable activity.[3]

9.2.3   Theoretical Arguments for the NFP Hospital Tax Exemption

Economic theory suggests that governments may want special tax treatment (either a subsidy or lower tax rate) for activities when a competitive market would fail to produce an efficient outcome. Market failures can arise from private agents underproviding public goods (i.e., goods that are nonrival in consumption) or goods that generate positive externalities. Hospital activities that may create positive externalities include research and development, community education, medical education (to the degree health care professionals do not capture these benefits through returns to human capital), and disease control. Since FP firms only enter markets with nonnegative expected economic profits, they may underproduce hospital outputs that are not profitable. If the social benefits of these outputs exceed their private returns, then a subsidy to encourage the provision of these outputs may be justified. While society might want to encourage goods with positive externalities, subsidies tied to the provision of these goods (when feasible) would be more effective at encouraging the desired behaviors than would income or property tax exemptions.

Another potential market failure that NFP hospitals may help solve is related to information problems in health care markets.[4] The NFP organizational form may reduce these information problems relative to FP firms. If NFP hospitals face other organizational disadvantages, such as lack of access to equity capital markets, then the tax exemptions may increase economic efficiency by encouraging the NFP form despite its other disadvantages. Hansmann (1981) argues that offsetting the not-for-profit's capital constraint is a more appealing argument for the tax exemption than administrative reasons or encouraging the provision of community benefits. However, using a general equilibrium model, Goodspeed and Kenyon (1993) conclude that the tax exemption is a second-best method to counter the capital constraint.

---

3. See Frank and Salkever (1994) for a brief description of some of the recent policy challenges to NFP hospitals.

4. Frank and Salkever (1994) review models in which NFP status creates trust with customers. Arrow (1963) and Pauly (1978) are seminal articles.

In addition to efficiency grounds, equity arguments are also made to support the NFP hospital tax exemption. The argument for redistributing resources through health care, rather than by directly transferring money to poor people, is that health care is a "merit" good. As with many of the efficiency arguments, this justification runs afoul of being inferior to more targeted policies. For example, Medicaid targets resources for the care of the poor much more directly than a property or income tax exemption.

Thus far, we have described theoretical arguments in favor of the tax exemption of NFP hospitals. Many of these arguments offer only weak support for the tax exemption since it is not directly tied to particular behaviors or desired outcomes. Claims justifying the tax exemptions for NFP hospitals based on the services they provide require that NFP hospitals are more likely than FP hospitals to produce the desired outputs. We address whether the different organizational forms produce different outputs in the next section.

Policies that benefit one organizational form over another often spur criticisms of "unfair competition." Managers of FP hospitals claim that they are at a competitive disadvantage because the NFP hospitals are exempt from taxes. Presumably, these managers would support replacing the tax exemption with policies tied to specific behaviors but independent of organizational form. While such policies might be more effective from the government's perspective for the reasons discussed above, the issue of unfair competition is more complex than just noting that a policy favors one organizational form over another.

First, the coexistence of two organizational forms providing similar services (though possibly not identical services) suggests that the alternative organizational forms have competing advantages and disadvantages.[5] While the NFP organizations may have tax and reputation advantages, the FP firms may have an edge in terms of access to equity capital or managerial efficiency (assuming the market for corporate control effectively disciplines FP managers). In addition, FP hospitals may take advantage of opportunities for "cream skimming" either by specializing in high-profit activities or by catering to high-profit patients.[6] Thus, the mix of firms in the industry depends on the size of the tax advantage for NFP hospitals relative to these other differential costs and benefits of the two

---

5. For a discussion of the merits of alternative organizational forms from an agency cost perspective, see Fama and Jensen (1983a, 1983b). Alternatively, the coexistence of the two organizational forms could be a disequilibrium phenomenon; however, despite the recent wave of conversions of NFP hospitals into FP hospitals, this explanation seems implausible given the persistence of the two forms.

6. Myerson (1997) discusses the trend toward specialized hospitals "designed to conquer a profitable niche," such as heart hospitals and cancer centers. While he claims that FP hospitals are more aggressive in seeking these opportunities, both organizational forms are participating in the trend. In addition, these specialty hospitals have increased the competitive pressures on all hospitals providing a given service.

organizational forms. Second, Rose-Ackerman (1982) argues that the competition offered by NFP hospitals is "unfair" only if it is unanticipated and creates windfall losses for investors in the FP enterprises; FP firms should include anticipated competition from NFP firms in their investment decisions, and hence, anticipated competition does not unduly burden the FP firms (though it may shift the composition of investment within the industry).

9.3   Patterns in Location, Size, and Function of NFP and FP Hospitals

Given the justifications for the tax exemption of NFP hospitals and the potential for unfair competition, we present some basic facts about the size and characteristics of hospitals that are related to these hypotheses. Understanding differences in hospital characteristics is helpful for evaluating the tax benefits of NFP hospitals and for determining whether the organizational forms differ in their provision of community benefits. We focus on nonfederal, general short-term hospitals in the 50 states and the District of Columbia using data from cost reports submitted to the Health Care Financing Administration (HCFA) for fiscal year 1995 by hospitals participating in Medicare.

Of these 4,996 short-term hospitals in the United States in 1995, 2,963 (59 percent) are not for profit, 724 (15 percent) are for profit, and 1,309 (26 percent) are governmental. As the NFP sector contains some very large teaching hospitals, nearly 70 percent (660,150) of beds are located in NFP hospitals. FP hospitals account for 12 percent (116,135) of beds, while the government hospitals account for the remaining 18 percent (169,680).

9.3.1   Regional Differences

The distribution of hospital types varies greatly by geographic region. In the Northeast, the NFP sector dominates. Connecticut, Maine, New Jersey, Rhode Island, and Vermont do not have any FP hospitals, and in Massachusetts, New York, and Pennsylvania, the percentage of beds in for-profit control is under 3 percent. The government sector is also small in the Northeast; the percentage of hospital beds in the government sector is less than 10 percent in every northeastern state. In contrast to the Northeast, the percentage of hospital beds in the FP sector exceeds 30 percent in seven states: Texas, Utah, Tennessee, Nevada, Florida, Delaware, and Louisiana. Nearly half (54,511) of all for-profit hospital beds are in just three states: Texas, Florida, and California.

Since hospital services are predominantly provided locally, the uneven geographic distribution of FP hospitals raises questions about how the different organizational forms interact. Obviously, in a market with no FP hospitals, the NFPs are insulated from competitive pressures induced by the potentially different objectives of FP hospitals.[7] At the other extreme, when FP hospitals have a large market share, they may be less able to exploit profit opportunities through segmenting the market since there are fewer NFP hospitals to serve the less-profitable patients. In general, the competitive interactions between organizational forms may depend on the market penetration of FP hospitals. For example, the presence of a single FP hospital in a market might not influence the behavior of the dominant NFP hospitals, but when FP firms have a large market share, the NFP hospitals might respond by changing some behaviors. Since FP hospitals are unevenly distributed across locations, it is unlikely that a single, simple model will capture the interactions between FP and NFP hospitals in these different markets.

9.3.2 Differences in Size

In table 9.1, we present the 25th percentile, the median, and the 75th percentile of the characteristics of the hospitals by control type. We summarize the data in this way to minimize the effect of what appear to be unrealistic values and to give an idea of the dispersion of the data as well as its central tendency. Panel A presents data on hospital size. At the 25th percentile, the NFP hospitals are smaller than the FP hospitals in terms of the total facility beds and the number of discharges, though the 25th percentile of the number of hospital employees is greater for NFP hospitals. At the median and the 75th percentile of the distributions, the NFP hospitals are larger than the FP hospitals across all three dimensions. For example, the 75th percentile of the total facility beds is 50 percent larger for the NFP hospitals than for the FP hospitals, and the 75th percentile of the total number of employees is 109 percent larger. Across all three size measures, government hospitals are the smallest of the three types. For each size variable, a Kruskal-Wallis test of equivalence of the distribution across hospital types is rejected at the 0.01 level.

In panel B of table 9.1, we describe hospital size by financial measures. Across all points in the distribution, NFP hospitals have the greatest amount of both fixed and total assets, followed by FP and then government hospitals. NFP hospitals at the median and the 75th percentile generate more net patient revenue than their FP counterparts, though at the 25th percentile, net revenues of NFP hospitals lagged behind those of the FPs. Revenues of government hospitals are the lowest of the three types. Kruskal-Wallis tests for each of the variables presented in the middle panel rejected the null of equal distributions at the 0.01 level.

---

7. Unless regulatory barriers prevent entry by FP hospitals, the NFP hospitals may be influenced by the threat of entry by FP competition even where FP hospitals have zero market share.

Table 9.1   **Hospital Characteristics by Type of Hospital Control**

	25th Percentile			Median			75th Percentile			K-W Test
	NFP	FP	Gov	NFP	FP	Gov	NFP	FP	Gov	
A. Hospital size										
Total facility beds	81.0	86.5	42.0	170	138	70	310	205	141	*
Total discharges	1,682	1,839	496	4,975	3,609	1,233	10,791	6,463	3,301	*
Length of stay	4.53	4.32	4.32	5.51	5.11	5.46	7.05	6.06	10.81	*
No. of employees	206	177	84	520	330	161	1,134	543	391	*
B. Hospital finances										
Total assets (10^6)	11.34	9.43	3.37	40.7	22.4	8.04	107.30	47.34	24.93	*
Fixed assets (10^6)	5.09	4.19	1.38	18.2	13.0	3.59	44.92	27.92	11.77	*
Net patient revenue (10^6)	12.03	13.30	3.75	37.2	28.4	8.04	89.40	51.17	23.66	*
Inpatient % total revenue	53.4	58.1	47.7	62.4	66.9	56.6	71.3	74.9	66.4	*
C. Types of patients										
Medicaid % days	5.47	4.74	4.90	10.5	10.9	11.7	18.9	19.9	24.7	*
Medicare % days	36.5	39.9	20.9	51.8	52.4	49.9	61.9	65.5	64.2	*
Case mix index	1.15	1.19	1.00	1.28	1.33	1.09	1.44	1.47	1.24	*
% ICU days	2.34	3.99	0	4.94	5.85	1.88	7.27	7.65	6.14	*

Source: Tabulation based on a sample of 4,996 general short-term hospitals from HCFA's public use file of Medicare cost reports, fiscal year 1995.

*The Kruskal-Wallis test of equivalent distribution of the variable across the three hospital types was rejected at the 0.01 level.

9.3.3   Characteristics and Complexity of Patients

Panel C of table 9.1 presents measures of the kind and complexity of the patients treated in the three types of hospitals. The first two rows of this panel present the percentage of patients insured by Medicaid and Medicare, respectively. If government insurance programs offer less generous reimbursement than private insurance, we would expect that profit-maximizing firms might have an incentive to "cherry pick" or avoid the treatment of patients covered by this type of insurance. Though the advent of managed care has made Medicare patients relatively more attractive to hospitals than they were in the past, this is less true for Medicaid patients, and it seems remarkable that the percentage of patients in the two types of private hospitals should be so similar. The final two rows of table 9.1 give some indication of the complexity of cases served by each hospital type as measured by a case mix index (CMI) and the percentage of inpatient days that were in the intensive care unit.[8] By these indices the FP hospitals tend to treat slightly more difficult cases than NFP hospitals.[9]

9.3.4   Comparison of Services Provided

As a result of different organizational objectives, tax benefits, differences in regulatory constraints, or perhaps simply the historical evolution of the hospital market, hospitals of different organizational forms may differ in the kind and intensity of services that they provide. We examine differences by hospital type in the provision certain services, both those described in the literature as "community benefits" and those we classify as "specialized" services.

Community Benefits

As FP hospitals have grown in number, potential differences across hospital types in the willingness to provide uncompensated care has received much attention. The motivation for these concerns is clear: In the absence of harmful reputation effects, one would expect profit-maximizing firms to avoid treating uninsured patients, for whom receipt of payment is unlikely. Moreover, NFP firms are expected to provide a reasonable amount of uncompensated care in exchange for their tax-exempt status, though in most states the level of uncompensated care required to maintain NFP status is vaguely specified. Although it is not possible to study these differences with the Medicare cost report data, which lack information on the provision of uncompensated care, two recent studies use data on California

---

8. Higher values of HCFA's CMI indicates a case load that is more expensive to treat.
9. Alternatively, the difference in CMI may come from FP hospitals systematically recording more difficult diagnoses than NFP hospitals for similar patients. This recording difference would maximize reimbursements from third-party payers.

hospitals to address this question. Norton and Staiger (1994) find that though NFP hospitals provide more uncompensated care, the difference between NFP and FP firms disappears when accounting for the endogeneity of the choice of organizational form. In other words, their results indicate that NFP and FP hospitals located in areas with similar characteristics would offer similar amounts of uncompensated care. Their study underlines the importance of treating the organizational form as endogenous in order to make strong predictions related to the effects of the organizational form on hospital behavior. Young, Desai, and Lukas (1997) find that uncompensated care in hospitals that underwent a transition from NFP to FP did not decline relative to a control set of NFP hospitals, though, consistent with Norton and Staiger (1994), the hospitals that were acquired had a lower baseline level of uncompensated care.

Using the Medicare cost report data, we present evidence on the presence of three additional hospital services viewed as community benefits: an emergency department, a delivery room, and a hospital teaching program.[10] In our description of the differences in service provision below, we do not purport to provide estimates of a behavioral model that accounts for the endogeneity of organization form. Rather, we seek to provide a basic description of the differences, how they might be partially accounted for by variables such as hospital size, and how this description is related to various hypotheses suggested by economic theory. We present statistics on these services in table 9.2. The first three columns of the table show the proportion of hospitals of each organizational form that provide the service or have the characteristic. In column 4, we present a chi-square statistic for the null hypothesis of equality in the proportion across organizational forms. Finally, column 5 reports whether statistical differences between organizational forms were maintained in a linear probability model where the presence of the service or characteristic was modeled as a function of (1) a constant; (2) four hospital size indicators; and (3) indicators for teaching status, government status, for-profit status, church affiliation, and status as a sole community hospital. We also included interactions of the two organizational form indicators with the four size indicators.

The first row of table 9.2 presents results on the presence of emergency room services by hospital type.[11] Uninsured patients are more likely to use emergency rooms for routine medical care than insured patients and the

10. The sample from the cost reports was limited to hospitals that reported "reasonable" values for total number of beds, number of employees, employees per bed, total discharges, return on fixed assets, fixed assets per discharge, return on total assets, net revenue per day, length of stay, inpatient share of revenue, and average wages.
11. As for each of the "service" variables, the emergency department variable is set to 1 if the hospital reported positive costs for the department.

296   William M. Gentry and John R. Penrod

Table 9.2   Presence of Hospital Services/Characteristics by Organizational Form

	Percent with Service				Regression Results (5)
	NFP (1)	FP (2)	Gov (3)	Chi-Square (4)	
Emergency room	97.8	93.2	99.0	0.001	[1][a]
Delivery room	74.7	62.7	72.8	0.001	[1]
Teaching program	29.2	12.7	9.1	0.001	[1]
ICU	79.6	87.3	52.8	0.001	[1]
CCU	24.5	13.2	10.8	0.001	[2][b]
Radiation therapy unit	24.4	10.5	9.9	0.001	[1]

Source: Based on the sample from Medicare cost reports for fiscal year 1995.

Note: Columns 1, 2, and 3 show percentages for each service by hospital type, and column 4 gives the chi-square for the test of equality of the proportions across organizational forms. Column 5 indicates where there were differences across organization forms in a linear probability model where the provision of the service is modeled as a function of a constant; four hospital size indicators; and indicators for teaching status, government status, for-profit status, church affiliation, and status as a sole community hospital. The two organizational form indicators were interacted with the four size indicators.

[a][1] indicates significant differences across organizational forms for some hospital sizes; see text.

[b][2] indicates no significant differences across organizational forms for any hospital size.

emergency department is a port of entry for hospital admission for more seriously ill uninsured patients.[12] Therefore, it is possible that profit-seeking hospital firms would seek to avoid providing these services. In the first three columns of table 9.2, we show the proportions of the three types of hospitals with an emergency department. Consistent with our expectations, 93 percent of FP hospitals provide emergency services, compared to 98 percent of NFP and 99 percent of government hospitals. The chi-square statistic indicates that the proportions are statistically significant. Controlling for potential confounding factors in the regression model, small FP hospitals (those with less than 75 beds) are 18 percentage points (*p* value of 0.0001) less likely to have an emergency room than their NFP counterparts, and FP hospitals with between 150 and 225 beds are 5.5 percentage points less likely to provide emergency services than their NFP counterparts. There are no statistically significant differences between FP and NFP hospitals with between 75 and 150 beds or between FP and NFP hospitals with more than 300 beds.

For reasons analogous to that for emergency rooms, profit-maximizing hospital firms might avoid the provision of newborn deliveries in order to avoid expending resources on births to uninsured or Medicaid-insured young mothers, especially since uninsured women are more likely to have

12. For example, Culhane and Hadley (1992) find that NFP psychiatric hospitals are more accessible through emergency services than their FP counterparts.

low birth weight children that could require expensive neonatal care.[13] In the second row of table 9.2, we present some statistics for provision of hospital delivery rooms by hospital type. Sixty-three percent of FP hospitals provide delivery services, compared to 73 percent of government and 75 percent of NFP hospitals. In the regression analysis, statistically significant differences between FP and NFP firms are present for the two smallest size categories. Relative to similarly sized NFP hospitals, FP hospitals with fewer than 75 beds are 28 percentage points less likely to have delivery services, and FP hospitals with between 75 and 150 beds are eight percentage points less likely to provide delivery services.

The future of hospital-based medical education programs in increasingly competitive hospital markets has been the subject of much discussion (see, for example, Reuter and Gaskin 1997). Culhane and Hadley (1992) show that NFP psychiatric hospitals are more likely to be involved in professional training than FP psychiatric hospitals. The third row of table 9.2 presents statistics for the presence of a teaching program in our sample of short-term general hospitals.[14] Twenty-nine percent of NFP hospitals have a teaching program, while only 12.7 percent of FP and 9.1 percent of government hospitals do. The regression analysis reveals that teaching status is very strongly related to size, and organizational form does not influence the probability of having a teaching program for hospitals with fewer than 150 beds. However, among the three largest categories, there were important (and statistically significant) differences between FP and NFP firms in the probability of having a teaching program. FP hospitals with between 150 and 224 beds were 16 percentage points less likely to have a teaching program. For hospitals with between 225 and 299 beds and hospitals with more than 300 beds, the differences were 29 and 36 percentage points, respectively.

Provision of Specialized Services

In rows 4 through 6 of table 9.2, we present statistics on the presence of three specialized service units: an intensive care unit (ICU), a coronary care unit (CCU), and a radiation therapy unit (RTU). We find that FP hospitals, perhaps surprisingly, are the most likely to have an ICU (83 percent), followed by NFP (78 percent) and government hospitals (50 percent). The regressions indicate that the statistically significant differences across organizational forms are concentrated in the smallest two hospital size categories. For the CCUs, NFP hospitals lead, with 24.5 percent having a CCU, with the proportions being 13.2 percent and 10.8 percent in FP and government hospitals, respectively. However, having a CCU is

13. Haas et al. (1993) describe differences in birth outcomes between insured and uninsured women in Massachusetts.
14. We classify hospitals as teaching hospitals if they indicated the presence of interns and residents on the Medicare cost report.

strongly associated with size and teaching status, and in the regression analysis, none of the indicators for organizational form or their interactions with the size indicators were statistically significant. The results for the RTUs are somewhat different, though the pattern of the raw proportions look similar to those of the CCUs, with 24.4 percent of NFPs, 10.5 percent of FPs, and 9.9 percent of government hospitals having RTU units. The regression reveals that the presence of a RTU is very strongly associated with size and teaching status. Once these are controlled for, there is no statistical difference between government and NFP hospitals. For the three smallest hospital size categories, there is no difference between FP and NFP hospitals, but there is a significant difference for the two highest categories. For example, a NFP hospital with more than 300 beds is 18 percentage points more likely, other things equal, to have an RTU than its FP counterpart.

These systematic differences in the outputs of FP and NFP hospitals may offer some justification for the tax exemptions for NFP hospitals if society values these differences and, for some reason, the FP organizational form underprovides these services. These differences in services may, in part, explain the differences in profitability that we document in the next section. However, the story of service differences across organizational form is complicated by the significant amount of within-organizational-form variation. For example, as defined by Clement, Smith, and Wheeler (1994), 20–80 percent of NFP hospitals do not provide a level of community benefit equal to the government's tax expenditure on them, and Culhane and Hadley (1992) find in their discriminant analysis that, based on the services provided and clientele served by their sample of psychiatric hospitals, some NFP psychiatric hospitals appear more like their FP counterparts than like the other NFP psychiatric hospitals.

9.4   The Exemption from Capital Taxes

A major portion of the tax advantage of NFP hospitals comes from the exemption from factor taxes on capital—the corporate income tax and the property tax. We begin this section by discussing general issues in analyzing factor taxes. We follow this general framework with imputations of the aggregate value of the exemption from income and property taxes and the heterogeneity in these benefits across hospitals.

9.4.1   General Issues in Analyzing Factor Taxes

Since the property tax and income tax are taxes on capital, the importance of the exemption from these taxes depends on how much capital hospitals use. To get an idea of the importance of capital for hospitals, table 9.3 compares the capital intensity of publicly traded FP hospitals and other broad industry groups for 1995. The data are from COMPU-

Table 9.3   **Hospital Capital Intensity and Profitability Relative to Other Industries, 1995**

Industry	Wages to Net PPE	Net PPE to Sales	Return on Assets (%)
Natural resources	0.292	0.864	6.8
Manufacturing	0.391	0.360	10.2
Transportation and utilities	0.313	1.157	8.4
Sales	0.402	0.182	8.7
Services	2.022	0.412	9.1
Hospitals	0.724	0.608	10.3

Source: Authors' calculations from Standard & Poor's COMPUSTAT database.

Note: The values are industry averages weighted by the size of the denominator (i.e., the sum of all firms' values for the numerator divided by the sum of all firms' values for the denominator). Net PPE is the net book value of property, plant, and equipment. The labor expense measure is missing for many firms.

STAT, a database of corporate financial statements. While the publicly traded firms may differ from their privately held or NFP competitors, these data are useful for making interindustry comparisons. Furthermore, the eight publicly traded firms with primary Standard Industrial Classification (SIC) code 8062 own the majority of for-profit hospitals.[15] The table reports two measures of capital intensity—wages divided by the net book value of property, plant, and equipment (PPE) as an approximation of ratio of labor-to-capital inputs, and the net book value of PPE divided by sales revenue as an approximation of the capital-to-output ratio.

In terms of the labor-to-capital ratios, hospitals appear much more labor intensive than firms in nonservice industries (a ratio of 0.72 for hospitals compared to 0.39 for manufacturing firms).[16] While these data indicate that hospitals are relatively labor intensive in terms of factor proportions of capital and labor, hospitals are in the middle of all firms in terms of asset-to-sales ratios. That the manufacturing sector has both low wage-to-asset and low asset-to-sales ratios suggests that material inputs play a larger role in manufacturing than in service industries, such as hospitals. Overall, the data offer some evidence that hospitals are relatively labor intensive and, therefore, would benefit less from a capital tax exemption than would firms in other industries.

15. According to the *Directory of Investor-Owned Hospitals, Hospital Management Companies, and Health Systems,* the eight publicly traded companies in the sample own 562 of the 740 (76.0 percent) nonspecialty investor-owned hospitals, which account for 101,879 of the 120,620 (84.5 percent) beds in these hospitals. For 1995, *Hospital Statistics* (from the American Hospital Association's annual survey) reports 752 for-profit community hospitals with a total of 106,000 beds.

16. The wage data include hospital employees but not payments made directly from patients to doctors, so they probably understate the relative labor intensity of health care services. For the manufacturing sector, a large fraction of the firms do not report the wage data.

While the corporate income and property taxes are both factor taxes on capital, the differences in their administration leads to crucial differences in how important the tax exemption may be for NFP hospitals. The corporate income tax is levied on the flow of income generated by the firm's assets; in contrast, the property tax applies to the stock of assets owned by the firm. For a given rate of return, it is possible to construct a property tax that has the same revenue as a tax on capital income (assuming that the property tax applies to all of the capital generating the income). For example, for a 10 percent return to capital, a 30 percent capital income tax raises the same revenue as a 3 percent property tax.

Several details of the actual tax systems affect the equivalence between income and property taxes. First, property taxes sometimes only apply to a subset of the firm's assets, such as land and structures. Second, for the corporate income tax, the returns that flow to bondholders do not face corporate taxation since interest expense is deductible. Third, since the income tax is an ex post capital tax, any returns generated as inframarginal returns (economic profit) or from good or bad luck are included in the tax base. Similarly, the income tax depends on the profitability of the management of the assets. If the firm chooses to deploy the assets in ways that are less profitable than it could otherwise use the assets, then it will pay less in income taxes for a given amount of assets; however, the property tax levy is not sensitive to these decisions. The same argument applies if management deploys the assets less efficiently. This difference in taxes is especially relevant if NFP hospitals provide less-profitable services that have unmeasured (from the perspective of the tax base) social benefits.

Since the income tax uses an ex post measure of the return to capital, the tax liability depends on the profitability of the firm. The third column of table 9.3 provides a simple comparison of the profitability of publicly traded hospitals relative to other sectors. The 10.3 percent return on assets for publicly traded hospitals in 1995 is similar to the return on assets in manufacturing (10.2 percent) and higher than the returns in the other sectors. For the period 1978 through 1995, hospitals had an average return on assets of 11.5 percent. These returns suggest that an exemption from a capital income tax could have substantial value for hospitals.

While the comparisons of the publicly traded FP hospitals with firms in other industries provide a useful benchmark for thinking about the magnitude of the tax break for hospitals relative to the tax liabilities in other industries, this sample of firms may not reflect the value to NFP hospitals. As discussed above, the organizational forms differ in their outputs. They may also differ in terms of their reliance on capital and their profitability. In terms of their reliance on capital, two potentially offsetting effects might lead to differences in input choices across organizational forms. First, the capital tax exemption may encourage NFP hospitals to choose more capital-intensive production methods or specialize in more capital-intensive outputs.[17] Second, since NFP hospitals cannot issue public equity, they may use less capital than FP hospitals. To compare the two types of hospitals, we return to the Medicare cost report data.

Table 9.4 compares the capital intensity and profitability of different types of hospitals. We have five measures of capital intensity: (1) employees per bed; (2) wages to fixed assets; (3) fixed assets to net patient revenue; (4) fixed assets per discharge; and (5) allocated capital costs as a fraction of total allocated costs. While the nonparametric statistical tests reject the null hypothesis that the distributions of the capital intensity variables are drawn from a common distribution, there are no strong patterns in capital intensity across types of hospitals. The distributions of the capital intensities have considerable overlap indicating that high capital intensity is not associated with a particular organizational form. At the median of their distributions, NFP hospitals have more employees per bed (3.30 for NFP hospitals to 2.44 for FP hospitals), higher wages relative to fixed assets (0.92 to 0.74), and lower capital costs relative to total costs (0.09 to 0.107). These differences suggest that NFP hospitals are less capital intensive than the FP hospitals. However, in terms of fixed assets relative to net patient revenues or discharges, NFP hospitals appear slightly more capital intensive than FP hospitals.

The second panel of the table compares the profitability of different types of hospitals. Our measures of profitability are: (1) net income; (2) return on assets (total income divided by total assets); (3) return on fixed assets (the difference between patient revenue and operating expenses divided by fixed assets); and (4) operating margins (net patient revenues less operating expenses divided by operating expenses). The government hospitals are clearly less profitable than the private hospitals. By all of the measures except net income, the NFP hospitals are less profitable than the FP hospitals. The median of the return on fixed asset distribution for NFP hospitals is zero compared to 10.4 percent for FP hospitals; the low return on assets suggests that the NFP hospitals might pay considerably less in income taxes than their FP counterparts. However, the different organizational forms are much more similar in terms of returns on total assets; one difference between the return on fixed assets and the return on total assets is the investment income earned on investments, an important source of income for NFP hospitals with large endowments.

The lower incomes of NFP hospitals are consistent with both of the

17. The idea of one organizational form specializing in a particular set of outputs depends on the coexistence of the two organizational forms within the same geographic market. For markets served only by NFP hospitals, one would expect that only the substitution of capital for labor for a given set of outputs would occur, since without an FP competitor, changing outputs implies changing the overall set of services received by the community.

Table 9.4   **Capital Intensity and Profitability by Type of Hospital Control**

	25th Percentile			Median			75th Percentile			K-W Test
	NFP	FP	Gov	NFP	FP	Gov	NFP	FP	Gov	
A. Capital Intensity										
Employees per bed	2.42	1.87	1.66	3.30	2.44	2.44	4.16	3.09	3.50	*
Wages to fixed assets	0.68	0.50	0.76	0.92	0.74	1.08	1.29	1.29	1.63	*
Fixed assets to net patient revenue	0.35	0.28	0.30	0.47	0.45	0.42	0.61	0.65	0.59	*
Fixed assets per discharge	2,623	1,913	2,028	3,852	3,522	3,204	5,444	5,721	5,030	*
Capital costs over total costs	0.070	0.083	0.053	0.090	0.107	0.070	0.113	0.133	0.091	*
B. Profitability										
Net income (thousands)	137	−54.5	−24.6	1,333	1,343	299	5,201	5,717	1,187	*
Return on assets (%)	1.1	−0.6	−0.5	4.4	6.9	4.2	7.9	19.3	4.9	*
Return on fixed assets (%)	−9.3	−4.6	−31.5	0.0	10.4	−7.0	8.3	34.4	4.9	*
Operating margin (%)	−4.2	−2.7	−12.0	−0.0	5.2	−3.3	4.1	16.8	2.4	*

Source: Tabulation based on a sample of 4,996 general short-term hospitals from HCFA's public use file of Medicare cost reports, fiscal year 1995.
*The Kruskal-Wallis test of equivalent distribution of the variable across the three hospital types was rejected at the 0.01 level.

competing theories stated above. Consistent with the intent of the NFP tax exemption, the NFPs could be distributing some of their "income" in the form of community benefits, or services provided at a price below average cost. Alternatively, the lower incomes could come from administrative inefficiency or excessive payments to factors of production. The lower incomes of the NFP hospitals may also reflect random differences across firms and years. Our analysis of cost report data focuses on 1995 when FP hospitals happened to be more profitable than NFP hospitals. While this difference is common, in some years, the different organizational forms have similar profitability (see Sloan 1997).[18] Thus, our comparisons of NFP and FP hospitals are somewhat sensitive to the choice of year.

These univariate comparisons of capital intensity and profitability do not control for other hospital characteristics, such as size and teaching responsibilities, that are correlated with organizational form. To control for some of these factors, we regress our measures of capital intensity and profitability on the number of beds in the facility and dummy variables for for-profit status, government ownership, church affiliation, rural location (sole community hospital status), and teaching (as proxied for by the presence of interns or residents). Table 9.5 presents the results from these descriptive regressions. In terms of capital intensity, a more clear picture emerges that FP are more capital intensive than NFP hospitals: On average, relative to NFP hospitals, the FP hospitals have 0.6 fewer employees per bed, 0.06 higher fixed-asset-to-revenue ratios, $838 more fixed assets per discharge, and 0.023 higher capital costs as a fraction of total costs.[19] If, as suggested by the regressions, NFP hospitals are less capital intensive than FP hospitals, then the value of the NFPs' exemption from capital taxes is less than the value of taxes paid by the FP hospitals. Furthermore, these regressions cast doubt on the hypothesis that the exemption from capital taxes leads the NFP hospitals to substitute capital for labor or to specialize in more capital-intensive forms of health care.

The regression results on profitability confirm the conclusions from table 9.4 that FP hospitals are more profitable than NFP hospitals. Relative to the NFP hospitals, the FP hospitals have $1.3 million more in net income, a 5.4 percentage point higher return on assets, a 15 percentage point higher return on fixed assets, and a 7.9 percentage point higher operating

18. While Sloan's analysis of total margins shows that FP and NFP hospitals are similar in some years, Cleverly's (1992) comparison of the return on equity of hospital systems indicates that FP hospital chains typically outperform NFP hospitals.

19. For the variables created from accounting measures of capital (either fixed assets or allocated capital costs), newer hospitals may have higher measured capital costs than older hospitals if depreciation allowances for accounting purposes are more generous than true economic depreciation. With accelerated depreciation, book values of capital will understate market values. If hospital age is correlated with organizational form, then these discrepancies could affect our results.

Table 9.5   Capital Intensity and Profitability Regressions

			Explanatory Variable				
	Constant	Beds (thousands)	For Profit	Government	Church	Rural	Teaching
Employees per bed	2.93**	0.702**	-0.59**	-0.33**	-0.0061	-0.13*	1.31**
Wages to fixed assets	1.27**	-0.42**	-0.087	-0.040	-0.13*	0.16**	-0.11*
Fixed assets to net patient revenue	0.52**	0.0024	0.060*	0.034	0.026	-0.049	0.039
Fixed assets per discharge	4,155**	726*	837**	-50.9	159	84.0	1,170**
Capital costs over total costs	0.087**	0.015**	0.023**	-0.011**	0.0056**	-0.0035*	0.0070**
Net income (000)	14.6	13.5**	1,366**	-275	1,302**	-110	2,823**
Return on assets (%)	3.1**	3.6**	5.4**	-0.016	0.63	1.8**	-0.81*
Return on fixed assets (%)	-3.2**	10.0**	15.0**	-7.9**	1.8	1.5	-3.9**
Operating margin (%)	-0.75*	4.0**	7.9**	-3.3**	1.1*	0.33	-1.9**

Source: The sample includes 4,555 general short-term hospitals from HCFA's public use file of Medicare cost reports, fiscal year 1995.

Note: Relative to the sample in tables 9.1, 9.2, and 9.4, we eliminated observations with implausible values.

*Significant at the 5 percent level.

**Significant at the 1 percent level.

margin. The results also indicate that larger hospitals are more profitable (both in terms of the level of income and the rate of return), government hospitals are less profitable than NFP hospitals, and teaching hospitals are less profitable than other hospitals (in terms of rates of return). Overall, these differences in profitability suggest that many NFP hospitals would not have large income tax liabilities since they are not profitable.

9.4.2 The Value of the Exemption from Income Taxes

As a starting point for analyzing the importance of the income tax exemption for NFP hospitals, we examine the income tax liabilities of publicly traded FP hospitals, the same sample we used in table 9.3 to compare capital intensity across industries. Table 9.6 presents summary measures of the importance of income taxes over time for publicly traded hospitals and across industries for 1995. For 1995, publicly traded hospitals reported $976 million in total income taxes.[20] Hospitals' tax liabilities have grown over time as the FP hospital sector has grown. Compared to earlier years, 1995 seems typical in terms of income taxes relative to assets, sales, and cost of goods sold. Relative to manufacturing firms, income taxes are a slightly higher fraction of hospital assets, sales, and cost of goods sold.

Since NFP hospitals may differ in terms of capital intensity and profitability, applying the taxes paid by the FP hospitals may not be a good indicator of the taxes that the NFP hospitals would pay if the income tax exemption were repealed. To get a sense of the potential tax liabilities of the NFP hospitals, we impute income tax liabilities from the HCFA cost report data. As an approximation of federal income taxes, we multiply each hospital's net income by 35 percent, the top corporate statutory marginal tax rate. For firms with negative net income, this imputation leads to a tax "refund." This refund can be used to offset income tax liability from either previous years (a carryback), future years (a carryforward), or other hospitals "owned" by the same taxable entity.[21] To calculate precise estimates of the value of the refunds associated with losses requires a complicated, dynamic program accounting for the probability of firms moving from positive to negative income in order to use their carryforwards. Our approach overstates the value of tax refunds to the extent that some NFP hospitals persistently have negative income. To incorporate state income tax rates, we include the top marginal state corporate income tax rate,

<hr>

20. These data are the income taxes reported for financial reporting purposes. They may differ from tax payments to the government due to differences in financial and tax accounting. For example, differences in the timing of depreciation allowances can affect the taxes reported in financial statements relative to actual payments.

21. The ability to offset losses against income of affiliated hospitals is obviously useful for the large FP hospital chains. However, most NFP hospitals are in relatively small groups. The repeal of the NFP income tax exemption would create incentives for NFP hospitals to consolidate in order to benefit from taxable losses generated by a single hospital.

Table 9.6   Summary Measures of the Importance of Income Taxes for Publicly Traded Hospitals

Year	Number of Firms	Income Taxes (Total in $millions)	Income Taxes to Book Value of Assets (%)	Income Taxes to Sales (%)	Incomes Taxes to Cost of Goods Sold (%)
1980	11	196	4.2	4.8	6.1
1985	17	620	3.3	4.4	5.6
1990	17	391	1.6	1.8	2.2
1994	12	926	2.9	3.9	4.8
1995	8	976	3.0	3.8	4.6
			Cross-Industry Comparison for 1995		
Manufacturing	3,218	162,162	2.9	3.0	4.3
Services	1,143	9,826	2.7	3.3	5.5

Source: Authors' calculations from Standard & Poor's COMPUSTAT database supplemented with Tenet Healthcare's *1996 Annual Report.*
Note: The ratios reflect total industry income taxes to industry book value, sales, and cost of goods sold.

Table 9.7 **Imputed Income Taxes by Type of Hospital Control**

	25th Percentile		Median		75th Percentile	
	NFP	FP	NFP	FP	NFP	FP
Federal income tax (thousands)	68.7	−3.5	514.5	583.3	1,861.6	2,135.4
Federal income tax to net patient revenue	0.47	−0.038	1.7	2.2	3.1	5.1
Federal income tax to total assets	0.46	−0.017	1.5	2.5	2.7	6.4
Total income tax (thousands)	79.2	−3.8	579.8	642.5	2,110.8	2,329.9
Total income tax to net patient revenue	0.54	−0.044	1.9	2.5	3.5	5.6
Total income tax to total assets	0.52	−0.017	1.8	2.7	3.1	7.1

Source: Data are from HCFA's public use file of Medicare cost reports, fiscal year 1995.

Note: The ratios of taxes to revenue and assets are expressed as percentages. We eliminated observations for which the return on assets or the return on fixed assets was greater than one in absolute value.

adjusted for deductibility of state income taxes for federal income tax purposes.[22]

Table 9.7 reports statistics on the imputed value of income taxes paid by NFP and FP hospitals, and the relative values of income taxes to net patient revenue and total asset value. We include the FP hospitals as a comparison for the NFP hospitals; unfortunately, the cost report data do not include a variable for taxes paid. The imputations for the FP hospitals also allow us to compare our imputed tax liabilities with the reported tax liabilities of publicly traded hospitals in table 9.6. The eight hospital firms in table 9.6 owned 562 hospitals and record $976 million in income taxes paid. For the 622 FP hospitals in our sample, we impute an aggregate income tax liability of $946 million, which suggests that our simple imputation does a reasonable job of capturing income tax liabilities.

While the median dollar values of federal income taxes are similar for the two types of firms ($514.5 for NFP hospitals compared to $583.3 for FP hospitals), much of this difference comes from differences in hospital size. In terms of income taxes relative to revenues or total assets, the median values for NFP hospitals are roughly two-thirds as large as the me-

22. We use state corporate tax rates from *Significant Features of Fiscal Federalism.* Since the last version of *Significant Features of Fiscal Federalism* has data for 1993, we update this data with information from the Federation of Tax Administrators.

dian values for FP hospitals. Since the NFP hospitals have lower (private) rates of return than the FP hospitals, they benefit less from the income tax exemption than would be expected by simply assuming that they would pay a similar share of net revenue or asset value in income taxes as the FP hospitals. Without the tax exemption, the median NFP hospital would pay income taxes of 1.9 percent of net patient revenues; in contrast, the median FP hospital pays income taxes of 2.5 percent of net patient revenues. If the repeal of the income tax exemption pushes the NFP hospitals to behave like the current FP hospitals, then the 2.5 percent represents the tax savings for NFP hospitals. The comparison of the value of the tax exemption with revenues suggests that the tax exemption provides considerable financial resources to undertake the NFPs' charitable mission. For the 2,801 NFP hospitals in our sample, the aggregate imputed income tax liability is $4.6 billion, with roughly $4.1 billion resulting from the federal income tax exemption and the remaining $500 million from the state tax exemption.

We impute the potential income tax liability by applying the tax rate to total net income, which is the sum of operating income and investment income. Unlike FP hospitals, some NFP hospitals have substantial endowments invested in financial assets. Thus, the NFP hospital is a combination of an operating business with a hospital and a portfolio of financial assets. In aggregate, the exemption from income taxes on investment income accounts for $1.4 billion of the total value of the exemption from income taxes, which is 30 percent of the total value of the income tax exemption. The value of the tax exemption on investment income is concentrated among hospitals with large endowments. For an NFP hospital with zero (or negative) operating income but an endowment yielding investment income, the income tax exemption only has value because the hospital is a tax-exempt investor in financial assets.

9.4.3   The Value of Exemption from Property Taxes

Based on data provided by hospitals for the fiscal year 1992, HCFA undertook a special project to analyze property tax payments by FP hospitals. HCFA's data indicate that the average amount paid in property taxes by FP hospitals in 1992 was 1.6 percent of fixed assets. We use this rate as our first estimate of the average property tax rate that would apply to NFP hospitals in the absence of the tax exemption. We apply this rate to the fixed assets of NFP hospitals in the 1995 cost report data and report summary statistics on the value of the tax exemption in table 9.8. The median hospital-level exemption is $295,139; the median exemption per bed is $1,769; the median exemption per discharge is $62; and the median exemption as a percentage of total revenues is 0.7 percent.

There are several potential problems with the above calculations as estimates of the size of property tax exemption. The most obvious is that FP

Table 9.8   **Imputed Property Taxes for NFP Hospitals in Total and for Three States**

	% Tax Rate on Fixed Assets	Property Tax Level	Property Tax per Bed	Property Tax per Discharge	Property Tax % Net Revenue
25th percentile					
New Jersey	1.36	358,704	1,525	44	0.5
Ohio	1.46	151,988	1,157	52	0.6
Wisconsin	2.37	125,990	1,299	97	1.1
United States[a]	1.60	82,357	922	42	0.6
Median					
New Jersey	1.62	649,414	1,876	57	0.6
Ohio	1.70	429,901	1,848	67	0.8
Wisconsin	2.81	277,397	2,945	126	1.4
United States[a]	1.60	295,139	1,769	62	0.7
75th percentile					
New Jersey	1.82	1,016,505	2,830	73	0.9
Ohio	1.91	819,896	2,835	89	1.0
Wisconsin	3.28	773,765	5,035	168	1.9
United States[a]	1.60	721,766	2,827	87	1.0

Total Imputed Property Taxes, NFP Hospitals
New Jersey	$64.34 million
Ohio	$117.86 million
Wisconsin	$83.66 million
United States	$1.705 billion

Source: Tabulations compiled from Medicare cost reports report on fixed assets and state tabulations on property tax rates.

[a]U.S. property taxes are based on a rate of 1.6 percent, the percentage of fixed assets paid in property taxes by hospitals paying property taxes, 1992.

firms and NFP firms may systematically locate in areas with different tax rates, so that the rate of 1.6 percent, developed from a set of FP hospitals, may not be an appropriate rate to apply to NFP hospitals. In particular, FP firms may locate in areas where property taxes are low. In addition, the uniform rate does not provide information on the heterogeneity in the tax rates and in the value of the exemption. For this reason, we expand our analysis to individual states.

Since there is no nationwide database providing the effective commercial property tax rates for each municipality, we set out to build our own by contacting the treasury departments in a large number of states. Three states—New Jersey, Ohio, and Wisconsin—provided *effective* tax rates for each municipality in the state.[23] Since FP hospitals represented a negli-

23. The Office of Revenue and Tax Analysis of the Michigan Department of Revenue has recently published a set of imputations of the value of the tax exemption for NFP hospitals in Michigan (Michigan Department of Treasury 1997). They reported that property taxes represented 45.2 percent of Michigan's $390.2 million in tax expenditures for not-for-profit hospitals in 1996.

gible part of the market in these three states in 1995, we cannot adequately address the question of whether property tax rates "faced" by FP and NFP firms are systematically different. However, our data from these states will give us some idea of the intrastate heterogeneity in the value of the tax exemption.

Our three states differ in the classification of fixed assets that are taxed. In Ohio, real property (land and buildings) is taxed at a different rate than business personal property (movable equipment, etc.), and in New Jersey only real property is taxed. Since the Medicare cost report data do not provide separate variables for real and business personal property, we use the information on capital cost of buildings and fixtures and movable equipment to determine the percentage of fixed assets in each of the two property categories. In each state, the property rate shows a fair amount of variation. Combining data from the Medicare cost reports and property tax rate data on the municipalities in which the hospitals reside, we calculate what the property tax bill of the NFP hospitals would have been had they not been exempt from taxation.

Results from the property tax imputations for NFP hospitals are given in table 9.8. We report the 25th percentile, the median, and the 75th percentiles for five measures of the property tax burden. The tax rate for the median hospital in each of the three states is higher than the national average for FP hospitals. For New Jersey, the difference is slight (1.62 percent versus 1.6 percent), but in Wisconsin, the median is 2.8 percent, 75 percent higher than the FP national average. In addition to the interstate heterogeneity, tax rates vary considerably within states. For example, in Wisconsin the 25th percentile tax rate is 2.37 percent, while the 75th percentile tax rate is 3.28 percent, an increase of 40 percent. Property tax levels move through a larger range, since this is largely a function of hospital size. Indeed, the Michigan Department of Treasury (1997) calculates that the 10 largest of the 172 NFP hospitals in Michigan account for over 40 percent of Michigan property tax expenditures. Columns 3, 4, and 5 present the imputed property taxes in ways that account for hospital size. In column 3, we can see that, at the median, property taxes per bed ranged from $1,848 in Ohio, which is just slightly above the median for the country as a whole ($1,769), to $2,945 in Wisconsin. Column 4 shows that the median imputed property tax per discharge ranged from $57 in New Jersey to $126 in Wisconsin, which is more than double the U.S. median of $62. In column 5 we see that, as a percentage of revenues, the median property tax ranged from 0.6 percent in New Jersey to 1.4 percent in Wisconsin.

At the bottom of table 9.8, we calculate the total property tax expenditure for general short-term NFP hospitals in the three states. The tax expenditure ranges from $64 million in New Jersey to $118 million in Ohio. Since we do know how well the property tax rates that "apply" to NFP hospitals in these three states represent those faced by NFP hospitals around the country, we use the average FP hospital property tax rate developed from the HCFA study to develop a nationwide estimate of the value of the property tax exemption. By this measure, the total property tax expenditure in the United States for fiscal year 1995 was $1.7 billion. As a proportion of capital tax exemptions given to NFP hospitals by state and local government, this property tax bill is three times the size of the $500 million we calculated as the value of the exemption from state corporate income taxes. The much higher federal corporate income taxes result in a high value of the federal corporate income tax exemption ($4.1 billion), even at the relatively low level of profitability of NFP hospitals. Thus, the value of the property tax exemption represents only 27 percent of the total 6.3 billion dollars of capital tax exemptions at all levels of government.

The relative size of the different types of assets also affects the value of the property tax and income tax exemptions. The income tax exemption excludes income generated both by assets employed in the provision of medical care and investment assets, but the property tax only applies to fixed assets (or a subset of fixed assets). From table 9.1 we can see that, at the median, nonfixed assets represent the majority of the assets of NFP hospitals. Since property taxes are based only on fixed assets, the value of the property tax exemption, at the median, applies to less than half of all hospital assets.

9.4.4 The Combined Value of Capital Tax Exemptions

How large is the value of the capital tax exemption relative to government budgets and other tax expenditures directed to the health care sector? If the tax exemption were abolished, how large would the revenue gain be relative to, say, the health care needs of the uninsured? In 1994, aggregate property taxes paid in the United States were $197 billion and aggregate corporate income taxes were $169 billion (U.S. Bureau of the Census 1997, table 478). Thus, with our assumption of no behavioral changes by the NFP hospitals, the $6.3 billion capital tax exemptions ($1.7 billion in property tax exemptions and $4.6 billion in income tax exemptions) extended to NFP hospitals represent about 1.7 percent of property and corporate income taxes paid.[24] Compared to other tax expenditures in the health care sector, the capital tax exemption for NFP hospitals is much smaller than the $60.6 billion tax expenditure on the exclusion of employer contributions for medical insurance, but it is larger than the $3.7 billion for deductibility of medical expenses and the $2.2 billion for de-

---

24. As we discuss below, our calculations are based on the assumption of static reaction of hospitals to the capital taxes. It is possible that the NFP hospitals could obtain profitability levels similar to FP hospitals in an environment where they are taxed.

ductibility of charitable contributions to the health care sector (U.S. Bureau of the Census 1995, table 523).

In 1995, approximately 41 million people in the United States lacked health insurance. Hence, the value of the capital tax exemption to NFP hospitals represents $154 for each uninsured person. In 1995, per capita hospitalization expenses totaled $1,283.[25] Assuming that the uninsured have hospitalization costs similar to the national average and that hospital output and prices are not sensitive to tax policy, then the extra tax revenue generated by taxing NFP hospitals could fund 12 percent of a program to extend hospitalization insurance to the uninsured.

9.5   Access to Tax-Exempt Bond Markets

The ability to borrow using tax-exempt bonds is another potential tax-related advantage for NFP hospitals. In this section, we address two issues related to the value of the access to tax-exempt bond markets. First, we document the importance of tax-exempt bonds for NFP hospitals. Second, we discuss how potential policy reforms would affect NFP hospitals' value of issuing tax-exempt bonds.

Table 9.9 reports data on the issuance of long-term nonrefunding tax-exempt bonds by type of issuer for 1988 to 1992: government, NFP hospitals, and other tax-exempt private activity. These data are unpublished Internal Revenue Service tabulations.[26] The data exclude refunding issues, which are associated with refinancing of existing debt. Thus, these data should reflect borrowing for new investment. For 1992, the $10.3 billion in NFP hospital bonds accounted for 7.8 percent of the total tax-exempt bonds issued. The average bond issue was for $29.3 million. While other segments of the tax-exempt bond market grew by 49 percent between 1988 and 1992, the value of NFP issues grew by 124 percent. To put this $10.3 billion in perspective, it is useful to compare the proceeds of the bonds with the size of fixed assets of NFP hospitals. For a sample of 2,838 NFP hospitals with cost report data in both 1994 and 1995 and no change in ownership status, total fixed assets in 1995 are $102 billion with a median value of $18.5 million. Furthermore, the aggregate change in fixed assets (i.e., a measure of net investment) for these hospitals is $4.2 billion. Thus, the aggregate bond issuance of $10.3 billion is large relative to the stock and flow of fixed assets of NFP hospitals.

While table 9.9 reports on the flow of new bond issues, the stock of outstanding debt depends both on new issues and the repayment of previous bonds. For information on the stock of outstanding bonds, we present

25. Data on the number of uninsured and per capita hospitalization expenses comes from the *Statistical Abstract of the United States 1997.*

26. We thank Marvin Schwartz of the Statistics of Income and Bruce Davie of the Treasury Department for assistance with the data.

Table 9.9   Long-Term Tax-Exempt Bond Issuance, by Type of Issuer

Year	Total		Government Bonds		NFP Hospitals		Other Private Activity	
	Number	Amount	Number	Amount	Number	Amount	Number	Amount
1988	11,217	86.9	9,245	53.5	208	4.6	1,764	28.8
1989	12,024	94.8	9,284	61.9	250	6.3	2,490	26.6
1990	12,646	106.8	10,317	70.6	265	6.6	2,064	29.6
1991	12,827	122.1	10,458	86.3	369	11.1	2,000	24.7
1992	11,877	132.9	9,937	97.5	352	10.3	1,588	25.1

Source: The data are from unpublished tabulations from the *Statistics of Income,* Internal Revenue Service.

Note: Dollar values are in billions of current dollars. The bonds are nonrefunding bonds.

data collected by the IRS from the balance sheets of tax-exempt organizations.[27] For 1994 (the most recent year with available data), NFP hospitals had $46.1 billion of outstanding tax-exempt debt. By comparison, these hospitals reported aggregate fixed assets of $191 billion and total assets of $281 billion. Thus tax-exempt bonds are an important source of financing for NFP hospitals.

These aggregate tabulations mask the heterogeneity in tax-exempt bond issuance among NFP hospitals. Only 19.7 percent of NFP hospitals have outstanding tax-exempt debt. Since issuing bonds has a fixed cost of underwriting, it is not surprising that the hospitals with outstanding tax-exempt bonds are much larger than the NFP hospitals without tax-exempt bonds; the hospitals with tax-exempt bonds have average fixed assets of $54.1 million compared to $14.6 million for those without tax-exempt debt. Conditional on having outstanding tax-exempt bonds, the median value of outstanding debt was $24.6 million. The median value of the ratio of outstanding tax-exempt debt to fixed assets was 0.769, which suggests that these hospitals are either highly leveraged or have substantial other assets. In support of the latter hypothesis, the median ratio of tax-exempt debt to total assets is only 0.336.

While these data indicate that tax-exempt bonds are an important source of financing for NFP hospitals, they do not give any information on the value of the tax "subsidy" from using tax-exempt bonds. Calculating the value of the subsidy depends on the alternative policy under consideration as well as how the NFP hospitals use the proceeds from borrowing. Under current tax law, investors are willing to lend to tax-exempt issuers at lower interest rates than they lend to issuers of taxable debt because they do not pay income taxes on interest from tax-exempt bonds. For example, the average current yield on AAA-rated tax-exempt municipal bonds is 5.29 percent for 20-year maturities; in contrast, 20-year U.S. Treasury bonds yield 6.68 percent. Thus, expressed as a percent of the yield on the taxable bonds, the tax-exempt bonds have a subsidy of 21 percent for a 20-year yield.

Morrisey, Wedig, and Hassan (1996) propose using this comparison of taxable and tax-exempt yields for valuing the tax benefit from tax-exempt borrowing. They impute the value of tax-exempt bonds as the interest rate differential between taxable and tax-exempt bonds times the amount of debt outstanding. Assuming a yield spread of 1.5 percentage points

27. The data are from the public use files of form 990 returns of tax exempt organizations for reporting year 1994. The data are a stratified random sample of NFP organizations with oversampling of large organizations. Since hospitals are larger than most NFP organizations, the sample has almost all major NFP hospitals. The data include weights for estimating population statistics. Unlike the HCFA data, we cannot separate the IRS data by type of hospital. Therefore, these data include long-term and specialty hospitals in addition to the general, short-term facilities that we discussed in previous sections.

(slightly higher than the spread between tax-exempt municipal debt and the relatively less risky U.S. Treasury bonds), this imputation implies that the \$46.1 billion of outstanding NFP hospital tax-exempt debt creates an annual tax benefit of \$691.5 million. This imputation approximates the value of issuing tax-exempt bonds in either of two situations. First, suppose that the policy alternative is to maintain the exemption from income taxes for NFP hospitals but to repeal their access to tax-exempt borrowing, and that NFP hospitals do not respond by borrowing less. Second, if the proceeds from the bonds are being invested in financial assets with higher rates of return than the tax-exempt bonds, then the yield spread captures the arbitrage profit from the investment strategy.

This imputation does not measure the value of issuing tax-exempt bonds if the proceeds are being used to increase fixed assets and the policy alternative is the repeal of both the access to tax-exempt bonds *and* the income tax exemption. Under this policy alternative, the NFP hospitals would face a higher interest rate, but their interest payments would be deductible from the corporate tax base. With this more global change in the tax status of NFP hospitals, the hospitals would face an after-tax cost of borrowing of $(1 - t_c)i$, where t_c is the firm's marginal corporate tax rate and i is the nominal interest rate on taxable bonds. As an example, suppose an NFP hospital can borrow at 1 percentage point above the current AAA-rated tax-exempt bond yield for 20 years for a total interest rate of 6.29 percent; in contrast, a taxable hospital that can borrow at 1 percentage point above the 20-year U.S. Treasury bond rate of 6.68 percent and faces a 35 percent marginal corporate tax rate has an after-tax cost of borrowing of 4.99 percent. Thus, the NFP hospital faces a higher after-tax cost of borrowing than its FP competitor. A full analysis of this problem also depends on the investor-level tax rates and the degree to which these tax rates are capitalized into bond prices. For a general treatment of how tax-exempt bonds affect the cost of capital for NFP hospitals, see Wedig, Hassan, and Morrisey (1996).

An important determinant of the value of issuing tax-exempt bonds is how the hospital uses the proceeds. Legally, the hospitals must demonstrate that the funds will be used for new construction and that they do not have access to other funds.[28] Despite these legal requirements, many of the NFP hospitals with tax-exempt debt outstanding also have endowments. Since money is fungible, one could argue that to the extent that the endowment could be used to pay off tax-exempt debt, these hospitals are engaging in tax arbitrage.

To get an upper bound on the amount of tax arbitrage undertaken by NFP hospitals, we use the IRS data on tax-exempt organizations to com-

---

28. The legal restrictions on the use of the proceeds from tax-exempt borrowing have grown more stringent over time.

pare the size of outstanding bonds with endowments. The value of the hospital's endowment is the sum of investments in securities, real property (held for investment purposes), and other investments. For hospitals with endowments that exceed their tax-exempt debt outstanding, we measure the amount of possible tax arbitrage as the outstanding tax-exempt debt. These hospitals could retire their entire bond liability by reducing their endowment. Overall, 5.2 percent of NFP hospitals have endowments that exceed their tax-exempt bond liabilities. For hospitals with endowments that are less than their tax-exempt debt outstanding, we measure the amount of possible tax arbitrage as their endowment. That is, these hospitals could only eliminate part of their bond liability by using their endowment.[29] Of NFP hospitals, 11.7 percent have endowments that are less than their tax-exempt bond liabilities and 2.8 percent have tax-exempt bond liabilities but report an endowment value of zero. This calculation indicates that $23.6 billion, or just over half of the aggregate tax-exempt bond liability, is potentially related to arbitrage rather than new construction. Valuing the tax benefit of the arbitrage with a yield spread of 1.5 percentage points suggests an annual tax benefit of $354 million. Since the yield spread depends on the tax rate of taxable investors, it increases with the level of the nominal interest rate. Thus, this tax advantage (either on the bonds associated with potential arbitrage or on all bonds, as in Wedig, Hassan, and Morrisey 1996) increases when interest rates are high.

In summary, tax-exempt bonds are an important source of financing for NFP hospitals. However, if one takes as the policy alternative the repeal of both the exemption from income taxes and access to tax-exempt bond markets, it is unlikely that the overall tax exemption reduces the after-tax cost of borrowing for NFP hospitals. Nevertheless, our examination of hospital balance sheet data from the IRS suggests that tax arbitrage may also lead to some of the tax-exempt borrowing. To the extent that hospitals are getting around the complicated tax code restrictions on such activity, they benefit from profitable tax arbitrage. Our calculations suggest that these concerns are potentially relevant for approximately half of tax-exempt borrowing by NFP hospitals.

9.6 Tax Benefits of Charitable Contributions

The final piece of the tax benefit puzzle is the ability of NFP hospitals to solicit tax deductible contributions. Since NFP hospitals are 501(c)(3)

29. Our calculations assume that the hospitals do not need their endowments as a form of working capital or for precautionary saving. To the extent that hospitals need to keep some investments for these purposes, we are overstating the amount of tax arbitrage. Also, gifts to the endowments sometimes come with restrictions on the disposition of the assets. We ignore these restrictions since they are potentially endogenous to the tax planning process. That is, the NFP hospital can use these restrictions to justify engaging in financial arbitrage.

organizations for tax purposes, donors deduct their gifts from their income (and estate) tax bases (if they file income taxes as an "itemizer"). This deduction lowers the after-tax price of charitable giving.[30] These contributions provide financing that is unavailable to FP hospitals. As with the use of tax-exempt bonds, we are interested in two questions. First, How important are charitable gifts as a source of financing? Second, How should we calculate the value of the tax exemption?

We have two sources of data on the importance of charitable contributions for NFP hospitals: (1) the cost report data include a variable on donations received; and (2) data from informational returns (Form 990) filed by NFP hospitals with the IRS. These different data sources lead to different conclusions regarding the importance of charitable contributions. The cost report data indicate that only 56 percent of NFP hospitals report receiving contributions. For 1995, aggregate contributions were $649 million (for our sample of 2,948 NFP hospitals), which amounted to 0.26 percent of total assets for all hospitals or 0.49 percent of the total assets of the hospitals that reported positive contributions. Conditional on receiving some contributions, the 25th percentile is only $11,831 in contributions, and the median is $60,878. However, conditional on positive contributions, the 95th percentile is $1.3 million, indicating that at least 83 hospitals received more than $1.3 million in donations in 1995. Overall, the cost report data suggest that contributions are a minor source of funding, except for a small set of hospitals.

In contrast, in the IRS data for 1994, 77 percent of 501(c)(3) hospitals received public contributions (not including government grants) totaling $3.2 billion. These contributions are 1.15 percent of total assets and 2.72 percent of fixed assets. Hence, the tax data suggest that charitable contributions are a nontrivial source of funds for NFP hospitals. Of the hospitals receiving contributions, the 25th percentile of the contribution distribution is $16,260 and the conditional median contribution is $71,820. These conditional values are similar to the cost report data values, albeit more hospitals report positive contributions to the IRS. The most striking difference in the two data sets is among large recipients; among hospitals reporting contributions to the IRS, the 95th percentile of the distribution of contributions is $2.82 million, suggesting that 200 hospitals receive contributions greater than this amount. This group of hospitals accounts for 3.85 percent of all hospitals but receives 71 percent of the charitable contributions. While the tax data include a broader set of hospitals, which may explain part of the difference in aggregate contributions, this sample difference is unlikely to explain the difference in contributions relative to assets.

---

30. For analyses of how taxes affect incentives to give to charity, see Clotfelter (1985) and Randolph (1995).

While the data sources disagree on the overall magnitude of charitable contributions, both sources indicate that charitable contributions are highly skewed toward a select group of hospitals. Auten, Clotfelter, and Schmalbeck (1997) provide further evidence on the importance of charitable contributions to hospitals. They report that of large individual charitable contributions of more than $5 million in 1996 (a total of $1.5 billion of gifts in all), 9.3 percent ($140 million) went to university-affiliated medical centers and 7.6 percent ($115 million) went to free-standing medical research institutions.[31]

In comparing charitable contributions with the fixed assets, we are implicitly assuming that contributions are used to finance capital expenditures. These comparisons, at least with the IRS data, suggest that contributions are a modest, but important, source of financing. Alternatively, contributions could pay for services for less-fortunate patients; however, contributions are quite small relative to overall patient revenues (less than 0.5 percent). The descriptions of the large gifts suggest that most large donations are for capital expenditures or large investments rather than covering operating expenses.

In estimating the value of the tax benefit of the deduction for charitable gifts, one needs to know the marginal tax rate of the donor. Given the information reported by Auten, Clotfelter, and Schmalbeck, it seems likely that most of the donations to NFP hospitals are from high-income taxpayers with high marginal tax rates. A static measure of the revenue cost of these provisions would be the marginal tax rate times the amount of the contributions. For example, if the average combined federal and state marginal income tax rate for donors is 35 percent,[32] then the $3.2 billion in charitable contributions reported in the IRS data imply a tax expenditure of $1.1 billion.[33] However, if tax rules singled-out NFP hospitals for a change in status, one would expect a large shift in where donors would give; also, one would expect universities and other medical centers to respond by setting up targeted foundations to serve specific needs, such as cancer research. Thus, it is difficult to imagine changing the tax policy

31. Auten, Clotfelter, and Schmalbeck (1997) use data compiled by the electronic magazine *Slate*. In contrast, the 1993 IRS data for all 501(c)(3) organizations reports that hospitals received 5.8 percent of total contributions and government grants (see Internal Revenue Service 1997). These data do not include most religious organizations. Since Hodgkinson and Weitzman (1989, 41–42, table 1.17) report that approximately two-thirds of household contributions go to religious organizations, hospitals' total share in deductible contributions is substantially less than the 5.8 percent.

32. This calculation assumes that all donors to hospitals itemize their deductions, which may lead to an overstatement of the tax expenditure. However, we ignore estate tax considerations, which could be quite important for wealthy donors.

33. Our tax expenditure calculation is substantially less than the $2.1 billion reported for 1994 in the U.S. federal budget (see U.S. Bureau of the Census 1997, table 523). Our calculation focuses on hospitals and excludes health research organizations.

toward charitable gifts for NFP hospitals without changing the tax treatment of all charitable organizations.

9.7 Dynamic Considerations and the Incidence of the Tax Treatment of NFP Hospitals

The estimates in the previous sections provide evidence on the relative magnitude of the elements of the tax treatment of NFP hospitals. This information helps us understand the "statutory incidence" of the tax exemptions—how much tax revenue the government loses and which agents would write checks to the government under alternative tax regimes. If prices and quantities remain unchanged by tax policy, then the static estimates of statutory incidence would also be the economic incidence (the ultimate beneficiaries after accounting for price and quantity changes) of the policy. One complication created by analyzing NFP organizations is that even with this set of static assumptions, it is unclear who benefits when the NFP organization has a tax windfall. In the context of a for-profit corporation, the shareholders are the assumed beneficiaries of such a windfall. Since NFP hospitals do not have shareholders, then the windfall will be distributed somehow through the various constituencies of the NFP hospital. In theory, these tax savings should accrue to the community through such benefits as uncompensated care. However, as we discussed above, it is unclear how the community benefits differ across organizational forms. An alternative possibility is that other stakeholders, such as doctors or other employees, benefit from the tax advantages.

While assuming static behavior simplifies estimating the tax benefits, the economic incidence cannot be discerned by calculating hypothetical tax payments. Instead, the economic incidence depends critically on the behavioral responses of NFP hospitals. Starting from the framework of no behavioral response, one needs to know how tax policy changes would affect prices, outputs, and inputs in the market for hospital services. In terms of outputs, tax policy may affect many different dimensions. The tax exemptions may decrease the price of health care or increase the quantity of health care provided. If the tax benefits are shifted forward onto consumers through lower prices, then it is less likely that the tax exemptions will generate resources for NFP hospitals to spend on other community benefits.[34]

Traditional public finance models of incidence (see Shoven and Whalley 1992 for a survey) suggest that taxing one sector less heavily than another

---

34. Some analysts have argued that lower prices are a form of community benefit (see Clement, Smith, and Wheeler 1994). Of course, lowering prices (and the associated income) automatically dilutes the value of the exemption from income taxes.

would lead to increased output in the lightly taxed sector. However, these models assume profit-maximizing investors allocating capital across sectors. For NFP hospitals, these traditional incidence channels probably do not work well. Even if the tax exemptions increase the quantity of health care, it is unclear whether this increase benefits needy people. The behavioral responses could also include changes in the quality of care (without a corresponding change in price) or the types of outputs provided (particularly a shift toward outputs whose social returns exceed their private returns).

These changes in the output market shift tax benefits forward onto consumers. Other behavioral responses would shift the tax benefits backward onto factors of production. The tax exemption could change the capital intensity of hospital production with the less heavily taxed NFP hospitals opting for a more capital intensive production function; however, our evidence in section 9.4 suggests that this effect is likely to be small. NFP hospitals could also respond by "distributing" the tax benefit in the form of higher wages or better working conditions. Better working conditions could include more workers per bed, as we document in table 9.4. Consumers may benefit if the increase in the number of workers results in higher quality care (a form of shifting of tax benefits to the consumer if the price does not increase); however, workers may also benefit if they work less intensely for the same pay. Lastly, the NFP hospitals can engage in behaviors that skirt the restrictions on private inurement and private benefit by attempting to distribute the tax benefits to insiders, such as managers or doctors. An example of such behavior is joint ventures between hospitals and physicians (for details on these joint ventures and the associated legislative concerns, see U.S. General Accounting Office 1993).

One additional behavioral response also deserves mention: The organizational form of hospitals may depend on the value of the tax exemptions. Gulley and Santerre (1993) examine this hypothesis using panel data on market shares of NFP and FP hospitals in different states. Consistent with expectation, they find that higher state corporate income taxes and higher local property taxes increase the market share of NFP hospitals. To the extent that organizational form is more than a label for tax purposes, these tax-induced changes in organizational form affect the characteristics of care provided in different markets.

In addition to incidence, public finance economists are concerned with the excess burden associated with tax policy. The excess burden of the tax exemption depends on how the lost revenue is raised. The low tax rate on the production of health care through NFP organizations must be compensated for by raising tax rates on other goods. To estimate the excess burden associated with this change in tax rates requires knowing the demand and supply elasticities for various types of goods. Estimating the excess burden associated with the tax exemptions is complicated by the possibility that the exemptions encourage the provision of community benefits. If the tax exemption serves as a corrective tax that encourages the production of goods with positive externalities, the excess burden is less than would otherwise be calculated by examining the elasticities of supply and demand for different goods. Thus, as with the question of economic incidence, understanding the excess burden associated with the tax exemption requires a model of the behavioral responses and social benefits of NFP hospitals.

In summary, our calculations focus on the relatively straightforward measurement of the statutory incidence of the tax treatment of NFP hospitals. These estimates provide a useful starting point for framing the debate on tax policy toward NFP hospitals. However, they are a starting point, rather than an ending point, for understanding the economic implications of tax policy toward NFP hospitals.

9.8 Conclusion

In this paper, we explore the size and heterogeneity of the tax breaks granted to NFP hospitals. The tax breaks include exemption from income tax, exemption from property tax, use of tax-exempt bonds, and the tax deductibility of contributions to the hospital. In terms of nontax characteristics, NFP and FP hospitals are similar in many ways, though there are some important differences across organizational forms. One striking difference between NFP and FP hospitals is their geographic location. Across states, FP hospitals' market share of beds ranges from zero to over 30 percent. The median NFP hospital is larger than the median FP hospital; however, the size distribution of NFP hospitals is quite dispersed, including some very small hospitals as well as the large, urban teaching centers. Patient characteristics as measured by the proportion of Medicaid and Medicare patients and the HCFA case-mix index are remarkably similar for FP and NFP hospitals. Analysis of the provision of several hospital services viewed to be either community benefits or specialized shows significant differences between forms, though we find significant intraform differences as well. The similarities across organizational forms suggest that the tax exemptions are not essential to the provision of health care; however, further research is needed to determine whether the incentive effects or distributional effects of the tax exemptions justify their existence.

The value of the exemption from capital taxes depends on capital intensity and, for the income tax, profitability. Despite technological advances in medicine, hospitals remain more labor intensive than nonservice industries. Perhaps surprisingly, given the capital tax break, FP hospitals are more capital intensive than their NFP counterparts. The FP hospitals are also more profitable than the NFP hospitals. For some NFP hospitals, investment income is a substantial portion of total income. Our estimates of the aggregate value of the capital tax exemptions for NFP hospitals are $4.6 billion from income taxes and $1.7 billion from property taxes.

The tax benefits of tax-exempt bond financing and charitable contributions are concentrated among a relatively small set of hospitals. Less than 20 percent of NFP hospitals have outstanding tax-exempt debt, and charitable contributions are highly skewed toward an elite group of hospitals. Compared to FP hospitals that pay higher interest rates but deduct interest payments from taxable income, it is unclear how much of an advantage tax-exempt bonds provide NFP hospitals for building new facilities. If, however, the tax-exempt borrowing allows the NFP hospitals to maintain their endowments while expanding their facilities, then the NFP hospitals benefit from tax arbitrage. We find that almost half of outstanding tax-exempt debt of NFP hospitals could be offset by their endowments, leading to an arbitrage benefit of $354 million per year. For charitable contributions in 1994, we estimate that the $3.6 billion of donations lowered the donors' tax liabilities by about $1.1 billion.

As emphasized in section 9.7, our estimates do not include the behavioral responses caused by the tax exemptions. A full understanding of the impact of the tax exemptions requires estimates of how NFP and FP hospitals respond to tax incentives. An important behavioral margin is the choice of organizational form, which depends on tax benefits as well as the costs and benefits of nontax characteristics of each form. The continuing trend of hospital conversions may offer one way to examine these issues using longitudinal data with changing organizational form.

References

Arrow, Kenneth. 1963. Uncertainty and the Welfare Economics of Medicare Care. *American Economic Review* 53:941–73.
Auten, Gerald E., Charles T. Clotfelter, and Richard L. Schmalbeck. 1997. Taxes and Philanthropy among the Wealthy. Duke University, Durham, N.C. Photocopy.
Bittker, Boris I., and George K. Rahdert. 1976. The Exemption of Nonprofit Organizations from Federal Income Taxation. *Yale Law Journal* 85 (3): 299–358.
Clement, Jan P., Dean G. Smith, and John R. C. Wheeler. 1994. What Do We Want and What Do We Get from Not-for-Profit Hospitals? *Hospital and Health Services Administration* 39:159–78.
Cleverly, William O. 1992. Financial and Operating Performance of Systems: Voluntary versus Investor-Owned; Voluntary Multihospital Systems. *Topics in Health Care Financing* 18 (4): 63–73.
Clotfelter, Charles T. 1985. *Federal Tax Policy and Charitable Giving.* Chicago: University of Chicago Press.
Culhane, Dennis P., and Trevor R. Hadley. 1992. The Discriminating Characteris-

tics of For-Profit versus Not-for-Profit Freestanding Psychiatric Inpatient Facilities. *Health Services Research* 27:177–94.

Fama, Eugene F., and Michael C. Jensen. 1983a. Separation of Ownership and Control. *Journal of Law and Economics* 26:310–25.

———. 1983b. Agency Problems and Residual Claims. *Journal of Law and Economics* 26:327–49.

Frank, Richard G., and David S. Salkever. 1994. Nonprofit Organizations in the Health Sector. *Journal of Economic Perspectives* 8:129–44.

Goodspeed, Timothy J., and Daphne A. Kenyon. 1993. The Nonprofit Sector's Capital Constraint: Does It Provide a Rationale for the Tax Exemption Granted to Nonprofit Firms? *Public Finance Quarterly* 21:415–33.

Gulley, O. David, and Rexford E. Santerre. 1993. The Effect of Tax Exemption on the Market Share of Nonprofit Hospitals. *National Tax Journal* 46:477–86.

Haas, Jennifer S., I. Steven Udvarhelyi, Carl N. Morris, and Arnold M. Epstein. 1993. The Effect of Providing Health Coverage to Poor Uninsured Pregnant Women in Massachusetts. *Journal of the American Medical Association* 269 (1): 87–91.

Hansmann, Henry. 1981. The Rationale for Exempting Nonprofit Organizations from Corporate Income Taxation. *Yale Law Journal* 91 (1): 54–100.

Hodgkinson, Virginia A., and Murray S. Weitzman. 1989. *Dimensions of the Independent Sector: A Statistical Profile.* Washington, D.C.: Independent Sector.

Internal Revenue Service. 1997. Charities and Other Tax-Exempt Organizations, 1993: Data Release. *Statistics of Income Bulletin* (spring): 122–34.

Marmor, Theodore R., Mark Schlesinger, and Richard W. Smithey. 1987. Nonprofit Organizations and Health Care. In *The Nonprofit Sector: A Research Handbook,* ed. Walter W. Powell. New Haven, Conn.: Yale University Press.

Michigan Department of Treasury. Office of Revenue and Tax Analysis. 1997. *Non-Profit Hospital Tax Expenditures.* Lansing, Mich.: Michigan Department of Treasury.

Morrisey, Michael A., Gerard J. Wedig, and Mahmud Hassan. 1996. Do Nonprofit Hospitals Pay Their Way? *Health Affairs* 13:132–44.

Myerson, Allen R. 1997. Hospitals Specialize to Increase Profits. *New York Times,* 7 October, D1.

Norton, Edward C., and Douglas O. Staiger. 1994. How Hospital Ownership Affects Access to Care for the Uninsured. *RAND Journal of Economics* 25: 171–85.

Pauly, Mark V. 1978. Is Medical Care Different? In *Competition in the Health Care Sector: Past, Present, and Future,* ed. Warren Greenberg, 11–36. Germantown, Md.: Aspen Press.

Randolph, William C. 1995. Dynamic Income, Progressive Taxes, and the Timing of Charitable Contributions. *Journal of Political Economy* 103:709–38.

Reuter, James, and Darrell Gaskin. 1997. Academic Health Centers in Competitive Markets. *Health Affairs* 16:242–52.

Rose-Ackerman, Susan. 1982. Unfair Competition and Corporate Income Taxation. *Stanford Law Review* 34:1017–39.

Sanders, Susan M. 1995. The "Common Sense" of the Nonprofit Hospital Tax Exemption: A Policy Analysis. *Journal of Policy Analysis and Management* 14: 446–66.

Shoven, John B., and John Whalley. 1992. *Applying General Equilibrium.* New York: Cambridge University Press.

Sloan, Frank A. 1997. Commercialism in Nonprofit Hospitals. Duke University, Durham, N.C. Photocopy.

U.S. Bureau of the Census. 1995. *Statistical Abstract of the United States 1995.* Washington, D.C.: U.S. Government Printing Office.

———. 1997. *Statistical Abstract of the United States 1997.* Washington, D.C.: U.S. Government Printing Office.

U.S. General Accounting Office. 1993. *Nonprofit Hospitals: For-Profit Ventures Pose Access and Capacity Problems.* Washington, D.C.: U.S. Government Printing Office.

Wedig, Gerard J., Mahmud Hassan, and Michael A. Morrisey. 1996. Tax-Exempt Debt and the Capital Structure of Nonprofit Organizations: An Application to Hospitals. *Journal of Finance* 51:1247–83.

Young, Gary J., Kamol R. Desai, and Carol VanDeusen Lukas. 1997. Does the Sale of Nonprofit Hospitals Threaten Health Care for the Poor? *Health Affairs* 16:137–41.

Asymmetric Information and the Not-for-Profit Sector
Does Its Output Sell at a Premium?

Tomas Philipson

10.1 Introduction

The not-for-profit sector is responsible for a large amount of economic activity that economists have considered to be of primary importance; it is estimated to conduct a fifth of research and development (R&D) and accounts for almost all production of high-skill human capital outside on-the-job training and the vast majority of the health care produced worldwide. In the United States, the growing not-for-profit economy employs about 10 percent of the labor force.[1] About half of the total employment in the not-for-profit sector is in health services, concentrated in hospitals, of which 85 percent of employment is not-for-profit. Education and research make up the second largest component of not-for-profit employment, about 20 percent, followed by social services, such as child care and job training, which make up about 15 percent of the not-for-profit labor force.

This importance of the not-for-profit economy in the United States and elsewhere has generated a large theoretical and empirical literature on the positive behavior and normative role of not-for-profit institutions in eco-

Tomas Philipson is professor of public policy, economics, and law at the University of Chicago, and a research associate of the National Bureau of Economic Research and the Stigler Center for the Study of the Economy and the State.

This paper has benefited greatly from research assistance by David Grabowski and Anup Malani. The author thanks the volume editor and conference participants, in particular the discussants, for input as well as Gary Becker, Merton Miller, Casey Mulligan, and Derek Neal. Financial support from the George Stigler Center for the Study of the Economy and the State and the Alfred P. Sloan Foundation Research Fellows Program is gratefully acknowledged.

1. See Rudney (1987).

nomic activity in general and in health care in particular.[2] The two major strands of this literature attempt to either qualitatively justify the efficiency role of not-for-profit regulations or to draw out and empirically investigate behavioral differences between these types of institutions and more traditional ones.

One of the major efficiency rationales put forward for the value of not-for-profit production in health care is that it solves an asymmetric information problem between uninformed consumers and informed producers.[3] The argument is that when quality of supply is unobservable, a producer who is constrained to not have profits has lower agency costs than an unconstrained producer. This agency explanation for the efficiency gains of not-for-profits is essentially an argument that the output of not-for-profit firms is not perfectly substitutable with that of for-profit firms. Although the empirical content of this argument, beyond the existence of not-for-profits, has not been the focus of previous analysis, this paper attempts to test the information asymmetry explanation of not-for-profits. Our basic argument is that there should be a not-for-profit premium if this asymmetry is important. We test this implication against the alternative prediction that regulatory status is perfectly substitutable on the demand side. Consumers do not care about the profit status of the firm per se, only indirectly through the price or the observable quality of its output.[4] A well-known equilibrium argument is that a *necessary* condition for two perfect substitutes to be sold in equilibrium—that is, for not-for-profits and profits to coexist—is that they be priced equally. Consumers would not hold the more expensive substitute. This implication holds in standard hedonic models as well, when consumers may have heterogeneous preferences regarding other attributes, as long as all consumers are indifferent between organizational forms per se. We apply this simple argument empirically to the case of the mixed production taking place in the U.S. long-term care market. Although the basic argument seems very general, there are a few caveats when applying it to the long-term care industry in the United States, the main one being supply constraints limiting consumer substitutability.

Testing the difference between the information asymmetry prediction and perfect substitutability is operationalized empirically as follows. In a cross section of firms, perfect substitutability implies that if one runs a hedonic price regression controlling for the observable qualities of the good, a dummy variable that indicates the not-for-profit status of the pro-

2. For general discussion see, e.g., Weisbrod (1977, 1987, 1988), Powell (1987), Hansmann (1980), Rose-Ackerman (1986, 1996), and the references contained therein. For discussion of not-for-profit behavior in health care, see, e.g., Newhouse (1970), Pauly and Redisch (1973), Becker and Sloan (1985), and Sloan (1997). Gertler (1989) and Gertler and Waldman (1992) address the nursing home industry discussed here.

3. See, e.g., Weisbrod (1987), Easly and O'Hara (1983), or the review in Hansmann (1987).

4. Indeed, one may conjecture that most consumers, like most economists, are unable to define exactly what a not-for-profit is.

ducer should have a zero effect. In other words, controlling for *observed* quality, price is not affected by organizational status. Note that this is a necessary condition of equilibrium with mixed production of both organizational forms. It says that if we observe two nursing homes that offer the same observable services, as controlling for quality in a regression attempts to do, then they must be priced the same, independent of the status of the producer. It is not a sufficient condition of equilibrium, since it may be that, as an implication of this perfect substitutability, we only observe the lowest-cost organizational form, as would be the case, for example, under the common assumption of constant returns to scale in industrywide cost functions. In contrast, if agency costs were lower in not-for-profits, in a mixed industry in which the two organizational forms were equally priced or in which for-profits sold at a premium, complete substitution toward not-for-profits would be observed. To summarize, in a hedonic price regression on quality and organizational form, the informational role of not-for-profits would imply a positive independent effect of a not-for-profit dummy.

We attempt to distinguish between these two implications using data on the U.S. long-term care industry during the last two decades. The empirical analysis is based on pricing behavior as reported in the two latest cross sections, 1985 and 1995, of the National Nursing Home Survey (NNHS). NNHS is a continuing series of national sample surveys of nursing homes, their residents, and their staff. The two years display somewhat different results regarding the premia for organizational form. Overall, 1985 provides more support for the argument that for-profit care sells at about a 5 percent premium, as opposed to 1995, which indicates support for the perfect substitutability implication of no premium in either direction. The results also differ across the types of care offered. In particular, for residential care, the premia for for-profit care are the largest and the most significant. However, for no year or type of care does the not-for-profit premium become significantly positive. Our main finding is therefore that if asymmetric information arguments about not-for-profits imply that they must sell at a premium in a mixed industry, this evidence does not seem to offer support for this implication.

The paper may be briefly outlined as follows. Section 10.2 briefly discusses econometric aspects of the not-for-profit effects of interest, centering on the particular effect discussed here concerning perfect substitutability. Section 10.3 then summarizes the aggregate trends in quantities and prices for the U.S. nursing home industry by for-profit versus not-for-profit status. These aggregates tend to provide the same results as the firm-level data. Section 10.4 thereafter considers the perfect substitutability hypothesis firm-level data on nursing homes using the National Nursing Home Survey. Lastly, section 10.5 concludes and discusses the limitations of the analysis as well as the potentially exaggerated role attributed to asymmetric information in shaping market outcomes in health care.

10.2   Types of Not-for-Profit Effects and Perfect Substitutability

In order to assess the existence of a not-for-profit premium, this section first describes the application of the standard potential outcome framework for the econometric analysis of the impact of not-for-profit status on firm behavior. Let (Y_0, Y_1) be two outcome vectors of a *single* firm, one occurring if that organization were to be a not-for-profit and the other if it were to be a for-profit. For example, the outcomes may represent input, output, or pricing behavior. The dummy D indicates organizational choice. If the organization chooses to be a not-for-profit firm, then we observe the outcome Y_0, and if it chooses to be a for-profit firm, we observe the outcome Y_1. For a given firm, then, we observe

$$Y = DY_1 + (1 - D)Y_0.$$

To discuss conversions over time, let Y denote such a pair of outcomes at a given time and Y' indicate outcomes at a later time. The central distribution of interest is then the joint distribution $F(y, y', d, d')$ over such pairs given the choices of organizational form over time.

As there have been many estimates of not-for-profit effects, it may be useful to make explicit the implicit identifying assumptions that link these effects and how they relate to the one of interest in detecting a not-for-profit premium. By definition of potential outcomes, we only observe the distributions $F(y_d|D = d)$ in the first period and $F(y_{d'}'|D = d')$ in the second period. However, many effects in which we are interested involve knowing the counterfactual distributions $F(y_d|D \neq d)$ in the first period and $F(y_{d'}'|D' \neq d')$ in the second. The missing data, by definition, is the behavior of the firms if they were not in their observed regulatory status. For example, we would not be able to observe the uncompensated care or debt level of a not-for-profit firm if the same firm was for-profit.

One may therefore distinguish between *observed* and *potential* effects of regulatory choice. Observed effects concern differences in behavior across firms in the regulatory status they have actually chosen, and potential effects concern differences between observed and counterfactual statuses. The first type of effect is key when testing positive theories of not-for-profit or for-profit choice as done in this paper; it focuses on how firms *do* behave in the data. The second type of effect focuses on how firms *would* behave under some other circumstances not observed in the data; it is therefore often key for evaluating new policy interventions, such as, for example, the effect of raised corporate income taxes on conversions.[5]

5. Observed versus potential effects have little to do with whether the analysis is cross-sectional across firms or longitudinal effects involving conversions of the same firm. Observable cross-sectional effects are concerned with comparing the outcomes of not-for-profits with for-profits, $F(y_0|d = 1)$ with $F(y_1|d = 1)$, as opposed to potential effects that require data, $F(y_1, y_0|d = 1)$ if looking at for-profits and $F(y_0, y_1|d = 1)$ when looking at not-for-profits. Likewise, observable longitudinal effects would compare $F(y_0|d = 0)$ with $F(y_1'|d' =$

Observed effects concern the properties of the equilibrium of firm behavior under regulations observed in the data. The observed effect of interest here concerns whether similar output in a mixed industry sells at a not-for-profit premium. A well-known argument in economics suggests that a necessary condition for two perfect substitutes to be sold in equilibrium is that they are priced equally. If they were not, consumers would not hold the more expensive substitute. Below, we will apply this simple argument to the case of the impact of organizational form in the mixed U.S. long-term care market. We operationalize this argument in a cross section of producers as follows. It implies that if one runs a price regression controlling for the observable aspects of the good affecting its value to the consumer, such as quality of services of homes, a not-for-profit dummy should have a zero effect. In other words, controlling for quality, price is not affected by organizational status.[6] Note that this is a *necessary* condition of equilibrium in the mixed long-term care market. It says that if we find two homes that offer the same services, as controlling for quality in a regression attempts to do, then they must be priced the same, independent of the status of the producer. It is not sufficient, since it may be that as an implication of this perfect substitutability, we only observe the lowest-cost organizational form. It is completely due to the demand side, as all it requires is that if two goods that are perfectly substitutable are to be held in equilibrium, they must be equally priced for demanders to hold them both.

It is well known that, generally, hedonic regressions do not identify demand schedules when both sides are heterogeneous; only when demand is homogeneous does the price function trace it out. However, here the argument is that although the demand side may be heterogeneous with respect to *other* quality attributes, under the null it is homogeneous with respect to organizational form; all consumers are perfectly willing to substitute the two given that the observable quality of the service is held constant. Consumers may value different types of services offered by nursing homes differently, although they all would be indifferent between a not-for-profit and for-profit home if they offered the same services. Although producers of different types may sort themselves due to differences in comparative advantages of care, when a not-for-profit firm and a for-profit firm end up providing the same service, they must do it at the same price because the hedonic equilibrium price function traces out the homogeneous indifference to organizational form.

---

1) when looking at not-for-profit conversions and $F(y_1|d = 1)$ with $F(y'_0|d' = 0)$ when looking at for-profit conversions. Potential longitudinal effects would concern how representative conversions were to changes in status of nonconverters.

6. Under perfect substitutability and equal prices, profit differences are only due to cost differences, which may be substantial given the difference in input markets between the two regulatory forms.

Lack of a not-for-profit premium is a cross-sectional independence restriction on outcome distributions across regulatory statuses. It says that price is independently distributed across regulatory status conditional on quality observable to consumers. Letting the outcome vector $Y = (p,q)$ discussed above represent price and quality, a weaker version of it only requires means, as opposed to the entire distributions, to be the same, as in

$$E[p_1|q_1 = q, d = 1] = E[p_0|q_0 = q, d = 0].$$

This cross-sectional observed effect does not claim to take a stand on what the potential effect is or what the longitudinal observed or potential effect is. In particular, longitudinal estimators that attempted to correct for "unobserved heterogeneity" would be particularly bad for addressing this equilibrium restriction.

The perfect substitutability implication differs from the not-for-profit premium implication due to asymmetry of information between demanders and suppliers. According to this argument, consumers are assumed to know the IRS status of the producer, but not to be able to know the full quality, both observed and unobserved, leading to an inequality replacing the equality above.

$$E[p_1|q_1 = q, d = 1] < E[p_0|q_0 = q, d = 0].$$

A priori, it seems that one would suspect that consumers knew more about the quality of output than the regulatory status of the firm. Nevertheless, a necessary equilibrium condition of a mixed industry would be that not-for-profits would then have to sell at a premium, since if they did not, output by for-profit firms would not be held.

10.3 Aggregate Trends in the U.S. Long-Term Care Industry

As background to the firm-level discussion of not-for-profit premia in the sale of long-term care to follow, this section first discusses the aggregate differences between the behavior of firms of different regulatory statuses.

Figure 10.1 shows the percentage trends in market structure and firm size during the last three decades. More precisely, it depicts the number of nursing homes, the average size of firms in terms of beds, and capacity in terms of occupancy rate.

According to these data, the total number of nursing homes in the United States increased during the mid-1970s, was fairly level during the late 1970s and early 1980s, and then decreased in the late 1980s and into the 1990s. However, the percentage differences in number of firms are rather small compared with the normalized value at year 1973. Occupancy rates have basically remained unchanged at very high levels, around 95 percent. However, the average firm size, beds per nursing home, has been

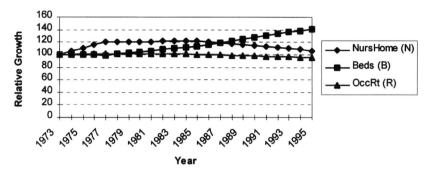

Fig. 10.1   Relative growth of number of nursing homes, beds per nursing home, and occupancy rates, 1973–95

Source: The data in this figure were constructed from several sources, including HCIA, the Health Care Financing Administration (HCFA), and annual censuses.

Note: The three trends above are all normalized to 100 in 1973. The actual values in 1973 are 16,700 for nursing homes, 75 for beds, and 91.4 percent for occupancy rates.

steadily increasing since 1973, with homes being about 40 percent larger now than in 1973. These three trends imply that output growth has mainly occurred through expanded firm size and not through expanded entry or capacity.

We first report aggregate state data on the observed premia and other differences between organizational forms. We use data from HCIA as reported for the years 1988–94 in the issues of the *Guide to the Nursing Home Industry.* This data set contains summary statistics for the universe of nursing homes in the United States that receive any reimbursement from Medicaid and Medicare, which is about 80 percent of the total universe of about 18,000 homes.

Table 10.1 shows the national evidence of the differences in output, input, and prices between for-profits versus not-for-profits as measured by the HCIA survey of homes.

The table reports both the absolute values as well as the relative values between the two groups. For example, it indicates that for-profits had, on average, 14 percent more beds in a home than not-for-profits in 1989. Consistent with other studies showing lower costs of for-profits relative to not-for-profits, the table reports lower staffing ratios and wages but a larger quantity of output as measured by patient days. For-profits use 87–91 percent of the full-time equivalents (FTEs) of not-for-profits, pay them 93 percent of not-for-profit wages, but take care of 11–13 percent more patient days. Since labor by far dominates the cost of production, on this high level of aggregation and not adjusting for quality and the type of patient populations for which these homes cared, for-profit homes are suggested to be lower cost. Despite these cost differences, and of relevance to our later analysis of pricing behavior, this aggregate data displays a *premium*

Table 10.1   National Quantity and Price Data by Year and Type of Nursing Home, 1989–1994

	1989			1990			1991			1992			1993			1994		
	FP	NFP	Ratio	FP	NFP	Ratio	FP	NFP	Ratio	FP	NFP	Ratio	FP	NFP	Ratio	FP	NFP	Ratio
Outputs																		
Patient days	34,565.5	30,754.9	1.12	34,518.05	31,355.32	1.1	34,423.15	31,325.76	1.1	34,995.95	31,063.25	1.13	34,818.99	31,040.77	1.12	34,306.35	30,453.04	1.13
Size (number of beds)	100	88	1.14	100	90	1.11	100	90	1.11	101	88	1.15	101	88	1.15	100	87	1.15
Capacity (occupancy rate)	94.7	95.75	.99	94.57	95.45	.99	94.31	95.36	.99	94.93	96.71	.98	94.45	96.64	.98	93.99	95.9	.98
Inputs																		
Labor																		
Full-time equivalents	.75	.86	.87	.76	.88	.86	.76	.88	.86	.8	.89	.9	.83	.91	.91	.84	.92	.91
Capital																		
Long-term debt to total assets	.57	.34	1.68	.6	.3	2	.6	.29	2.07	.54	.31	1.74	.51	.32	1.59	.56	.26	2.15
Age of plants	6.4	12.76	.5	7.07	12.97	.55	8.25	12.43	.66	8.28	13.42	.62	8.64	13.4	.64	8.96	14.07	.64
Depreciation	6.24	2.82	2.21	6.16	2.91	2.12	5.74	3.07	1.87	6.5	2.92	2.23	6.67	3.29	2.03	6.96	3.63	1.92
Prices																		
Outputs																		
Private price per day	35.72	31.35	1.14	41.50	35.51	1.17	35.53	25.64	1.39									
Public price per day	65.41	65.41	1	69.49	69.49	1	74.58	74.58	1									
% publicly priced days	69.55	67.18	1.04	71.49	69.04	1.04	73.06	71.82	1.02	72.81	71.54	1.02	72.20	71.27	1.01	71.66	70.14	1.02
Inputs																		
Wages	15,628	16,818	.93	17,321	18,626	.93	18,606	19,335	.96	20,133	20,615	.98	20,966	21,445	.98	21,801	22,162	.98

Source: National Nursing Home Survey, 1989–1994.

Note: FP represents for-profit, and NFP not-for-profit, nursing homes. Ratio indicates the for-profit divided by the not-for-profit values.

for for-profit care. At this level of aggregation, private prices are higher, not lower, for care in for-profit homes relative to not-for-profit homes.

Since the regulation and subsidization of this industry varies greatly across states, as Medicaid is administered and partly funded by the states, it is useful to consider the aggregate state evidence regarding the differences between for-profit and not-for-profit care within states. Table 10.2 shows the aggregate state-level evidence on the differences between for-profits versus not-for-profits corresponding to the national evidence in table 10.1. Using a state as the unit of observation, it reports the distribution across states of the relative ratio of the measured variables. If this average is unity without any variance, then this means that, across all states, the two forms of organization have identical outcomes. The larger the variance and the further away this mean is from unity, the less alike the two forms are across states.

This unconditional data on the distribution of differences in averages across states shows that they are less pronounced than the national differences, so that part of the national differences is the result of aggregation bias with respect to heterogeneous states. Within a state, the two sectors appear to be more similar. For example, although for the nation as a whole, for-profits are about 14 percent larger in bed size, on average, they are 10 percent larger within a state. Although by definition, average public prices do not vary across organizational form within a state, the private prices are remarkably similar within states. This similarity does not of course control for any quality characteristics or other factors that may drive price, but it suggests that even on this broad level of aggregation, output tends to be priced similarly, as would be suggested by the perfect substitution hypotheses.[7]

10.4   Firm Level Analysis of the Not-for-Profit Premium

These aggregate data are only suggestive of the differences in behavior across firms of different organizational forms. In this section, we go on to consider the substitution hypothesis versus information hypothesis using firm-level data on prices from the two latest cross sections, 1985 and 1995, of the National Nursing Home Survey (NNHS). NNHS is a continuing series of national sample surveys of nursing homes, their residents, and their staff. Four nursing home surveys have been conducted: 1973, 1977, 1985, and 1995.[8] Although each of these surveys emphasized different top-

7. The observed effects were upper bounds on the counterfactual effects under the theory of choice of organizational form discussed in Lakdawalla and Philipson (1997). The ratio above therefore represents upper bounds of the differences given this level of aggregation; actual potential effects would be smaller than in the table under the theory.
8. These surveys were preceded by a series of surveys from 1963 through 1969 called the "resident places" surveys.

Table 10.2   Distribution of State Differences in Aggregate Quantities and Prices by Year and Type of Nursing Home, 1989–1994

	1989				1990				1991				1992				1993				1994			
	Mean	S.D.	Min.	Max.	Mean	S.D.	Min.	Max.	Mean	S.D.	Min.	Max.	Mean	S.D.	Min.	Max.	Mean	S.D.	Min.	Max.	Mean	S.D.	Min.	Max.
Output																								
Patient days	1.08	.29	.5	1.92	1.06	.26	.51	1.76	1.06	.25	.5	1.82	1.05	.28	.75	2.24	1.05	.27	.75	2.21	1.05	.27	.74	2.19
Size (number of beds)	1.1	.3	.53	1.9	1.09	.27	.53	1.84	1.08	.26	.53	1.84	1.07	.3	.76	2.42	1.06	.28	.76	2.3	1.06	.28	.75	2.3
Capacity (occupancy rate)	.98	.03	.91	1.03	.98	.03	.91	1.01	.98	.03	.91	1.03	.98	.02	.93	1.04	.99	.02	.94	1.04	.99	.03	.94	1.04
Inputs																								
Labor																								
Full-time equivalents	.85	.09	.61	1.04	.87	.1	.64	1.06	.86	.11	.56	1.08	.9	.08	.72	1.04	.91	.08	.73	1.06	.92	.07	.75	1.03
Capital																								
Long-term debt to total assets	1.49	.92	.05	4	1.54	.98	.25	4.1	1.55	1.2	.13	5.57	1.46	.6	.55	3.25	1.47	.81	.46	4.4	1.33	.53	.28	2.68
Age of plants	.6	.23	.19	1.14	.66	.22	.26	1.19	.72	.25	.28	1.24	.76	.19	.35	1.18	.77	.16	.4	1.09	.77	.15	.54	1.07
Depreciation	1.56	.55	.69	3.39	1.47	.59	.15	3.32	1.44	.45	.65	2.5	1.37	.34	.81	2.21	1.33	.36	.89	2.26	1.22	.29	.77	2
Prices																								
Outputs																								
Private price per day	.97	.24	.33	1.37	1	.69	.13	4.62	.88	.28	.16	1.28	.96	.23	.35	1.45	1.04	.2	.61	1.41				
Public price per day	1	0	1	1	1	0	1	1	1	0	1	1	1	0	1	1	1	0	1	1				
% publicly priced days	1.13	.18	.9	1.58	1.16	.2	.94	1.58	1.15	.16	.93	1.54	1.12	.14	.97	1.56	1.11	.12	.98	1.53				
Inputs																								
Wages	.97	.09	.73	1.38	.97	.09	.69	1.17	.99	.12	.73	1.52	1	.05	.9	1.1	.99	.04	.89	1.1	.99	.03	.9	1.05

Source: National Nursing Home Survey, 1989–1994.

Note: Summary statistics refer to the for-profit divided by the not-for-profit variable values.

ics, they all provided some common basic information about nursing homes, their residents, and their staff. For our purposes in investigating pricing, we only utilize the 1985 and 1995 cross sections because those were the only ones that contained prices. The survey is that of repeated cross sections and thus does not allow for longitudinal comparison. However, the pricing implication of interest concerns the observed cross-sectional equilibrium distribution at a particular point in time. It asks whether, at a given time, similar outputs sell at different or the same prices dependent on organizational status. Therefore, it does not put clear restrictions on the longitudinal data in terms of changes in prices over several periods. Therefore, the fact that NNHS is not a panel survey is not of primary importance for the question addressed here.

The frame of the NNHS includes all nursing and related care homes in the United States. Places that only provide room and board are excluded, as are places with fewer than three beds. All nursing home facilities included in the survey are freestanding or are nursing care units of hospitals, retirement centers, or similar institutions where the unit maintains financial and resident records separate from those of the larger institution. The two earlier surveys, conducted in 1985 and in 1977, are similar because they both included nursing care homes, personal care homes, and domiciliary care homes. These surveys represent a broadening in scope over that of the 1973–74 survey, which excluded facilities providing only personal care or domiciliary care. However, because personal and domiciliary care homes constitute such a small proportion of the 1977 and 1985 surveys, no special adjustments need to be made when comparing the three surveys.

The data were sampled using a stratified two-stage probability design. The first stage was a selection of facilities, and the second stage was a selection of residents and employees of the sampled facilities. In the 1985 survey, only registered nurses were sampled. The sampling frame for employees was the list of all staff members, including those employed by contract. Only staff members involved in direct patient care (administrative, medical, therapeutic, and nursing staff) were sampled. Survey data were collected using a combination of personal interview and self-enumerated forms.

The summary statistics of the data for the two cross sections 1985 and 1995 of the NNHS are contained in tables 10.3 and 10.4. As before, for each year, the data are reported by the tax status of the home.

Similar to the aggregate data discussed before, these summary statistics are grouped into categories of output and input, along with their corresponding prices. The variable that divides up the data in each cross section is a for-profit dummy that indicates the tax status of the home. Due to the different designs of the survey, the 1985 categorization of not-for-profit includes only private firms but the 1995 categorization contains both public and private firms. The 1985 data are generally better suited than the 1995 data for investigating our question concerning price differences

	For-Profit (N = 752)[a]		Not-for-Profit (N = 336)	
	Mean	SD	Mean	SD
Control variables				
Hospital-owned home[b]	0.002	0.05	0.07	0.25
Member of group of homes[b]	0.62	0.48	0.34	0.47
Output variables				
Quantity-patient days	42,404	23,516	52,249	30,827
Percent days subsidized				
Medicaid skilled	0.22	0.29	0.23	0.3
Medicaid intermediate	0.42	0.35	0.37	0.33
Medicare	0.02	0.07	0.03	0.11
Scale—number of beds	121	60	131	70
Admissions	118	102	108	123
Discharges	110	100	94	118
Output prices				
Private price per day				
Skilled	64	15	70	18
Intermediate	53	12	55	14
Residential	43	17	40	16
Public Medicaid price per day				
Skilled	50	11	58	14
Intermediate	42	8	45	10
Quality variables				
Medicaid certified				
Skilled[b]	0.68	0.47	0.72	0.45
Intermediate[b]	0.86	0.35	0.8	0.4
Percent of measured resident services				
provided[c]	0.70	0.14	0.72	0.13
Location				
City[b]	0.69	0.46	0.67	0.47
Northeast region of U.S.[b]	0.19	0.39	0.29	0.46
North central region of U.S.	0.30	0.46	0.43	0.49
South region of U.S.[b]	0.36	0.48	0.18	0.39
West region of U.S.[b]	0.15	0.37	0.1	0.3
Input variables				
Number of MDs				
Full time	0.08	0.79	0.59	3.05
Part time	0.34	1.56	1.10	3.03
Number of nurses				
Full time	4.60	5.24	10.48	14.44
Part time	3.15	4.16	6.13	6.79
Number of nurses' aides				
Full time	33.75	25.75	50.84	47.77
Part time	11.35	12.78	18.75	20.09

[a]Note that missing observations will decrease the sample size for certain variables summarized below.
[b]Variable is a dummy, with Yes = 1 and No = 0.
[c]This is a quality index that represents the fraction of 18 measured services the nursing homes provide. These measured services are medical, other medical, nursing, mental health, physical therapy, speech or hearing therapy, occupational therapy, special education, personal care, social services, nutrition, hospice, sheltered employment, vocational rehabilitation, transportation, prescription/non-prescription medications, equipment/devices, and any other resident services. Note that specifying these services as separate dummy variables did not significantly alter the findings.

Table 10.4   **Summary Statistics of Nursing Homes for 1995 National Nursing Home Survey by Ownership Status, NNHS 1995**

	For-Profit ($N = 924$)[a]		Not-for-Profit ($N = 485$)	
	Mean	SD	Mean	SD
Control variables				
Member of group of homes[b]	0.66	0.47	0.34	0.47
Output variables				
Scale—number of beds	122	52	108	59
Admissions	137	152	134	169
Output prices				
Private price per day				
Skilled	124	69	137	61
Intermediate	98	29	102	35
Residential	80	30	81	45
Public Medicaid price per day	88	72	105	98
Public Medicare price per day	181	76	165	68
Quality variables				
Certified[b]	0.98	0.16	0.94	0.23
Percent of measured resident services				
provided[c]	0.76	0.11	0.75	0.11
Located in city[b]	0.69	0.46	0.69	0.46
Input variables[d]				
FTEs: Administrators	1.41	0.99	1.7	1.51
FTEs: Registered nurses	8.77	8.52	15.52	18.27
FTEs: Licensed practicing nurses	13.53	10.48	19.21	24.95
FTEs: Nurses' aides	43.12	28.39	64.31	59.94
FTEs: Doctors	0.45	1.62	1.03	4.48
FTEs: Dentists	0.1	0.33	0.13	0.4
FTEs: Dental hygienists	0.05	0.38	0.06	0.25
FTEs: Physical therapists	1.16	2.31	1.02	2.11
FTEs: Speech	0.56	0.92	0.41	0.98
FTEs: Dietitians	0.98	1.76	1.18	1.54
FTEs: Podiatrists	0.14	0.4	0.15	0.47
FTEs: Social workers	1.47	1.36	2.25	2.08

[a]Note that missing observations will decrease the sample size for certain variables summarized below.

[b]Variable is a dummy, with Yes = 1 and No = 0.

[c]This is a quality index that represents the fraction of 20 measured resident services the nursing homes provide. These measured services are dental, help with oral hygiene, home health, hospice, medical, mental health, nursing, nutrition, occupational therapy, personal care, physical therapy, podiatry, prescription/non-prescription medications, sheltered employment, social services, special education, speech or hearing therapy, transportation, vocational rehabilitation, and equipment/devices. Note that specifying these services as separate dummy variables did not significantly alter the findings.

[d]An FTE is a full-time equivalent employee.

across similar services; they contain more detailed categorization of prices as well as better controls on the cost of production in the homes.

There are three levels of service provided by a nursing home in these data, and both private and public pricing differentiates between them. These three levels are skilled, intermediary, and residential, ranging from the most to the least acute care offered, and hence from the most expensive to the least expensive. In 1995, the market is divided roughly in half between skilled and intermediate care, 46 versus 50 percent of consumers, with residential care making up the remaining 4 percent.[9] Although the type of services differs across these three levels of care, in the 1995 NHHS, the fraction of residents within an average home using particular services were as follows: 17 percent for dental care, 88 percent for medical services, 14 percent for mental health services, 96 percent for nursing services, 69 percent for nutritional services, 14 percent for occupational therapy, 25 percent for physical therapy, 93 percent for prescribed and nonprescribed medication, 64 percent for social services, 7 percent for speech and hearing therapy, 22 percent for transportation services, and 8 percent for other types of services not documented.

There is a large share of consumers that are publicly subsidized by the Medicaid program for the poor and the Medicare program for the old. Medicare subsidies are not means tested and are only for about three months of more acute skilled nursing care after hospitalization; this represents a very small fraction of total days, in terms of a few percent. Medicaid subsidies are means tested but are for both skilled and intermediary care; this represents a very large fraction of total days—often more than two-thirds. Furthermore, states differ substantially in how they spend and regulate the nursing home industry through Medicaid. The main impact of this is through the daily price they pay for subsidized consumers—the per diem prices of skilled or intermediary Medicaid patients.

Since prices reflect the cost of production of the quality of care provided, it is important to control for quality when assessing price differences across organizational form for similar services. The two waves of the NNHS contained rather detailed measures of quality, both in terms of the type of labor employed (accounting for about 90 percent of overall production costs) as well as the services provided to consumers in the home. About 20 different types of services were measured in both years, and we created an index representing the fraction of these measured services that were provided within a home.

Tables 10.5 and 10.6 consider cross-sectional price differences for similar outputs for the years 1985 and 1995. The equilibrium effect of organizational form is estimated controlling for service offered in terms of the type of consumer population served, labor inputs, size and quality of insti-

9. See National Center for Health Statistics (1997).

Table 10.5   **Perfect Substitution Tests, NNHS 1985**

	Public Price (1)	Output, Control (2)	Input (3)	Quality (4)
Dependent Variable: Private Price Per Day—Skilled				
For-profit	0.03	0.05	0.07	0.06
	(1.73)	(2.19)	(3.10)	(3.13)
Sample size	487	413	413	413
R^2	0.53	0.54	0.58	0.62
Dependent Variable: Private Price Per Day—Intermediate				
For-profit	.05	.05	.07	.07
	(1.73)	(2.42)	3.50)	(3.58)
Sample size	478	405	405	405
R^2	0.43	0.49	0.53	0.60
Dependent Variable: Private Price Per Day—Residential				
For-profit	0.26	0.20	0.26	0.27
	(4.64)	(2.73)	(3.46)	(3.58)
Sample size	154	132	132	132
R^2	0.19	0.32	0.38	0.42

Note: The specifications (1–4) correspond to the blocks of variables found in the summary statistics in table 10.3. Each subsequent specification includes all those variables included in the previous specifications (e.g., specification 2 includes both the output/control variables and public prices). Coefficient estimates of the for-profit variable (1 = for-profit, 0 = not-for-profit) are reported with *t*-statistics in parentheses below them. All price variables (both public and private) are logged in these regressions.

tution, as well as other variables that may determine the value of the product to consumers. The tables report four specifications with successively larger and inclusive conditioning sets. These conditioning sets correspond to the sets reported in the summary statistics in tables 10.3 and 10.4.

The key effect of interest for the perfect substitution or asymmetric information hypothesis is that of the for-profit dummy that indicates how price changes with the tax status, controlling for quality of care. Only these price effects of organizational form are reported across the four specifications.[10] This effect concerns the observed effect of the equilibrium distribution of homes choosing their actual status; it has little to say about the potential effects when the equilibrium would change under alternative incentives than those prevailing when the data was collected.

The two years display somewhat different results regarding the premia for for-profit care. Overall, 1985 provides more support to the argument that for-profit care sells at about a 5 percent premium, as opposed to 1995, which indicates support for the perfect substitutability implication of no premium in either direction. The results also differ across the types of care

10. The entire tables are available from the author upon request.

Table 10.6   Perfect Substitution Tests, NNHS 1995

	Public Price (1)	Output, Control (2)	Input (3)	Quality (4)
Dependent Variable: Private Price Per Day—Skilled				
For-profit	−0.02	0.01	0.04	0.17
	(−0.70)	(2.562)	(1.8)	(2.06)
Sample size	912	834	821	821
R^2	0.40	0.40	0.43	0.45
Dependent Variable: Private Price Per Day—Intermediate				
For-profit	−0.004	0.008	0.03	0.04
	(−0.18)	(0.37)	(1.14)	(1.56)
Sample size	623	568	557	557
R^2	0.40	0.43	0.46	0.48
Dependent Variable: Private Price Per Day—Residential				
For-profit	0.16	0.14	0.17	0.02
	(2.32)	(1.80)	(2.06)	(0.80)
Sample size	217	198	195	195
R^2	0.13	0.17	0.23	0.27

Note: The specifications (1–4) correspond to the blocks of variables found in the summary statistics in table 10.4. Each subsequent specification includes all those variables included in the previous specifications (e.g., specification 2 includes both the output/control variables and public prices). Coefficient estimates of the for-profit variable (1 = for-profit, 0 = not-for-profit) are reported with *t*-statistics in parentheses below them. All price variables (both public and private) are logged in these regressions.

offered. In particular, for residential care, the premia for for-profit care are the largest and the most significant. The asymmetric information argument would seem to imply that not-for-profit output should sell at a premium relative to for-profit output when they are both demanded in a competitive economy. However, for neither year and neither type of the three types of care offered does the premium for for-profit care become significantly negative.

These results have several obvious limitations and should therefore be viewed as suggestive, and not conclusive, in demonstrating the empirical relevance of perfect substitutability of organizational form. The first limitation is the lack of quality controls available in the data, particularly in terms of not being able to assign geographical locators of homes in great detail. Second, it is well known that there are barriers to entry in U.S. health care markets, particularly in long-term care, where certificate of need (CON) laws seem to have had a great impact and are often monitored and enforced with respect to measures such as beds per old individual in the region.[11] Noncompetitive markets may have less substitution than assumed throughout the discussion here, as public regulations may inflate

11. See Lakdawalla and Philipson (1997) who uses the differences in the restrictiveness in CON laws to explain not-for-profit shares across states.

for-profit premia. Without such regulatory barriers that may allow for-profits to mark up more aggressively, both perfect substitutability or information asymmetry would imply that if for-profits mark up more, then full substitution toward the equally or more preferred output of not-for-profits should take place in the long run.

To address these concerns to the largest degree feasibly allowed by these data, although not by any means ideally, table 10.7 reports the estimated premia by region and interacts them with city versus rural location within those regions. The table indicates that the premia are of similar order, although efficiency is reduced and the coefficients are freed up to vary across regions.

Many observers of health care and other regionally based markets tend to believe that regional market power is less pronounced in city markets; that is, city markets are more competitive than rural markets. Therefore, if competition lowers the for-profit premium because market power is less pronounced, one would expect the for-profit premium to be lower in the city markets than in rural markets. However, the city interaction in column 5 of table 10.7 seems to indicate that the for-profit premium is *higher* in the more competitive city markets, especially in intermediary care. The raw or unconditional interaction, the second specification within each region, has a negative but most often insignificant effect. However, when controlling for quality as done before, the interaction is either insignificantly different from zero or significantly positive. At this level of aggregation, this raises questions about whether less-restrictive entry barriers would eliminate the for-profit premium.

10.5   Concluding Discussion

A necessary condition of equilibrium with mixed production under the asymmetric information rationale for not-for-profit production is that their output sells at a premium. However, we found that data from the National Nursing Home Survey in 1995 seem to support perfect substitutability and that data from 1985 even indicate the existence of a *for-profit* premium. The empirical analysis here was naturally tentative and illustrative. In addition, the U.S. long-term care industry has potential barriers to entry in some states, making the free entry assumption required for price equalization difficult. However, we hope the main message of the exercise is clear: Theoretical arguments about not-for-profit production, in particular the role of asymmetric information, need to be confronted with supporting data before acquiring their current level of acceptance.

More generally, it may be that asymmetric information plays a less important role in determining outcomes in health care markets than is often argued by economists (see Arrow 1963). Indeed, for mortality-inducing or chronic health conditions, it is difficult to think of any other goods or service markets in which consumers know *more* about available alterna-

Table 10.7   **Perfect Substitution Tests within Regions, NNHS 1985**

	Public Price (1)	Output, Control (2)	Input (3)	Quality (4)	Within-City Effects (5)
	Dependent Variable: Private Price Per Day—Skilled				
Northeast Region					
For-profit	.068 (2.58)	.071 (2.02)	.060 (1.57)	.061 (1.59)	.091 (1.058)
For-profit*City	—	—	—	—	−.036 (−.394)
Sample size	117	93	93	93	93
R^2	.53	.63	.64	.66	.66
North Central Region					
For-profit	.025 (.987)	.058 (1.842)	.078 (2.418)	.073 (2.244)	.016 (.358)
For-profit*City	—	—	—	—	.096 (1.759)
Sample size	194	160	160	160	160
R^2	.31	.44	.50	.50	.51
South Region					
For-profit	.006 (.168)	−.050 (−1.041)	−.040 (−.791)	−.031 (−.615)	−.003 (−.024)
For-profit*City	—	—	—	—	−.035 (−.270)
Sample size	128	116	116	116	116
R^2	.50	.59	.61	.63	.63
West Region					
For-profit	.041 (.753)	.029 (.310)	−.003 (−.033)	.008 (.076)	.652 (3.135)
For-profit*City	—	—	—	—	−.784 (−3.392)
Sample size	48	44	44	44	44
R^2	.09	.27	.46	.47	.65

Dependent Variable: Private Price Per Day—Intermediate

Northeast Region					
For-profit	.092 (3.59)	.096 (2.80)	.110 (2.986)	.109 (2.922)	.208 (2.505)
For-profit*City	—	—	—	—	-.117 (-1.332)
Sample size	115	91	91	91	91
R^2	.26	.31	.44	.46	.47
North Central Region					
For-profit	.033 (1.317)	.038 (1.246)	.054 (1.770)	.046 (1.497)	.052 (1.175)
For-profit*City	—	—	—	—	-.010 (-.192)
Sample size	194	161	161	161	161
R^2	.26	.40	.48	.50	.50
South Region					
For-profit	.051 (1.369)	.001 (.010)	.011 (.221)	.029 (.612)	.059 (.580)
For-profit*City	—	—	—	—	-.039 (-.334)
Sample size	123	111	111	111	111
R^2	.46	.59	.62	.67	.67
West Region					
For-profit	.059 (1.194)	.035 (.438)	-.006 (-.071)	-.010 (-.110)	.437 (2.210)
For-profit*City	—	—	—	—	-.546 (-2.483)
Sample size	46	42	42	42	42
R^2	.04	.32	.51	.51	.62

Note: The specifications (1–4) correspond to the blocks of variables found in table 10.3 (with the exception that the region dummies in specification 4 have been omitted). Each subsequent specification includes all those variables included in the previous specifications (e.g., specification 2 includes both the output/control variables and public prices). Specification 5 is identical to specification 4 except that it includes an interaction term (FP*City). Coefficient estimates of the for-profit variable (1 = for-profit, 0 = not-for-profit) are reported with *t*-statistics in parentheses below them. All price variables (both public and private) are logged in these regressions.

tives. Chronic illness allows time to learn and, as a consequence, the level of information among chronically ill about available treatments is astounding. It is not uncommon that it is at least on par with that of doctors not specializing in the disease. The growth in disease-specific web pages and electronic support groups will only spur this knowledge. Although foreign to the working assumptions of economists analyzing health care markets, this is not surprising, since when decisions are important, people will inform themselves about their consequences. In the face of these strong incentives for acquiring information by the demand side, tracing out the empirical content of the proposed impacts of asymmetric information in health care markets seems important, particularly since the conviction of economists of their importance often is based on theoretical citations rather than on the facts those citations help explain.[12]

References

Arrow, K. 1963. Uncertainty and the Welfare Economics of Medical Care. *American Economic Review* 53 (5): 941–73.
Becker, E., and Frank A. Sloan. 1985. Hospital Ownership and Preference. *Economic Inquiry* 23 (1): 21–36.
Cawley, J., and T. Philipson. 1999. An Empirical Examination of Information Barriers to Trade in Insurance. *American Economic Review,* forthcoming.
Easly, D., and M. O'Hara. 1983. The Economic Role of the Nonprofit Firm. *Rand Journal of Economics* 14:531–38.
Gertler, P. 1989. Subsidies, Quality, and the Regulation of Nursing Homes. *Journal of Public Economics* 39:33–53.
Gertler, P., and D. Waldman. 1992. Quality-Adjusted Cost Functions and Policy Evaluation in the Nursing Home Industry. *Journal of Political Economy* 100: 1232–56.
Hansmann, Henry B. 1980. The Role of Nonprofit Enterprise. *Yale Law Review* 89:835–901.
———. 1987. Economic Theories of Non-Profit Organizations. In *The Non-Profit Sector,* ed. W. Powell. New Haven, Conn.: Yale University Press.
HCIA. 1996. *The Guide to the Nursing Home Industry.* Dallas, Texas: Arthur Andersen.
Hoerger, Thomas J. 1991. Profit Variability in For-Profit and Not-for-Profit Hospitals. *Journal of Health Economics* 10 (3): 259–89.
Lakdawalla, D., and T. Philipson. 1997. The Non-Profit Sector and Industry Performance. Working paper. University of Chicago, Chicago, Ill.
National Center for Health Statistics. 1997. Characteristics of Elderly Nursing Home Residents: Data from the 1995 National Nursing Home Survey. *Advance Data,* no. 289.
Newhouse, J. 1970. Towards a Theory of Non-Profit Institutions: An Economic Model of a Hospital. *American Economic Review* 60 (1): 64–74.
Pauly, M., and M. Redisch. 1973. The Non-Profit Hospital as a Physician Cooperative. *American Economic Review* 63:87–100.

12. For an elaboration of this argument, see Cawley and Philipson (forthcoming).

Philipson, T., and G. Becker. 1998. Old-Age Longevity and Mortality Contingent Claims. *Journal of Political Economy* 106 (3): 551–73.
Powell, W. 1987. *The Non-Profit Sector.* New Haven, Conn.: Yale University Press.
Rose-Ackerman, S., ed. 1986. *The Economics of Non-Profit Institutions.* New York: Oxford University Press.
———. 1996. Altruism, Non-Profits and Economic Theory. *Journal of Economic Literature* 34 (2): 701–28.
Rudney, G. 1987. The Scope and Dimensions of Non-Profit Activity. In *The Non-Profit Sector,* ed. W. Powell. New Haven, Conn.: Yale University Press.
Sloan, F. 1997. How Do Not-for-Profit and For-Profit Hospitals Differ? Paper presented at NBER preconference on Non-Profit Hospitals, Cambridge, Mass.
Weisbrod, B. 1977. *The Voluntary Non-Profit Sector: Economic Theory and Public Policy.* Lexington, Mass.: Lexington Books.
———. 1987. Non Profit Organizations. In *The New Palgrave: A Dictionary of Economics.* New York: Stockton Press.
———. 1988. *The Non-Profit Economy.* Cambridge, Mass.: Harvard University Press.

Comment on Chapters 9 and 10   Judith K. Hellerstein

Introduction

The two papers I discuss here, "The Tax Benefits of Not-for-Profit Hospitals" by Gentry and Penrod (hereafter GP), and "Asymmetric Information and the Not-for-Profit Sector: Does Its Output Sell at a Premium?" by Philipson, seem at first glance to have little in common other than that they both examine aspects of organizational form (for-profit versus not-for-profit) within health care. Upon closer inspection, however, there are many interesting features of the papers that are similar, from their attention to detail in discussing the institutions they study to the similar implications that can be drawn from both papers about the effects of organizational form in health care, implications that are not the focus of either paper.

The remainder of my discussion will consist of four sections. In the next section, I discuss how the two seemingly disparate papers are actually similar in many ways, and how together they bring to light some important implications about organizational form in health care. In the third section, I comment briefly on GP alone, while in the fourth section I comment briefly on Philipson. The fifth section concludes.

Linking the Papers

While both the GP and Philipson papers consider aspects of organizational form in health care markets, they seek to answer completely differ-

Judith K. Hellerstein is assistant professor of economics at the University of Maryland and a faculty research fellow of the National Bureau of Economic Research.

ent questions in very different markets within health care. GP examines the implications of the tax benefits of not-for-profit hospitals in the United States, and provides ceteris paribus benchmark estimates of the dollar value of the benefits to not-for-profit hospitals of the various aspects of their tax exemption. Philipson, on the other hand, examines empirically whether consumers are willing to pay a premium for not-for-profit care in nursing homes, which is what agency theories of the benefits of not-for-profits suggest.

Moreover, even though both papers are concerned with aspects of organizational form (for-profit versus not-for-profit) in health care, the markets they examine are different. Nursing homes can be thought of as providing long-term health care for the elderly, and short-term general hospitals (those considered by GP) can be thought of as providing short-term health care for the general population. Importantly, as Philipson notes, there is a fundamental difference between them in the United States: Hospitals are primarily not-for-profit, while in nursing homes, the for-profit organization predominates.

One might expect, then, that the two papers would have little in common. And yet there are striking similarities between them. The first similarity is stylistic, but it bears mentioning because it is quite important. The two sets of authors both pay careful attention to the important details of the institutions they study. GP, in considering the magnitudes and implications of the tax benefits of not-for-profit hospitals, explain clearly the tax implications of not-for-profit status. They also document in great detail similarities and differences in the structures of not-for-profit versus for-profit hospitals, including tabulations across organizational forms of inputs and outputs (facility beds, employees, length of stay, assets, patient composition, available technologies, etc.) and financial information, including measures of profitability. Philipson, in focusing on long-term health care facilities, also documents in detail differences across organizational form in inputs and outputs such as facility beds, types of employees, and types of services offered. Both papers therefore serve useful purposes as references for readers interested in learning more about the economics of organizational form in short-term and long-term care in the United States, and may help inspire future research about these markets.

GP identify the three common justifications for the existence of not-for-profits. Perhaps the most compelling justification, at least from an economic standpoint, is that there are information asymmetries in the provision of health care. Since consumers of health care cannot fully evaluate the quality of the services they are purchasing, for-profits will have an incentive to both underprovide quality and overprovide quantity, as both of these can increase profits. The existence of not-for-profits, then, helps solve this agency problem. It is this justification for not-for-profits that forms the basis for the Philipson paper. If consumers cannot, in fact, fully evaluate the quality of health care they are receiving, they should be willing, in theory, to pay for the elimination of this agency problem. In other words, consumers should be willing to pay a premium for the services of a not-for-profit provider, and Philipson provides an empirical test of this hypothesis in nursing homes.

While not-for-profits do enjoy tax benefits because of their organizational form, GP point out that they may be disadvantaged in two ways. First, they may have a harder time accessing capital than for-profits because they cannot issue equity, and second, they may not enjoy the managerial efficiency that for-profits enjoy because of principal-agent problems. In fact, both papers provide evidence that is at least consistent with both of these issues.

GP provide ample evidence that for various sensible measures of capital intensity (or its inverse), for-profit hospitals are more capital intensive than not-for-profit hospitals. This is shown most convincingly in the descriptive multivariate regression results in table 9.5, where for-profits have significantly lower employee-to-bed ratios in addition to significantly higher ratios of fixed assets to net patient revenues, fixed assets per discharge, and capital costs over total costs. Philipson only provides summary statistics of characteristics of not-for-profit and for-profit nursing homes and provides no statistical tests for differences between the two, so it is slightly harder to tell whether capital intensity really varies statistically across organizational form. Nonetheless, from the statistics he does present in table 10.1, which are derived from national data for 1989–1994, for-profits have higher bed sizes but fewer employees, so that the employee-to-bed-size ratio is smaller in for-profit than not-for-profit nursing homes. In addition, for-profits also pay lower wages and therefore have much higher labor costs per bed size.

What is most striking across the two papers, however, is the consistent results on differences in profitability across organizational form in hospitals and nursing homes. GP find that for-profits have statistically significant higher net income, return on assets, return on fixed assets, and operating margins than not-for-profits. Philipson, meanwhile, finds in regressions of price on measures of what might be termed quality plus an organizational form dummy, that prices charged by for-profits are at least as high as, if not higher than, those charged by not-for-profits. Moreover, this is true even though for-profits have lower labor costs, something that is also true in GP's hospital results. Since, as Philipson notes, labor costs are by far the biggest cost of production in nursing homes, these results imply that for-profit nursing homes are more profitable than not-for-profit nursing homes.

These profitability results are at least consistent with the hypothesis that for-profits in health care are able to take advantage of managerial efficiency to increase profits. Further research is needed to confirm the results of these papers (particularly using data from other years) and to study explicitly whether managerial efficiency is the reason behind the profitability of for-profit hospitals and nursing homes. Moreover, further research into the mechanisms by which for-profits achieve this profitability should be a priority.

Both papers do provide evidence that should be taken as a starting point for further research. It appears that for-profits are able to achieve higher profitability by adjusting both along the output price and input cost margins in ways that go beyond keeping labor costs down. GP provide evidence that for-profit hospitals have consistently lower lengths of stay for all types of patients (which leads to lower input costs), yet they report that their case-mix index is higher than not-for-profits. The lower length of stay result suggests that for-profit hospitals are successful in reducing input costs per patient, while the case-mix result may imply that for-profits are better able to "game" the insurance reimbursement system,[1] which can be thought of as a way of adjusting along the output price margin. Philipson's results, if taken at face value, show that for-profit nursing homes are able to adjust prices directly, charging more in many cases to private patients than not-for-profits.[2] One has to wonder what the implications of these results are for patient welfare in particular, and social welfare in general.

The Behavioral Response Problem in Computing Tax Benefits of Not-for-Profit Status

GP should be applauded for their attention to detail in considering the many facets of the tax status of not-for-profit versus for-profit hospitals, and in attempting to carefully estimate the dollar magnitude of the tax benefits of not-for-profit status. This was no small task. As GP note, however, almost all of their estimates are based on the assumption that there would be no behavioral responses to the elimination of the tax benefits for not-for-profit hospitals. The authors do consider many possible ways in which not-for-profit hospitals might respond to losing their tax-exempt status, and conclude the paper by suggesting that the trend toward hospital conversions to for-profit status may provide evidence on the magnitudes of behavioral responses. This seems overly optimistic, unfortunately, for two reasons.

First, there is ample evidence that for-profits make strategic decisions about where to locate (e.g., Norton and Staiger 1994). This should be the case if indeed they are acting as profit maximizers, and hospital conversions should occur for strategic reasons as well. If hospital conversions occur nonrandomly, trying to infer behavioral responses of comprehensive

---

1. For evidence of how and why this might happen, see McClellan (1997).
2. How for-profit nursing homes are able to do this is not clear, and I return to this point below.

tax reform from longitudinal changes in the behavior of converted hospitals may be very misleading. If one cannot control for all of the factors that lead a hospital to convert, one will not get an accurate picture of behavioral responses to tax-exemption status.

Second, the behavioral response of hospitals to a global change in tax policy may be very different from the behavioral response of a given not-for-profit hospital when it converts to for-profit status. A change in tax policy would affect every not-for-profit hospital in a given market (albeit not uniformly, obviously), while a change in the tax status of one hospital via conversion affects other hospitals only indirectly through market competition. There is no reason to believe that the behavioral responses of hospitals to these two very different changes to the structure of market competition will be comparable.

In the end, then, one is confronted with the fact that actually estimating the behavioral responses to changes in the tax exemption status of hospitals is a formidable task. Given the complexity involved in modeling the market structure of hospitals, it may well be that estimating such a behavioral response will require some sort of fortuitous "natural experiment"-type policy change.

Do For-Profit Nursing Homes Really Charge Higher Prices?

Philipson provides evidence from hedonic regressions that the agency justification for not-for-profit status does not hold up empirically in his data. Indeed, for many specifications, for-profit nursing homes actually charge statistically significant higher prices than not-for-profits, even conditional on the other observable characteristics of nursing homes in his data. The economic differences in prices are also substantial: The estimates range from a 6 percent price premium to a 27 percent price premium in 1985, although the estimates are smaller and not always significant in 1995.

One is left to wonder, then, how it is that for-profit nursing homes are able to charge a premium over not-for-profits. One possibility is simply that this is an artifact of the data. In particular, the quality measures that the National Nursing Home Survey contains are somewhat crude as they measure formal services provided by the nursing homes. Indeed, adding the quality variables into the regression does not change the R^2's much, so these quality variables (the coefficients of which are not reported) do not explain much of the variation in nursing home prices. It may well be that consumers (either nursing home patients or their families) also value highly many less formal services provided by the nursing homes, services that are harder to measure in a survey filled out by nursing home administrators but that may well be correlated with the organizational status of the nursing home. In particular, a for-profit nursing home will specialize in providing some aspects of these unmeasured quality variables if doing so allows it to provide a differentiated "product" for which consumers are willing to pay a premium and for which profits are increased.

Another possibility for the finding that for-profit nursing home prices are higher is that consumers do not have full information about price and quality when choosing a nursing home for themselves or a family member. Given the circumstances under which such choices are made, this may well be the case. This is, of course, exactly the type of agency problem that is used to justify the existence of not-for-profits, because while not-for-profit nursing homes may not have an incentive to exploit this information asymmetry, for-profit nursing homes will want to take advantage of consumers' lack of information. While Philipson argues that this problem should lead consumers to use not-for-profit organizational form as a signal of the nonexploitation of consumers, there may be other signals that consumers infer from organizational form (such as managerial efficiency or interest in complying with the demands of longer-term residents).

The data set used in this paper will not be enough to get to the bottom of the puzzle of why or whether for-profits are able to charge a premium for long-term care. Patient satisfaction surveys, more attention to the process by which nursing homes are chosen, and more detailed surveys of the services (formal and informal) provided by nursing homes are needed, all in combination with good price data.

Conclusion

Both the paper by GP and the paper by Philipson provide food for thought about a variety of topics. While the papers set out to examine very different aspects of not-for-profit health care and look at different types of care (short-term hospitals versus long-term nursing homes) for different populations, they find consistent patterns along a number of dimensions. The most interesting of these is the finding that for-profits are consistently more profitable than not-for-profits. Assuming this empirical result holds up upon further examination, it has the potential to have large implications for patient and consumer welfare, implications that should be considered in future research. This is particularly important as these markets rapidly evolve in response to changes in the structure of health insurance, changes in federal and local policy toward the provision of health care, and the aging of the population.

References

McClellan, M. 1997. Hospital Reimbursement Incentives: An Empirical Analysis. *Journal of Economics and Management Strategy* 6 (1): 91–128.

Norton, E. C., and D. O. Staiger. 1994. How Hospital Ownership Affects Access to Care for the Uninsured. *Rand Journal of Economics* 25 (1): 171–85.

Comment on Chapter 10   William B. Vogt

In his chapter, "Asymmetric Information and the Not-for-Profit Sector: Does Its Output Sell at a Premium?" Tom Philipson estimates a hedonic price function in order to assess the degree to which not-for-profit (NFP) nursing homes provide higher quality care than do for-profit (FP) nursing homes.[1] He motivates this empirical project by noticing that the substantial representation of not-for-profit firms in the production of health services is normally explained by recourse to (often implicit) agency models. The idea is that not-for-profits have different objectives than do their for-profit counterparts. Perhaps they value not only profit but also the delivery of high-quality goods. These preferences may cause them to deliver high-quality goods in circumstances where for-profit firms would choose to deliver low-quality goods. Not-for-profits do not cheat on (unobserved) quality because they do not want to cheat.

The paper reasons that, if not-for-profits do, indeed, deliver higher quality care than do for-profits, then consumers, recognizing this, will be willing to pay higher prices for the not-for-profits' services. This greater willingness to pay should show up in data as a higher selling price for not-for-profits' services.

The paper's empirical implementation consists of a hedonic price regression performed on data for a sample of nursing homes in the United States in the years 1985 and 1995. Price is regressed on a large array of observable characteristics, including prices paid by public payers, scale, input use, and quality indicators. The results indicate that, unconditionally, not-for-profits receive higher prices than do for-profits. However, when the array of control variables is entered into the regression, this result either disappears or reverses itself. The paper concludes that, in 1995, there was no difference in willingness to pay, and in 1985, there appears to be higher willingness to pay for for-profit firms.

This paper represents an interesting attack on a problem that has seen too little serious empirical investigation. The question it addresses is provocative and timely, the methodology employed is thought provoking, and the results of the analysis are fascinating. In my comments, I would like, first, to examine in a little more detail the assumptions undergirding the analysis, and, second, to suggest that the results admit alternative explanations.

Although the paper does mention many of the assumptions that lie behind this type of exercise, I think it is worth emphasizing again what assumptions ensure that a regression of this kind produces results interpret-

William B. Vogt is assistant professor of economics and public policy at the H. John Heinz III School of Public Policy and Management, Carnegie Mellon University.

1. I confine my comments to this paper because my knowledge of public finance is limited enough that my comments on Gentry and Penrod would not likely be useful.

able as willingness-to-pay measures. For the sake of explicitness, let us examine a utility function for long-term care (LTC) services. Suppose consumers make a discrete decision about the firm at which to consume LTC and that, after this, the utility of the choice is revealed to them:

$$U_{ij}(X_{1j}, X_{2j}, X_{3j}, \text{NFP}_j, I - p_j) =$$
$$\beta'_{i1} X_{1j} + \beta'_{i2} X_{2j} + \beta'_{i3} X_{3j} + \beta_{i\text{NFP}} \text{NFP}_j + \alpha(I - p_j).$$

Here U_{ij} is the utility to consumer i of going to firm j; X_{1j} are the characteristics of firm j observable to consumers and the econometrician; X_{2j} are the characteristics of firm j observable to consumers but not the econometrician; X_{3j} are the characteristics of firm j observable to neither; NFP is an indicator variable for NFP status; p_j is firm j's price, I_i is consumer i's income, and β_i represent the weights assigned to various characteristics by consumer i. Since consumers cannot see X_{3j}, they form expectations over them, so that their behavioral utility function will be:

$$U_{ij}(X_{1j}, X_{2j}, \text{NFP}_j, I - p_j) =$$
$$\beta'_{i1} X_{1j} + \beta'_{i2} X_{2j} + \beta'_{i3} E(X_{3j} | X_{1j} X_{2j}, \text{NFP}) + \beta_{i\text{NFP}} \text{NFP}_j + \alpha_i(I - p_j).$$

This can be inverted to produce, for consumer i, prices that keep him indifferent between firms. I drop both I and the level of utility since they are unimportant for our purposes.

$$p_{ij}^D(X_{1j}, X_{2j}, \text{NFP}_j) =$$
$$\frac{1}{\alpha_i}(\beta'_{i1} X_{1j} + \beta'_{i2} X_{2j} + \beta'_{i3} E[X_{3j} | X_{1j} X_{2j}, \text{NFP}] + \beta_{i\text{NFP}} \text{NFP}_j).$$

Price is superscripted by D to show that it is a relationship that creates indifference for consumer i on the demand side (as opposed to being an equilibrium relationship between price and characteristics). The object the paper is interested in is

$$\frac{1}{\alpha_i} \beta'_{i3}(E[X_{3j} | X_{1j} X_{2j}, \text{NFP} = 1] - E[X_{3j} | X_{1j} X_{2j}, \text{NFP} = 0]).$$

The empirical strategy is to run the following regression:

$$p_j = \gamma'_{i1} X_{1j} + \gamma_{\text{NFP}} \text{NFP}_j + \varepsilon_j.$$

The coefficient γ_{NFP} is then (in essence) interpreted as:

$$\frac{1}{\alpha_i} \beta'_{i3}(E[X_{3j} | X_{1j} X_{2j}, \text{NFP} = 1] - E[X_{3j} | X_{1j} X_{2j}, \text{NFP} = 0]).$$

The identification of γ_{NFP} with the underlying structural information relies on three conditions being true:

1. That the equilibrium price relationship, $p^*(X_1, X_2)$, reveals the indifference curves of consumers;
2. That $(1/\alpha_i) \, \beta'_{i3} \, (E[X_{3j}|X_{1j} X_{2j}, \text{NFP} = 1] - E[X_{3j}|X_{1j} X_{2j}, \text{NFP} = 0])$ is a constant; and
3. That the omission of X_2 creates no bias.

The first condition is required if the regression is to be interpreted as revealing demand information. The second and third conditions are required for the regression to be properly specified.

The first condition, that a hedonic price function reveals demand information, is known to be true if:[2]

1. There is perfect competition.
2. There is no heterogeneity among consumers.
3. All observed firms are in the same market.

These are strong assumptions in any case, and they are particularly strong here. Since the sample is drawn from the United States as a whole, the third assumption amounts to assuming that nursing home services are sold on a national market. The paper deals with this in the best way these data allow, by analyzing separate regions separately. As to the second assumption, the paper notes that if $(1/\alpha_i) \, \beta_{3i}$ is constant across consumers, then the hedonic price function identifies demand information for this characteristic.

As to the first assumption, this is problematic for two reasons. First, as I mentioned above, these products are geographically differentiated, and since it is reasonable to believe that consumers have relatively strong preferences over their residential location, the firms in the sample are likely to have some market power owing to this differentiation. Second, and as the paper notes, CON laws limit both entry and capacity expansion in this industry. This, combined with the fact that nursing homes have very high capacity utilization and the anecdotes of waiting lists for some homes, should give us pause in assuming the costless spot market that is part of perfect competition.

The second condition requires two assumptions. First, that $\beta_{iNFP} = 0$ and that $E(X_{3j}|X_{1j} X_{2j}, \text{NFP})$ be linear in NFPs. The third condition contains, again, the assumption that geographic and other unmeasured differentiation are not important in these markets. It is, in general, very difficult to "sign" the bias that the failure of any of these assumptions might

---

2. Here, I am assuming that there is a single market for nursing home services and that the stochastic element in the statistical model arises exclusively from measurement error in prices. For discussion, see Rosen (1974). For discussion in a multimarket context with richer stochastic specification than I consider, see Epple (1987).

Table 10C.1   **NFP Premium and Control Variables**

Year	None (%)	Cost (%)	Cost, Quality (%)
1985	+9	−3	−6
1995	+10	2	−17

cause, and sorting out which of these assumptions is true and what implications for the interpretation of the results any failures have must wait for future work, probably with different data.

Before passing on to an alternative interpretation of these results, I'd like to expand a bit on what the results say. In table 10C.1, I reproduce the results from the sample means and from the regression analysis, expressed as the NFP price premium for skilled care. The columns in the table correspond to unconditional means, specification 1 from the paper ("public price"), and specification 4 from the paper ("quality"). I have interpreted the public price variables as cost controls, since in many states (at least in 1985) Medicaid paid on a "cost plus" basis.

What the results say is that, in the raw data, NFPs enjoy a 9 or 10 percent price premium. Once costs are controlled, NFPs have a much smaller (or negative) premium, and once cost and quality are controlled, NFPs have a negative premium. The paper, since it tells a demand-side story, is either interpreting the cost controls as proxies for X_2 or as controls for the fact that the market is defined too broadly.

In addition, there are some other facts in the unconditional means that bear comment. Assuming that public price is a cost proxy, NFPs in both 1995 and 1985 have higher costs than do FPs. Furthermore, using input levels and the indicators reported as quality measures, NFPs provide, in general, higher quality care. (This is consistent with other work on nursing homes; see Gertler and Waldman 1992, for example.)

I will now spin a story that rationalizes these results, using the "NFPs are different" conventional wisdom. My point is not that this story is more correct than the one the paper spins, but that the data and mode of analysis at hand do not distinguish between them.

Consider the pricing equation of an FP firm in an imperfectly competitive market:[3]

$$p^{FP} = MC(q) - D(p,q)\bigg/\frac{\partial D}{\partial p}.$$

3. It is easiest to think of this as a model of monopolistic competition. For an interpretation as an oligopolistic model, consider the demand to be residual demand, after solving out for the responses of rivals.

Here, MC are marginal costs, D is the demand curve, and q is the quality of the good produced.

An NFP with conventional preferences ("profit deviating" in the language of Philipson and Lakdawalla 1997; see also Newhouse 1970) has a utility function

$$U = \pi + \lambda_1 Q + \lambda_2 q,$$

where π are profits, Q is output, and q is quality. Its pricing equation is:

$$p^{\text{NFP}} = MC(q) - \lambda_1 - D(p, q)\Big/\frac{\partial D}{\partial p}.$$

In discussing these two pricing equations, I'll proceed intuitively; however, it is not very difficult to write down a formal model rationalizing the intuition. Since the NFP has a preference for quality, per se, it is likely that it will choose a higher quality. (This is most obvious when quality is unobservable, when FPs will choose the lowest feasible level.) Consider now whether the NFP will price higher or lower than does the FP. The preference for output, λ_1, tends to decrease price; whereas the higher quality raises marginal costs and likely also raises the third, "market power," term, tending to increase price. So, the effect of NFP preferences on price is indeterminate.

When costs are controlled, NFPs will appear to have a smaller price premium than they do when costs are not controlled (since they have higher costs). Removing MC from the FP and NFP equations above leads to FPs' prices increasing relative to NFPs' prices. If we think of the residual covariation in price and quality remaining after costs are controlled as arising from the market power term, then controlling for quality should cause NFPs' prices to fall further, relative to FPs' prices. In fact, once MC and market power are gone from the pricing equation, all that is left to differentiate the two is λ_1. Thus, with cost and quality controlled for, NFPs should have a lower price than do FPs, because of their preference for output.[4]

So, a model in which NFP nursing homes are imperfect competitors with profit-deviating preferences appears to produce predictions consonant with the results found in the paper and reported in table 10C.1 and its accompanying text. What is at issue here is whether the regression reported in the paper identifies demand-side behavior, supply-side behavior, or some mixture. The story I tell above relaxes assumption 1 (perfect competition). With an imperfectly competitive market, price is a choice vari-

---

4. Obviously, all of this discussion proceeds as if the right-hand-side variables are exogenous, which they are not.

able of firms, they have some scope in setting it, and their objectives and costs appear in their choices (thus in prices).

"Asymmetric Information and the Not-for-Profit Sector: Does Its Output Sell at a Premium?" opens an important discussion of the strategies one might employ in evaluating empirically the validity of theories of not-for-profit behavior. The potential gains to the careful application of economic theory to a critical appraisal of agency and profit-deviating theories of not-for-profit behavior are large and, although this paper does not produce conclusive results on the matter, it is valuable in that it establishes a reference point for future investigation and helps to set the agenda for future work.

References

Epple, D. 1987. Hedonic Prices and Implicit Markets: Estimating Demand and Supply Functions for Differentiated Products. *Journal of Political Economy* 95:59–80.

Gertler, P., and D. Waldman. 1992. Quality-Adjusted Cost Functions and Policy Evaluation in the Nursing Home Industry. *Journal of Political Economy* 100: 1232–56.

Newhouse, J. 1970. Towards a Theory of Non-Profit Institutions: An Economic Model of a Hospital. *American Economic Review* 63:87–100.

Philipson, T., and D. Lakdawalla. 1997. Nonprofit Production. Department of Economics, University of Chicago, Chicago, Ill. Mimeograph.

Rosen, S. 1974. Hedonic Prices and Implicit Markets: Product Differentiation in Pure Competition. *Journal of Political Economy* 82:34–55.

Contributors

Susan Athey
Department of Economics
E52-251B
Massachusetts Institute of Technology
Cambridge, MA 02139

Laurence C. Baker
Department of Health Research &
  Policy
School of Medicine
HRP Redwood Bldg, Rm T253
Stanford University
Stanford, CA 94305

David Bates
Brigham & Women's Hospital
75 Francis Street
Boston, MA 02115

Christopher J. Conover
Center for Health Policy, Law and
  Management
Duke University
125 Old Chemistry
Box 90253
Durham, NC 27708

David M. Cutler
Department of Economics
Harvard University
Cambridge, MA 02138

Sarah Feldman
Assistant Professor of Obstetrics,
  Gynecology and Reproductive
  Biology
Harvard Medical School
25 Shattuck Street
Boston, MA 02115

Richard Frank
Department of Health Care Policy
Harvard Medical School
180 Longwood Avenue
Boston, MA 02115

William M. Gentry
Graduate School of Business
Columbia University
3022 Broadway Street, 602 Uris Hall
New York, NY 10027

Bradford H. Gray
New York Academy of Medicine
1216 Fifth Avenue
New York, NY 10029

Judith Hellerstein
Department of Economics
Tydings Hall
University of Maryland
College Park, MD 20742

Frederick L. Hiltz
66 Washington Street
Stoneham, MA 02180

Jill Horwitz
Ph.D. Program in Health Policy
Kennedy School of Government
Harvard University
79 JFK Street
Cambridge, MA 02138

M. Katherine Kenyon
Deaconess Billings Clinic
2825 Eighth Avenue North
P.O. Box 37000
Billings, MT 59107

Frank R. Lichtenberg
Graduate School of Business
Columbia University
3022 Broadway, 726 Uris Hall
New York, NY 10027

Mark B. McClellan
Office of Economic Policy
Department of the Treasury
1500 Pennsylvania Avenue, NW
Room 3454
Washington, DC 20220

David Meltzer
Section of General Internal Medicine
University of Chicago
5841 S. Maryland, MC 2007
Chicago, IL 60637

Karen Norberg
Department of Child and Adolescent
    Psychiatry
Boston Medical Center
818 Harrison Ave.
Boston, MA 02118

John Penrod
Montreal General Hospital
Research Institute
1650 Cedar Avenue
Montreal, PQ H3G 1A4 Canada

Tomas Philipson
Department of Economics
University of Chicago
1126 East 59th Street
Chicago, IL 60637

James B. Rebitzer
Department of Economics
Weatherhead School of Management
Case Western Reserve University
10900 Euclid Avenue
Cleveland, OH 44106

David S. Salkever
Department of Health Policy and
    Management
School of Hygiene and Public Health
Room 429, Hampton House
Johns Hopkins University
624 North Broadway
Baltimore, MD 21205

David S. Scharfstein
Sloan School of Management
Massachusetts Institute of Technology
Room E52-433
50 Memorial Drive
Cambridge, MA 02142

Jonathan S. Skinner
Department of Economics
6106 Rockefeller Hall
Dartmouth College
Hanover, NH 03755

Frank A. Sloan
Center for Health Policy Research
    and Education
Duke University
Box 90253
Durham, NC 27708

Douglas O. Staiger
Dartmouth College
Department of Economics
Rockefeller Hall, Room 322
Hanover, NH 03755

Scott Stern
Sloan School of Management
Massachusetts Institute of Technology
50 Memorial Drive, E52-554
Cambridge, MA 02142

Donald H. Taylor, Jr.
Center for Health Policy, Law and
    Management
125 Old Chemistry
Box 90253
Duke University
Durham, NC 27708

William B. Vogt
H. John Heinz III School of Public
    Policy and Management
Carnegie Mellon University
Pittsburgh, PA 15213

Alan Weil
The Urban Institute
2100 M Street, NW
Washington, DC 20037

John E. Wennberg
Center for the Evaluative Clinical
    Sciences
Dartmouth Medical School
7251 Strasenburgh Hall
Hanover, NH 03755

Catherine Wolfram
Department of Economics
Harvard University
Littauer 113
Cambridge, MA 02138

Author Index

Subject Index

Acute myocardial infarction (AMI), 5, 96–98, 102–3
American Hospital Association (AHA): annual survey, 201

Capital: capital intensity in for-profit and not-for-profit hospitals, 301–5, 347; capital intensity in hospital industry, 298–99; comparison of use by publicly traded hospitals and other industries, 298–301; cost of capital in hospital conversions, 33–37
Community benefits: as requirement for not-for-profit hospitals, 82
Competition: among for-profit, not-for-profit, and government hospitals, 1; in not-for-profit hospital market, 208–9
Conversions. *See* Hospital conversions

Data sources: analysis of advanced emergency response systems, 124–30; for analysis of differences in quality of managed care, 232–33; for analysis of hospital characteristics, 291; for analysis of hospital ownership changes (1985–96), 17, 18–20; charitable contributions to not-for-profit hospitals, 317; for differences in treatment of patients in managed care and fee-for-service plans, 231; for hospital conversion analysis, 18–20; for hospital performance analysis, 96–97; information about health outcomes, 273–74; to

measure quality of emergency response services, 115, 163; National Nursing Home Survey, 349; Standard & Poor's Compustat database, 298–99

Efficiency: allocative, 170, 188; in health care, 176–79; productive, 169–71
Emergency response systems: Basic 911 and Enhanced 911 (E911), 114; effect of 911 system on productivity of, 120; indirect effect on patients, 114; role in health care outcomes, 113, 116; role in hospital selection, 113–14, 116, 120–21. *See also* 911 systems

Factors of production: in hospitals compared to other industries, 298–99; issues in taxing of, 298–305
Fee-for-service (FFS) health plans: differences between managed care plans and, 8, 229–30; volume-outcome relationship as quality measure, 274–80
Foundations: created to allocate hospital sales in North and South Carolina, 26–27; cy pres proceeding for use of restricted funds, 48
FP. *See* Hospitals, for-profit

Health care. *See* Medical care
Health care industry: changes affecting all facets of, 80–81; role of Medicare in, 81–82. *See also* Medical care

365

Health care plans: accreditation by NCQA, 229; provider networks of, 278
Health care quality: categories of measurement, 273–74; measurement by NCQA, 229; research examining patient outcomes, 230; research examining process of health care, 230; volume-outcome relationship as measure of, 274–80
Health maintenance organizations (HMOs): conversion of not-for-profit to for-profit, 80; Medicare HMOs, 220; in Minneapolis, 220
Herfindahl-Hirschman Index (HHI): future values of output concentration, 20; for hospital output concentration, 19, 82–83
Hospital conversions: Columbia-HealthOne, 50–54, 62–63, 76–77, 81–82, 85–88; in context of health care industry, 80–81; effect on health care market, 63–78, 83–85; effects in North and South Carolina and Tennessee (1990–96), 27–32, 87–89; factors influencing, 46; further research, 42; mechanics of, 47–49; methodology for change of ownership analysis, 17–22; nonfinancial returns in North and South Carolina, 38–41; in North and South Carolina (1985–96), 17–18, 87; from not-for-profit to for-profit, 1, 4–5, 45, 54–56; rates of return and cost of capital in North and South Carolina, 33–37; reasons for, 57–60, 84–85; reasons for in North and South Carolina (1985–96), 22–23; by region, 56; Wesley Medical Center sale, 49–50, 61, 64–73, 86
Hospital industry: capital intensity compared to other industries, 298–99; effect of changes in market for, 1; effect of managed care on, 42; mergers in Denver, 50–54; not-for-profits' strategy for market share, 208–9; trends in market for services, 196–202
Hospital performance: in care of AMI and IHD cases, 97–99; comparisons across hospitals using RAMRs, 99; measures of, 93–95. See also Hospital quality
Hospital quality: measurement of, 5–6, 156–58; quality-of-care information, 166–67; risk-adjusted mortality rates as measure of, 99–103, 157–58, 165–66

Hospitals: choice of organizational form, 2–4; computing fair transaction prices in sale of, 16; decline in number of beds (1985–95), 222; fair price for, 15; mergers, 1; ownership in community, 196–97; payment-cost margins (1984–97), 197–98; risk-adjusted mortality rates based on AMI admits, 100–102; spending for uncompensated care, 201–2; supply of public goods, 3, 221; volume, 233
Hospitals, community: effect of PPS on revenues and treatment patterns, 197–98; revenues (1981–96), 197–98
Hospitals, for-profit: bed share, 13–14, 196–97; characteristics of patients in, 293–95; comparison of capital intensity and profitability with not-for-profit hospitals, 301–5, 347; conversions of not-for-profit to, 45, 54–56; differences in quality of care from not-for-profit hospitals, 94; diversification and joint ventures, 1, 200–201; exploitation of Medicare loopholes, 5, 47, 82; for-profit hospital chains, 14; importance of income taxes for publicly traded, 305–8; location, size, and function of, 291–98; owned by publicly traded firms, 299; profitability compared to not-for-profits, 46–47; property tax payments, 308–11; quality of care, 3; services provided, 294–98; specialization, 290; spending for uncompensated care, 201–2; as suppliers of public goods, 3
Hospitals, government: budget issues related to, 3; conversion to for-profit and not-for-profit in North and South Carolina, 23–26; conversion to not-for-profit, 14; current share of beds in, 13–14; as suppliers of public goods, 3
Hospitals, not-for-profit: access to tax-exempt bond market, 312–16; acquired by public hospitals in North and South Carolina, 23–26; bed share, 13–14, 196–97; characteristics of patients in, 293–95; comparison of capital intensity and profitability with for-profit, 301–5, 347; conversion from public to, 14; conversion rules, 47–48; conversion to for-profit, 1, 4–5, 45, 54–56; conversion to for-profit in North and South Carolina, 23–26; decline in number